On the History of Film Style

David Bordwell

Harvard University Press
Cambridge, Massachusetts, and London, England
1997

Printed in the United States of America

Designed by Annamarie McMahon

Library of Congress Cataloging-in-Publication Data

Bordwell, David.
On the history of film style / David Bordwell.
p. cm.
Includes bibliographical references and index.
ISBN 0-674-63428-4 (cloth : alk. paper). — ISBN 0-674-63429-2 (pbk. : alk. paper)
1. Motion pictures—Aesthetics. 2. Motion pictures—Historiography. I. Title.
PN1995.B6174 1997
791.43′01—dc21
97-4016
CIP

Ala combriccola di Pordenone

Acknowledgments

This book was begun with the aid of a fellowship from the John Simon Guggenheim Memorial Foundation. I am grateful to the Foundation for its support. Most of the manuscript was written while I was a Senior Fellow at the Institute for Research in the Humanities at the University of Wisconsin–Madison. I very much appreciate the scholarly camaraderie provided by my Institute colleagues, particularly the energetic and good-humored director, Paul Boyer. The book was completed with the help of funding from the University of Wisconsin–Madison Graduate School Research Committee under the auspices of the Wisconsin Alumni Research Foundation.

This book owes its existence to many archivists who have provided access to films and printed documents. These include Mary Corliss and Charles Silver of the Museum of Modern Art (my oldest archivist friends); Enno Patalas, Klaus Volkmer, and Gerhardt Ullmann at the Munich Film Museum; Masaioshi Ohba and particularly Hisashi Okajima at the Film Center of Tokyo; Elaine Burrows of the National Film and Television Archive of the British Film Institute; the irrepressible Chris Horak and Paolo Cherchi Usai, both then presiding over the Motion Picture Collection of the George Eastman International Museum of Photography; and archivist extraordinaire Maxine Fleckner-Ducey of the Wisconsin Center for Film and Theater Research. I am especially grateful to Gabrielle Claes, director of the Cinémathèque Royale de Belgique, who has loyally supported my work for many years. The Cinémathèque's cheerful staff—Clémentine, Liliane, Alain, Jean-Victor, Axel, and all the rest—have made it a wonderful place to conduct research.

I must also thank Michael Campi, Jerry Carlson, Seymour Chatman, Charlie Keil, Alison Kent, Hiroshi Komatsu, Richard Koszarski, Graziella Menechella, Mike Pogorzelski, Tony Rayns, Donald Richie, Andreas Rost, Patrick Rumble, Ben Singer, Meier Sternberg, and Lindsay Waters for assisting this project in various ways. Two among the revered old guard of film studies died while I was revising the manuscript. Both John Gillett of the British Film Institute and William K. Everson of New York University shared their love of cinema with all who came in touch with them, and books like this have benefited greatly from their spontaneous generosity. I also want to recall the friendship of Jeanne Allen and David Allen; on Thanksgiving 1976 they presented me with Hegel's *Aesthetics*, the gift that keeps on giving.

Several students in my 1994 seminar on film style offered me new insights. Tino Balio, Don Crafton, Vance Kepley, J. J. Murphy, and other Wisconsin colleagues regularly enrich my understanding of film. A manuscript draft was criticized in detail by Kristin Thompson, Yuri Tsivian, Ed Branigan, and Dana Polan, reader for Harvard University Press. Kristin also supplied some of the frame enlargements and printed up all the illustrations, proving once more that love forgives folly.

I must single out four more friends. Noël Carroll's extensive and probing comments on the manuscript fundamentally reshaped my arguments. Noël offered me so many good criticisms that I have had to save some of them for another book. Lea Jacobs and Ben Brewster let me sit in on their seminar on early film, permitted me to interject the occasional monosyllable, and listened patiently to my remarks on matters they know far more about than I. Ben also read this book and corrected important matters of fact. Finally, Tom Gunning gave me dozens of thoughtful suggestions on the manuscript. He was at his most generous when I was criticizing arguments he has made.

This book originated in an article written for *Film History* in 1994. Portions of the book were presented as lectures at MIT and the University of Hong Kong, and I thank the people who invited me, Henry Jenkins and Patricia Erens respectively, along with the listeners who offered comments.

Paolo Cherchi Usai, Lorenzo Codelli, Piero Colussi, Andrea Crozzoli, Livio Jacob, Carlo Montanaro, Piera Patat, Davide Turconi, and the rest of the Pordenone crew are largely responsible for opening my eyes to the splendors of early film. Perhaps this volume will partly repay them for all the acts of kindness they have bestowed on so many cinéphiles.

Contents

You can observe a lot by watching.

Yogi Berra

1.1 *Accidents Will Happen* (W. R. Booth? 1907).

1.2 *Red and White Roses* (William Humphrey? 1913).

1.3 *The President* (Carl Theodor Dreyer, 1919).

1.4 *The President.*

1.5 *The President.*

chapter 1

The Way Movies Look: The Significance of Stylistic History

If you had gone to the movies around 1908, most of the fictional films you saw would have played out their dramas in images like that of Fig. 1.1. The actors are arranged in a row and stand far away from us. They perform against a canvas backdrop complete with wrinkles and painted-on decor. The shot unfolds uninterrupted by any closer views. Today such an image seems startlingly "uncinematic," the height of theatricality.

Only half a dozen years later, a moviegoer would have seen something much more naturalistic (Fig. 1.2). A man is seduced by a woman in a parlor. There is still no cutting to close shots of the characters, but the shot space is quite volumetric. The man stands fairly close to the camera, and the furnishings, tiger skin and all, stretch gracefully into depth, culminating in the distant figure of the woman, outlined sharply against her bedroom.

Visiting a movie theater around 1919, you would have seen quite different images. A wealthy young man is struck by the beauty of a young working woman; they study each other. The key action is played out in less depth than in the 1913 shot (Fig. 1.3). As if to compensate, the action is broken up into several shots. The erotic exchange takes place in a pair of closer views (Figs. 1.4, 1.5). And for the shot of the woman, the camera angle changes sharply, putting us "in between" the actors.

Now skip ahead to 1950 or so. Husband and wife confront each other across a staircase landing (Figs. 1.6, 1.7). As in the 1919 scene, a series of shots penetrates the space, changing the angle to accommodate the participants. But now the camera's angle heightens the pictorial depth, yielding foreground, middle ground, and background planes reminiscent of those in our 1913 case. Although the foregrounds are not in crisp focus, each shot yields a close-up of one figure and a long-shot view of the other.

1.6 *Crows and Sparrows* (Zheng Junli, 1949).

1.7 *Crows and Sparrows.*

A dozen years later, another woman confronts another man. She invites him to take a meal in her restaurant. The tramp starts to take off his hat (Fig. 1.8). Cut in to him as he continues his gesture (Fig. 1.9)—apparently, a cut to a close-up like that in our 1919 example. But suddenly the man is no longer standing by the doorway; he is taking off his hat as he sits down at the table. The camera reveals the actual situation by moving diagonally back to include the woman as she serves him (Fig. 1.10). The cut is disconcerting in a way not evident in our earlier scenes. Either the tramp took off his hat twice, or, in this story's world, characters' continuous movements can somehow span breaks in time and space.

Drop in at a theater around 1970 and you may have a sense of *déja vu.* For on the screen there unfolds a story told in images reminiscent of those seen circa 1910 (Fig. 1.11). The furnishings are somewhat more three-dimensional, and the framing is not quite so roomy, but the image is defined by a faraway wall and distant figures strung out somewhat like clothes on a line.

Although our specimens represent a range of film-producing nations (Britain, the United States, Denmark, China, France, Soviet Georgia), none comes from an acknowledged classic. Yet these largely unknown films encourage us to ask fundamental questions about the history of moving images.

What leap most readily to the eye are the differences: one shot versus several; single versus multiple camera positions; fairly flat versus relatively deep compositions; distant views versus closer ones; spatial and temporal continuity versus discontinuity. Can we pick out plausible patterns of change running from our earliest image to our most recent one? Are there overall principles governing these differences? Disclosing such patterns and principles only sharpens our appetite. How and why did these changes take place? Why did the "clothesline" method of 1910 fall into disuse? And why, after the changes in intervening decades, does a 1971 film apparently revert to it? How, that is,

1.8 *Une aussi longue absence* (Henri Colpi, 1960).

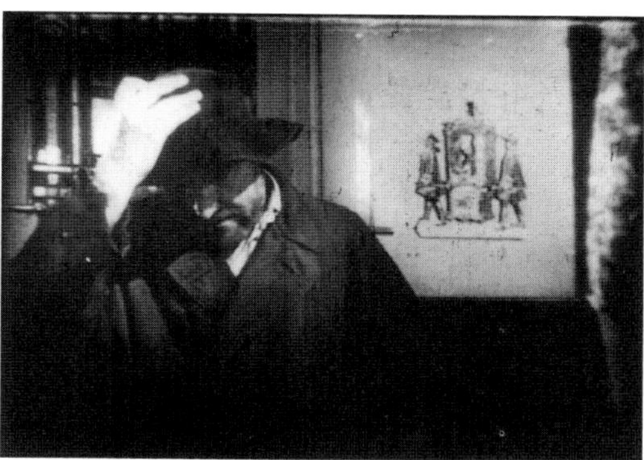

1.9 *Une aussi longue absence.*

1.10 *Une aussi longue absence.*

1.11 *Pirosmani* (Georgy Shengelaya, 1971).

can we *explain* the changes we discern? We are asking the cinematic counterpart of the question that opens E. H. Gombrich's *Art and Illusion:* Why does art have a history?

A little reflection leads us to another line of inquiry. Not everything in our sample sequences changes from epoch to epoch. The three-shot scene of the young man's erotic appraisal of his servant, filmed over seventy-five years ago, remains perfectly intelligible to us. So does the pair of images of husband and wife on the landing. Moreover, if we are surprised by the shift in time and space when the tramp doffs his hat (Figs. 1.8–1.10), it is probably because we assume that most cuts will connect time and space smoothly. Which is to say that these specimen images also hold certain techniques and principles of construction in common. Our investigation of film history will have to take account of the continuities that crisscross particular cases.

A few examples cannot suggest all the ways in which film images have been constructed across a hundred years. Our images provide mere traces of trends, hints of complex and overlapping developments. For now they serve to highlight simple facts too often forgotten. The way movies look has a history; this history calls out for analysis and explanation; and the study of this domain—the history of film style—presents inescapable challenges to anyone who wants to understand cinema.

In the narrowest sense, I take style to be a film's systematic and significant use of techniques of the medium. Those techniques fall into broad domains: *mise en scène* (staging, lighting, performance, and setting); framing, focus, control of color values, and other aspects of cinematography; editing; and sound. Style is, minimally, the texture of the film's images and sounds, the result of choices made by the filmmaker(s) in particular historical circumstances. Carl Theodor Dreyer had the option of filming the exchange of looks (Figs. 1.3–1.5) in a single shot like that of Fig. 1.2, but he chose to emphasize the characters' expressions by cutting to closer views.

Style in this sense bears upon the single film. We can of course discuss style in other senses. We may speak of *individual* style—the style of Jean Renoir or Alfred Hitchcock or Hou Hsiao-Hsien. We may talk of *group* style, the style of Soviet Montage filmmaking or of the Hollywood studios. In either case we will be talking, minimally, about characteristic technical choices, only now as they recur across of a body of works. We may also be talking about other properties, such as narrative strategies or favored subjects or themes. Thus we might include as part of Hitchcock's style his penchant for suspenseful treatments of dialogue or a persistent theme of doubling. Nonetheless, recurring characteristics of staging, shooting, cutting, and sound will remain an essential part of any individual or group style.

The history of film style is a part of what is broadly taken to be the aesthetic history of cinema. This umbrella category also covers the history of film forms (for example, narrative or nonnarrative forms), of genres (for example, Westerns), and of modes (for example, fiction films, documentaries). Film scholars commonly distinguish aesthetic history from the history of the movie industry, the history of film technology, and the history of cinema's relations to society or culture.

These sorts of history are not easy to mark off sharply, and any particular research project will often mix them. It is probably best to conceive of writing film history as driven by *questions* posed at different levels of generality. As a first approximation, the lesson of our miniature case studies can be formulated in just this way. Historians of film style seek to answer two broad questions: What patterns of stylistic continuity and change are significant? How may these patterns be explained? These questions naturally harbor assumptions. What will constitute a pattern? What are the criteria for significance? How will change be conceived—as gradual or abrupt, as the unfolding of an initial potential or as a struggle between opposing tendencies? What kinds of explanation can be invoked, and what sorts of causal mechanisms are relevant to them?

Probing these assumptions is part of the business of the chapters that follow. For now, we should recognize that the enterprise itself—the effort to identify and explain patterns of stylistic continuity and change—constitutes a central tradition in film historiography.

To defend this tradition today is to risk looking ossified. Since the rise of new trends in film theory during the 1960s, exploring the history of style has been routinely condemned as "empiricist" and "formalist." The student of technique has been accused of naively trusting in data rather than in concepts and of locking film away from what really matters—society, ideology, culture.[1] The postmodernist will add that to try to write a history of film style is to indulge in the fantasy of a "grand narrative" that will give meaning to what are, in our current circumstances, only fragments of experience, a flotsam of isolated artifacts and indefinitely indeterminate documents.

These objections, at least as usually voiced, seem to me ill founded. For instance, to call stylistic history empiricist is simply inaccurate. Empiricism is an epistemological doctrine that holds that experience is the only source of knowledge. This view has often been accompanied by the claim that experience arises from the mind's passive registering of impressions. No significant film historian ever believed such things. The chapters to come will show that conceptual frames of reference have guided even the most traditional historians of style in selecting their data and mounting their arguments. True, historians unavoidably make *empirical* claims—that is, claims that are subject to modification in the light of further information. But critics and theorists make empirical claims too. "Empiricism" as a philosophical or psychological doctrine should not be confused with an appeal to claims that are empirically reliable.

Something similar goes for charges that anyone who studies the history of film artistry is a "formalist." A further implication is that practitioners of stylistic history hold the view that film art, or art in general, is autonomous from other spheres. But one need not hold an autonomist view in order to practice aesthetic history; many historians of style argue that changes in film art are bound up with other media and with many nonartistic practices, such as social and political changes. To choose an area of study is not automatically to vote for the best way of studying it. To frame research *questions* about such formal processes as style is not to commit oneself to a belief that the ensuing *explanations* are wholly of a formal order. It is perfectly possible to find that the formal phenomena we're trying to explain proceed from cultural, institutional, biographical, or other sorts of causes. Indeed, we cannot predict where a question about style will lead us. It is, as we say, an empirical matter. Of course, someone can urge us to ignore form and style altogether, but this is a dogmatic gesture for which I can imagine no plausible grounds.

What of the postmodernist suspicion of "grand narratives"? If we conceive a grand narrative as a deterministic or teleological one, in which early events carry the seeds of later developments, we must acknowledge that some historians have held that film style develops in some such way; but not all have. A teleology is not a necessary component of a history of film style. Alternatively, if a grand narrative is one that subsumes a variety of distinct events to an overarching long-term logic, one can point out that postmodernist doctrine traces its own grand narratives: the passage from realism to modernism to postmodernism, or from early capitalism to late capitalism, or from the nation-state to the global market. More positively, we can note that not all enlightening historical accounts of film style are grand in this sense. Much of the most exciting "revisionist" research into style over the last two decades has avoided the sweeping picture and revealed a wealth of fine-grained causal processes operating within a brief period.

Most important, any historical narrative, grand or not so grand, is best conceived as an effort to answer some question. Revisionist accounts are attractive not so much because they work on the smaller scale as because they constitute strong answers to the questions they pose. An inquiry into film style must stand or fall by its plausibility compared to that of its rivals, and if a "grand narrative" addresses a problem more convincingly than a "microhistory" does, we cannot dismiss it out of hand for theoretical incorrectness. A research project that is cogently posed and carefully conducted will command serious attention no matter what scale it works upon.

This book maintains that the tradition of stylistic history of film withstands the sorts of skepticism I have just mentioned. I will have occasion to elaborate on some of these theoretical challenges more thoroughly later. Even if stylistic history were passé, though, it would still be worth studying. For it has constituted one of the most influential visions of cinema circulating around the world.

Part of this tradition's influence is due to its sheer intellectual appeal. Writing stylistic history has engaged some of the best minds ever to reflect upon cinema: Georges Sadoul, Jean Mitry, and above all André Bazin. During the 1970s and 1980s much of the most original and penetrating film research focused upon problems of style, particularly in pre-1920 cinema. Read simply as intellectual inquiry, the historiography of film style is precise and provocative to a degree that contemporary film theory, for all its aspirations, usually is not.

The study of style has profoundly shaped the ways in which we understand the history of cinema. The periods into which we divide that history, the kinds of influences and consequences we take for granted, the national schools we routinely name (German Expressionism, Italian Neorealism): such conceptual schemes were bequeathed to us by stylistic historians. The historiography of film style was concerned not only to divine the great works and to amass data about them; it also promoted frames of reference that still guide our thinking. The most up-to-date scholar studying film theory or cultural reception inherits a great deal of conceptual furniture from this tradition.

Furthermore, historians of film style have created a checklist of notable films, a canon running from *A Trip to the Moon* (1902) and *The Great Train Robbery* (1903) through *The Battleship Potemkin* (1925) and *Citizen Kane* (1941) to *Breathless* (1960) and beyond. This "masterpiece tradition," as it has been dubbed by Robert Allen and Douglas Gomery, continues to exercise widespread authority.[2] It is taught in film classes and disseminated through museum screenings, television broadcasts, popular documentaries, videocassette rentals, and those arts-center events at which a silent classic is accompanied by organ or orchestra. Many of the "great films" circulating in today's media environment were brought to notice by historians of style.

The canon and conceptual frameworks laid out by historians' enterprises have also shaped the ways in which films have been made. Ideas of cinematic specificity at large in the literature have influenced the thinking of directors from the silent era to Robert Bresson, Ingmar Bergman, and Luchino Visconti. Since the 1920s, directors and screenwriters have realized that their work can also be defined by self-conscious reference to stylistic traditions. It is likely that our example from *Une aussi longue absence* (Figs. 1.8–1.10) pays a modernist homage to the cutting experiments of the Soviet Montage school. Film brats like Martin Scorsese and Francis Ford Coppola presented themselves as heirs to the French New Wave. From behind the video rental counter Quentin Tarantino watched those *films noirs* and Jean-Luc Godard movies acclaimed as stylistic breakthroughs. The historiography of film style has become an important part of the history of filmmaking.

Granted, historians of style might have exercised great influence and still have been wholly wrongheaded. But such is not the case. They have seized upon genuinely important questions about cinema—questions that cannot be dismissed as remnants of theoretical naiveté or outdated positivism. To understand why, consider the very act of watching a film. However much the spectator may be engaged by plot or genre, subject matter or thematic implication, the texture of the film experience depends centrally upon the moving images and the sound that accompanies them. The audience gains access to story or theme only through that tissue of sensory materials. When we pronounce Fig. 1.2 tense, or recognize the erotic charge passing between the characters in Figs. 1.3–1.5, or sense a reserved poise in Fig. 1.11, all these intuitions stem from style. However unaware spectators may be of it, style is working at every moment to shape their experience.

From a filmmaker's perspective, images and sounds constitute the medium in and through which the film achieves its emotional and intellectual impact. The organization of this material—how a shot is staged and composed, how the images are cut together, how music reinforces the action—can hardly be a matter of indifference. Style is not simply window-dressing draped over a script; it is the very flesh of the work. No wonder that rich craft traditions have grown up to guide filmmakers in choosing technical means that best serve stylistic ends. By centering our inquiry on film style, we are trying to come to grips with aspects of cinema that matter very much to how films work. No adequate theory of film as a medium can neglect the shaping role of style.

In certain respects, the images and sounds that filmmakers have created vary across times and places; in other respects, they are stable. This state of affairs opens up a new realm of questions. How and why do some stylistic factors vary? How and why do others stabilize? And what are the implications for the ways in which filmmakers and audiences have conceived of how movies might work? There are no more important and more exciting problems for film scholars to tackle.

Indeed, stylistic history is one of the strongest justifications for film studies as a distinct academic discipline. If studying film is centrally concerned with "reading" movies in the manner of literary texts, any humanities scholar armed with a battery of familiar interpretive strategies could probably do as well as anyone trained in film analysis. This is especially true as hermeneutic practices across the humanities have come to converge on the same interpretive schemas and heuristics.[3] But if we take film studies to be more like art history or musicology, interpretive reading need not take precedence over a scrutiny of change and stability within stylistic practices.

In this effort we can learn a great deal from our predecessors. Over some eighty years scholars of distinction have bequeathed us a rich historiography of film style. The next three chapters trace the development of this research tradition. Throughout these chapters I conceive of a research tradition as constituted by a broadly marked-out field of inquiry, an approximate agreement on central problems in that field, and common methods of inquiry. Thus the historical study of film style is defined by its object—change and stability in film technique over time. It is also defined by a core set of problems about chronology, causality, affinity, influence, and the like. The study is also governed by shared methods, most centrally those of stylistic analysis.

A research tradition can harbor different, even conflicting, research *programs*. This term, rather than "theory," captures the sense that film historians, while deploying conceptual structures, characteristically concentrate on research, not on theory-building.[4] Within the tradition I am surveying, three research programs developed distinct conceptions of stylistic history. These programs shared a sense of the essential story to be told, but they organized that story in varying ways and sought different explanations for the changes and continuities they detected. In the process, they brought to light new phenomena, proposed fresh patterns of cause and effect, and sharpened our sense of how particular questions could be posed.

Within research programs, we can pick out particular research *projects*. For example, a scholar might focus on explaining why at a certain period filmmakers began consistently to break scenes into closer views of the action, as in Figs. 1.3–1.5. Often a scholar will not bother to spell out the research program she undertakes. Nonetheless, her research project will usually contribute to a tacit program shared with other workers in the field.

The research tradition explored in this book seeks to identify and explain significant patterns within the international history of style. I thereby rule out "chronicle" histories, which aim only to record the flux of phenomena.[5] I also rule out most versions of biographical history, for these do not attempt to trace large-scale patterns of change or stability. Most of my historians paint with a broad brush; their aims are synoptic and international.

In this regard these historians inherit certain premises and conceptual routines of art history more generally. For example, proponents of what I shall call the Standard Version of stylistic history plotted the history of film as a progressive development from simpler to more complex forms, treated according to that biological analogy of birth/childhood/maturity so common among art historians since Vasari. Some film historians likewise embraced the idea, proposed as long ago as Aristotle, that an art form reaches perfection by disclosing its essential and most distinctive qualities. And many film historians, like their counterparts in music and the visual arts, sought to explain the emergence of the canonical works, the masterpieces that demonstrated the highest possibilities of the medium.

Film historians looked to the sort of explanations invoked by art historians: national temperament, idiosyncrasies of artists, and impersonal principles of development lying latent within the medium. In particular, we shall see that several assumptions deriving from the historiography of modern art—the need for perpetual breaks with academicism, the possibility that an art work can pursue a "radical" interrogation of its medium—informed accounts of film's stylistic history.

And we shall watch film historians wrestle with what we might call the problem of the present. If visual art, including cinema, develops progressively, how do we understand what is occurring now? One option, articulated by Standard Version historians, is to take the present as a moment of decline, overshadowed by the glories of past achievements. This accords with the rise-and-fall pattern that often accompanies the biological analogy; maturity inevitably gives way to old age. Another alternative is to postulate the present as a moment of ripeness, the full flowering of aesthetic possibilities; this is the line pursued by 1920s writers and by Bazin and his contemporaries. Whatever option is chosen, the historian has a problem. Since no one can foresee the future, tomorrow's stylistic developments may confound the trajectories the historian has plotted.

The problem of the present has a special urgency in a twentieth-century art; change has seemed to hurtle ever faster toward us. Stylistic movements like Neorealism and the French New Wave each lasted only about five years (like Fauvism and Parisian Cubism). Across a mere twenty years, from 1908 to 1928, film style altered as dramatically as musical style had in the second half of the nineteenth century. Many film historians worked as journalists reviewing new releases, and they grew sensitive to current small-scale changes in technique. We shall see the protagonists of our research tradition try to understand a protean art in a protean century.

Chapters 2 through 4, then, survey the Western historiography of film style. Some of this material will be familiar to film historians, but I have tried to supply some fresh insights into the conceptual underpinnings of the research programs, as well as sidelights on their historical contexts.

Not only did many of these historians believe that the film medium progressed; they believed that historical inquiry did as well. The fruits of their research tradition, I suggest in Chapter 5, make this a plausible claim. If we take progress to mean an enlarging fund of empirical knowledge, few will doubt that film historians have made progress. We know much more about the history of cinema than our predecessors did. Historiographic progress, however, involves more than amassing data; it demands an increasing skill in formulating and solving problems. While the ultimate payoff is usually empirical—that is, a wider and richer understanding of historical events—the conceptual schemes elaborated by the tradition have guided concrete inquiry in productive directions.

Chapter 5 seeks to defend this cluster of claims by offering a review of revisionist stylistic history during the 1970s and 1980s. This surge of energy was partly made possible by scholars' self-conscious awareness of earlier research programs. The chapter also examines critically a parallel development, which I call "culturalism": the effort to subsume stylistic history to a broader theory of social experience in modernity or postmodernity. In particular, I raise some objections to the idea that alterations in a culture's "ways of seeing" can play a central role in explaining stylistic change.

One way to show the viability of the main tradition is to try to contribute to it. This I undertake in the final chapter, a case study of the history of depth staging. Long though it is, Chapter 6 remains sketchy; my treatment of the problem is essayistic and exploratory, not exhaustive. I mean only to offer an example of how a contemporary researcher might draw upon the tradition while also criticizing, extending, and refining it.

Some last chores and caveats: Films are usually cited by their most familiar U.S. titles; original titles will be found in the index entry for the film. Instead of a bibliography, I have incorporated bibliographic comments into the beginning of each chapter's endnotes. These remarks can serve as a guide for further reading.

Most books on film (even, alas, on film style) use not frame enlargements but "production stills," photographs taken during filming. A production still does not accurately represent the image seen in the finished film. The photographs that illustrate this book are all frame enlargements, taken from prints of the films discussed. Because prints survive more or less well, the quality of reproduction will vary, but the frames are essential as documentation of key points in my argument. Often the captions carry part of the argument too.

I concentrate upon fiction films. The possibility of writing a stylistic history of documentary was explored very little in the tradition I am considering, and I lack the expertise to pursue it. The stylistic history of documentary may differ considerably from that of the fiction film.[6]

Finally, the bad news is that the tradition I discuss has largely neglected the contribution of sound to film style. The good news is that astute researchers are today exploring this problem.[7] I shall be satisfied if what follows yields a better understanding of moving images across the last hundred years.

chapter 2 Defending and Defining the Seventh Art: The Standard Version of Stylistic History

What fancies were spawned by that cinema of the heroic period! Its muteness seemed like a virtue to us. Its infirmity made its devotees believe that it was going to create an art out of nothing but moving images, painting in motion, dramaturgy without words, which would become a language common to all countries.

René Clair, 1962

By the end of World War I, cinema had established itself as a powerful mass medium. At the same time it was coming to be recognized as a distinct art. Embraced by millions, it was also championed by intellectuals who believed themselves to be witnessing, for the first time in recorded history, the birth of a new form of creative expression. Film, many thought, would be the defining art of the new century. It cast a spell over avant-garde novelists, composers, painters, and poets. Reinhardt and Antoine, as well as Brecht, Piscator, and Meyerhold; Virginia Woolf and Blaise Cendrars; H. D. and Cocteau; Léger and Rodchenko, Mayakovsky and Duchamp, Schoenberg and Milhaud, Dalí and Kathe Köllwitz, Alexandra Exter and Moholy-Nagy—if such a diverse lot of modern artists could be united by a passion for the cinema, what intellectual could doubt that the new medium harbored genuine creative possibilities?

These possibilities, advocates insisted, were not on full display in tasteful adaptations of the classics—those pieces of filmed literature or theater with which many producers hoped to lure a middle-class audience. No; *The Birth of a Nation* (1915), *The Cabinet of Dr. Caligari* (1920), *The Last Laugh* (1924), *The Battleship Potemkin* (1925), and other masterworks triumphed partly because they exploited the new medium's unique resources. Even when a film failed to be a masterpiece, it might remain important because it contributed to the medium's artistic development. Both the silent-film canon and emerging notions of artistry thus depended upon conceptions of the medium's historical evolution.

The canon established during the 1910s and 1920s remains with us today. It is the substance of most film history textbooks, most archives' repertory programming, most video releases of silent classics. Behind this canon stand assumptions about the nature of film, its artistic potential, the specificity of art, and the causes of historical change.

A Developing Repertoire: The Basic Story

The history of cinema is most commonly understood as a narrative that traces the emergence of film as a distinct art. Call this the Basic Story. Stretches of the Basic Story are now questionable, but, tacitly or explicitly, it has been the point of departure for the historical study of film style. The Basic Story tells us that cinematic style developed by abandoning the capacity of the motion picture camera to record an event. According to the Story, in the course of the 1910s and 1920s particular film techniques were elaborated that made cinema less a pure recording medium than a distinct means of artistic expression.

The saga begins with cinema as a record of everyday incidents, as in the *actualité* films of Louis Lumière (Fig. 2.1). Cinema was also used to capture theatrical performances, such as pageants representing the life of Christ (Fig. 2.2). A decisive step away from mere recording was taken by Georges Méliès' fantasy films. By stopping the camera and rearranging the figures and settings, Méliès created magical effects (Figs. 2.3, 2.4). Méliès' compères turned heads into musical notes, and his scientists blasted a rocket into the eye of the Man in the Moon. According to the Basic Story, Méliès' "artificially arranged scenes" launched truly cinematic spectacle, one based upon creative use of the camera's potential. Taking his work as a point of departure may have inclined cinéphiles to treat the fictional narrative film as the prototype for all cinema, as well as to assume that film art must transform the filmed event into something imaginary and unreal.

In the Basic Story, the early films of Edwin S. Porter mark the next advance in narrative technique. *The Life of an American Fireman* (1903) is credited with creating a story out of separate pieces of film, or shots, combined in a coherent fashion. *The Great Train Robbery* (1903) was widely believed to press still further in this direction. The bandits' escape and the rousing of the townspeople—two roughly simultaneous actions—are presented through cutting (Figs. 2.5, 2.6).

D. W. Griffith is usually credited with perfecting the enduring artistic resources of the story film. His work at the American Biograph Company displays comparatively subtle performance styles (Fig. 2.7). The Basic Story also credits him with inventing or perfecting elements of "cinematic syntax." He utilized flashbacks and faded scenes in and out. He is said to have developed analytical editing, the practice of breaking a scene down into shots that show closer views of faces, gestures, or props (Figs. 2.8, 2.9; compare Figs. 1.3–1.5.) In addition, Griffith's use of cross-cutting, known at the time as "alternating views" or "switch-backs," enabled him to build last-minute rescues to an unprecedented pitch of suspense. In the Basic Story, *The Birth of a Nation* (1915) is often considered cinema's first masterpiece, the consumma-

2.1 The camera records the world: *Arrivée d'un train à La Ciotat* (Louis Lumière, 1897).

2.2 A prototype of "theatrical" staging and filming: *The Passion Play of Oberammergau* (U.S., 1898).

2.3 In *La lune à un mètre* (1898), Méliès bedevils an old astronomer: the moon barges into his observatory, and when he tries to assault it . . .

2.4 . . . the moon mockingly withdraws back into the firmament.

2.5 Crosscutting in *The Great Train Robbery:* While the bandits escape with their booty . . .

2.6 . . . the townsfolk dance unawares.

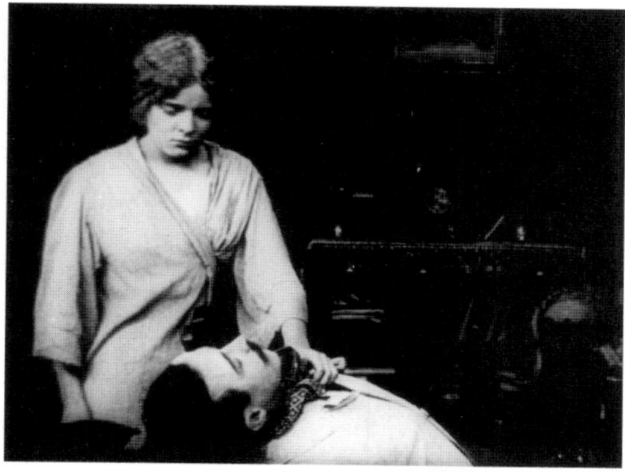

2.7 In *The Painted Lady* (1912), Blanche Sweet discovers that she has accidentally shot her lover. Instead of hurling herself into flamboyant despair, she gulps.

2.8 In *The Lonedale Operator* (1911), Griffith cuts from a long shot . . .

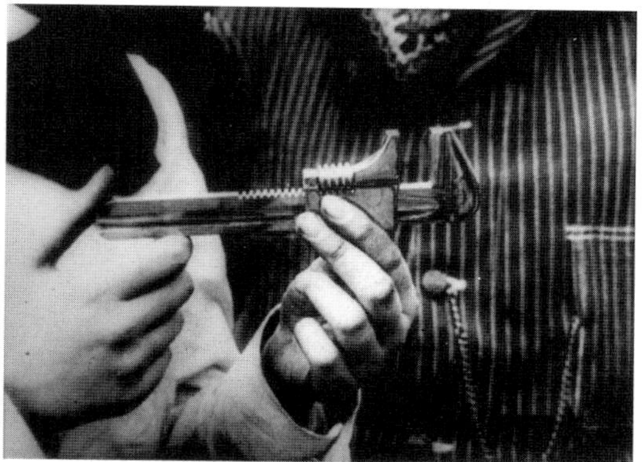

2.9 . . . to a close-up, revealing that what the robbers thought was a revolver was actually a wrench.

tion of all Griffith's innovations. Its successor, *Intolerance* (1916), takes editing to new heights by cross-cutting four historical epochs.

The Basic Story identifies the post–World War I period as one in which various Western countries made distinctive innovations. After Griffith had refined performance and developed new editing devices, European directors created distinctive national styles. Commentators credited the Swedes with bringing out the natural beauty of landscapes and drawing upon their literature with dignity and intelligence (Fig. 2.10). The French filmmakers, notably the Impressionist school, were seen as advancing the ways in which cinema can present stylized, subjective imagery, as in the works of Abel Gance, Marcel L'Herbier, and Jean Epstein (Fig. 2.11).

Throughout the 1920s, critics put German films at the front line of cinematic art. First, there were the Expressionist masterworks, most notably *The*

2.10 In Sjöström's *Terje Vigen* (1916), the hero's chores harmonize with a romantic Swedish landscape.

2.11 A husband who has abandoned his family contemplates returning; he decides against it when he imagines his mother-in-law as a bloated mole (*Feu Mathias Pascal,* L'Herbier, 1925).

2.12 A prisoner locked in a stylized cell in *The Cabinet of Dr. Caligari* (Robert Wiene, 1920).

2.13 *Metropolis*: The city of the future.

Cabinet of Dr. Caligari, which convinced critics that cinema could represent mental states with the disturbing force of contemporary painting and theater (Fig. 2.12). Historical and mythological films showed German designers' skill in creating magnificent, overpowering sets, as in Fritz Lang's *Metropolis* (1927; Fig. 2.13). Germany also produced works exploring a new realism of setting, performance, and story. *Backstairs* (1921) and *Sylvester* (1923) became prototypes of the slow, intense drama of *Kammerspiel,* or "chamber play." In addition, *The Last Laugh* (*Der letze Mann;* 1924) and *Variety* (1925) became famous for their dynamic and fluid camera movements (Fig. 2.14).

Near the end of the decade, another national cinema had its turn in the spotlight. *The Battleship Potemkin* (1925), *Mother* (1926), *The End of St. Petersburg* (1927), *October* (aka *Ten Days That Shook the World;* 1928), *Storm over Asia* (1928), *Arsenal* (1929), and *Earth* (1930) swung the world's attention

2.14 The startling camera movement that opens *The Last Laugh* descends in the hotel elevator, as shown here, and then rushes across the lobby and out through the revolving door.

2.15 After the battle in *The New Babylon* (1929), Grigori Kozintsev and Leonid Trauberg show the conscience-stricken soldier turning from the troops' destruction of the Commune . . .

2.16 . . . while bourgeoisie watching from the safety of a hill applaud. The sequence never shows all the characters in the same frame at once.

to the Soviet Union. These films established dynamic cutting, under the rubric of "montage," as a new creative resource for film art.

The concept of montage included various sorts of editing. Most generally, it referred to the ways in which the joining of two shots yielded an effect or meaning not evident in either shot alone. Thus Soviet directors exploited "constructive montage," which manages to suggest that characters are interacting with other characters or with objects while never including all the relevant visual elements in the same frame. (See Figs. 2.15, 2.16.) Sergei Eisenstein became famous for using montage to invoke abstract concepts, as in the famous "For God and Country" sequence of *October* (Figs. 2.17, 2.18). The Ukrainian Aleksander Dovzhenko was celebrated for more poetic and evoca-

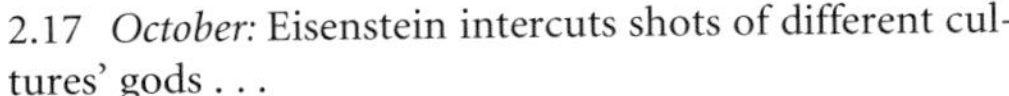

2.17 *October:* Eisenstein intercuts shots of different cultures' gods . . .

2.18 . . . in order to cast doubt on all deities.

tive juxtapositions of images. And all Soviet directors exploited the rhythmic discoveries of Griffith and the French Impressionists. In order to build up a climax or intensify an emotion, a cascade of shots might be cut in an accelerating fashion, culminating in images only fractions of a second long (Figs. 2.19–2.21).

The 1920s witnessed more radical avant-garde trends as well. Dada films such as *Entr'acte* (1924) and *Cinéma anémic* (1926), "Cubist" works such as Fernand Léger and Dudley Murphy's *Ballet mécanique* (1924; Fig. 2.22), and "purist" experiments such as the abstract films of Oskar Fischinger, René Chomette, and Walter Ruttmann also contributed to the exploration of the medium (Fig. 2.23). Nonetheless, the Basic Story typically treated experimental works as secondary to the narrative films produced within the mainstream of national film industries.

According to the Basic Story, the flowering of the silent film was abruptly cut off by the arrival of "talking pictures." Henceforth filmmakers would have to find a style appropriate to the sound cinema, and only a few imaginative creators responded to the challenge. In Germany, Fritz Lang's *M* (1931) daringly presented two lines of action simultaneously, one through the images and another on the soundtrack (Fig. 2.24). René Clair created musical fantasies such as *Sous les toits de Paris* (1930). In Hollywood Ernst Lubitsch mixed operetta conventions with more "filmic" editing rhythms in *Monte Carlo* (1930), as did Rouben Mamoulian in *Love Me Tonight* (1932; Fig. 2.25). For many observers, Walt Disney's cartoons showed that talking pictures could properly integrate the pictorial dynamism of the silent cinema into an audiovisual unity. On the whole, however, the Basic Story asserts that talkies triggered a reversion to film's "theatrical" mode and a loss of visual values.

Because of the vicissitudes of international film commerce, the silent-film canon varied a little from country to country. *The Birth of a Nation* did not ar-

2.19 As the czarist troops ride down the demonstrators in *Mother* (1926) . . .

2.20 . . . V. I. Pudovkin presents clashing shots of the horsemen . . .

2.21 . . . including virtually abstract views.

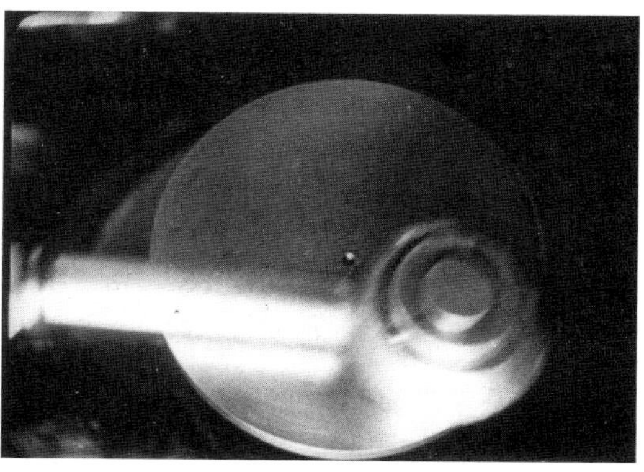

2.22 Stylization of the machine in Fernand Léger and Dudley Murphy's *Ballet mécanique.*

2.23 Painting-in-motion: Ruttmann's *Opus III* (1924).

2.24 *M:* While we hear a police analyst describe the insanity of the serial killer, Lang shows him experimentally changing his expression.

2.25 *Love Me Tonight:* Maurice Chevalier saunters among his neighbors while their morning routines tap out an infectious rhythm.

rive in Paris until the 1920s, so French writers tended to celebrate Cecil B. DeMille's *The Cheat* (1915), the great Hollywood revelation for war-bound Paris intellectuals. For similar reasons, American writers neglected *Sylvester* in favor of other German films of the period. Chauvinism also played some role in the constitution of many historians' canons. Jean-Georges Auriol, editor of a 1932 anthology of film history, eagerly dotted a contributor's essay with reminders that breakthroughs credited to other nations had actually been made earlier by French directors.[1] Still, there is enough agreement among writers of the period for us to speak of a consensus version of silent film history.

In its most abstract outline, the Basic Story traces some familiar patterns. Like an organism, cinema has a life course that goes through phases. The increasing sophistication of the silent film, followed by an artistic regression with the arrival of talking pictures, gave cinema a trajectory comparable to that posited for the visual arts by Vasari, Winckelmann, Hegel, and their successors. The birth-maturity-decline pattern, easily mapped onto a notion of rise and fall, allowed critics to posit that peak of development called "classic."[2] The masterpieces of the 1920s became celebrated as the mature classics of the medium.

In addition, many proponents of the Basic Story subscribed to the commonplace neo-Hegelian belief that in art a nation's spirit *(Volksgeist)* expresses itself.[3] Accordingly, the Basic Story highlighted distinctions among nations. Book-length studies often surveyed film history country by country.[4] It seems likely that the war's effects in dividing markets and distinguishing films by place of origin encouraged the idea of what the director Victorin Jasset called national "schools."[5] Moreover, many writers conceived of film history along lines parallel to current conceptions of modern painting. Art historians' rubrics—Parisian Cubism, German Expressionism, Soviet Constructivism, and the like—found their counterparts in film historians' outline of cinema as a succession of national movements.

National difference played a large role in the Basic Story; so did differences among individual creators. By the end of the silent era, the major dramatis personae of the tale were well known.[6] A 1932 survey is characteristic: Méliès is "the father of cinematic spectacle"; France benefited from the work of Max Linder, Louis Feuillade, and Emile Cohl; American film is the creation of Griffith, Thomas Ince, DeMille, Mack Sennett, and Charlie Chaplin; and so on.[7] Although the idea of the director as the artist responsible for the film is often associated with Parisian criticism after World War II, it emerged as early as the 1910s. The Basic Story takes as axiomatic the principle articulated in 1926 by a British critic: "It is obvious that, as regards any one particular film, the director is the man of destiny, the one supremely important person."[8]

All these tendencies find compact expression in Paul Rotha's 1930 *The Film till Now,* the most ambitious and influential English-language film history of the era. A short chapter surveying the development of the film as a means of artistic expression points to several milestones: *The Great Train Robbery* as launching the story-based film; the Film d'Art; the work of Griffith; *The Cabinet of Dr. Caligari* as the decisive break with realism; *The Last Laugh,* which "definitely established the film as an independent medium of expression";[9] and the Soviet masterworks. In the remainder of the book Rotha devotes a chapter to each significant film-producing nation, organizing his account according to the oeuvres of major directors.

From nation to creator to individual work: by the end of the silent era, this basic art-historical breakdown had become commonplace in synoptic film histories. More surprisingly, in certain respects the development of this mass-market entertainment seemed to parallel the history of modernism in other arts. Like contemporary art historians who glanced from country to country in search of the latest break with tradition, champions of the new medium presumed that the Basic Story would exhibit those "leaps from vanguard to vanguard" that pushed an art forward.[10] In the 1920s, the ball of cinematic progress seemed obviously to pass from America to Germany to France to the USSR. Ever since the Basic Story was articulated, each research program has had to reconstruct the idea of aesthetic modernism in a fresh way.

Film Culture and the Basic Story

Within thirty-five years of the invention of cinema, critics around the world had arrived at a remarkable consensus on the medium's achievements. How did the Basic Story come to be disseminated so widely? Certainly not only through such monographs as Rotha's; before 1940 very few book-length histories of cinema were published. Instead, institutions created by international film culture served to maintain and update the Basic Story.

Periodicals played a key role. National film industries had their catalogues and trade journals, which during the 1900s and 1910s often discussed the emerging canon and tested out aesthetic ideas as well. Publicity and trade journalism often helped a film achieve classic status. The reputation of Griffith, for instance, was forged outside the rarefied precincts of film historians. When Griffith left Biograph in 1913, his publicist ran an advertisement in the *New York Dramatic Mirror* claiming that his films were responsible for "revolutionizing Motion Picture drama and founding the modern technique of the art."[11] The advertisement credited Griffith with introducing the close-up, parallel cutting, suspense, the fade-out, and restrained acting. *The Birth of a Nation* was later greeted in the same paper with the headline "Summit of Picture Art."[12]

Occasionally the stylistic innovations that historians picked out were also promoted by the industry. For example, once *The Last Laugh* had been recognized for its fluid camera movement, Ufa could publicize other films that employed *die entfesselte Kamera* ("the flying camera") and celebrate Murnau's film as the first to "break through the limitations that the cinema had hitherto placed upon the gaze of the spectator."[13] Technical novelty, then as now, could help sell a movie.

The Basic Story was also supported by contemporaneous film journalism. The canonical works were celebrated time and again in the small film magazines that proliferated during the 1920s. France's *Cinéa* (founded in 1921) was followed by Germany's *Filmwoche* (1923), Austria's *Filmtechnik* (1925), Belgium's *Camera* (1932), Scotland's *Cinema Quarterly* (1932), and England's *Sight and Sound* (1932) and *Film Art* (1933). In the United States there were *Cinema Art* (1923), *Movie Makers* (1928), and *Experimental Cinema* (1930), among others. Perhaps the most internationally important journal was *Close-Up,* founded in 1927. Published in Switzerland, where uncensored versions of films were comparatively easy to see, *Close-Up* promoted European art cinema, Soviet film, and the international avant-garde.[14]

With a hundred years of cinema behind us, it is difficult for today's readers to appreciate the fascination that the Basic Story held for the writers of the little film magazines. Aware of only a dozen or so years of film production, writers in the mid- to late 1920s incessantly returned to the same films and directors. Open the handsome oversize journal *Photo-Ciné* for January 1928 and you will find debates on L'Herbier and René Clair, script extracts from Gance's *Napoléon,* a study of Epstein's Impressionist experiment *La glace à trois faces* (1928), an article on E. A. Dupont, and a long essay on Fritz Lang's career, illustrated with superb stills from *Siegfried* (1923) and *Metropolis.*

During the 1920s, this conception of silent-film artistry was sustained by the metropolitan film society, or ciné club. Paris became the center of the movement. Informal groups founded by Louis Delluc and Riccioto Canudo in 1920 were merged with Moussinac's Le Club Français du Cinéma (founded in 1922) to create Le Ciné-Club de France in 1924. A year later Charles Léger founded La Tribune Libre du Cinéma, and in 1928 Moussinac and associates created the left-wing club Les Amis du Spartacus, the venue for banned Soviet films. By 1929, with eight clubs in Paris alone and others in cities all over the nation, there emerged an association, La Fédération Française des Ciné-Clubs.

Clubs sprang up elsewhere. The United Kingdom's most famous club was the Film Society, a London venue founded in 1925. In Germany, several left-wing clubs devoted themselves to showing Soviet works. The most powerful group was Berlin's Volksverband für Filmkunst, which was said to have had over forty affiliates and 50,000 members across the nation.[15] Amsterdam's Filmliga, founded by Joris Ivens and others in 1927, made its journal a clearinghouse for information on other countries' clubs.[16]

Specialized theaters began catering to the demand for classic or prestigious films. In Paris, Jean Tedesco's Vieux-Colombier (a legitimate theater converted to a cinema in 1924) showed not only recent avant-garde work but also older films discussed in the journals. Tedesco's example was followed by Armand Tallier's Studio des Ursulines, which opened in 1926. In Berlin, the Kamera dedicated itself to a policy of showing artistic films, regardless of age.[17] In the United States, a "little cinemas" movement modeled on the "little theater" trend emerged in the mid-1920s. In New York there appeared the International Film Arts Guild, which had strong ties to *Close-Up*. By 1929 the United States had a loosely affiliated chain of alternative cinemas, with New York's Little Carnegie linked to kindred venues in Buffalo, Rochester, and Chicago.

In these clubs and specialized theaters, the key works of the still-emerging Basic Story would be premiered or reshown. The Vieux-Colombier screened current releases and revived *Caligari*, early works of Chaplin, *Sir Arne's Treasure* (1919), *Siegfried*, and *Broken Blossoms* (1919). London's Film Society mixed older films with more recent works. In 1928 the Society screened the 1907 *Ben-Hur*, Chaplin's *Kid Auto Races at Venice* (1914), *Nosferatu* (1922), Pudovkin's *Mother*, and Ruttmann's *Berlin: Symphony of a Great City* (1927). The Film Arts Guild of New York imported *Potemkin* and brought back *Intolerance*, *Waxworks* (1924), and *Backstairs*.

While the journals, clubs, and theaters were attracting audiences, intellectuals' efforts to have cinema recognized as one of the fine arts began to be acknowledged by more established cultural institutions. During 1921–1923 the Salon d'Automne of Paris included film sections in its prestigious annual gallery shows, and in 1924 the Grossen Berliner Kunstausstellung did the same. Both exhibits featured photographs and designs from outstanding national productions by Gance, L'Herbier, Lang, and the like. In 1925 the Exposition des Arts Décoratifs in Paris and the Kino und Photo Ausstellung in Berlin displayed graphic material from European film classics. Other international exhibitions were held in The Hague and Stuttgart.[18]

Just when cinema was winning official recognition as a fine art, sound movies arrived. With a shock, cinéphiles realized that their beloved classics would probably vanish from the screens. It took the death of the silent film to drive home to intellectuals that motion pictures would need to be preserved for future generations.

From the ciné-club movement came many of the men and women who established the world's first film archives. The Cinémathèque Française, founded by Henri Langlois, Georges Franju, and Jean Mitry in 1936, grew out of the Cercle du Cinéma, a club that had shown silent classics. The Museum of Modern Art Film Library, created in 1935, was headed by Iris Barry, one of the founders of London's Film Society. A Brussels ciné club, Le Club de l'Ecran, became the basis for the Belgian cinémathèque. "Each of these archives," wrote Langlois, "is the last creation of that great movement of opinion that, from 1916 to 1930, had arisen in defense of the cinema."[19]

Other film archives appeared in Sweden (1933), Germany (1934), London (1935), and Milan (1935). Most took as their mission the preservation of the country's film heritage and the dissemination of national film culture, but they also maintained the canon that had emerged in the silent era.[20] *The Birth of a Nation* was one of the first two films Langlois acquired.[21] The initial public screening sponsored by London's National Film Library included *The Great Train Robbery,* a Lumière short, a Chaplin film, and *The Birth of a Nation.*[22]

The Museum of Modern Art Film Library in New York illustrates how a prominent archive could grow out of 1920s film culture and consolidate the Basic Story. In 1932 Alfred H. Barr insisted that film have a place in the new museum he would direct:

> People who are well acquainted with modern painting or literature or the theatre are amazingly ignorant of modern film. The work and even the names of such masters as Gance, Stiller, Clair, Dupont, Pudovkin, Feyder, Chaplin (as director), Eisenstein, and other great directors are, one can hazard, practically unknown to the Museum's Board of Trustees . . . The only great art peculiar to the twentieth century is practically unknown to the American public most capable of appreciating it.[23]

Despite MOMA's commitment to modernism, the Film Library focused comparatively little on cinema's avant-garde—the films made in the wake of

Cubism, abstraction, Dada, and Surrealism. Instead, the collection came to center upon those Hollywood and European classics that had already been praised by historians. This was partly because there was no comparably elaborated historical account of the still-young avant-garde cinema. In addition, Barr's choice for film curator was someone for whom the development of mainstream cinema provided the impetus of film history.

Reviewing movies for London newspapers during the 1920s, Iris Barry had showered praise on Griffith, Sjöström, Lubitsch, Lang, Murnau, Dupont, and other canonized directors. As a member of the Film Society board, she had helped the Soviet classics circumvent censorship and find an audience among the British intelligentsia. Barry had then moved to New York and started working at the museum in 1932. When MOMA created its Film Library in 1935, she was appointed librarian, and her husband, John Abbott, was named director.

Barry and Abbott set out to acquire major early films, quickly purchasing titles by Méliès, Porter, and Griffith. By 1937 the Film Library held seven hundred titles. Barry also sought to educate the public. She arranged for an extension course to be offered at Columbia, where lectures by Hitchcock and King Vidor were accompanied by extracts from their work. Scholars were also featured. Barry recalled a lecture by Erwin Panofsky: "The fact that Panofsky had evidently long studied and esteemed movies, that he cited the pictures of Greta Garbo and Buster Keaton as familiarly and learnedly as he customarily referred to medieval paintings, really made a dent. What snob could venture now to doubt that films *were* art?"[24]

In 1939 MOMA opened in new quarters on 53rd Street, and as part of the occasion the Film Library launched a cycle of seventy films surveying "the main body of film-making from 1895 onwards."[25] The thirty programs presented an overview of the Basic Story, including "The Development of Narrative" (1895–1902), programs on early American masters, "The German Film: Legend and Fantasy," "The Swedish Film," and ending with a potpourri of sound-film genres. Now that MOMA had a theater of its own, Barry began daily screenings from the collection, thereby making the Film Library the first archive to offer regular public exhibition.

Inevitably, vagaries of availability and notoriety slanted the MOMA canon. The Film Library had access to relatively few films from the major French silent directors, so Feuillade, Delluc, and their contemporaries were scantily represented. Whereas some archivists believed in seeing and collecting as much as possible, Barry was highly selective. Eisenstein, Pudovkin, and Dovzhenko formed MOMA's great Soviet troika, while Dziga Vertov, Boris Barnet, Lev Kuleshov, Sergei Yutkevich, and the Fex collaborators Grigori Kozintsev and Leonid Trauberg were virtually ignored. Because of MOMA's holdings, U.S. cinéphiles could view Fridrikh Ermler's *Fragment of an Empire* (1929), but Kozintsev and Trauberg's *New Babylon* (1929) remained unknown for decades. Dreyer was known through *Leaves from Satan's Book* (1920) and *La Passion de Jeanne d'Arc* (1928), not through *The President* (1919) or *Mikael* (1924) or *Thou Shalt Honor Thy Wife* (aka *The Master of the House;* 1925).

Confident in her tastes, Barry rejected films by major directors. Griffith, however, held a place apart. He was, she claimed, "the ruling planet of the birth of motion picture production."[26] During the 1930s she acquired many of his Biograph titles, and Griffith gave MOMA a large collection of personal papers. In 1940 Barry mounted the first retrospective of his work and accompanied it with a major catalogue. There she praised his Biograph films for seeking to liberate the motion picture from the theater by means of changing camera distances and alternating scenes.[27] For Barry, creative editing began with *The Great Train Robbery* and culminated in *The Birth of a Nation* and *Intolerance;* Griffith's techniques laid the foundation for Soviet Montage a decade later. There is little doubt that Barry's efforts lifted Griffith's reputation enormously.[28]

Perhaps the Film Library's most influential activity was its circulation of 16mm prints to colleges and museums. The programs aimed to "illustrate the history, technique, and aesthetics of this new art."[29] Prefaced by explanatory titles written by Barry and accompanied by program notes, the MOMA programs became staples at public libraries and college campuses. In 1938 the Library won an Academy Award in honor of these efforts to make available to the public "the means of studying the motion picture as one of the major arts."[30]

At a period when most archives seldom opened their doors to researchers, U.S. scholars and teachers relied almost exclusively upon Barry's circulating programs. Ince's *Civilization* (1916), Erich von Stroheim's *Blind Husbands* (1919) and *Foolish Wives* (1922), the comedies of Douglas Fairbanks and Harold Lloyd, *Caligari, The Phantom Chariot* (1920), *Potemkin, Mother,* and other MOMA classics came to typify the silent cinema for generations of Americans.[31] Well into the 1970s, American scholars' study of silent film history rested largely upon the Basic Story as recast by the MOMA Film Library. For example, Lewis Jacobs' *Rise of the American Film* (1939), which elaborates the international version of the Basic Story, was researched with the assistance of Barry and her staff. The influence of the MOMA programs also marks Arthur Knight's popular survey, *The Liveliest Art* (1957). Knight, who worked at MOMA for a time, acknowledges that he hit on the idea for the book after he had given a lecture illustrated by screenings of *The Great Train Robbery,* a Griffith Biograph, a reel from *The Last Laugh,* and the Odessa Steps sequence from *Potemkin.*[32]

MOMA was only one of many institutions that disseminated the Basic Story throughout international film culture.[33] To a large extent that story founded the tradition of inquiry into film style. At the same time, and in the same forums, historians were proposing conceptual schemes that refined the accepted canon and chronology. These writers created the first research program dedicated to film's stylistic history.

The Standard Version: Central Assumptions

Our art is reproved for being specifically cinematic: "You are not literary enough! You are not dramatic!" But a film ought to be filmic, or it is not worth making. Actors, directors, designers, write on your banner in bold letters the most important commandment of film art: the cinema's language is cinematographic!

Lev Kuleshov, 1918

The Basic Story is largely a chronicle of technical progress. It traces a development toward growing expressivity, subtlety, and complexity in telling a story on film. Cinéphiles believed that, in the silent era at least, changes in film style yielded a gradual enrichment of technical resources. The complementary concepts of geographical school and individual master, commonplace in art history since Vasari, enabled film historians to ascribe the accumulating contributions to particular artists and circumstances.

In what I am calling the Standard Version, however, stylistic history was not treated simply as a growing body of contributions. Historians argued that film style could be understood as a development toward the revelation of cinema's inherent aesthetic capacities. To the linear conception of stylistic progress historians added the idea of the medium's unfolding potential. Panofsky put it crisply: "From about 1905 on, we can witness the fascinating spectacle of a new artistic medium gradually becoming conscious of its legitimate—that is, exclusive—possibilities and limitations."[34]

Panofsky's assessment sums up nearly twenty-five years of reflection on the nature of cinema, but he also links reflection on cinema to a venerable tradition in other arts. Critics had long equated a medium's "legitimate" powers with its "exclusive" ones—that is, those which only it possesses. Furthermore, the recognition of a medium's "possibilities and limitations" was central to assessing its subjects, themes, and expressive resources. Such reflections were at the heart of aesthetic theory at the turn of the century and remained crucial to debates about modernism in all arts.

Cinema could be regarded as a reproduction system, a way of capturing fleeting reality or staged performances and then presenting the action at other sites. But in 1910 hardly anyone was prepared to argue that a recording technology constituted an artistic medium. There was no art to the telegraph or the telephone. Zola's formulation rang in critics' ears: Art is not nature, but nature seen through a temperament. "The cinema, as a perfecting of photography," wrote Paul Souday in 1917, "is fated to reproduce reality mechanically. Yet art is not a mechanical copy but an intelligent interpretation of that reality."[35] The defenders of cinema as an art, like the defenders of photography before them, felt obliged to deny that the camera merely reproduced what was put before it.[36] They had to show that the medium—lens, film stock, cutting—somehow played a creative role.

Moreover, if film were to be an art, it would have to be a *distinct* art; if not, why invent it in the first place? Since antiquity, and particularly in the Renaissance, art theorists had routinely indulged in *paragone*—the comparison of the range and resources available to different arts.[37] Aestheticians several centuries later sought to create a "system of the arts," and in this effort distinctions among the arts became a central conceptual tool. Perhaps the most elaborate of such efforts was Hegel's hierarchy, ranking arts according to their reliance upon physical material, their philosophical possibilities, and so on.

Under the influence of Kantian and neo-Kantian doctrines, differences among the arts became the basis for claims about the aesthetic "essence" of each medium.[38] This sort of reasoning can already be seen in Lessing's distinction between spatial media such as painting and timebound media such as poetry. The nineteenth-century German philosopher Mauritz Lazarus wrote of music: "A musical work consists of measured tones with definite tonal relations; these tones—and nothing more—are contained in it, or, conversely, they alone contain what is musical and what is aesthetic in the work. There is no other content to be discovered, and with every postulation of such, the danger is immanent of deception or of transgression beyond what is musical."[39] According to this line of thinking, any art's essence was to be found in the medium's distinctive possibilities for creating forms or evoking feelings.

Often avant-gardists urged the artist to safeguard the purity of each medium. "Remember," warned the Symbolist painter Maurice Denis in 1890, "that a picture—before being a battle horse, a nude woman, or some anecdote—is essentially a plane surface covered with colors arranged in a certain order."[40] In a manifesto, "The Word as Such," the Russian Futurists Alexander Kruchenykh and V. Khlebnikov declared: "Before us language was required to be: clear, pure, honest, melodious, pleasant (tender) to the ear, expressive (vivid, colorful, juicy) . . . We think rather that language must be first of all *language*."[41] Notoriously, the Cubist advocate Roger Fry saw a radical difference between dramatic or narrative representation and those "spatial values" which were the essence of pictorial art. He concluded that a picture such as Rembrandt's "Christ before Pilate" actually mixes two distinct arts, the art of "illustration" and that art of "plastic volumes" appropriate to painting as such.[42]

Centuries of conversation about the arts thus presented the defenders of cinema with a double-barreled problem. How could one show that cinema did not merely reproduce reality? And what medium-specific factors made film a distinct art? In practice, the two issues yielded a single solution. If one could show that moving photography possessed unique features, then one could point to those as evidence that the medium truly *mediated*—that something creative interposed between the reality photographed and the image that resulted.

Remarks along these lines can be found as early as 1908. "Every art has its peculiar advantages and disadvantages growing out of the particular medium in which it expresses itself," observed American film journalist Rollin Summers. "It is the limitations and advantages of its particular means of expression that give rise to its own particular techniques."[43] Summers went on to argue that the lack of dialogue in a film required it to express emotion by means of pantomime, "scenic changes," and close views.[44]

Medium-specific views quickly became widespread. In 1911 Ricciotto Canudo, soon to become a prominent figure in French film culture, announced that cinema was becoming the basis of a new "plastic art in motion."[45] Another early theorist, Alexander Bakshy, argued that cinema's peculiar power lay in its ability to express life in "rhythmic motion," and the fact that the movement is produced by an automatic mechanism is irrelevant. "The cinematograph will rise to the level of art when men of great intelligence and insight express themselves in forms determined by the natural properties of this new medium."[46] In a 1916 book, Hugo Münsterberg declared that he would study "the right of the photoplay, hitherto ignored by esthetics, to be classed as an art in itself."[47]

What sort of art was cinema? Some observers held it to be a synthesis of older arts. Canudo believed that the three rhythmic arts (music, poetry, and dance) and the three plastic arts (architecture, painting, and sculpture) had found their synthesis in cinema, the seventh art.[48] The American Victor Freeburg set forth a comparable position.[49] At the other extreme, some believed that cinema owed nothing to any other medium. This purist position was often held by avant-garde filmmakers experimenting with light, shape, and movement divorced from storytelling.[50]

The most common view, and the one that had the most influence upon the writing of film history, kept to the middle of the road. For most cinéphiles, theirs was not an art of abstract shape and pure motion. It was centrally a narrative medium. Most observers assumed that from the start filmmakers sought to tell stories, and the progress of film technique was bound up with the discovery of ways in which cinema could present dramatic action clearly and engagingly. The line of descent from Méliès to Porter to Griffith and beyond presupposed an increasing skill in explicating the dramatic action and wringing more intense emotion from the audience.

Since cinema told its stories in dramatized form, the case for film's distinctiveness rested principally upon the manifest and manifold differences between film and theater. Like a play, a story film presented human actions through performance. Yet cinema's specific means broke with theatrical convention. "The task of the present moment," wrote a Russian intellectual in 1913, "is to distinguish cinema from theatre, to determine precisely the basic creative elements of each and thus to set each on its own true path."[51] In the same year Georg Lukács argued that the power of theater derived from the real presence of the actor, while the potential of cinema was based upon its ability to turn reality into "a life without a soul, pure surface."[52] An American journalist proposed that film's essential quality was a rapid accumulation and shifting of images impossible on stage: it was "art by lightning flash."[53]

Looking back, we may think that early cinema's massive debt to the stage led guilty intellectuals to deny that the finest films owed anything to the contemporary theatrical spectacle. But the polemical exaggerations also proceeded from a passionate belief that cinema was not merely a transmission medium. If the new art harbored its own expressive resources, a film could not be merely a copy of what was set before the lens.

Nothing proved this more decisively, many critics thought, than those cases in which a film's plot derived from the theater but a gifted director transformed dialogue into silent imagery. In *The Marriage Circle,* one critic remarked, Lubitsch had "shown, not told, the story. Everything is visualized, all the comedy is in what the characters are seen or imagined to be thinking or feeling, in the interplay, never expressed in words, of wills and personalities."[54] In this milder variant, the specificity argument is still with us. Films derived from plays are expected to translate dialogue into visual action, to "ventilate" the dramatic locale by expanding its purview, and to find cinematic equivalents for theatrical conventions, as in the stylized limbo of Peter Brook's *Mahabharata* (1989).

Like all other arts, the silent-era cinéphiles admitted, cinema had its limitations. But as Summers had pointed out in 1908, discovering what a medium *cannot* do is a salient way to define its artistic resources. "The limitations of an art give to it individual character," wrote another critic. "In the limitations of the medium, the artist finds a means of stimulating rather than of restricting his expression."[55]

The most influential argument that cinema's power derived from the medium's deficiencies was put forward by Rudolf Arnheim. Arnheim proposed that cinema not only fails to copy physical reality accurately; it does not faithfully record our visual experience either. We see the world as a spatial and temporal continuum, but a film's frame cuts the image free of that. Although we see a three-dimensional array, cinema presents its subject as a flat, geometrical display. Our vision organizes sensory data into recognizable forms and characteristic views, but cinema often presents ambiguous shapes and depicts objects from uncharacteristic angles. Yet, Arnheim argued, these very distortions of perceptual reality offered creative possibilities to the film artist. The ways in which cinema fell short of perfect recording marked out the royal road to genuine art.[56]

Along with reigning ideas of medium-specificity, current conceptions of artistic progress informed the historical explanations central to the Standard Version. In speaking of cinema's unfolding potential as having reached a "grand climax," Panofsky recalls the enduring idea that an art progresses by gradually unfolding its inherent potential until it attains, as Aristotle had said of tragedy, its "natural fulfillment."[57] The reformulation of this idea within the Hegelian tradition led many historians of painting and music to believe that the history of an art may be understood as stages in the revelation of the art's characteristic powers. A kindred idea guided students of the new medium of film.

In the early years, critics claimed, cinema was still too young to have discovered its true vocation. They presumed that the medium's virtues would unfold only in the fullness of time. Later, critics took the canonized films of the Basic Story as displaying technical discoveries that gradually revealed the specific resources of "film language." According to Léon Moussinac in 1925, the distinctive laws of cinema had been "revealed little by little thanks to the slow efforts of a few good craftsmen."[58]

Cinéphiles now had theoretical grounds for seeing the earliest films as insufficiently artistic. The Lumière *actualités* were mere records of what had happened in front of the lens, while most fictional films of the time simply reproduced the conventions of theater. By contrast, the Ku Klux Klan's rescue of besieged Southern whites in *The Birth of a Nation* became a *locus classicus* of the Standard Version in large part because Griffith's cross-cutting would have been impossible to replicate on the stage.

Similarly, a writer could comment that during the late 1920s Hollywood cinema seemed to have returned to theatrical conventions, whereas the Soviet directors had revived "the very elements of the moving picture . . . constructive cutting."[59] A French critic praised Kuleshov's *By the Law* (1926) for creating a "specifically cinegraphic language" of enlarged details and hyperbolic performance (Figs. 2.26, 2.27).[60]

From today's standpoint, such definitions and defenses of the seventh art look decidedly forced. In particular, the idea of medium-specificity has not aged well. It seems unlikely that any medium harbors the sort of aesthetic essence that silent-film aficionados ascribed to cinema. There are too many counterexamples—indisputably good or historically significant films that do not manifest the theorist's candidate for the essence of cinema. Indeed, the very idea of an essence, which is perhaps best understood as a set of jointly

2.26 At the climax of *By the Law,* Kuleshov cuts from the stark silhouettes, poised for the hanging . . .

2.27 . . . to a large close-up of the Bible in the hand of the vengeance-crazed woman.

necessary and sufficient conditions, is probably insupportable when applied to as variegated a medium as cinema.[61]

Similarly, the idea of cinema's history as an unfolding potential treats the medium as holding at the outset the seeds of future growth. Yet the later developments to which the historian points are always a mere sampling of the uses that have been made of the medium; if the historian picked different instances, she might be forced to posit a different essence *ab initio.* Worse, the unfolding-essence argument risks turning the result of historically contingent factors into a necessary product of forces somehow incipient from the very start. In using cross-cutting Griffith did not fulfill the essence of cinema; he applied the medium to certain tasks and thereby showed that it could function in certain ways.

Problematic as it was, though, the belief in an unfolding essence proved to be productive. The search for intrinsically cinematic qualities encouraged cinéphiles to analyze the techniques of the medium. In the course of this they isolated stylistic options that remain central to our thinking about film as an art.

For instance, several of cinema's technical devices required the artist to manipulate what was put in front of the camera: acting, stylized settings, expressive lighting. Those critics who believed that the essence of cinema was movement were particularly hospitable to experiments in performance and *mise en scène.* Even the apparently theatrical *Caligari* could be considered a tribute to cinematic dynamism: "The picture is a continual rush of movement. We feel emotion rising from motion as an immediate experience. That is the quintessence of cinematographic art."[62] Arnheim pointed out that Chaplin's pantomime revealed unexpected formal congruences among objects.[63] In *The Gold Rush,* when Charlie eats his boot (Fig. 2.28), he transforms it by turns into a fish carcass (by neatly filleting the sole), a chicken (by sucking the nails

2.28 Charlie aristocratically prepares to dine on his bootlace (*The Gold Rush*).

as if they were bones), and a plate of pasta (by twirling the bootlace as if it were spaghetti).

Most cinéphiles were hostile to even these traces of theatrical technique; Chaplin, for all his genius as a performer, was often considered an "uncinematic" director. Consequently, historians tended to search for stylistic progress in the "specifically cinematic" domains of camerawork and editing. They regarded close-ups, landscape shots, unusual angles, and camera movements as uniquely filmic devices, their resources revealed in such classics as *Intolerance, The Last Laugh,* and *The Battleship Potemkin.* "In *Variety,*" wrote a French critic, "the actors no longer plant themselves in front of the lens; instead it shifts with and for them, it turns around them, it puts itself before or behind them, above or below them, seizing upon their smallest expressions at the fraction of a second that is the most significant."[64] Dupont's flamboyant camera movements (Fig. 2.29) became the very prototype of German cinematography, bringing the audience into close relation with the protagonist's experience.

The change from shot to shot was also regarded as a key source of artistry. The metaphor of "film language" tended to imply that editing juxtaposed shots in the manner of cinematic "words" or "phrases." Terry Ramsaye claimed that under Griffith, "the close-up, the dissolve, the fade-out, the cut-back and such optical items were fitted into the syntax of the screen and given a new importance as tools of the picture narrator."[65]

Pioneered by Méliès, established by Porter, refined by Griffith, dynamized by Gance and his French colleagues, editing was brought to its apogee by the Soviet Montage school. For many historians, the Soviets demonstrated that editing was the central and distinctive film technique, since it most completely

2.29 *Variety:* The view from the trapeze.

liberated cinema from its dependence upon the theater. At the close of the silent era, V. I. Pudovkin's 1926 pamphlet *Film Technique* introduced readers to the "experiments" of Lev Kuleshov at the Soviet film school. Kuleshov had shown that single shots could be combined to create a scene without any basis in reality.[66] He filmed two actors, each in a different part of Moscow, and cut together the shots so that they seemed to be greeting one another; he added a close-up of two other actors shaking hands; and he then showed the two original performers looking offscreen; this shot was followed by an image of the White House in Washington, D.C.[67] The editing created the event: the actors and buildings did not have to exist in the same space and time. "The viewer himself," wrote Kuleshov, "will complete the sequence and see that which is suggested to him by montage."[68]

In cinematography and editing many writers thought they had found the answer to the problem of defining film as a distinct art. For these techniques unmistakably mediated between what was put in front of the lens and what the viewer eventually saw. They shaped and stylized photographed reality in order to create an artistic effect. No wonder that, confronted with the virtuosic camera movements and editing of the 1920s canon, many observers believed that the silent cinema had finally begun to display its full creative possibilities. Late silent films such as *La Passion de Jeanne d'Arc* (1928) seemed to exemplify everything to which motion picture art had been aspiring: subtle, intimate acting; stylized setting and lighting; an unprecedented freedom of camera angle; rhythmic and lyrical camera movements; and a "purely cinematic" space created through intercut close-ups, often without any establishing shots (Figs. 2.30, 2.31).

The Standard Version of history developed alongside the canon-building of the Basic Story. Guided by a notion of what film art was, what would count as progress in the medium, and how national schools might contribute to

2.30 In *La Passion de Jeanne d'Arc,* close-ups of Jeanne . . .

2.31 . . . followed by shots of her interrogators create an abstract terrain of gesture and facial expression.

a grand scheme, critics and journalists could insert current films into an ongoing narrative. Moussinac's *Naissance du cinéma* (1925), a collection of his 1920–1924 essays, identified the key works of film history, from DeMille's *The Cheat* and Griffith's *Broken Blossoms* (1919) to *Sylvester* and L'Herbier's *L'Inhumaine* (1924), and singled out the major artists: Chaplin, Ince, Griffith, Gance, Stiller, Sjöström, Robert Wiene, Lupu Pick, and others. Moussinac even provided a list of "steps" in evolutionary progress, all of them films canonized by trade papers, journalism, and ciné clubs. He went on to discuss major national schools (United States, Sweden, France, Germany) in more detail.[69] When Moussinac wrote a book on Soviet cinema a few years later, he claimed that Eisenstein and Pudovkin had moved still further toward disclosing cinema's distinctive resources.[70]

According to the Standard Version, the creative filmmaker was charged with revealing and exploring the aesthetic resources of the medium, chiefly by finding new ways of telling stories more clearly or powerfully. The accumulated contributions of national schools and individual artists were said to yield a "cinematic language" that was visible both in mainstream commercial products and in more avant-garde works.

Coming to Terms with Sound

The canon and chronology of the Basic Story were sketched in the silent era, in the very period when the Standard Version was being constructed. The coming of synchronized sound posed acute problems. What would now be the canonical works? What progress could be discerned? How could sound be taken as a further unfolding of the medium's unique artistic possibilities?

Here we touch on a feature of film historiography that we will encounter again and again. A synoptic history of the film medium was expected to take account of the most recent developments. A book surveying centuries of painting or music might be forgiven for devoting little space to contemporary work; developments in Surrealism or Art Deco could hardly challenge interpretations of Raphael or Rembrandt. Cinema, however, was still so young, and its artistic range was still so uncharted, that any argument about broad tendencies could be scotched by the film released last month. Thus the Standard Version was crafted to provide an explanatory scheme suitable to the diverse national schools and filmmakers of the period 1915–1928. But now cinéphiles were called to attention by the emergence of a new technology, and they had to accommodate the talking picture to their story and their explanatory scheme.

Some observers chose to ignore the chatter of the "100 percent talkie." They hoped that directors would explore the "creative use" of sound. A few filmmakers did stylize dialogue, introduce doses of silence, and employ markedly unrealistic music and noise. For instance, in René Clair's *Le Million,* men struggling for a coat containing a winning lottery ticket are accompanied by the crowd noises and referee whistle of a soccer match. Raymond Spottiswoode praised Clair's as "the gayest and freest films that have been made. His songs, his choruses and his commentative music emancipate the action from the plodding rhythms of conversational speech. He lives in a borderland world between fact and fancy."[71]

For the hard-line critics of the period, a film's soundtrack became problematic if it degenerated into that mere recording which was the antithesis of genuine art. Commentators sought theoretical principles that would assure the aesthetic primacy, or at least the equality, of the visual track in sound films. The Soviets suggested that sound be treated as a montage element, creating an audiovisual "counterpoint," or auditory montage.[72] In one sequence of *Deserter* (1933), as we see bourgeois citizens riding in a car, Pudovkin abruptly alternates children's voices and sweet music, creating jarring sonic "crosscutting." Suddenly we hear a woman's voice shouting, "The truth about the strike!" before we see her handing out leaflets. The sound bridge creates a disjunctive interruption similar to that of a rapidly flashed intertitle. Later, as soldiers march strikebreakers into the factory, the only sound is that of a single man's moaning voice, a kind of threnody for the workers. For many cinéphiles such sonic montage—much more hard-edged and disorienting than Clair's ingratiating auditory metaphors—pointed the way to true sound technique.

Yet no one could write a comprehensive history of the sound picture by commenting on a handful of daring movies. Most talkies seemed bare and clumsy by comparison with the dazzling inventions of the late silent cinema.

Acting styles often coarsened, camera positions became far more limited, editing options were reduced. Faced with what could only seem wholesale regression to staginess, the cinéphile might hope that talkies would be used for canned theater, while more visually engaging silent films would continue to be made. Other observers foresaw the end of silent movies. For some, this meant the end of cinema as such. The film of the future, Arnheim predicted, would include sound, realistic color, and three-dimensional images, thereby leaving the domain of art and becoming an unprecedentedly realistic transmitter of stage performances.[73] Less demanding cinéphiles kept going to the pictures, hoping that the sound film would partly recapture some of the pictorial expressivity of the silent days.

The pessimism triggered by the new technology is sharply visible in one of the most acute writers of the time. Gilbert Seldes established himself as a leading advocate of popular culture in *The Seven Lively Arts* (1924), an exuberant defense of movies, vaudeville, popular song, and comic strips. Throughout the 1920s and 1930s Seldes reflected at length on the silent movie and its successor.

Seldes maintained that the distinguishing characteristic of cinema was "movement governed by light."[74] Quite early, he argued, American film manifested this quality in scenes of combat and pursuit, in alternating editing, in more intimate acting styles, and particularly in slapstick comedy. He summarized the Basic Story in these terms. *The Birth of a Nation* was a key work in film history because it revealed fully what light in motion could accomplish: "Griffith made *The Birth* with the camera, not with fiction, not with stage-acting, not with scenes made 'according to the laws of pictorial composition,' not as sculpture or music."[75] Seldes praised *The Last Laugh* because it translated its story wholly into dynamic visual action. He saw the Soviet films as using purely cinematic symbols, such as *Potemkin*'s Odessa Steps and *Mother*'s thawing river.

When sound arrived, Seldes joined his contemporaries in denouncing it as a reversion to theater. Speech, he argued, halted the movies' visual momentum; now things were told instead of being shown. Still, Seldes sought to be conciliatory. The talkie was no real rival to the silent film, he indicated in a 1928 article. Each could flourish alongside the other as long as the talkie defined itself against both the stage and the silent film. Invoking the medium-specificity premise, Seldes demanded that directors exploit the talkie's unique resources and constraints.[76]

A year later, recognizing that the silent film was doomed, Seldes pleaded for an "intermediate form" in which the talking picture would become a "movie" again. He suggested that because the sound film was too realistic, it invited spectators to apply to it the standards of everyday life. What the talkie needed was less redundancy, more freedom of the camera to wander from the sound source, and some conventions that would stylize its dialogue. Seldes suggested radio as a source of inspiration.[77] In 1935 he was still objecting that sound film had not forged a new set of conventions, save in the gangster film and in Disney's *Silly Symphonies*.[78]

This conclusion dodged the real problem. If cinema was essentially visual, and the visual possibilities of cinema stood fully revealed at the end of the 1920s, how could sound films manifest any stylistic development? Seldes believed that the most important current changes were to be found in modes and genres created by the talkies: the musical, the gangster film, and the animated cartoon. Here too his attitude was widely shared. Refusing to explore the technical continuities between the silent and sound eras, and unable to find significant stylistic innovation in the sound film, many observers discovered the most salient historical developments in American sound genres.

Seldes was less a film historian than a cultural commentator. Nonetheless, his belief that the medium had an essence, his sense of cinema's aesthetic resources unfolding across a series of silent masterworks, and his anxiety about talking pictures were typical of contemporary film culture. A more elaborate and influential refinement of the Standard Version was offered by the major synoptic history of world cinema composed after the arrival of sound. Here problems of stylistic continuity and change were worked out on a grand scale.

Bardèche, Brasillach, and the Standard Version

In 1934 two young Frenchmen set out to write a history marking cinema's fortieth anniversary. Robert Brasillach was a poet, novelist, critic, and fascist sympathizer. He and his friend Maurice Bardèche were film fans, but they had been children when most of the silent classics appeared. In writing their book they relied upon fan magazines, interviews (one with an impoverished Méliès), screenings arranged by the Gaumont company, and the still-flourishing ciné clubs and repertory theaters.[79] Having grown up during the transitional years 1925–1934, Bardèche and Brasillach were forced to address the question of how the history of film style was to be written after the coming of sound.

Bardèche and Brasillach's *Histoire du cinéma* (1935) codifies central tendencies of the Standard Version. There is the division into national schools, the emphasis upon celebrated creators, and the proposition that the history of film is best understood as a search for the distinctive qualities of film as an art. Furthermore, Bardèche and Brasillach assert that it did not take long for filmmakers to discover the medium's "language" *(langage);* what took time was the emergence of cinema as an independent mode of artistic expression.

In particular, cinema had to overcome its theatrical tendencies. According to Bardèche and Brasillach, a lucky accident made the earliest cinema silent. Lacking spoken language, film was forced to become a visual spectacle, and this impelled artists to explore the design and ordering of images. But the arrival of sound created a regressive dependence on the theater. The authors leave open the prospect of a distinctive aesthetic for the sound cinema, but they suspect that intensified commercial pressures will make the creation of truly artistic work highly unlikely.

The customary division into national cinemas led many writers to postulate that a country's culture and character were the primary sources of film art.[80] Bardèche and Brasillach adhered to these *Volksgeist* beliefs all the more passionately because of their commitment to the "integral nationalism" promoted by Charles Maurras and his Action Française group.[81] Nonetheless, instead of writing self-contained histories of each people's filmmaking, they set out periods based upon broad international trends.

According to Bardèche and Brasillach, until 1908 or so film technique was ruled by Méliès and his cinematic sleight-of-hand. Through his technical audacity he pioneered stop-motion, cutting, the dissolve, the double exposure, and variable-speed filming. In the years 1908–1918, as cinema became more respectable, filmmakers in several nations broke with theatrical cinema and disclosed film's distinctive means. During the same period, intellectuals and artists became attracted to cinema.

Bardèche and Brasillach go on to assert that between 1919 and 1924 the cinema became an autonomous art. Several national schools (most prominently the French avant-garde, the Scandinavians, the Germans, and the Hollywood directors) discovered how to use devices that belonged to cinema alone. Editing, changes in camera angles, superimpositions, and similar resources were systematically exploited so as to provoke emotion or suggest ideas. The masterpieces of the late 1910s and early 1920s furnish examples of "a serious and complex art."[82]

The period 1924–1929 is that of the "classic" silent cinema, dominated by the masterworks of the major producing countries. Curious though it sounds today, Bardèche and Brasillach see no significant progress during these years. As a reaction against the self-conscious flourishes of the early 1920s, such as *Caligari*'s sets and *La Roue*'s rhythmic editing, filmmakers now made technique less noticeable. "Henceforth, technical skill would be hidden, almost invisible."[83] This claim flies in the face of the extravagant virtuosity on display in *Napoléon* (1928) and *La Passion de Jeanne d'Arc* (1928), not to mention the special effects of Murnau's *Faust* (1926), but Bardèche and Brasillach prefer to treat the waning years of silent cinema as a period of mature stability. By the time sound arrived, the silent film had completed its stylistic development and had become confident enough of its means to flaunt them no longer.

Earlier formulations of the Basic Story had presented it as a nation-by-nation survey. Historians marked off periods within a country's production largely on the basis of external events such as World War I or the arrival of new decades.[84] Bardèche and Brasillach instead propose a truly transnational stylistic history. Their four periods rest upon the biological metaphor commonly encountered in historical writing: Birth and Infancy, Childhood, Youth, Maturity. (The earliest stage, that of 1895–1908, is even called "Film's First Steps.") In their invocation of the "classic" period of the silent cinema, Bardèche and Brasillach also recall the common art-historical conception of classicism as a dynamic stability in which innovations submit to an overall balance of form and function.

Sound upset this equilibrium. "Five or six happy and triumphal years, brutally interrupted by the discovery that halted cinema on its royal road and instantly took back its fundamental laws and its aesthetic autonomy."[85] The early auditory innovations of Clair and Vidor were not taken up, and sound did not revolutionize film art. By and large, Bardèche and Brasillach's version of the rise-and-fall arc treats the "mature" talkie as merely a mundane silent film accompanied by spoken language, a species of filmed theater.

The first edition of the *Histoire* appeared soon after Clair and others had begun to reveal distinctive audiovisual possibilities in the sound cinema, and Bardèche and Brasillach single out a few directors whose creative powers had been augmented by sound.[86] But they spend far more time deploring the money-hungry producers who have elevated profits over artistry. The elegiac tone recalls Arnheim. "Even today, can one truly love this art without knowing it in the silent days? We cannot separate those last years from the years of our youth . . . We who witnessed the birth of an art may also have seen it die."[87]

The *Histoire* was seldom cited or translated, undoubtedly because of the authors' fascist commitments.[88] During the German occupation Brasillach proved a notoriously enthusiastic collaborator. In 1941 he was nearly appointed *commissaire* of the cinema, a post that would have given him control of the French film industry. The 1943 revision of the *Histoire* contains several anti-Semitic passages, as well as approving citations of Goebbels on national culture and an epilogue arguing that fascism could rejuvenate an enervated bourgeois society.[89] Immediately after the war, Brasillach was executed for collaboration. Bardèche married Brasillach's sister and devoted much of his life to sustaining a cult around his confrère. He completed the 1948 edition of the *Histoire* and updated it periodically.

Despite its political taint, for at least a decade the *Histoire* was the most prominent aesthetic history of film in any language. It brought cinema into the tradition of popularized appreciative art-historical writing, exuding something of the cozy belletrism of Elie Faure's multivolume *Histoire de l'art* (1909–1921). Building on twenty years of film journalism and chronicle histories, the young authors of *Histoire du cinéma* offered the Standard Version in a compact, compelling form.[90]

The volume's influence stretched across the Atlantic to the young Museum of Modern Art. In 1938 Iris Barry published an English translation, supplemented by a foreword by John Abbott indicating the importance of the Film Library in collecting and preserving "the steps through which this new and pervasive art has developed."[91] MOMA's collection and its 16mm programs reflect many of the precepts laid out by Bardèche and Brasillach.

The *Histoire* also influenced the eminent French film historians who began publishing after World War II. The communist Georges Sadoul stood as an ideological antithesis to the young fascist authors. He disdained their *Histoire* as "pamphlétaire,"[92] and he provided alternative explanations of certain phenomena. For example, both Sadoul and his rivals consider economic factors to be important causes of stylistic stability or change, and both cast this in an art-versus-commerce framework, but they differ on how economic causes are to be understood. Bardèche and Brasillach attribute the financial constraints on film artists to a cadre of businessmen eager to make a fortune out of the new mass entertainment. By contrast, Sadoul seeks to tie aesthetic factors to class interests. He argues that cinema developed artistic ambitions in the 1910s because it addressed itself to the bourgeoisie.[93]

Despite such divergences in explanations, Sadoul owes many debts to his two predecessors. His acclaimed one-volume *Histoire du cinéma mondial* (1949) and his multivolume *Histoire générale du cinéma* (published 1948–1954, with posthumous volumes in 1975) adhere rather closely to Bardèche and Brasillach's period scheme.[94] It is likely that Sadoul's work popularized their periodization. More generally, the "problem-space" that Sadoul confronted was defined by the stylistic tendencies enunciated by Bardèche and Brasillach and their predecessors.

Naturally, many aspects of the Basic Story and the Standard Version receive more detailed treatment at Sadoul's hands. For instance, he nuances the Bardèche/Brasillach conception of theatrical cinema by including not just Méliès but Albert Capellani and Danish directors of melodramas. The Standard Version's search for the development of "film language" enables him to bring forward the earliest British filmmakers as important contributors. He highlights the "Brighton School" of around 1900 for the directors' use of close-ups, cut-ins, tracking shots, and camera ubiquity. To the usual emphasis on Griffith's work at the Biograph company Sadoul counterpoints the Vitagraph studio, which "revolutionized the style and technique of the film" through close-ups and changing camera positions.[95] Sadoul is thus able to treat Griffith less as a pure original than as a synthesizer of European and American developments.

Sadoul's research occasionally yields an anticanon, as when he declares Alfred Collins' *Runaway Match* (1903) to be a repository of "almost all the resources of modern technique" and thus superior to the "palpable wretchedness" of *The Great Train Robbery*.[96] More often, though, his research aims to disclose the sources of already-recognized artistry. Griffith remains a great director even if he did not invent all the techniques he used. In Sadoul's work, the Standard Version became a research paradigm guiding more local, fine-grained accounts of the Basic Story.

Sadoul's books carried enormous authority. The synoptic *Histoire du cinéma mondial* ran through six editions in twelve years and was widely translated.[97] After Sadoul had begun to publish his works, René Jeanne and Charles Ford, Pierre Leprohon, and Jean Mitry produced major surveys, all of them variants upon the Standard Version.[98] Several international surveys written by other European film historians developed the Basic Story in congruent ways.[99] Well into the 1970s, the canon and period scheme found in both popular and academic accounts of silent and early sound-film style were not very different from those set out by Bardèche and Brasillach in 1935.

Today it is easy to criticize the Standard Version historians. Most of their assumptions, along with a good many of their conclusions, have been forcefully challenged by their successors. But we should remember the constraints under which they labored. They had virtually no chance to study any film closely, and many had to rely on decades-old recollections. They could therefore hardly develop an incisive critical vocabulary for discussing style. Even the finest writers pursuing this program often bequeathed us loose and inaccurate stylistic descriptions.

Forced to concentrate on an inherited canon, writers in this tradition could seldom stray toward that vast body of work consigned to obscurity. The acknowledged first times, the received opinions that favored Porter and Griffith and other luminaries, the neglect of those important films that did not wriggle through borders and blockades into ciné clubs and circulating programs—all these liabilities handicapped Standard Version historiography. For the most plodding practitioners, writing film history amounted to little more than lining up the Basic Story classics, perhaps reviewed in 16mm MOMA prints or on the screen of the Paris Cinémathèque, and commenting on them afresh.

Beyond constraints arising from a lack of primary research, there were problems with the conceptual scheme undergirding the Standard Version. In committing themselves to a specifically cinematic essence, Standard Version historians tended to sponsor a teleological conception of history. Delighted to discover a complexity of expression in the silent classics, they declared editing, "pure movement," or other qualities of those advanced works to be essentially cinematic. They then projected that essence back onto cinema's origins, treating most significant changes in style as developing toward that goal. As a result, Standard Version historians tended to ignore any event that did not fit their scenario. The disparities of cutting to be found in Porter's films, the ways in which Griffith's work does not anticipate the editing practices that would come to be standardized, the strategies of depth staging that emerged in the 1910s, the moments when Eisenstein's cuts are resolutely nondialectical—all these divergences from the path of cinema's necessary trajectory are simply ignored.

Part of the difficulty stems from the problem of the present, the inclination to take the contemporary moment as the ideal vantage point. The saliency of camerawork and editing in certain 1920s masterworks encouraged historians to measure cinema's progress in relation to them. Because early sound films seemed crude along those dimensions, writers fell back upon a birth-maturity-decline dynamic. Attuned to change rather than to continuity, Standard Version historians saw the advent of sound as an extrastylistic force; businessmen's desire for a technological novelty made technique regress. They did not consider the possibility that sound also promoted and reconfigured certain stylistic tendencies that had come to the fore in the silent cinema, such as spatial realism, temporal continuity, and dialogue-based scene construction.

Up to the arrival of sound, these writers presume, the history of cinema was largely a linear ascent in sophistication and complexity, a development from primitive forms to more refined ones. But the historians, by committing themselves to a search for a single overarching pattern, tend not to treat historical actions as shaped by a multitude of factors. When Panofsky writes that the medium itself gradually became conscious of its unique capacities, all contingent causes are swept aside by the inexorable advance of filmic expression, a kind of demiurge of Cinema. The essence of film art, seeking forms through which it can manifest itself, is embodied in works that actually came into being for very diverse concrete reasons. And what if this essence is very different than the Standard Version supposes? What if cinema does not have an essence at all?

The Standard Version eagerly accepted the biological analogy. But the very terms of youth-maturity-death presuppose what needs to be discovered through concrete investigation: the patterns among the works themselves. There is no reason to believe that stylistic change obeys any large-scale laws. A style may develop from simplicity to complexity, or from complexity to simplicity. Besides, as Truffaut pointed out in a review of a 1950s edition of

Bardèche and Brasillach's *Histoire,* orthodox film historians seemed grimly predisposed to tell a story of decay: "Decline of the European émigrés in Hollywood, decline of the great directors of the silent era, decline, always, of those who had the audacity to debut with a masterpiece."[100] Posit a phase of "mature classicism" at any point, and what follows is likely to seem a slide toward decadence.

Most abstractly, the Standard Version faces objections that afflict any variant of what E. H. Gombrich has called "Hegelianism without metaphysics."[101] This tradition maps purely conceptual distinctions onto a pattern of historical development, picking out artworks as more or less adequate manifestations of the favored qualities. Lumière and Méliès can be taken to instantiate cinema's inherent duality of reality and fantasy, while the abstract possibilities of editing are eventually revealed in Soviet uses of montage. Treating film history as the exfoliation of the *a priori* categories of an aesthetic system becomes a scaled-down version of Hegel's idea that artistic change, like other cultural developments, embodies the unfolding of the spirit.

We could go on adducing criticisms of the Standard Version. It conflated levels of stylistic continuity and change: the level of sheer technical devices, of formal systems recruiting those devices, of genres and traditions mobilizing those systems. The model focused on creative individuals rather than on institutions and collective norms, thereby offering no systematic explanation of how innovations were encouraged, blocked, spread, or sustained. The Standard Version was also heavily prescriptive; those directors who most keenly grasped cinema's essence won the highest praise.

Yet the faults of this research program should not lead us to forget how radical it was. For many years after the invention of cinema, most well-educated people thought that film could acquire prestige only by aping great works of drama or literature. The Standard Version was progressive in showing that unabashedly popular films by Griffith, Chaplin, and other creators were fresher and more venturesome than many productions with loftier ambitions. Even today, it is startling how many intellectuals identify film art with "quality cinema," the latest Shakespeare adaptation or Merchant/Ivory vehicle, rather than with more vigorous and cinematically complex movies in popular genres. Nevertheless, the Standard Version fell prey to elite assumptions by expecting film to develop in accord with high-art models. As a twentieth-century art, film style was fated to follow the scenario laid down by modernism: the medium discovered its nature by subordinating realism to self-conscious artifice.

The first robust rival to this research program accepted some of its premises, particularly an essentialist conception of film art and a belief that the medium's possibilities unfolded in a historical sequence. The key point of dispute centered upon the Standard Version's assumption that artistic progress depended upon cinema's development away from realism and recording. The most energetic advocate of this view was a practicing critic. Watching movies as they were released day by day, he imagined a history that took a fuller measure of contemporary changes in film technique.

chapter

3 Against the Seventh Art: André Bazin and the Dialectical Program

The cinema is not an eternal art. Its forms are not unchanging. Each of the aspects that it reveals is linked inevitably to the psychology of a period. Its successive faces vanish into the shadows when other ways of thinking rise up, when new techniques make earlier ones marginal.

Alexandre Astruc

The inquiry into stylistic history begun in the silent era sustained a research program of great longevity. Many historians of film style followed Lewis Jacobs and Georges Sadoul in providing fine-grained expansions and corrections of the Basic Story, often guided by ideas proposed in the Standard Version. Nonetheless, there have been two other significant research programs. While their proponents have not rejected the Standard Version wholesale, they have also come to grips with difficulties bequeathed them by their predecessors. These programs recast the patterns of change and stability identified in the Standard Version. They added to the canon and offered some fresh causal accounts. Most notably, these research programs addressed the problem of the present. In trying to accommodate contemporaneous stylistic developments, they broke with some long-standing assumptions.

The first full-blown alternative to the Standard Version was launched by André Bazin and his contemporaries. During a career that stretched from the mid-1940s to the late 1950s, Bazin offered the richest elaboration of this program. Yet he wrote no history of film on the scale of Bardèche and Brasillach's synoptic volume. His essays were predominantly high-level journalism, spur-of-the-moment communiqués from the movie houses of his day. Accordingly, his reflections on film history are usually embedded in articles on particular films and directors. Bazin's most wide-ranging historical study, "The Evolution of the Language of Cinema," was published only at the end of his life.[1]

Bardèche and Brasillach grew up in the golden era of silent cinema. Bazin, born in 1918, was a child of the talkies. He and his contemporaries sought to rethink basic problems of film style in the light of developments of the 1930s and 1940s. Out of the rich cinematic culture of postwar Paris, Bazin and other critics created a fresh conception of film as art, and this conception fostered a new model of the history of style.

Comfortable in occupied France, Bardèche and Brasillach updated the 1935 edition of their *Histoire.* Now one could take the proper distance on the talkies and periodize the sound era more carefully. In their 1943 revision Bardèche and Brasillach distinguish a 1929–1933 phase, during which some filmmakers undertook auditory experiments. After 1933, avant-garde movements disappeared, and artists and intellectuals largely gave up the medium. Bardèche and Brasillach argue that the stylistic stability of 1933–1939 was sustained by the routinized process of making a sound film. In commercial filmmaking, the division of labor and the power of the producer made it unlikely that a director would be able to stamp a personal style on a project. The authors echo Gilbert Seldes in indicating that the chief progress of American sound cinema lay in its genres and cycles; formulaic variations of plots had replaced stylistic innovation. The authors speculate that 1939, the threshold of the war, marked the apogee of this "classicism of the 'talkie.'"[2] In sum, after 1933 film style had ceased to develop.

It seems likely that the collaborationist version of the *Histoire du cinéma* (subtitled "Edition définitive") encapsulated the Standard Version for Bazin and his contemporaries. In particular, it bequeathed postwar writers a problem. If film technique halted its progress around 1934, how could one write a contemporary history of style?

French film culture awoke quickly after the German surrender. By the end of 1945, several film weeklies had resumed publication. The prestigious *Revue du cinéma,* which had vanished in 1931, was revived, and *L'écran français,* clandestine during the Occupation, became a gathering point for new film journalism. There was a burst of books on film, most notably the initial volumes of Sadoul's massive history and the first edition of his indispensable *Histoire du cinéma mondial* (1949), destined to replace Bardèche and Brasillach. Soon there appeared the influential journals *Cahiers du cinéma* (founded in 1951) and *Positif* (1952).

There was also a new audience. Young people enthusiastically joined ciné clubs. By 1954 France boasted 200 clubs with more than 100,000 members. Probably the most famous club was Objectif 49, formed by Bazin with the support of Jean Cocteau, Raymond Queneau, and other major figures. Film festivals became major international events, with the revival of the Venice festival in 1946 and the launching of festivals at Cannes, Locarno, Karlovy Vary, and Berlin. In the late 1940s, the European public rediscovered film as an international art.

New films played a central role in this renaissance. Parisian cinéphiles flocked to those Hollywood films blockaded by four years of German occupation: the *films noirs,* the vibrant Technicolor musicals, the historical sagas, the works of Hitchcock and Preston Sturges, and above all Orson Welles's *Citizen Kane* (1941) and *The Magnificent Ambersons* (1942) and William Wyler's *The Little Foxes* (1941) and *The Best Years of Our Lives* (1946). At the same moment appeared the early films of Italian Neorealism, such as Roberto Rossellini's *Open City* (1945) and *Germany Year Zero* (1947), Vittorio De Sica's *Shoeshine* (1946) and *Bicycle Thieves* (1948), and Luchino Visconti's *La terra trema* (1948). There were also important new works by the emerging French directors Robert Bresson, Roger Leenhardt, and Jacques Tati. Finally, the ciné clubs and specialized theaters revived important films from the 1930s. Jean Vigo's *Zéro de conduite,* André Malraux's *Espoir* (1939), and Renoir's *Une partie de compagne* (1936) all had their premieres after the war.

From this rush of cinephilia emerged a fresh attitude to film art. In the pages of the magazines, in the debates after ciné-club screenings, in the cafés of Cannes and Venice, a new conception of the nature and history of cinema arose. What was called *la nouvelle critique* (long before the "New Criticism" associated with 1960s Structuralism) went into battle against upholders of the silent cinema as the Seventh Art.

Some sources of the new criticism run back to the 1930s. Two playwrights, Marcel Pagnol and Sacha Guitry, had welcomed sound cinema as a means for bringing theater to the screen.[3] Both men polemicized fiercely against the reigning aesthetic of the silent image. "The talking film," Pagnol insisted, "is the art of recording, preserving, and diffusing theater."[4] He was proud that his *Marius* (1930) and *Césare* (1936) relied heavily upon conversation.

Guitry had attacked the silent avant-gardists since the mid-1920s, largely because they laid it down that film should be free of dramatic traditions. Guitry's plays, as cool and urbane as Pagnol's were unembarrassedly provincial and emotional, were brought to the screen throughout the 1930s and 1940s. Like Pagnol, Guitry was accused of promoting "canned theater," but his most famous film was audaciously novelistic. *Le roman d'un tricheur* (1936) utilized voice-over narration for almost its entire length; the commentator (Guitry in a frame story) recited all the characters' dialogue himself. This experiment, which relied upon prerecording the film's soundtrack and playing it back during filming, attacked that primacy of the image so valued by silent-era partisans. For Guitry, as for Pagnol, the purpose of the sound cinema was to render human action and psychology through speech. The story goes that when a cameraman suggested starting a scene by framing a chandelier before moving the camera down to the table, Guitry answered: "But my dear friend, the chandelier has no dialogue!"[5]

Men of the theater, Pagnol and Guitry had little influence upon critics still promulgating the silent-film aesthetic. Other voices were somewhat more persuasive. In the mid-1930s Roger Leenhardt, a member of the group around the philosopher Emmanuel Mounier, began to articulate a fresh aesthetic of the sound cinema. He learned the importance of the soundtrack while working as a cutter, and in Mounier's journal *Esprit* he published a series of articles tutoring readers in basic film aesthetics. Leenhardt believed that the cinema's essence lay in its realism, not in its aesthetic deformation of actuality.

Leenhardt's views were echoed from a more prestigious quarter. The left-wing novelist André Malraux grew interested in the cinema, seeking to adapt his *La condition humaine* (1933) and finally directing a version of his 1937 novel about the Spanish Civil War, *Espoir* (1939; Fig. 3.1). In 1940 Malraux published in the fine-arts magazine *Verve* his influential essay "Outline of a Psychology of the Cinema." Malraux's discussion of silent film adhered to the Basic Story, but he also claimed that far from destroying silent film, sound changed it into another sort of art.[6]

In 1947, in his hugely popular *Le musée imaginaire,* Malraux amplified his case. He argued that the doctrines of turn-of-the-century modernism, according to which the creator dominated reality by means of a style, were valid only for a brief moment in the history of art. The cinema, he claimed, was heir to the long tradition of descriptive painting. While modernism liberated painting from narrative demands, cinema took over those illustrative purposes that had been paramount from the Renaissance to the end of the nineteenth century.[7] Malraux thereby implied that cinéphiles had erred in trying to align film with modernism. The sound cinema was pledged to realism by its very place in the history of the visual arts.

Leenhardt and Malraux, both born around 1900, belonged to Sadoul's generation; silent films lived vividly in their memories. But for Alexandre Astruc, who was four years old when *The Jazz Singer* was released, movies meant talkies. His precocious, acerbic postwar essays mocked nostalgia for the silent classics. The world of the silent film, Astruc announced, "which sleeps in the dry pages of film history books, which revivals and retrospectives try uselessly to resuscitate, has for us the odor of things long dead."[8]

Astruc's most influential idea was his demand that the motion picture become an art of sheer personal creation, as direct and immediate as the novelist's pen.[9] This conception of the *caméra-stylo* helped lay the groundwork for that idea of "authorship" which emerged so powerfully in the pages of *Cahiers du cinéma* in the early 1950s. Against the Standard Version's idea that film was born as an art in the 1910s and 1920s, Astruc suggested that, with the revelations of Renoir, Welles, and others, cinema ceased to be a spectacle and became "a form of expression."[10] The sound cinema of the late 1930s and 1940s most fully revealed the artistic possibilities of the medium.

The most significant member of *la nouvelle critique* was André Bazin. By 1950

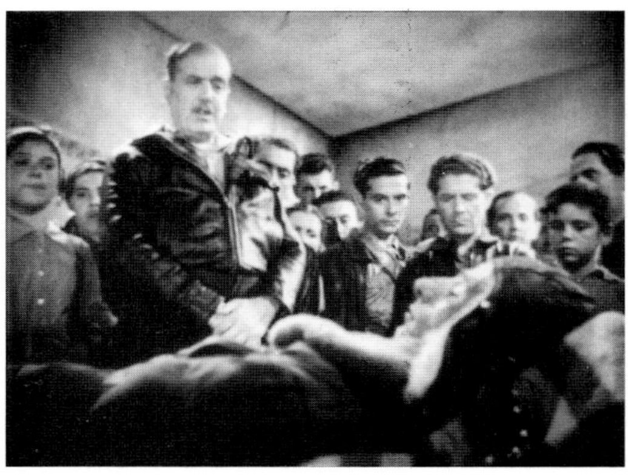

3.1 A Spanish general pays homage to a dead pilot in Malraux's *Espoir.*

he had moved to the center of his nation's film criticism—writing for most of the journals, reviewing for *Le Parisien libéré,* organizing Objectif 49 and Le Festival du Film Maudit, founding *Cahiers,* becoming president of the French film critics' association, and publishing a book on Welles. As Leenhardt and Astruc took up directing films, Bazin became the most acute and subtle proponent of the new generation's alternative to the Standard Version of film history.

The writers of *la nouvelle critique* advanced three main ideas. First, they attacked the belief that cinema gains its artistic power by stylizing or transforming reality. Instead, the critics claimed that recent films proved the fundamentally realistic vocation of the medium. Second, they argued that cinema was not like music or abstract painting; it was a storytelling art, and its closest kinship was with the novel and the theater. Finally, the 1940s critics argued that the aesthetic of silent-film artistry had too often neglected commercial cinema and its audience. By contrast, the young critics held cinema to be a popular art. They believed that Hollywood displayed high-level achievements and that the real "avant-garde" was the advanced studio filmmaking of the sound era. Each of these three precepts warrants a more detailed look.

By the mid-1940s it was chiefly historians and critics who subscribed to the silent-film aesthetic. The Soviet directors had long since recanted radical montage; Luis Buñuel, Jacques Feyder, Clair, Lang, and Cocteau had turned to more conventional techniques.[11] Surveying this situation, the *nouvelle critique* writers concluded that the aesthetic of the silent era was a dead end. "The charms of the Image, with a capital I, are exhausted," wrote Leenhardt in 1945.[12] Even the sacrosanct avant-garde of Surrealism and "pure cinema" had, Bazin argued, contributed very little to the development of cinema. Aiming at an elite audience and resisting the realistic nature of the medium, the experimental film had worked in a vacuum.[13]

In his *Verve* essay Malraux had considered the sound cinema not as the silent film plus dialogue but rather as a union of photographic recording with the radio play, which manipulated recorded sound with the freedom available to the silent film's visual track. "The sound film stands to the silent as painting does to drawing."[14] Several postwar critics pushed the idea further. The mistake of the orthodox view, they maintained, was emphasizing film's stylization of reality. In trying to make cinema a modern art, theorists had elevated style over content.[15] By contrast, the *nouvelle critique* writers argued, cinema's artistic possibilities lay exactly in that domain which the silent-cinema adherents despised: representational fidelity.[16] According to the young critics, the coming of sound had shown silent cinema to be narrow and incomplete as an artistic medium.

Broader changes in the arts probably helped turn the postwar critics away from the purism of the silent-era aesthetic. During the 1920s and 1930s, while the prewar Cubists and abstractionists were becoming consecrated as official museum art, realism was returning to favor. Germany's New Objectivity and the official Nazi art that followed, accompanied by the purge of "bolshevist" and "degenerate" modern tendencies; Stalin's Socialist Realism and his elimination of "decadent" and "reactionary" experimentation; Mussolini's state style; Piscator's and Brecht's "documentary realism" as well as the Popular Front style of the 1930s; the efforts by neoclassicizing painters and the School of Paris to supersede Cubism; the return to figurative art by Balthus, Picasso, and Beckmann; the work of the Mexican muralists and the U.S. Federal Art Project—everywhere one looked, artists of left, right, and center were turning to realism. Wartime propaganda contributed to the same tendency.[17] At the end of the 1940s debates about "existential realism" and Soviet-supported Social Realism surrounded the Parisian painters André Fougeron and Bernard Buffet, while Sartre's call for "engaged" art was often interpreted as a plea for artists to bear witness to contemporary life. In addition, the postwar resurgence of semidocumentary filmmaking in Germany, France, Italy, and Eastern Europe turned many progressive film critics sharply against the pictorialist aesthetic of the silent era.

According to *la nouvelle critique,* one index of sound cinema's new realism was the decline of montage. In French, *montage* denotes cinematic editing in general.[18] For writers of this period, though, montage also implied a particular sort of abstract, conceptual, or rhythmic cutting. Through montage the director assembled a meaningful totality out of fragmentary shots. Although the Soviet silent films were widely perceived as realistic (for their use of locations and nonactors), their cutting technique came to define the most artificial aspects of montage. The Soviets had, after all, demonstrated that it was possible to create a scene simply by cutting together details that might never have coexisted in actuality (Figs. 2.15, 2.16). Similarly, Eisenstein's "montage of

3.2 Classical découpage in Howard Hawks's *Twentieth Century* (1934): After Lily shoos her maid out of her train compartment . . .

3.3 Hawks cuts to a medium two-shot of Lily and her importuning mentor, Oscar Jaffe.

3.6 . . . flinging herself furiously onto the sofa.

3.7 Cut to Jaffe's reaction, and then . . .

attractions" did great violence to reality by assembling shots solely to generate an idea (Figs. 2.17, 2.18).

An alternative conception of editing came to be called *découpage.* Again, the term harbors two meanings. In film production, the découpage is the shot breakdown or shooting script that precedes filming. For the new critics, *découpage* also designated the sort of editing that dissects the scene, analyzing the action into brief shots. Unlike montage, which brings together heterogeneous fragments, découpage breaks a spatiotemporal whole into closer views.[19] We have already seen examples from *The President* and *Crows and Sparrows* (Figs. 1.3–1.5 and 1.6, 1.7).

Malraux had called Griffith's dissection of theatrical space "découpage," as had Bardèche and Brasillach.[20] In the postwar years, however, French critics often identified silent-film editing with montage and sound-film cutting with découpage. Astruc, for instance, argued that the silent film achieved its poetic

3.4 As Lily begins to throw a tantrum . . .

3.5 . . . Hawks cuts back to the *plan américain,* matching on her movement. This prepares for her action of . . .

3.8 . . . an eyeline-match reverse shot conveys Lily's response.

effects from a montage of disparate images, whereas the talking film was dominated by découpage, a technique "no longer poetic but theatrical, no longer a forced confrontation but an organized linkage."[21] This marks a crucial shift of values. Standard Version historians had praised Griffith's analytical cutting as antitheatrical because it broke up the continuous "theatrical" recording of the scene; but now découpage was praised for being more "theatrical" than montage, since it respected the temporal and spatial integrity of the action.

A large part of sound cinema's realism, therefore, depended upon the unobtrusive analytical editing, shot/reverse-shot cutting, and smooth camera movements characteristic of most countries' studio cinemas since the mid-1930s. Figs. 3.2–3.8, from *Twentieth Century* (1934), illustrate several tactics of "theatrical" découpage of the era.

The turn away from the orthodox aesthetic toward a realism-based conception of the medium was accompanied by a second basic idea. Although the

Basic Story and the Standard Version tacitly took the development of film style to manifest a growing power in storytelling, extreme partisans of the Standard Version often minimized this tendency and celebrated cinema as "the music of light" or "pure movement" (as Seldes had suggested). The *nouvelle critique* writers denounced this as pure, and purist, illusion. The arrival of sound and the death of the silent avant-garde demonstrated that cinema's richest tradition lay in the realm of narrative.

In her 1948 study *L'âge du roman américain,* Claude-Edmonde Magny traced the influence of film on the American novel. She held that a film was essentially a story, like the novel, and she argued that the two media shared techniques of temporal arrangement and point of view. Contemporary novelists like Dos Passos and Faulkner had understood this, borrowing such cinematic devices as alternating episodes. Correlatively, Magny pointed out, recent films had become more literary in their use of flashbacks and first-person narration.[22] Bazin agreed, claiming that the postwar period had forged a "novelistic" cinema in such works as Leenhardt's *Les dernières vacances* (1948) and Bresson's *Diary of a Country Priest* (1951).[23] By running counter to the position that film was an autonomous art, the young critics were led to unprecedentedly subtle discussions of cinema's use of literary devices of ellipsis and flashback construction.[24]

The realistic techniques of découpage enhanced the structural affinities between cinema and fiction. Bazin put it simply: "To make cinema today is to tell a story in a clear and perfectly transparent language."[25] Contrasting the mature sound cinema with the image-based silent era, Leenhardt wrote: "As in the novel, where the writing, subordinate and often distracting, must not be noticed, on the screen the technique of the camera is making itself little by little invisible . . . Only ten years will be needed for cinema to affirm its real power and nature: to be the most efficient, most complete of all narrative modes."[26] Whereas the advocates of the Standard Version had presumed that the film artist told the story through a personal, highly "poetic" use of the medium (Figs. 2.11, 2.12), the *nouvelle critique* writers stressed the analogies between cinema's mainstream "invisible" style and the unobtrusive narration furnished by laconic prose.

Even more unorthodox was the new critics' conviction that the modern cinema owed a debt to theater. Astruc saw sound cinema's découpage as inherently theatrical.[27] Bazin agreed: in a modern film, the editing did little more than emphasize key actions and follow the flow of a stagelike performance.[28] Calling cinema a "polymorphic" art, Leenhardt suggested that the sound cinema ought to collaborate with its old rival, the stage. Bazin pushed the point further, contending that now the cinema was sure enough of its means to adapt plays without fearing the stigma of "filmed theater." He praised the theatrical Pagnol for exploiting the rich *Midi* accent and putting dialogue at the center of the intrigue.[29] In a long, intricate essay Bazin argued that cinema was well suited to rendering the conventions that lay at the heart of theater.[30]

Inherently realistic and committed to storytelling, the cinema was also irrevocably a popular art. In the mid-1930s, Leenhardt had criticized "advanced" artists for esoteric formal experiments. He believed that the worldwide triumph of cinema proved that ordinary people could quickly become adept in the conventions of a new art. It was the intellectuals whose tastes were limited, since they could not see the manifold beauties of popular cinema.[31] Fifteen years later, in a statement inaugurating the ciné club Objectif 49, Bazin argued that the silent avant-garde was crippled by undertaking farfetched experiments comprehensible to only a few admirers.[32] Throughout his career, he believed that cinema's dependence on mass tastes was one source of its vitality.

To defend cinema as an inherently popular art was inevitably to defend Hollywood. The *nouvelle critique* writers reminded their readers that modern, "theatrical" découpage was forged in American studios. In 1946 Astruc summed up this Yankee "classicism."

> After ten years of talking pictures, [Hollywood's] technicians brought to perfection the most economical and transparent technique possible. A film was made of a series of sequences in *plan américain* [knees-up framing], with some camera movements and a constant play of shot and reverse-shot. Montage, which had been of the essence in the silent era, was abandoned and replaced by découpage. The movements of the camera were utilized in very precise framings: the tracking shot to give the impression of depth, the pan shot to give a sense of breadth.
>
> On the sound stages of Hollywood there was passed along a sort of empirical grammar formed from the long experience of highly devoted artisans. They knew, for example, that near the end of a film it was better to increase the number of close-ups in order to raise the degree of emotion. They also knew that the *plan américain* was the most efficient shot, permitting the greatest economy of editing.
>
> This technique may have lacked ambition, but it was faultless and sure. It would still be interesting today to analyze its smallest details.[33]

The Hollywood of the 1930s, despised by Bardèche and Brasillach as a factory bent on destroying originality, became a guild in which superb craftsmen, sharing a rich tradition, labored anonymously to create works of art.

This tradition was imitated around the world. "The formation of a sort of international style took place only after the cinema put sound in place," claimed Leenhardt. "The triumph of *talkies* gave us a 'Hollywood' type of film turned out in Paris, Berlin, even Moscow."[34] If we define avant-garde artists as those who open up paths that their successors are *obliged* to follow, Bazin proclaimed teasingly, the real avant-garde toiled in the commercial cinema, and many of its innovators came from California.[35]

Much of the case for cinema's realism, narrative propensities, and mass popularity rested upon the medium's most recent accomplishments. Like their predecessors, members of *la nouvelle critique* were obliged to come to terms with the cinema of their moment. For those critics newly freed of the Occupation, the contemporary cinema stretched back to 1939 and comprised the works of Renoir, Welles, Wyler, and the Italian Neorealists.

These contemporary directors relied upon a distinctive technique: *profondeur de champ.* Usually translated as "depth of field," in the critical discourse of the period the term actually denotes two significantly different technical options. Most often it designates the capacity of the camera lens to render several planes of action in sharp focus (Fig. 3.9). This technique, the product of decisions about staging, lighting, film stock, and manipulation of the lens, is often, somewhat problematically, translated as "deep focus." But *profondeur de champ* also embraces the possibility of what we call staging in depth—placing significant objects or figures at distinctly different distances from the camera, *regardless of whether all those elements in the scene are in focus.* For example, Renoir's 1930s films frequently arrange scenes in depth without keeping all planes crisply focused (Fig. 3.10). Nonetheless, the postwar Parisian critics considered Renoir a forerunner of the modern technique of *profondeur de champ.* As used by French critics, the term presumes depth staging, whether or not all planes are in focus.

Although films had exploited *profondeur de champ* since the beginning of cinema (see, for example, Fig. 1.2), the technique was almost completely ignored by critics of the 1920s and 1930s. Proponents of the Standard Version considered such staging a regression to a "theatrical" mode. But then came *Citizen Kane.*

Film critics' discovery of *profondeur de champ* was almost certainly initiated through the self-conscious promotional efforts of Orson Welles and his cinematographer, Gregg Toland. Just as Griffith's self-proclaimed invention of cross-cutting and close-ups boosted him into the standard histories, the publicity around *Citizen Kane* declared it a stylistic turning point. During the film's American release, Toland signed several articles explaining how *Kane* broke the rules.[36] He claimed as his chief innovation a technique he called "pan-focus."

> Through its use it is possible to photograph action from a range of eighteen inches from the camera lens to over two hundred feet away, with extreme

3.9 Staging in marked depth, with faces in focus from the foreground into the background (*Justice est faite,* 1954).

3.10 A famous shot from Renoir's *Partie de compagne* (1936), with deep staging and out-of-focus foreground planes.

> foreground and background figures and action both recorded in sharp relief. Hitherto, the camera had to be focused either for a close or a distant shot, all efforts to encompass both at the same time resulting in one or the other being out of focus. This handicap necessitated the breaking up of a scene into long and short angles [that is, long shots and close-ups], with much consequent loss of realism. With pan-focus, the camera, like the human eye, sees an entire panorama at once, with everything clear and lifelike.[37]

In more technical discussions in the trade press, Toland emphasized that pan-focus allowed him to meet Welles's demand for what critics would later call *long takes*—shots that ran to uncommon lengths and did duty for a series of briefer shots. "Welles' technique of visual simplification might combine what would conventionally be made as two separate shots—a close-up and an insert—in a single, non-dollying shot."[38] (See Fig. 3.11.)

Well before *Citizen Kane* premiered in Paris, Bazin and his contemporaries knew of Welles's and Toland's experiments. Sartre saw the film in the United States, and his essay on it was published nearly a year before the film appeared in France.[39] After *Kane*'s Paris release in July 1946, *La revue du cinéma* energetically promoted Welles, printing extensive reviews of *Kane* and *Ambersons,* along with script extracts, portions from a book on Welles's career, and an article by Toland explaining pan-focus and illustrating it with deep-focus stills from *Kane* and *The Little Foxes.*[40]

Parisian cinéphiles were entranced by the new style. A 1948 summary of recent developments in cinema praised Wellesian *profondeur de champ* as a milestone.[41] Jean-Pierre Melville composed a shot in his *Silence de la mer* (1949) in homage to *Kane*'s famous deep-focus shot of the glass and bottle in the foreground (Fig. 3.12). Leenhardt's *Les dernières vacances* made use of the sort of fluid depth found in *The Magnificent Ambersons* (Figs. 3.13–3.15).

3.11 "Pan-focus" and the long take: Kane is about to sign his newspapers over to his former guardian.

3.12 *Silence de la mer:* Melville pays homage to Welles; compare Fig. 3.21.

3.13 *Les dernières vacances:* Gabarde and Juliette dance past Jacques, first with him in the background . . .

3.14 . . . then, after a pan following them . . .

3.15 . . . the camera discovers Jacques's jealous reaction in the foreground.

Members of the *nouvelle critique* group were quick to grasp the implications of the technique. Welles's and Toland's claims to "realism" appealed to Leenhardt, Astruc, and Bazin. Allied with the long take, staging and shooting in depth was simpler and more natural than classical découpage. It permitted the director to present the action directly, as a skillful novelist narrates a scene.[42] Depth of field also raised new dramaturgical possibilities, as Bazin pointed out: the single shot with varying points of interest could build tension and create a denser ensemble performance.[43]

Similar arguments were mounted for Wyler's *Little Foxes* and *The Best Years of Our Lives.* Both were shot by Toland and bore the stamp of his "pan-focus." At a period when Sadoul was venerating John Ford, Leenhardt offered a rude provocation in his cry "À bas Ford! Vive Wyler!" He argued that to prefer Wyler was to align oneself with the most progressive forces in the "Hollywoodian *new look.*"[44]

In discussing both Welles and Wyler, the *nouvelle critique* writers claimed that *profondeur de champ* allowed the spectator freedom to scan the frame for significant information. Astruc declared that *profondeur de champ* "obliges the spectator's eye to make its own technical découpage, that is, to find for itself within the scene those lines of action usually delineated by camera movements."[45] Bazin argued that both *The Best Years of Our Lives* and *Citizen Kane* coaxed the viewer into participating in just these ways. The critics may have been aware of Wyler's own assertion that using depth and the long take "lets the spectator look from one to the other character at his own will, do his own cutting."[46]

Other Hollywood offerings confirmed the importance of Welles's and Wyler's innovations. Deep-focus and the long take seemed to define the future of cinema. Hitchcock's *Rope* (1948), consisting of a mere eight shots, suggested that far from being the essence of cinema, editing could be almost completely suppressed. Now a film could be rendered suspenseful and expressive solely through the choreography of characters and camera.[47]

Astruc, Bazin, and Leenhardt believed that Welles's and Wyler's discoveries had completed cinema's stylistic development. After montage and an aesthetic reifying the silent image, after découpage and the sound cinema's consolidation of transparent technique, there arrived *profondeur de champ* and the long take. These devices rendered the cinema a fully flexible medium of artistic expression.

To opponents who accused them of a fixation upon form, members of *la nouvelle critique* replied that the efflorescence of sound-film style allowed directors to confront new challenges of subject and theme. Now Cocteau, Olivier, and Melville were adapting plays in an aesthetically sophisticated way, producing neither ordinary films nor canned theater (Fig. 3.16). Even in the

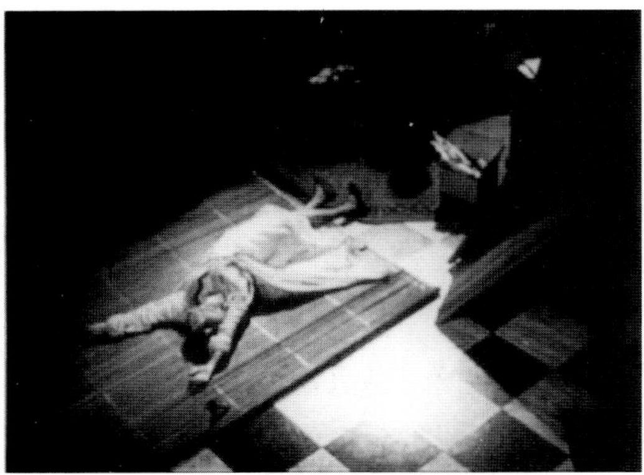

3.16 Enhanced theatricality: the curtain goes up on a bedroom in Melville's adaptation of Cocteau's *Les enfants terribles* (1950).

3.17 The priest is confronted by the tormented Chantal in Bresson's brooding, remorseless adaptation of Bernanos' *Diary of a Country Priest* (1951).

3.18 Daily routine and patrimony in *Farrebique.*

commercial American cinema, the ten-minute takes in *Rope* could be seen as an experiment in filming stage drama. By adapting novels to the screen, Malraux, Bresson, and Leenhardt were creating a cinema with the psychological density of modern literature (Fig. 3.17). Alain Resnais was making essayistic films about works of art; Georges Rouquier's *Farrebique* (1946) recorded a year in the life of a farm family (Fig. 3.18). And the Italians were utilizing the new technical resources in a splendid variety of ways.

Just as Bardèche and Brasillach took the coming of sound to mark the end of stylistic progress, the *nouvelle critique* writers posited that in the late 1940s the sound film had reached a kind of final state. New technologies would be introduced, but color and widescreen could only reinforce the tendency toward a realistic, storytelling cinema reliant on depth, camera movement, and the long take. The problem for the immediate future was the exploration of new domains: social reality, works of art in adjacent media, and that path toward personal expression signposted by Astruc's idea of the *caméra-stylo.*

The Evolution of Film Language

Only a few months after the publication of Bardèche and Brasillach's Occupation *Histoire du cinéma,* André Bazin, writing in a Parisian student magazine, commented upon the waning of cinephilia among young people. He reminded his readers that the coming of sound had alienated intellectuals, and he traced their disenchantment to the fact that they no longer had any influence over an increasingly commercial industry.[48] The twenty-five-year-old Bazin did not mention Bardèche and Brasillach, but his indictment pointedly recalls their generation's despair at the rise of the talkies. His charge that intellectuals of the previous decade had displayed an "absence of all effort at systematic thought in regard to the cinema" might well have been addressed to them.[49]

In 1943 Bazin accepted the commonplace that sound cinema had halted innovation. "The curve of [cinema's] stylistic evolution already shows a downward path."[50] After the war, however, the new films from America, Italy, and some French directors suggested that the medium had been reborn. From 1946 until his death in late 1958, Bazin challenged the program of the Standard Version. Naturally he drew upon the ideas circulating among his comrades of *la nouvelle critique.* But his manner of synthesis and the conclusions he drew were more original, more systematic, and more influential than anything offered by his contemporaries. His framework, which I shall call the Dialectical Version of the Basic Story, offered an optimistic, wide-ranging account of cinema's stylistic path.

Bazin's revision starts from the idea that the Basic Story includes not one trend but two. One tendency follows the scenario laid down by the Standard Version: some filmmakers did seek to free cinema from photographic reproduction. The national schools of the 1920s put their faith in manipulations of the image through camera tricks or abstract montage.[51] But Bazin finds a second tendency running alongside the first, stretching back to the "primitive" cinema and emerging in the work of Robert Flaherty, F. W. Murnau, and others. These filmmakers put their faith in the camera's ability to record and reveal physical reality. The result was a realism of time and space that was no less artistic than the stylization yielded by Expressionism and montage.

The coming of sound, then, halted only one tendency, the cinema of excessive artifice. Bazin claims that sound promoted a moderate realism of staging and cutting, continuing the tradition of analytical editing founded by Griffith. The "invisible découpage" seen in all countries' films of the mid-1930s respected real space and made the celebrated montage techniques of the silent era seem overwrought. Although many accounts of Bazin's theory counterpose montage and *mise en scène* as exclusive alternatives, he agrees with his contemporaries in distinguishing two sorts of editing: the abstract montage characteristic of the silent era and the découpage characteristic of the sound film. Proponents of the Standard Version deplored the "theatrical" sound cinema of découpage, but Bazin argued that it was a reasonable compromise between silent stylization and the more realistic cinema to come. The stabilizing of Hollywood genres and the perfecting of découpage helped create a "classical" equilibrium of style during the 1930s.

Realistic in its portrayal of spatial relations, classical découpage nonetheless was obliged to elide or stretch real time. A cut might trim a few seconds of dramatically irrelevant action or exaggerate a gesture through a slight overlap. (See Figs. 3.4, 3.5.) Classical editing thus retained traces of an "intellectual and abstract" rhythm.[52] This drawback was overcome by means of a "dialectical step forward in the history of film language."[53] That step was taken by Renoir, Welles, Wyler, and Italian Neorealist directors. Bazin identifies this new phase with the long take and the shot in depth, which preserve temporal continuity as well as spatial unity.

It was *Citizen Kane* that prompted Bazin's effort to trace the "evolution of the language of cinema." From the perspective of the Standard Version, the film could seem merely a pastiche. Sadoul, for instance, dismissed all claims for the film's novelty. He declared *Kane* "an encyclopedia of old techniques" and criticized Welles for reviving silent-era Expressionism.[54] To these objections Bazin replied that *Kane*'s depth of field defined new functions for its inherited techniques. Bazin went beyond merely itemizing these devices, as Sadoul had, and sought to account for their contextual uses.

He points out that early cinema spontaneously exploited *profondeur de champ* well before the arrival of analytical editing (Fig. 3.19). In this period, cuts served only to link spaces, not to break a scene into closer views. But when directors began to employ analytical cutting, deep-focus camerawork gave way to shallow focus. Selectivity of focus was the most effective way to guide the viewer's attention within close shots (Fig. 3.20). The depth of the primitive shot gave way to Griffith's tactics of guiding the spectator's attention, and these devices were the basis of classical découpage.

Bazin now gives his argument a subtle twist. He claims that the deep focus of the 1940s created a "vast geological displacement" in film language. How? By assimilating into the *single* image the *principles* of analytical cutting.[55] Bazin's key example is the scene of Susan's aborted suicide in *Citizen Kane* (Fig. 3.21). A 1930s découpage-based director would have cut from Kane outside Susan's room, banging on the door, to Susan gasping in bed, and then to the glass and

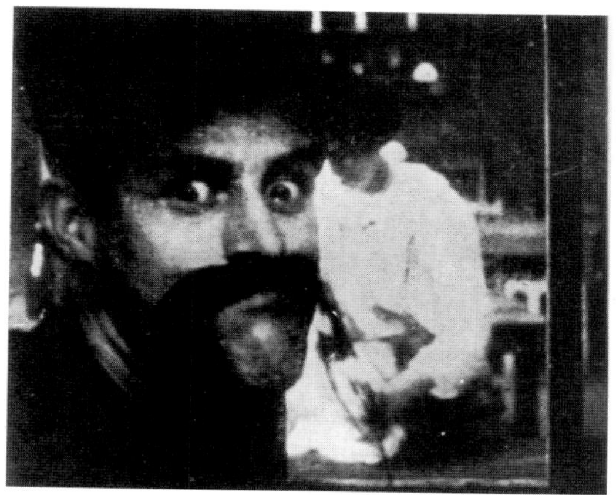

3.19 A shot from an unidentified 1910 entry in the *Onésime* series, used by Bazin to illustrate "primitive" *profondeur de champ.*

3.20 An out-of-focus background highlights the face in this close-up from Lubitsch's *Lady Windermere's Fan* (1925).

3.21 Susan's attempted suicide (*Citizen Kane*).

bottle. This string of shots would allow us to infer that she has taken an overdose of medicine. But Welles jams all the elements into a single frame.

> Far from being . . . a return to the "static shot" employed in the early days of cinema by Méliès, Zecca and Feuillade, or else some rediscovery of filmed theatre, Welles's sequence shot is a decisive stage in the evolution of film language, which after having passed through the montage of the silent period and the *découpage* of the talkies, is now tending to revert to the static shot, but by a dialectical progress which incorporates all the discoveries of *découpage* into the realism of the sequence shot.[56]

A one-shot scene in the early cinema would not so sharply isolate the key elements. While a tableau shot would probably put the door in the background, both the bed and the bottle would probably be situated in the middle

3.22 In *Judex* (1916), the photograph turned from us on the desk in the lower front is significant, but Feuillade does not isolate it in a foreground "close-up" plane as Welles has emphasized the glass and bottle in Fig. 3.21.

3.23 As Homer and Butch play in the foreground, Al smiles appreciatively in the middle ground, and the barstool boys express their appreciation; the important dramatic action, however, takes place in the far-off booth, where Fred phones Al's daughter, Peggy.

ground, in a welter of other scenic detail. (For a somewhat comparable case, see Fig. 3.22.) The three striated zones of action in Welles's shot highlight the key ingredients of the scene, but without cutting. "The fixed shot of *Citizen Kane* could be conceived only after the era of montage; Griffith's analysis had to reveal clearly the anatomy of presentation before Welles or Wyler, with a cameraman of Gregg Toland's class, could remodel the unity of the image much as a sculptor might do."[57]

Accepting the chronology and canon of the Basic Story, Bazin reorganizes it by means of a quasi-Hegelian account of the development of film style. The opposing strains of the 1920s, Expressionism-plus-montage and photographic realism, find a temporary synthesis in 1930s classical cutting. But this synthesis still falls short of true realism. The conflicting tendencies within classical cutting—time-abstracting découpage versus the urge to respect real time—yield a new synthesis in Welles's deep-focus long take.

Bazin also insists that in certain directors this "geological displacement" had far-reaching aesthetic consequences. His celebrated discussion of a climactic scene in Butch's bar in *The Best Years of Our Lives* shows how the scale of planes is in inverse ratio to the significance of the action taking place on them. Here Homer's piano-playing in the foreground furnishes a "diversionary action" in tension with the scene's crux, the phone call that Fred makes in the distant booth (Fig. 3.23).[58]

Bazin demonstrates that the same principle can obtain when depth is exploited much less vigorously. In *The Magnificent Ambersons* Fanny's breakdown at the kitchen table stands out against a "pretext action." The salient zones are not stacked in depth, but we must still scan the frame; otherwise George's prattle

3.24 "Pretext action" and real action in *The Magnificent Ambersons.*

as he wolfs down cake will distract us from Fanny's twinge of distress (Fig. 3.24).[59] Renoir's restlessly panning camera in *La règle du jeu* creates a similar effect. In sum, the revolution in film language of the 1940s demands that the spectator cultivate viewing skills that go beyond those elicited by classical cutting. The viewer will have to scan the image, seek out salient points of interest, and integrate information into an overall judgment about a scene.

While Bazin's contemporaries often treated *profondeur de champ* as an all-purpose replacement for cutting and shallow focus, he argued that a single film might fruitfully incorporate these antithetical elements. Within *Citizen Kane,* he points out, Welles mixes long takes, which "crystallize" dramatic time, with montage sequences, which represent a more conceptual duration. Welles thus creates a "narrational dialectic [*dialectique du récit*]."[60] Now the time-abstracting qualities of editing find contextually appropriate functions. "Far from wiping out once and for all the conquests of montage, this reborn realism gives them a body of reference and a meaning. It is only an increased realism of the image that can support the abstraction of montage."[61]

Similarly, in studying *The Little Foxes,* Bazin showed that when a film used *profondeur de champ* constantly, the conventional soft-focus background could become an aesthetically significant choice. In a climactic scene, Horace has refused to lend his wife, Regina, the money she needs for her schemes. During their quarrel, he is stricken with a heart attack (Fig. 3.25). After she refuses to bring him his medicine, he staggers out of the parlor and starts upstairs (Fig. 3.26). As Regina sits unmoving, facing the audience, Horace can be glimpsed collapsing on the steps in the background; he is in darkness, and his figure is out of focus (Fig. 3.27). After Horace has lost consciousness, Regina whirls to her feet (Fig. 3.28) and starts toward the stair; only now does Wyler shift focus to present him clearly (Fig. 3.29). The alert viewer of *The Best*

3.25 *The Little Foxes:* Horace convulsed by his heart attack.

3.26 Cut in to the immobile Regina. Starting out of the room, Horace stumbles against the rear wall, out of focus.

3.27 In an out-of-focus silhouette, Horace collapses on the staircase.

3.28 As Regina rises and turns, Toland racks focus.

3.29 She runs to Horace, with the entire background now in focus.

Years of Our Lives must concentrate on Fred far away in the rear of Butch's bar, but at least there the figure is crisply focused (Fig. 3.23). In the *Little Foxes* scene the crucial action is all but indiscernible. Thanks to selective focus, Bazin claims, "the viewer feels an extra anxiety and almost wants to push the immobile Bette Davis aside to get a better look."[62]

While Leenhardt, Astruc, and others seized by polemical zeal might speak of *profondeur de champ* as marking the end of classical découpage, Bazin was more prudent. He refused to take depth and the long take as absolute values. Within a film these techniques could always enter into a dynamic relation with editing, selective focus, and other resources.

At the same moment Bazin was analyzing the style of Welles and Wyler, the films of Italian Neorealism were being released in Paris. Bazin was particularly concerned with Neorealism's "phenomenological" realism and, like Magny, with its novelistic use of ellipses and ambiguity. He also enlisted the Italians in the trend minimizing classical découpage. Visconti's *La terra trema* showed that Wellesian depth yielded magnificent results outside the studio:

> *Profondeur de champ* has naturally led Visconti (as it led Welles) not only to renounce editing [*montage*] but literally to reinvent découpage. His "shots," if one can still speak of shots, are unusually long—often three or four minutes; in each, quite naturally, several actions are taking place at once. Visconti also seems to have wanted systematically to base his construction of the image upon the event itself. A fisherman rolls a cigarette? No ellipsis is granted us; we see the whole operation. It will not be reduced to its dramatic or symbolic meaning, as is usual with editing [*montage*].[63]

In the opening scenes of *La terra trema,* for example, Visconti establishes the family's daily routine in leisurely fashion, employing long takes and striking depth (Fig. 3.30).

The revelations of Welles, Wyler, and the Neorealists made Renoir appear all the more farsighted. "He alone," wrote Bazin, "forced himself to look back beyond the resources provided by montage and so uncovered the secret of a film form that would permit everything to be said without chopping the world up into little fragments."[64] Renoir seemed to have pioneered the *profondeur de champ* later exploited by Welles and Wyler (Fig. 3.10). Less obviously, his freely moving camera provided a horizontal equivalent of depth, a "lateral depth of field" that suggests a seamless world enveloping the action (Figs. 3.31–3.33).[65]

Bazin wrote about the Hollywood "avant-garde" immediately after the war, ending this phase of his career with his 1950 book on Welles. He spent his remaining years preparing a monograph on Renoir, "the most visual and sensual of filmmakers."[66] With the installation of Renoir as precursor and

3.30 *La terra trema:* Casual zigzag depth for the family's morning routines.

3.31 *La règle du jeu:* As Schumacher moves through the crowd of servants looking for Lisette, Renoir's camera pans rightward with him . . .

3.32 . . . picks up St.-Aubin in the act of seducing Christine . . .

3.33 . . . and, still moving right, catches up with Schumacher in another doorway, only to reveal André in the foreground, seething at Christine's flirtation.

supreme exponent of the dialectical step forward in film language, Bazin's historical scheme was compete.

Toward an Impure Cinema

In descriptive precision and attention to the ways techniques can function across a film, Bazin's dialectical history of style far surpasses its Standard Version predecessors. Furthermore, his synoptic scheme created a more discriminating and comprehensive version of the Basic Story. Now the international history of silent film harbored two tendencies. Either a filmmaker sought to overcome the realism of the medium through expressive artifice and stylization, or the filmmaker sought to enhance the realistic capacities of film

3.34 *Tabu:* Islanders paddle out to greet the ship that will carry away the heroine.

by recording and revealing concrete actuality. For Bazin, the stylizing tendency proved barren. With the coming of sound, the artifice of the "high" silent era drew to a close, and the cinema's "realistic vocation" was gradually revealed, first in the triumph of classical découpage and then in the revolution wrought by Renoir and his successors. Bazin thus extended the stylistic history of cinema beyond the dead end posited by the Standard Version.

He also reconfigured the canon in significant ways. Bazin's "reality trend" assigned expanded roles to certain players in the Basic Story. Flaherty, obliging the audience to wait on the ice with Nanook for the seal to grab his line, understood how cinema could record the reality of duration. So did Stroheim, each of whose films, Bazin claims, could just as well have been shot in a single, relentless close-up. Murnau emerged from the shadows of Expressionism as the director whose compositions in *Nosferatu, Tartuffe* (1926), and especially *Tabu* (1931) obliged reality to reveal its "structural depth" (Fig. 3.34).

Wyler's reputation soon slumped despite Bazin's and Leenhardt's enthusiasm, but certainly in backing Welles *la nouvelle critique* helped him into the pantheon. Bazin recalled that *Citizen Kane* had been for his generation what *The Cheat* had been for the 1915 Parisian intelligentsia—the sign that Hollywood was in the forefront of world cinema. He watched with satisfaction when the major directors of the 1950s, such as Nicholas Ray, freely acknowledged Welles's importance.[67] Bazin did not live to see the final fruits of his generation's efforts: the consecration of *Citizen Kane,* in poll after poll since the 1960s, as the greatest film ever made.[68]

Probably the most spectacular rise in prestige, however, was Renoir's. He had been making films since 1925, but for the most part Standard Version historians ignored him. Of his mature work, only *La grande illusion* (1937) garnered wide praise; even Bardèche and Brasillach's 1943 *Histoire* treated it as one of the finest French films of its decade. On the whole, this painter's son was considered a wealthy amateur lacking a flair for the cinema. Leenhardt complained that *La Marseillaise* (1938) succumbed to Renoir's typical carelessness: "diffusion, lack of focus, disorder (especially in the camera movements)."[69] *La règle du jeu* (1939) aroused strong opposition on its initial release, and Renoir's absence from France during the Occupation made him a marginal, slightly suspect figure.

After the war, however, his reputation began to rise. Revivals of *La grande illusion* and of *La règle du jeu* won praise, and both circulated widely among ciné clubs. The official journal of the clubs ran a special issue on Renoir's work in 1948, and *The River* (1951) won a major prize at Venice. By the time *Cahiers* published a special Renoir number in 1952, he had become the *nouvelle critique*'s candidate for the best director in history. The critics' campaign succeeded. A 1959 restoration of *La règle du jeu* (dedicated to Bazin) swept the world, and since the 1960s it has been considered one of the finest films ever made.

In recasting the canon of the Basic Story, Bazin suggests a solution to the problem that vexed the Standard Version as he knew it: What style is most suitable for the sound cinema? He replies that the mature sound cinema assimilated the "revolution" of the long take, the shot in depth, and fluid camera movement—technical avenues quite different from the "creative use of sound" advocated in the early 1930s. Moreover, particular films revealed a formal interaction among découpage, montage, and the new stylistic tendencies, with the contrasts themselves becoming a source of fruitful aesthetic effects (as in *Kane* or *The Little Foxes*). And although stylistic progress had all but ceased, cinema would develop by tackling new subjects and setting itself new formal problems, such as adapting works in other media to the screen.

Bazin's research program replaces the idea of stylistic progress as accumulated resources with a more dialectical dynamic of inner tensions and partial syntheses. This move is made possible by extending the transnational generalizations already outlined in Bardèche and Brasillach's period scheme. Bazin's predecessors had often emphasized national cultures as wellsprings of film art, but he traces cinematic innovation to supranational forces at work across the history of representation. He offers, in fact, two developmental schemes—one largely technological, the other involving the history of visual representation. Both locate cinema outside orthodox histories of modern art.

Bazin's technological history treats movies as manifesting an age-old "myth of total cinema." In the nineteenth century, he claims, tinkerers and artisans dreamed of a representation that would be a complete simulacrum of reality, "a perfect illusion of the outside world in sound, color, and relief." The history of cinematic technology gradually approaches this ideal. Arnheim had noted this with anxiety, but Bazin presumes from the start that one should not treat the silent film as a culmination of the medium's capacities. "The primacy of the image is both historically and technically accidental . . . Every new development added to the cinema must, paradoxically, take it nearer and nearer to its origins. In short, cinema has not yet been invented!"[70]

This technological progress, largely a product of the nineteenth century, is accompanied by a representational impulse running much further back. Bazin suggests that pictorial art springs from a "mummy complex," an ancient, transcultural urge to freeze time. The mummy, its wrappings molding the human figure they bind, is the prototype of all visual representation. The mummy is not a copy of the dead one; it *is* the dead one. Thereafter sculpture and painting tried in vain to approximate this identity of representation and object. Eventually the plastic arts "sublimated" their desire to embalm the moment, contenting themselves with combining realistic resemblance and purely symbolic representations. Bazin hazards that medieval art achieved the purest balance of these tendencies.

With the invention of perspective in the Renaissance, the scales tipped decisively toward realism. The Baroque painters went still further, straining to capture transitory movement. Photography, claims Bazin, freed art from this hopeless effort to freeze time. The mechanical lens, automatically producing an image of the fleeting instant, surpasses painting in authentic realism. Like a mold or a fingerprint, the photograph is the physical trace of the object represented. The invention of photography grants painting its "aesthetic autonomy." With Cézanne, for instance, pictorial design no longer obeys perspective, and form and color become the painting's *raison d'être.* Cinema, on the other hand, extends photography's objectivity by recording temporal flow as well as spatial layout. "The film delivers baroque art from its convulsive catalepsy. Now, for the first time, the image of things is likewise the image of their duration, change mummified as it were."[71]

Bazin concludes that the aesthetic basis of cinema and the driving force behind stylistic change both stem from cinema's reproductive power. Whereas other arts present reality through symbols, cinema's photographic basis permits it to reproduce tangible, unique events. From this capacity to record the world springs the specific qualities of filmic "realism." The stylistic options selected by Renoir, Wyler, Welles, and the Neorealists harmonize with the essential nature of the medium. By exploiting deep-focus imagery, long takes, and camera movement, these directors respect the spatial and temporal continuum of the everyday world—exactly the quality that motion picture photography is best equipped to capture. Of course these directors employ artifice; how could they not? But the sort of artifice they press into service is consonant with cinema's mission of exposing and exploring phenomenal reality.

According to modernist orthodoxy, the conquest of appearances began in the Renaissance, passed through the Baroque era, and culminated in the academic realism of the nineteenth century. Then Manet and the Impressionists—ambivalently, both optical realists and champions of pure patches of paint—challenged canons of representational realism. Cézanne launched the criticism of appearances which gave rise to such twentieth-century movements as abstraction, Expressionism, and Cubism. As a result, most film historians had tried to justify cinema as a quasi-modernist art by virtue of its ability to stylize reality.

Bazin, however, places cinema quite outside the modernist success story. Like Malraux, he grants that self-conscious artifice triumphed in the plastic arts, and he accepts the commonplace that photography freed painting from its need to produce likenesses. Yet for him photography, cinema included, is a distinct medium, which does not have to justify itself by its formal transformation of reality. Turning the Standard Version on its head, Bazin proposes that the medium's essence lies exactly in its recording capacity.

Cinema is thus not the seventh art. It will not find a niche in a revised system of the fine arts, nor is it a synthesis of other arts, as, say, opera synthesizes drama and music. Cinema is a medium first, an art only secondarily. Its specificity resides in its ability to retain the light rays bouncing off the world into the camera lens. Whereas Bardèche and Brasillach begin their history with Chinese shadow plays and the magic lantern, Bazin starts with the mummy. For Bardèche and Brasillach cinema is only contingently photographic, but for Bazin it is essentially so.

Bazin accordingly adjusts film's relation to the traditional arts. As a medium, cinema welcomes the opportunity to record anything—not only staged fictions but random incidents, even artworks in other media. Bazin thus considers what cinema can add by presenting—literally, re-presenting—famous paintings, classic novels, great plays. Deliberately provoking the silent film partisan, he argues for an "impure" cinema that can preserve and expand all the other arts' greatest achievements.

Perhaps nothing more dramatically illustrates the novelty of Bazin's position than his esteem for "theatrical" cinema. He will not dismiss even canned theater, but he reserves special praise for those films, like Olivier's *Henry V* (1945), which present theatrical conventions by means of intelligent use of cinema's recording capacities. Good filmed theater does not transform stage material, Bazin maintains; it refracts and amplifies it, respecting and intensifying its sheerly theatrical qualities. When Cocteau's *Les parents terribles* (1954) expands the play's original one-room setting to encompass the entire apartment, this is no mere "ventilation" of the script. Cocteau exploits camera movements through the cramped rooms in order to retain the sense of suffocation that pervades the play.

Bazin's challenge, then, involves not only widening the canon and proposing new, long-range causes of stylistic change. He also rejects the aesthetic preferences of the Standard Version, elevating an "ontological" realism over the aesthetic stylization prized by the silent-era aficionados. Still, he does not challenge other aspects of the Standard account. Many of his protagonists—Murnau, Flaherty, Stroheim, Dreyer—were already heroes of the Basic Story. The revival of silent classics in ciné clubs and in Langlois's Cinémathèque Française made the canon familiar. And, thanks to the publicity surrounding *Kane,* it did not take the panegyrics of *la nouvelle critique* to convince intellectuals that Toland and Welles were in the forefront of American cinema.

There are also intriguing congruences between Bazin's account and that offered by Bardèche and Brasillach. The latter posited an international "classicism" at the end of the 1930s and traced the stylistic stability of American sound cinema to the emergence of genres and cycles. Both premises became indispensable points of departure for Bazin's arguments about depth of field. In addition, the 1943 edition of Bardèche and Brasillach's *Histoire* highlighted Ford and Wyler as the outstanding American directors, particularly emphasizing *Stagecoach* (1939), *Dead End* (1937), *The Letter* (1940), and *The Little Foxes.* Even though Bardèche and Brasillach did not discuss the films' stylistic qualities, Bazin's generation was primed to see these works as salient.

Bazin's basic assumption that stylization contrasts with realism can be found in earlier literature too. Most proximately, in the epilogue to their *Histoire* Bardèche and Brasillach posit two opposing tendencies traversing the history of the medium: "to escape as far as possible from reality" and "to accentuate the most realistic properties of the photographic image."[72] This formulation became a cliché, embalmed in the textbook split between Méliès and Lumière, formalism and realism. Bazin subtly revises this schema, but it was put conspicuously on the horizon by the most notable French history of cinema.

More broadly, Bazin's position converges with some of the Standard Version's aesthetic principles. Like Arnheim and others, he assumes that film technology is evolving toward greater reproductive fidelity. For him as for his predecessors, cinema has an essence, and a properly artistic use of the medium should exhibit it. And all agree that some filmmakers understand cinema's essence and assist the medium in developing toward its proper aesthetic goal.

These shared assumptions open Bazin up to the same sorts of criticisms that Standard Version teleologies face. Filmmakers working on very different projects and problems are drafted into a large-scale, impersonal advance that has as its aim the fullest manifestation of cinema's intrinsic nature. But again we have no good reason to believe that the medium has an essence. Even if it does, why must filmmakers respect it? More specifically, Bazin's ontological realism is suspect as a candidate for film's essence: cinema can exist perfectly well without photography. We have cartoons which are animated drawings, or which are drawn directly on film, or which are generated on computers.[73]

In significant ways Bazin is even more Hegelian than his predecessors. He recasts the history of art in the light of the advent of cinema, tracing photography back to ancient impulses that only now find fulfillment. He posits not only progress in cinema's self-realization but also a struggle between the "image" trend and the "reality" trend. This clash eventually produces a synthesis, a "dialectical step forward in film language"—the long-take, deep-focus image that fuses "primitive" depth with the analytical breakdown of space pioneered by découpage. Once more, the tangible goals of concrete agents are swept up into a momentum governed by an abstract idea of evolution; once more, trends that do not suit the historian's teleology are ignored.

One flagrant instance: Bazin introduces the concept of classical découpage in order to show how the conflict between the "image" trend and the "reality" trend was initially resolved in the sound era. But as a system of techniques découpage goes back to the 1910s, and it becomes dominant during the 1920s. Arguably, both Soviet and French montage develop out of Hollywood continuity even as they provide alternatives to it. An adequate account of the post-1915 silent cinema would have to acknowledge the centrality of "Griffithian editing." If forced to include this in his scheme, Bazin could consider it either as a third alternative alongside the "image" and "reality" trends or as a comprehensive system that sustained both tendencies. (*Caligari* and *La roue* depend upon it no less than does *Nosferatu* or *Greed.*) In either case, however, he would have to explain how and why découpage gains a new significance in the sound era and why we should consider it to mark the reemergence of the reality trend.

Similarly, Bazin tends to ignore scenes and shots that do not fit into the dialectical sweep of his scheme. Despite his allowance for conflicting tendencies within a single film, he tends to play down the nonrealistic components of many of his most cherished works—the constructive cutting and florid music in many Neorealist films, or the Expressionistic grotesquerie and Soviet-style montage in Welles's work after *Ambersons.* In general, Bazin tends to miss the extent to which even his favored directors depend heavily upon editing. Renoir reserves his long camera movements for only certain scenes of *La règle du jeu;* the early portions rely on cross-cutting and shot/reverse-shot editing, thus creating a "hybrid" découpage.[74] Bazin claims that Flaherty respects the concrete reality of time by giving us Nanook sitting patiently on the ice until he finally catches a seal. But in every print of *Nanook of the North* I have been able to see, a jump cut elides Nanook's wait, and we are suddenly confronted with a huge, distinctly dead seal already hauled onto the ice. There is likewise more cutting in the scene of Horace's heart attack *(The Little Foxes)* than Bazin allows. Presumably because Stroheim was Hollywood's most committed "realist" in subject matter and locale, Bazin feels obliged to treat him as if he were a "realist" long-take director as well; in fact Stroheim organizes his scenes around a hectic découpage.

Bazin did not have the machinery or the access to prints that would have allowed him to check such details. Nevertheless, he is to some extent the victim of the new standards he set: the remarkable finesse of his analyses invites just such corrections. Unfortunately, they are often corrections that cast doubt on the plausibility of an evolutionary scheme even more grandiose than that offered by the Standard Version.

From Stylistic History to Thematic Criticism

The Standard Version of stylistic history has been taken up, amplified, and revised extensively over sixty years, but Bazin's Dialectical Version has not been mined in any thoroughgoing fashion. This neglect is due in part to the rather fragmentary way in which the account was assembled, in a series of essays over a decade and a half. In addition, authoritative scholars within Bazin's milieu doubted his historical scheme. Despite Bazin's counterarguments, Sadoul clung to the belief that Renoir and Welles simply reverted to older techniques. He was fond of pointing out that Lumière's *Arrivée d'un train* (1895) presents its action in dynamic depth and "utilizes all the resources of a lens having a great depth of field."[75] (See Fig. 3.35.) Bardèche proved somewhat less grudging: his 1948 edition of *Histoire du cinéma* treats depth of field and the long take as major discoveries of 1940s cinema. He nonetheless adds that Welles's innovations had little influence on production, which retained the shooting methods standardized during the 1930s.[76]

I only came to this idea of coming before or after very late. When Rohmer, who was a professor at the time, used to talk about Flaubert, he knew that, logically, Flaubert came after Homer or Saint Thomas Aquinas. But when he saw Nicholas Ray's *Bigger than Life* and a film by Murnau, I'm not so sure that he talked about them with the clear notion that Ray came after Murnau.

Jean-Luc Godard

Many of Bazin's insights were assimilated piecemeal, creating what we might call a Revised Standard Version. Instead of taking up the Dialectical program, either to refine it or to extend it to new domains, historians deployed Bazin's particular critical insights in order to extend the Basic Story into the 1930s, 1940s, and 1950s by incorporating the work of Renoir, Welles, Wyler, and the Neorealists. Accordingly, the "unfolding essence of the medium" component of the Standard account was played down when writers discussed sound cinema.

3.35 "Wellesian" depth à la Lumière: *Arrivée d'un train à La Ciotat.* This is a later stage of the shot shown in Fig. 2.1.

Bazin's historical account of the "evolution of film language" had its most powerful influence on young writers associated with *Cahiers du cinéma.* But they recast his ideas to suit an agenda focused on critical interpretation and appraisal. The "cinemaniacs" *(cinémanes)* or "Young Turks" fervently defended Hollywood and valorized a conception of modernity in film. Most generally, they drew upon certain of Bazin's ideas to forge an ahistorical conception of film style that could sustain their practical criticism. Because this conception came to exercise great influence, and because in a roundabout way it shaped a third historiographic tradition, it is worth pausing over here.

The *Cahiers* team is most widely known through those members who became important directors: Eric Rohmer (né Maurice Schérer), Jean-Luc Godard, Claude Chabrol, Jacques Rivette, François Truffaut, Luc Moullet. Formed by the ciné-club movement of the postwar years, deeply grateful to *la nouvelle critique* for guiding them toward a new aesthetic, these young men were also at pains to differentiate themselves. From 1950 on, in the short-lived *Gazette du cinéma* and then under Bazin's tolerant eye in *Cahiers du cinéma,* they proceeded to lay out what became known as the *politique des auteurs.*

For several decades French critics had argued about authorship in the cinema; during the 1930s the film's *auteur* was often assumed to be the scriptwriter.[77] Debates on the subject intensified after the war.[78] The *Cahiers* writers' "policy of authorship" held the director to be the key artist in the filmmaking process; even Hollywood directors could achieve personal expression through their handling of film technique. Auteurism was overtly evaluative as well, ranking directors and oeuvres. The Young Turks delighted in elevating commercial directors and creating a new canon. Now Hitchcock, Hawks, Preminger, and Nicholas Ray were held superior to Pabst, Clair, even Ford. Now the great Murnau films were *Tabu* (1931) and *Sunrise* (1927) rather than *Nosferatu* and *The Last Laugh;* Lang's American films, such as *The Big Heat* (1953), were preferred to *M* and other German classics.

By the mid-1950s the Young Turks held editorial control of *Cahiers* and made it almost completely a vehicle of *auteur* criticism. *Cahiers* found master strokes in such contemporary works as Hawks's *Monkey Business* (1952), Ray's *Party Girl* (1958), and Preminger's *Exodus* (1960). In 1958, countering an international poll naming the ten best films of all time, the *Cahiers* offered its own list, in which Welles was represented by *Mr. Arkadin* (1956), Dreyer by *Ordet* (1955), and Hitchcock by *Under Capricorn* (1949).

Bazin played a central role in this revolution, usually by positive influence, occasionally as an orthodoxy that the Young Turks could reject. For one thing, he and his colleagues gave the younger writers a rationale for celebrating Hollywood. Astruc's conception of Hollywood as an *atelier* of sturdy craftsmanship was expanded by Bazin, who offered the scandalous claim that the technical perfection of the American studios gave the filmmaker, for the first time in history, the working conditions hospitable to genuine artistry.[79]

More generally, Bazin's realist program supplied concepts that could be tailored to the auteur aesthetic. The "transparency" and laconism that Bazin and Leenhardt had praised in 1940s films were easily applicable to the work of Hawks—for many *Cahiers* writers, the very personification of fluent classicism. In *Rope* and *Under Capricorn* Hitchcock pursued the long take in ways that the *Cahiers* critics could treat as a consequence of the discoveries of Renoir and Welles.[80] The idea of découpage as a sound-cinema convention, broached by Bazin and his contemporaries, also proved central to the 1950s debates. For the "Hitchcocko-Hawksians" of *Cahiers,* analytical editing and the shot/reverse shot became not stereotyped formulas but expressive devices that the finest directors used to maximal effect. Openly challenging Bazin, Godard offered a "Defense and Illustration of Classical *Découpage,*" in which he argued that the cut was unsurpassed in its power to convey certain psychological and emotional states.[81]

The same arguments were applied to conceptions of modern cinema. Largely ignoring the Neorealist classics, the cinemaniacs concentrated upon later works such as Antonioni's *Cronaca di un amore* (1950) and Rossellini's *Voyage to Italy* (1954). In discussing the latter, Rivette reproached Bazin's generation for failing to notice that the cinematic "liberation" they had proclaimed led to this masterpiece (Fig. 3.36).[82] For Rohmer, contemporary filmmaking was opening the way toward the only true modernity—classicism, understood as an archetype of eternal beauty. Renoir's *The Golden Coach* (1953), Hitchcock's *I Confess* (1953), and Hawks's *The Big Sky* (1952) confirmed that in the 1950s, not in 1939, cinema entered its mature "classical" phase.[83]

3.36 The beginning of modern cinema, according to the young *Cahiers* critics: Rossellini's *Voyage to Italy.*

Above all, the Young Turks treated *mise en scène* as a criterion of value. Astruc's use of the term proved most influential. "We have come to realize," he wrote in 1948, "that the meaning which the silent cinema tried to give birth to through symbolic association exists within the image itself, in the development of the narrative, in every gesture of the characters, in every line of dialogue, in those camera movements which relate objects to objects and characters to objects."[84] For most of the *Cahiers* critics, *mise en scène* was the art of felicitously displaying the human body. The director's task was to relate the body to its surroundings, using the shot to unfold the action and create a visual rhythm.[85]

Astruc's definition denies editing, or at least "symbolic" editing, a place in *mise en scène.* Cutting now had to be justified through its role in supporting or sustaining the body's movement in space. Godard argued just that in 1956, asserting that editing is an essential component of *mise en scène,* particularly when there is a need to express such qualities as abrupt hesitation or to intensify the moment when characters exchange looks.[86] The *Cahiers* writers praised Hollywood directors for understanding that the material in front of the camera dictates, by its internal tempo or narrative development, the placement of cuts. It is noteworthy that Eisenstein was revered by the Young Turks, but principally for his compositional sense: elevating *Ivan the Terrible* (1944) over Eisenstein's silent classics, they turned the great *montageur* into a great *metteur en scène.*

For the *Cahiers* critics, *mise en scène* became the almost mystical precondition for cinematic art. What makes *Voyage to Italy* modern, declared Rivette, is its objective, behavioral *mise en scène:* the film presents not psychology but merely the glances and gestures of the characters. Rohmer lamented the fact that sound découpage replaced the sustained *mise en scène* of Griffith, Murnau, and other silent masters with an aesthetic of the glimpse. In sound cinema, the shot was too often determined by the needs of dialogue, not by a respect for the integrity of space.[87]

Western directors like Hitchcock, Hawks, Lang, Dreyer, Ray, Preminger, Rossellini, Ophuls, and Renoir did not have a monopoly on brilliant *mise en scène.* When Japanese films began to arrive at festivals in the early 1950s, the *Cahiers* critics discovered in Kenji Mizoguchi not only exoticism but a dazzling deployment of bodies in space. *The Life of Oharu* (1952) was for Philippe Demonsablon a revelation of lengthy takes, camera movements, calm rhythm, and staging in depth; Mizoguchi's plastic sense, he maintained, was worthy of Murnau.[88] Luc Moullet declared *Ugetsu monogatari* (1953) at once the world's simplest and most complex film.[89] "These films," wrote Rivette, "in a language we do not know, presenting stories totally foreign to our customs and habits, in fact speak to us in a very familiar language. Which one? The only one to which a director must aspire: that of *mise en scène.*"[90] For example, in a single shot of *Ugetsu* Mizoguchi charges a mundane space with supernatural presence. Modestly following the character, the camera takes us into a spiritual world, no less tangible than the physical one (Figs. 3.37–3.40).

The discovery of Mizoguchi, along with the rediscovery of Keaton, Feuillade, and others, seemed to confirm the probity of *mise-en-scène* criticism. So too did the new widescreen processes. For Astruc they proved that cinema was "an art of *mise en scène.*"[91] Much the same attitude was taken by the Young Turks around *Cahiers,* who saw in CinemaScope a confirmation of the primacy of the action staged for the camera. Not that editing was now eliminated; instead, it became the servant of *mise en scène.* Charles Bitsch, for example, praised *A Star Is Born* (1954) for its synthesis of techniques: "Notice: fast cutting, ten-minute takes, the most skillful camera movements, the most daring match-cuts, the most difficult framings—everything is there. We finally have the material proof that in CinemaScope everything is possible."[92] For the *Cahiers* critics, the widescreen format enhanced Hollywood's expressive resources while still respecting the integrity of the narrative event. The emergence of widescreen technology probably helped consolidate the *mise-en-scène* aesthetic generally.

To all of these lines of argument Bazin offered quiet resistance. He could not accept Hitchcock and Hawks, let alone Ray and Preminger, as great filmmakers. He argued against what he regarded as the extremes of auteurism, laying particular emphasis on the need to appraise works singly.[93] His theory of cinema's photographic basis led him to embrace a wide range of films, from documentaries like *Kon-Tiki* (1951) and *Le mystère Picasso* (1956) to fantasies like *Le ballon rouge* (1956). For him, the camera could record and reveal phenomenal reality of all sorts, in all its ambiguity and richness.

3.37 In *Ugetsu,* Genjuro the potter returns home to find the hearth cold.

3.38 Mizoguchi's camera follows him through the cabin.

3.39 The camera drifts along the wall, paced to his walk outside.

3.40 But when Genjuro reenters, the hearth is warm, and his resurrected wife tends the fire.

The Young Turks made Bazin's writings the basis for a connoisseurship. *Mise-en-scène* criticism narrowed a broad theory of cinema to a rationale for superior artistic effects. Whereas Bazin's realism emphasized the concreteness of actual behavior (the Neorealist actor *is* before he performs), the Young Turks emphasized skilled performance. Godard asserted that all the cinema could reveal of an inner life are "the precise and natural movements of well-trained actors."[94] Bazin's conception of realism, which grounded stylistic choices in an ontology of the medium and thereby challenged ordinary conventions of verisimilitude, became a new aesthetic, a canonized style. His standards for a good film, as much metaphysical and moral as artistic, were replaced by criteria characteristic of classical art—harmony, naturalness, subtlety, and unobtrusive control.

In addition, the concept of *mise en scène* enabled the younger generation to launch a hermeneutics of film. Although Bazin favored stylistic analysis over thematic commentary, the *Cahiers* critics were among the first to undertake quasi-literary interpretations of film style—by no means a common practice before the 1950s. Significantly, the discovery of expressive individuality in Hollywood filmmaking coincided with the rise of "art cinema" in Europe, Scandinavia, and elsewhere. As a result, the auteur critics imported into their discussion of Hollywood films many reading protocols favored by art cinema. Style became an abstract gloss on story.[95]

The path marked out by the *Cahiers* writers was taken by many other cinéphiles, most notably Andrew Sarris in the United States and the group around the British journal *Movie.* During the early 1960s auteurism and the interpretation of *mise en scène* became, in several variants, the dominant form of serious discourse about cinema. In the same period cinema enjoyed a new popularity among intellectuals and young people. Film journals proliferated in Paris, New York, Berlin, London, and Montreal; ciné clubs and "art theaters" cultivated the new audience of university students. The writings of the *Cahiers* critics provided a central impetus for this cinephilia.

Partly as a result of the Young Turks' revision of *la nouvelle critique,* the effort to mount a stylistic history of cinema was replaced by an interpretive criticism. The frequently brilliant analyses offered in the pages of *Cahiers, Movie,* and New York's *Film Culture* deliberately lifted films out of their historical contexts. Style was a vehicle for thematic meaning, largely isolated from broader patterns of aesthetic continuity and change. The *politique des auteurs* became an antihistoriography.

Malraux had observed that in contemporary life the visual arts dwelt within a *musée imaginaire.* In the age of photographic reproduction, "art" had become a vast agglomeration of individual images, cut off from their traditions and uses, assembled in a virtual display that permitted the perceiver to pick out endless similarities and differences. This sense of history as a simultaneous order presides over the 1950s and 1960s *Cahiers* writings. Griffith is a contemporary of Resnais; Feuillade, of Cukor. Mizoguchi's ties to Japanese culture are ignored because, according to Luc Moullet, masterpieces are outside time and place.[96] The canon proposed by the Standard Version assigned each work a role in some stage of the unfolding of cinema's essence, while Bazin located his canonical works within the grand conflicts and syntheses of dialectical evolution. The auteurist canon, however, is a timeless collection of great films, hovering in aesthetic space, to be augmented whenever directors create more masterworks.

The Cinémathèque Française, where Langlois's programming delightedly juxtaposed works from radically different traditions, provided a hospitable setting for the imaginary museum of the *Cahiers* generation.[97] Ironically, one argument pushed by *la nouvelle critique* may also have inclined the younger generation to take an ahistorical stance. While Bazin always treated aesthetic problems historically, he also believed that by 1950 the stylistic development of the cinema had largely run its course. This view may have encouraged his juniors not to seek further changes. The development of widescreen technologies soon confirmed their belief that the long take, depth of field, camera movement, and kindred techniques marked the end point of stylistic evolution. The Dialectical Version of stylistic history provided a coherent and persuasive narrative of aesthetic change and continuity. According to this account, stylistic change was finished. Once the cinemaniacs of *Cahiers* began to envision history as squeezed down to a single point in which directors and films existed in a simultaneous array, all that remained was to celebrate the classics and watch for further evidence of personal expression through *mise en scène.*

Very soon, though, this view had to be modified. Critics were again confronted by the problem of the present—the need to account for current filmmaking. Around 1960, strong evidence emerged that the stylistic history of film had not ended. And in a curious echo of the debates around silent film, this evidence suggested that a fresh conception of artistic modernism could best account for stylistic developments in contemporary cinema.

chapter

4 The Return of Modernism: Noël Burch and the Oppositional Program

There were many modern filmmakers in silent films: Eisenstein, the Expressionists, and Dreyer too. But I think that sound films have perhaps been more classical than silents. There has not yet been any profoundly modern cinema that attempts to do what cubism did in painting and the American novel in literature, in other words a kind of reconstitution of reality out of a kind of splintering which could have seemed quite arbitrary to the uninitiated.

Eric Rohmer, 1959

Around 1960, European directors launched what came to be recognized as a modernist cinema. Alain Resnais's *Hiroshima mon amour* (1959), Jean-Luc Godard's *À bout de souffle* (1960), Michelangelo Antonioni's *L'avventura* (1960), Federico Fellini's *8 1/2* (1963), Jean-Marie Straub's *Nicht versöhnt* (*Not Reconciled,* 1965), Ingmar Bergman's *Persona* (1966), Alexander Kluge's *Abschied von Gestern* (*Yesterday Girl,* 1966), and other major works seemed to deviate both from classical découpage and from Bazinian realism. They even mobilized techniques strikingly similar to silent-era montage.

Still more innovative were the products of the revitalized experimental film of Europe and America. Some veterans like Hans Richter and Oskar Fischinger continued to work, but the most prominent figures were Maya Deren, Stan Brakhage, Kenneth Anger, Peter Kubelka, and other newcomers. Shooting in 16mm or even 8mm, these filmmakers forged a cinema of personal expression and formal experiment. The "New American Cinema" was only one manifestation of a worldwide urge to make films that were comparable in experimental audacity to contemporary poetry and painting.

A growing number of institutions began to support filmmaking outside the Hollywood mainstream. New festivals held at Pesaro, Italy, Hyères, France, and Knokke-le-Zout in Belgium encouraged young filmmakers. As the 1920s had witnessed an efflorescence of ciné clubs and specialized theaters, during the 1960s museums, campus film societies, and "art theaters" made experimental work available. Film magazines and book series flourished, and many of them discussed the new European directors and the revivified avant-garde.

Bazin died in 1958, just before these developments crystallized. He and his contemporaries had been impelled, by their belief in the Renoir-Welles-Neorealist line, to recast the stylistic history of sound film. But now the realism of the 1940s and 1950s had given way to a new stylization. A fresh model of stylistic history emerged, one that reread the past in ways that made the present intelligible.

Implicit within the Basic Story was a distinction between a filmmaking practice that derives from popular culture and appeals to a mass audience, and an avant-garde cinema tied to the fine arts and aiming at an educated elite. Bazin ignored the canonized avant-garde, seeing its exploitation of artifice and stylization as a misguided aping of the traditional arts. The avant-garde played a somewhat larger role in Standard Version accounts, since its explorations of film technique were thought to yield discoveries that expanded the resources of the medium. Nonetheless, because most historians assumed that film was centrally a narrative art, they relegated most experimental cinema to the margins of history.

In what I shall call the Oppositional Version of the development of style, the duality between the avant-garde and the mainstream narrative cinema becomes the primary organizing principle. Noël Burch's work offers a striking exemplar of this tendency. Although Burch has written no single synoptic history, his monographs and articles from the 1950s to the early 1990s cumulatively delineate a broad research program. Throughout, his strategy has been to study Western filmmaking from the vantage points of oppositional modes that "denaturalize" the conventions of mainstream technique and that suggest other ways in which films might be made.

Burch has recently turned away from the sort of stylistic history with which this book is concerned, but his research before the early 1990s remains the most important instance of the oppositional program. Over the last twenty-five years, this comparative approach has given a fresh force to the effort to write an international history of style. Not only has it allowed historians to disclose a revival of modernism in the efforts of Godard, Resnais, and the like; it has also enabled researchers to rethink silent cinema's modernism and its role in the Basic Story.

Radicalizing Form

Art is something subversive . . . Art and liberty, like the fire of Prometheus, are things one must steal, to be used against the established order.

Picasso

Modernist experimentation did not vanish during the 1930s, but the political movements of that period and the propaganda demands of World War II promoted accessible art and didactic realism. After the war, modernism returned with a vengeance. The hostility to avant-garde art displayed by Hitler's and Stalin's regimes seemed to confirm modernism as the proper contemporary art for the Free World. Thanks to government patronage, corporate commissions, and foundation grants, avant-garde movements gained an unprecedented cultural centrality. News magazines and television informed citizens about Abstract Expressionism, the New Novel, "twelve-tone" music, and the "Theater of the Absurd." In nearly every medium, the most prestigious work exemplified what Harold Rosenberg called "the tradition of the new."

To a considerable extent, postwar modernists took up the issues broached by their elders. The Cubists, the Surrealists, Pound, Eliot, Kafka, Stravinsky, Schoenberg, Berg, and other figures from the 1910s and 1920s became heroes for a new generation. Exponents of the *nouveau roman*—Robbe-Grillet, Butor, Sarraute, and their peers—looked back to Roussel, Gide, Kafka, and Joyce. Brecht, given his own ensemble in East Berlin, won fame with his productions and stimulated new interest in his prewar theories of "epic theater." In France, where neoclassical composition reigned, the atonal music of the Viennese school came as a thunderclap to Pierre Boulez and his contemporaries. The tradition of abstract painting, kept alive by Klee in Switzerland and by Richter and others in the United States, became the predominant trend in the late 1940s with New York "action painting" and the *abstraction chaud* of Paris.

But postwar modernists did not simply recycle ideas from the 1910s. For one thing, the widespread public acceptance of modernism encouraged artists to surpass the canonized avant-garde. Trained in the quasi-Hegelian assumptions of prewar art and art criticism, these "progressivist" modernists believed in always "taking the next logical step." In addition, new conceptions of the nature of modernism cast contemporary work in a specific role. One of these conceptions is suggested in Boulez's remark that his teacher Olivier Messiaen worked "to radicalize his language—to go as far as possible, that is to say, in discovering and exploiting new resources."[1]

Calling on the specificity-of-the-medium tradition, modernists undertook a self-conscious quest for the bases of form. Boulez, Stockhausen, and their contemporaries held that musical composition could be radicalized through "total serialism." They sought to subject every musical parameter to the integral logic of the tone-row, or "series." The composer could make the series govern not only pitch but also rhythm, harmony, even tone color and attack. Believing themselves to be taking the necessary step beyond Webern, the advocates of total serialism concentrated on the fundamental materials and structures of composition. Now each piece originated its own form and became an utterly singular object.

A comparable aesthetic radicalism seemed to many at the core of Brecht's ideas. Contrasting "Aristotelian" theater with "epic" theater, Brecht had since the 1920s argued for a form of representation in which the spectator was "distanced" from the spectacle and the events were "made strange" (the *Verfremdungseffekt*). Brecht assumed that this strategy would promote critical thinking about society. But many commentators saw Brecht's chief contribution as a stripping of theatrical performance down to its basic components. His work became a model of "presentational theater," showing how to incorporate such antinaturalistic effects as direct address, impersonal recitation of lines, and frank display of the mechanics of lighting and staging.

According to one influential conception of modernism, then, the artwork was obliged to acknowledge the materials and structures of its medium, to "lay bare the device," in the phrase of the Russian Formalists. For critics of the visual arts, Clement Greenberg's formulations of this aesthetic position proved most influential. Since 1939, Greenberg had analyzed modern painting as a string of efforts to articulate the features characterizing the medium, as opposed to concealing the medium in pursuit of illusion. Throughout history, Greenberg argued, the masters reconciled the tension between illusory depth and painterly surface, but modern artists gave up the effort to create an appearance of three-dimensional bodily space. Modernist painting seeks to determine its own "unique and proper area of competence"—the shape of the support, the properties of form and color, and above all the flat surface, a property unique to pictorial art.[2]

So far, Greenberg's position constitutes an ascetic version of integrity-of-the-medium arguments. But he also seeks to show that painting's development is a quasi-philosophical quest: art now explores the conditions of its own possibility. "The essence of Modernism lies, as I see it, in the use of characteristic methods of a discipline to criticize the discipline itself, not in order to subvert it but in order to entrench it more firmly in its area of competence."[3] Greenberg sees this process of self-criticism as akin to Kant's probing of the subject's conditions of knowledge, but it is also Hegelian in identifying an art's progress as a development toward increasing self-awareness.

Many critics and theorists accordingly came to see the modernist work in any medium as critically engaging with other works and traditions. The serial musical work attacked orthodox tonality; the *nouveau roman* dismantled the detective story and the psychological novel. Modernism was to be art about art—its premises, patterns, and procedures. "The artist," wrote Greenberg, "deliberately emphasizes the illusoriness of the illusions which he pretends to create."[4] The modernist work could thus set in fruitful tension both illusion and materiality, absorption and contemplative distance, representation and a critique of representation. This dialectic within the work was writ large in the modernist tradition's strategy of "radicalization"; the return to fundamentals offered an implacable opposition to academic or popular norms of art-making.

Some artists and commentators delineated other conceptions of a postwar modernism, such as a realistic depiction of the existential problems of contemporary life, or an assimilation of popular culture and commercial imagery. For our purposes, though, the formally ascetic strand of modernism is most important. Within filmmaking and film historiography, it exercised a decisive force.

Filmmakers inclined toward modernist critique had an obvious target. By the 1950s the quasi-realistic, literary-theatrical cinema of Hollywood, Europe, and the USSR enjoyed unprecedented influence. American cinema swiftly regained its dominance of the continental market, and many critics identified it as an enemy of any and all modernisms. Commentators, audiences, and amateur filmmakers were growing ever more aware of the conventions of this cinema. Astruc's and Bazin's descriptions of the premises of classical découpage were echoed in a host of treatises explaining the standard way to stage, light, shoot, and cut a narrative film.[5] Several training academies were founded to supply professionals to national industries. What had been craft lore was now spelled out in curricula; transmitted through the classroom, artisanal rules of thumb became academic formulas.

By contrast, an obvious candidate for cinematic modernism was the re-emerging experimental film movement in Europe, Canada, and the United States. Some avant-garde filmmakers were allied to prewar traditions of *cinéma pur* or Dada and Surrealism; more distinctively postwar trends included Brakhage's development of the "lyrical film." On the whole, most participants in the postwar avant-garde saw themselves as opposed to a slick, mechanical efficiency typified by the Hollywood film. In the 1960s, as avant-gardists began to form cooperatives to distribute their films, the sense strengthened that the avant-garde was an energetic alternative to the commercial cinema.

Not surprisingly, much of the writing around the "New American Cinema" drew upon conceptions of modernism circulating in the world of the visual arts. Critics often traced parallels between Brakhage's work and Abstract Expressionist painting.[6] Greenberg's conception of modernism had a particularly strong influence.[7] P. Adams Sitney, for instance, praised George Landow's devotion to "the flat-screen cinema, the moving-grain painting."[8]

Far more commercially successful than the experimental movements was that other broad challenge to standardized mainstream film, the "art cinema" of Europe, Asia, and Latin America. In the face of American domination, several governments protected domestic film industries in the name of national culture, including indigenous modernist trends. The world's conception of cinematic modernism was largely founded upon that body of work running from late Neorealism and early Bergman through the films of Antonioni, Bresson, Fellini, and Buñuel, to all the "Young Cinemas" of the 1960s, most notably France's *nouvelle vague*. Bazin's ideal of objectivity and the *Cahiers'* elevation of sober, elegant *mise en scène* were confronted by a cinema of fragmentation, ambiguity, distanciation, and flagrant aesthetic effects.

4.1 *Hiroshima mon amour:* An ambivalent eyeline cut carries us from the heroine in the present, looking . . .

4.2 . . . "at" herself in the past, imprisoned by the vindictive villagers.

For many observers, Resnais's *Hiroshima mon amour* (1959) proved that the European modernist cinema had come of age. The script by Marguerite Duras juxtaposed the landscape of contemporary Hiroshima with a French woman's recollections of her love affair with a Nazi soldier during the Occupation. The abrupt, laconic flashbacks to the woman's memories of Nevers, as well as the elliptical recounting of her present affair with a Japanese man, suggested that Resnais had recast Soviet cutting for purposes of psychological revelation. "Montage," Bazin had opined, "by its very nature rules out ambiguity of expression,"[9] yet the disjunctive editing of *Hiroshima mon amour* yielded lyrical ambivalences of plot and theme (Figs. 4.1, 4.2). During a roundtable discussion, a group of *Cahiers* critics placed the film firmly in a modernist context, linking it to existentialism, the *nouveau roman,* Stravinsky, Picasso, Matisse, and Braque. They concluded that *Hiroshima* renewed the Soviet legacy while flaunting its own formal operations in the modern manner. "Montage, for Eisenstein as for Resnais, consists in rediscovering unity from a basis of fragmentation, but without concealing the fragmentation in doing so."[10]

Hiroshima mon amour was an early signal of *Cahiers*' own renewal. Throughout the 1960s the journal developed an ever-stronger taste for modernist filmmaking. The American auteurs were passing from the scene, and a new generation—the "Young Cinemas" of Europe and Latin America—demanded attention. The journal opened its pages to literary intellectuals such as Barthes and the *Tel quel* group. Paris's second *nouvelle critique,* that of the Structuralist theorists, became central to *Cahiers* debates. As the idea of *mise en scène* was replaced by notions of reflexivity and disjunctive construction, Bazin's ideas of objectivity and photographic realism came under fire. In one essay, while paying obeisance to Bazin ("the father of us all"), Michel Delahaye maintained that the Young Cinemas worked to deny the narrative "transparency" that the postwar critics had prized.[11]

In discussing both the noncommercial experimental cinema and the commercial art cinema, critics began to elaborate the idea of modernism as an oppositional filmmaking. For example, Marie-Claire Ropars-Wuilleumier developed an aesthetic based upon the innovations of Antonioni, Godard, and Resnais.[12] Against the "communicative film" *(film véhiculaire),* which transmits a definite message through the identification of a prior reality, she set the film of *écriture* ("writing"), in which disjunctive montage generates a dynamic play of meanings. Bazin had seen classical découpage as a step toward an integral realism of time and space; by contrast, Ropars held that new meanings were produced only when montage juxtaposed discrete fragments. This process was at work in *Hiroshima, 8 1/2,* the films of Eisenstein and Bresson, even *Citizen Kane.*[13] In a view that recalls Boulez's demand that each work find its own form, Ropars considered montage the means through which the film of *écriture* created a unique system, a singular interplay of representation and meaning.

At the same period Raymond Durgnat pointed out that the reemergence of modernism made it easier to grasp mainstream cinema as only one way to make films, and an academic one at that. In a series of essays exploring some stylistic conventions underpinning the "Old Wave," Durgnat drew deftly upon the Standard Version and Bazin, but he noted that contemporary experiments challenged both programs. He suggested that by 1950, the technique of shot/reverse shot had "straitjacketed" Hollywood style, and that more fluid cutting, entering cinema via television, displayed strong affinities with the intellectual montage of Eisenstein. As a result of this new style, "half-pictorial, half-abstract," "the story film is acquiring something of the novel's power of discursiveness."[14]

Noël Burch's writings were also marked by oppositional lines of thought. Born in 1932 in San Francisco, he went to France in 1951. Taking a degree in filmmaking at the Institut des Hauts Etudes Cinématographiques undoubtedly acquainted him with the norms of postwar "classicism." While making experimental films, he translated books by the musicologist André Hodeir.[15]

Burch's essays advocated a stringent modernism. He dismissed most early New Wave features as shapeless and technically backward. He chose as the most promising figures Resnais (as much for his documentaries as for *Hiroshima*) and the all but unknown Marcel Hanoun. As early as 1959 Burch offered an explanation of film form that was at once anti-Bazinian and redolent of the transformative aesthetic of the silent era. "The essence of cinema is the abstraction of the purely concrete, the integration of the elements of 'everyday,' concrete reality into elaborate, artificial, and abstract patterns in such a way that these elements lose their 'significance' without losing their identity."[16]

During the 1960s Burch elaborated a film aesthetic that, like the one proposed by Ropars, counterposed mainstream popular cinema to a rigorous, self-conscious modernism. Yet whereas Ropars relied on a literary analogy *(écriture)*, Burch developed his theory along lines indicated by his praise of Hanoun: *Une simple histoire* (1958) demonstrated that "the seventh art is capable of a discipline and a degree of abstraction comparable to that of contemporary painting or music."[17] Whereas Bazin welcomed literature and theater as models for filmmaking, Burch echoed 1920s debates about "the seventh art" in suggesting that cinema's proper stylization lies close to that of music and the visual arts.

Burch's 1969 book *Praxis du cinéma* collected a series of articles that appeared in *Cahiers du cinéma* in 1967–68. This book, along with occasional articles earlier in the decade, delineates a "theory of film practice" that opposes an academic or "zero-degree" style to artistic projects that explore and expose the formal possibilities of the medium. The zero-degree film subordinates formal organization to narrative demands, while in the modernist film "découpage articulations [will be] determining the 'scenario's' articulations as much as vice versa."[18]

In surveying the possibilities open to formal exploration, Burch treats the techniques of the medium as "parameters." Each parameter exists as a binary alternative. Thus one parameter is soft-focus/sharp-focus imagery; another is "direct" sound versus postsynchronized sound. In *Praxis du cinéma*, an exhaustive survey of cinema's parameters, Burch pays particular attention to editing. He reviews the spatial and temporal options opened up by any cut, and he argues that the contemporary director must take responsibility for organizing the continuity or discontinuity created through "matches" *(raccords)* from shot to shot. In conceiving every cut as inevitably disruptive, Burch redefines découpage as the overarching organization of montage. This enlarged découpage, the total spatiotemporal organization of a film's shots, constitutes the very texture (*facture* or *écriture*) of the finished work.[19]

Recall, for example, our early extract from *Une aussi longue absence* (Figs. 1.8–1.10). The tramp starts to remove his hat in the doorway but completes the movement at the dinner table. This cut is polyvalent; it suggests that the scene's action continues, but it also marks the start of a new sequence. The cut creates both gestural continuity and spatiotemporal discontinuity, at once serving the story and becoming a discrete stylistic event which cannot be wholly subsumed to narrative realism.

Like the *Cahiers* writers, Ropars, and others, Burch sets such modernist montage against continuous takes and open *mise en scène*. But in his effort to mount a comprehensive inventory of options, he also subjects Bazinian techniques to binary treatment. Thus he proposes that the frame creates a polarity of onscreen/offscreen space. He goes further to suggest six zones of offscreen space, each of which can be activated through characters' entrances and exits, glances, or partial framings. For Burch, the fluid framing and character movement of *La règle du jeu,* celebrated by Bazin as presenting a teeming phenomenal reality, can be dissected into a formal play of specific parameters.

Beyond itemizing such technical polarities, *Praxis du cinéma* argues that the advanced film will develop "dialectical" relations among those parameters it activates. Thus Hanoun's *Une simple histoire* sets up an interplay among elliptical editing, the relation of commentary to the image, and the bare, bleak story being told. Sometimes the voice-over narration anticipates the action, sometimes it is completely synchronized with it, and sometimes it follows it.

The most fully achieved film will in turn organize its parameters and dialectical relations according to some larger structure. In some cases the cinematic texture may develop apart from the story, as a kind of cadenza. But this approach, Burch warns, risks becoming merely decorative. He prefers that the dialectical play of parameters be "organic," sustaining or challenging the narrative action while also displaying rigorous abstract principles. Fritz Lang's *M* provides Burch's most fully worked-out example. Here, he claims, the most disjunctive cutting appears in the opening sequence, and the film gradually moves toward sequences built around temporal continuity. This movement not only supports the action taking place in each scene but also presents a broader survey of parametric options (Figs. 4.3–4.5).

Burch's theory draws on Umberto Eco's contemporaneous discussion of the "open work," on the combinatory theories advanced to explicate the *nouveau roman,* and above all on theories of serial musical composition. The very term "parameters," derived from musicology, was given currency by Boulez. Burch's conception of dialectical organization is indebted to Hodeir's and Boulez's discussions of "musical dialectics" in Schoenberg and Webern. Boulez had argued that Western tonality represents a hierarchy subordinating rhythm, timbre, and other musical parameters, much as Burch claims that mainstream formal choices promote the script over the *facture* of technique. Serial works, however, do not rank parameters a priori, and by analogy Burch suggests that all cinematic materials can become as salient as narrative principles.[20] Indeed, he conceives the future film as "a totally immanent object," much as Boulez's follower Pierre Schaefer sought to understand compositions as "musical objects."[21] Still, Burch is careful to point out that the musical analogy is useful only up to a point, since a film can never be as completely organized as a musical piece.

Serial ideas circulated throughout film culture during the 1960s. Rivette wrote in 1962 of "that definitively *atonal* cinema which announces all the

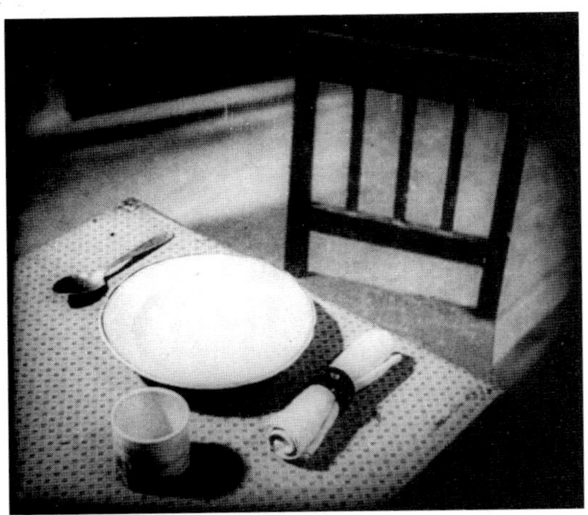

4.3 In *M,* the opening sequence cuts between the dinner awaiting the tardy schoolgirl . . .

4.4 . . . and an oblique presentation of her death at the hands of Becker.

4.5 By contrast, the murderer's trial and final confession are rendered in long takes.

great works of today."[22] The Viennese filmmakers Peter Kubelka and Kurt Kren conceived frames and shots as units that could be permuted across an entire film.[23] Jean-Daniel Pollet also explored permutational editing in his short feature *Méditerranée* (1967).[24] Nonetheless, Burch's book remains the most thoroughgoing attempt to subsume cinematic modernism to a serial aesthetic, and his ideas proved influential for some time.[25] In the years immediately after the French publication of *Praxis,* however, Burch modified his theory and began to translate it into a historiography of style.

Several circumstances shaped his efforts. The general effect of the orthodoxy/modernism opposition was to make standardized filmmaking seem more a contingent construction than a natural norm. From the standpoint of the experimental cinema, mainstream style could seem arbitrary, and some filmmakers of the 1960s suggested as much.[26] At the same time, the study of film semiotics had the effect of relativizing mainstream practices. In the early 1970s Christian Metz proposed that all films, including those of the dominant narrative cinema, were woven out of codes, none of which had a privileged access to reality.[27] Similarly, the increasing research into pre-1920 filmmaking and the recent avant-garde suggested alternative histories.[28] Once scholars realized that cinema might well have been quite different, they were able to look at ordinary movies as strange and contingent things.

In addition, the "political modernism" emerging in the late 1960s encouraged a socially critical use of experimental techniques. Borrowing principally from versions of Brecht's early writings, critics and theorists argued that modernism could subvert orthodox conceptions of social reality. Formal experimentation challenged the illusion-based pleasures of Hollywood entertainment. From 1969 on, for example, *Cahiers* and other Parisian journals published articles arguing that the techniques of orthodox filmmaking reinforced a belief that the world is as it appears; orthodox cinematic spectacle, according to these writers, reproduced bourgeois ideology.[29] Many who adhered to this version of Marxist aesthetics believed that the modernist insistence on montage, collage, and other disorienting techniques could expose the "ideology of the visible."

Some theorists quickly pointed out that sheer formal experiment could not sweep away ideological mystification, that political commitment or socially relevant content would have to guide progressive work. As early as 1966 the art critic Annette Michelson linked the modernist conception of "radicality" to the political sense of the term, insisting that the problem of Resnais, Godard, and their successors was "to raise, or rather accommodate, ideological content to the formal exigencies of the modernist sensibility."[30] Godard's *La Chinoise* (1967) and *Vent d'est* (1969) and Straub and Huillet's *Chronicle of Anna Magdalena Bach* (1967) and *Othon* (1969) seemed to many critics instances of just such an accommodation (Fig. 4.6).

With the resurgence of Marxist theories of film came a questioning of orthodox historiography. The "empiricism" anathematized by Louis Althusser seemed flagrantly on display in Sadoul and Mitry, while Bazin's belief in cinema's power to reproduce reality looked to be a pure case of "idealism." The most thoroughgoing critique was offered by Jean-Louis Comolli in an unfinished series of articles running in 1971 and 1972 in a newly Marxist *Cahiers du cinéma.* Comolli argued that the history of cinema was not a string of scientific discoveries or aesthetic breakthroughs. Instead, cinema was from the start "overdetermined" by interactions among signifying sys-

4.6 *La Chinoise:* Politicized subject matter and themes—students studying Mao's Cultural Revolution—manifest Godard's experimental form.

tems, ideological demands, and economic activities. At the nexus of these forces was that "impression of reality" prized by early filmmakers, sought by mainstream representational practices, and celebrated by Bazin. According to Comolli, the camera was not a neutral instrument but a repository of signifying conventions derived from Renaissance painting, still photography, and an idealist world view. Any changes in style would necessarily support or contest the ideology of transparent realism. Only a theoretically informed, nonlinear, "materialist" history of the cinema could capture this dynamic.[31]

Such debates moved Burch toward a distinctive version of politicized modernism. In a 1973 preface to the English translation of *Praxis du cinéma,* he declared that the "illusionist" approach to filmmaking evoked a response comparable to the "identification" that Brecht had deplored. But Burch did not yet assign a determining role to political content or purpose. Linking Brecht with Eisenstein, he declared that "a complete reading of the artistic process, including the conscious perception of form, is a liberating activity."[32] Modernist cinema could break with zero-degree style even if it did not transmit political messages.

Assimilating current ideas about illusionism, identification, and the ideological effects of formal parameters, Burch turned his attention to a study of film history. Like Bazin and the Standard Version writers, he was openly evaluative and prescriptive. He aimed to show, he claimed later, that mainstream cinema "naturalized" its mode of representation and that some alternative film styles offered models for radical film practice under Western capitalism.[33] By the mid-1970s this idea had become fairly commonplace,[34] but Burch elaborated the most detailed and far-reaching oppositional research program. In rejecting Bazin's "idealism" and insisting that cinema developed within an ideology of realism and the economic milieu of capitalism, Burch's work answered Comolli's call for a self-consciously "materialist" history of film style.

The Institutional Mode and Its Others

When the bourgeoisie had to find something other than painting or the novel to conceal reality from the masses, that is, to invent the ideology of the new mass communications, they called it photography.

Jean-Luc Godard

The 1970s spawned many taxonomies of oppositional cinema. An influential *Cahiers* article proposed no fewer than seven types of films, based upon the possibilities of transmitting or challenging the dominant ideology.[35] One critic contrasted progressive cinema with "narrative-representational-industrial" filmmaking.[36] Burch's research projects sketch another typology. There is, he proposes, mainstream illusionist cinema; a "primitive" cinema that preceded and overlapped with it; a significantly different practice in Japan; and, on the fringe of Western illusionist cinema, a "crestline" (*ligne de faîte;* the term is Boulez's) of "deconstructive" films and directors.[37] Studying alternative practices enables the historian to "relativise and analyse [illusionism] for what it is: i.e., a *construction.*"[38]

Burch dubs the illusionist cinema of Hollywood and most national film industries the "Institutional Mode of Representation" (IMR). Recasting Bazin's conception of "total cinema" along class lines, he suggests that the nineteenth-century bourgeois intelligentsia dreamed of "the Recreation of Reality . . . a perfect illusion of the perceptual world." This goal was pursued not only in painting and drama but also in wax museums, dioramas, and photography. Like Bazin and proponents of the Standard Version of stylistic history, Burch anchors the cinema's historical identity in the effort to record reality; but he sees this effort as driven by class struggle and ideology, not by scientific or spiritual impulses. Indeed, he argues that Marey's and Muybridge's urge to analyze physical movement was actually opposed to the bourgeoisie's taste for an integral illusion.[39]

Most generally, in an echo of 1930s Soviet cultural theory, Burch asserts that a rising class demands more realistic representational media than its rivals have put in place.[40] In nineteenth-century Europe and America this tendency emerged in new techniques of illusionism. Rejecting a transcultural "mummy complex," Burch calls this impulse the "Frankenstein" ideal, a notion of vanquishing death through creating life mechanically.[41] Paradoxically, however, the bare recording of reality could not satisfy the bourgeois appetite for illusion; the distant views and opaque stories of the earliest films proved uninvolving. Filmmakers had to create psychologically convincing representations.

The first step was constructing an autonomous fictional world on screen. By drawing upon realist devices already established in literature and drama, the

IMR sought to build an intelligible narrative centering on character and promising self-sufficiency and closure. According to Burch, the ideology that founded the IMR considers the individuated person to be at once prime mover and center of attention. The characters' psychological depth, so prized by orthodox criticism, defines the narrative world, or "diegesis," they inhabit.

In order for this world to become convincingly real, the IMR must make technique "invisible" or "transparent." The zero-degree style attacked in *Praxis du cinéma* is now described historically, as emerging out of an ideology of illusionism. The IMR creates recognizable ("iconic") images possessing simple, easily grasped compositions. These shots are arranged in a spatially and temporally linear fashion. Actors are encouraged not to look at the camera, since that would suggest that the narrative world was no longer sealed off from the spectator's gaze. From painting the IMR borrows tricks of suggesting three dimensions—modeled lighting, perspectival sets, and oblique camera positions. Even those codes of editing which emerged over the medium's first two decades support the illusion of depth. Cutting into a scene, especially with a change of angle, creates the sense of a three-dimensional, "haptic" space. Cecil B. DeMille's *The Cheat* offers an early instance of how characters looking just off the lens axis suggest a voluminous area we could enter (Figs. 4.7, 4.8).

How does the IMR affect the spectator? Its illusionist devices generate identification with the characters by emphasizing what they see and how they react. Burch further claims that cutting within a scene or cross-cutting between locales creates a "ubiquitous subject," a "motionless voyager."[42] Along with the conventions of Renaissance perspective, the editing codes serve to "center" the viewer, creating the illusion of being an invisible, all-knowing witness to events. Yet the film's space is always phenomenologically grounded in the spectator's bodily perception: in obedience to continuity editing principles, the imaginary world of the narrative is oriented around the viewer's left and right.

What began as a machine for reproducing perceptual reality became a vehicle of fantasy, even hallucination. Burch writes that shot composition, lighting, and editing made the spectator lose a sense of the flatness and circumscription of the screen, with a resulting "interiorisation of the picture as an *environment,* centred around the spectator's illusory self."[43] By masking the ways in which particular cinematic techniques endowed flat images with volume and human presence, the IMR offered at once the illusion of reality and a visual experience organized according to the priorities of a specific ideology. Of all media, only film could completely and unobtrusively fulfill the bourgeois dream of replication.

According to Burch, the IMR began around 1904. The earliest sort of editing, the direct cut in to enlarge a detail (or "axial match"), contributed to

4.7 "Haptic" space through eyeline matching in *The Cheat:* The distraught businessman comes to the sliding door . . .

4.8 . . . and the Japanese and the socialite look back at him across an imaginary space on either side of us.

centering the spectator. Directors began to link shots by contiguous spaces; in chase films, pursuers and pursued pass through a shot, emptying it before arriving to fill the next (Figs. 4.9–4.11). By 1910, directors had largely mastered the technique of matching screen direction for frame entrances and exits. That is, when characters exit one locale by crossing a frame edge, they enter the next space by crossing the opposite edge (Figs. 4.12, 4.13). Matching screen direction supported that idealized orientation of left/right spatial relations demanded by the "motionless voyage." During the same period, alternating editing started to signal simultaneity. In the 1910s track-ins and reframings became more common, as did a breakdown of the scene into detail shots. Dreyer uses this sort of editing in *The President* (Figs. 1.3–1.5), as does Griffith in presenting the wrench in *The Lonedale Operator* (Figs. 2.8, 2.9).

From 1915 (the year of *The Cheat,* Ralph Ince's *The Italian,* and Griffith's *The Birth of a Nation*) through 1917 (Maurice Tourneur's *A Girl's Folly*), the IMR's visual system became consolidated as the dominant style of advanced cinema.[44] By 1922, in Lang's *Dr. Mabuse der Spieler,* the system could brazenly display its economy and subtlety.[45] The arrival of synchronized sound brought illusionism to fruition. According to Burch, despite filmmakers' efforts to create a substitute reality in the silent film, the middle class still regarded cinema as a poor second to the theater. Only the arrival of talking pictures, which presented characters as rich psychological beings, won the bourgeois class to cinema. The result was the "canned theater" of the 1930s, a tradition that continues to form the basis of the IMR's products.

Rather than positing a continuous stylistic progress, as the Standard Version historian did, or dialectical tensions and syntheses as Bazin had suggested, Burch sees the IMR's development as broken by detours and backward steps. The bourgeois dream of perfect reproduction provided a drive toward a goal.

4.9 In *Le cheval emballé* (Ferdinand Zecca, 1907), the runaway horse gallops through a market, knocking down stalls . . .

4.10 . . . and is pursued by brawling market vendors until the shot is empty.

4.11 Cut to a view of the stall with the horse arriving.

4.12 Direction matching in *The Warning* (1914): The woman leaves the first shot on frame left . . .

4.13 . . . and runs into an adjacent space from frame right.

The Brighton school, Porter, Griffith, DeMille, and other pioneers of the IMR sought a total illusion incorporating movement, depth, color, sound, and the sense of human presence. Other factors, however, rendered progress more wayward. For instance, the early Passion plays mark an advance by linking shots into a narrative; but by copying famous paintings the filmmakers tended to crowd the frame with distracting detail (Fig. 2.2).[46]

Internationally, the IMR displayed comparably uneven development. Before illusionism became dominant, films relied on forms derived from circus, vaudeville, lectures, and other popular entertainments. The expansion and refinement of the IMR depended upon the growing power of the middle class within the cinematic institution, and this power varied according to the circumstances of the class struggle in the major film-producing nations. In Britain, for instance, the bourgeoisie's control over working-class leisure made it natural for middle-class entrepreneurs to become directors. Burch argues that Britain's early progress toward the IMR was indebted to the tradition of lantern-show programs, an entertainment dominated by middle-class entrepreneurs. In the United States, the desire to bring films into bourgeois venues, first through vaudeville and then through nickelodeons, hastened the rise of the IMR. Griffith's ascendancy was predicated on his experience in "artistic" theater. By contrast, the middle and upper strata in France avoided the cinema until around World War I, and so directors there maintained a "primitive" tableau style longer.

Proponents of the Standard Version had argued that the development of "film language"—close-ups, cross-cutting, naturalistic acting, and the like—resulted from a felicitous synchronization among filmmakers around the world. Bazin likewise saw classical découpage as an international effort, a compromise struck in the 1930s between the image-based and reality-based trends. What he played down was the fact that filmmakers arrived at the principles of this découpage long before the sound era. Burch argues that the growing power of the IMR installed classical découpage as the new international norm by the 1920s. Of course, it was not the universal language envisaged by René Clair and his contemporaries. However widely it was adopted, "film syntax" was only one, ideologically determined way of making films. Burch explains its rise by appealing to the composition of audiences, the social origins of producers and directors, and the representational traditions deployed. His explanations thus go beyond Sadoul's rather sketchy Marxist analyses and make class-based causes central to the rise of "transparent" storytelling cinema.

Alongside the IMR, Burch claims, there has developed a tradition of oppositional filmmaking—a "crestline" of critical films. Many of these became Basic-Story masterpieces, but only through a misunderstanding. Instead of

4.14 *Caligari:* The doctor advances from the depth of the shot, but the spidery lines of the painted decor seem to be scratched right across the image surface.

contributing to the development of mainstream "film language," as the Standard Version historians supposed, the crestline works have actually challenged the illusionist cinema "though a 'deconstruction' and 'subversion' of the dominant codes of representation and narrativity."[47]

By "deconstruction" Burch does not mean exactly what Derrida does. Like the modernist works described in *Praxis du cinéma,* the crestline films incorporate a norm and simultaneously criticize it, citing the code in order to expose it as a code. In the manner of Greenberg's painter, the filmmaker at once produces an illusion and displays it as such. For example, critics traditionally praised *The Cabinet of Dr. Caligari* for conveying a madman's fantasy through Expressionist sets and acting. Burch, however, treats the film as a rejoinder to the newly achieved IMR. Invoking the modernist tension of represented depth and pictorial surface, *Caligari* combines realistic movement of figures in volumetric sets with a flatness of performance and composition harking back to the "primitive" tableau (Fig. 4.14). *Caligari*'s modernism is not solely attributable to its rigorous parametric organization, as *Praxis* might have argued. For Burch the historian, *Caligari* is the first crestline work because its "dialectical" form lays bare the artificiality of the IMR by juxtaposing it with the pictorial system it sought to replace.[48] The most advanced, "limit-works" of the crestline go further, absorbing all relevant parameters into a more organically structured formal system.

The crestline films, Burch argues, have posed various alternatives to the IMR, depending on the codes they activate. In the Soviet Union during the 1920s and early 1930s, for instance, the Montage school presented a variety of responses to the IMR. Kuleshov, Boris Barnet, and other directors recast the narrative conventions of American genres in order to create a socialist popular cinema. Other directors worked more thoroughly on stylistic parameters.

4.15 In *L'argent,* the camera often spins and meanders through the vast spaces commanded by the businessman.

Through various systems of disjunctive editing, guided by a materialist conception of representation and history, Pudovkin, Eisenstein, and Vertov all attacked the conception of a unified story world and the rules of correct matching. Each one, in idiosyncratic ways, deconstructed the IMR's editing codes and created new, organic works.

Burch uses the same oppositional approach in appraising the historical significance of specific works and oeuvres. Marcel L'Herbier's *L'argent* (1928), ignored or dismissed since its appearance, anticipates the découpage principles later explored by Welles, Kurosawa, Bergman, Antonioni, and Resnais.[49] In defiance of the codes of motivated tracking shots exploited by Griffith and Murnau, L'Herbier's camera often moves arbitrarily, in order to create a rhythm within or between shots (Fig. 4.15).[50] Similarly, Burch treats the career of Carl Theodor Dreyer as a forty-year dialogue with the IMR. At the end of the silent era, *La Passion de Jeanne d'Arc* was a rigorous experimental film, creating diegetic space wholly through the eyeline match and laying bare "the essential two-dimensionality of spatial rendering in film."[51] According to Burch, Dreyer's last film, *Gertrud* (1964), proved itself equal to the second generation of postwar masterworks. It strictly varied its shot-changes, created a dialectic of movement and fixity, and harked back to *Caligari* in its interplay of flatness and depth (Figs. 4.16, 4.17).

Modernists have always sought predecessors; in 1911 a concert of Satie's oldest music was predicated on the idea that he had "a prescience of the modernist vocabulary."[52] Burch's reconfiguring of the Basic Story creates a distinguished oppositional tradition for the postwar art cinema and experimental film. Although Burch does not provide a historical account of the development of the modernist works of the 1950s and 1960s, he evidently believes that they could be assimilated to the long-range project of "decon-

4.16 The tension of flatness and depth in *Gertrud:* After a lengthy scene before the back wall of the parlor . . .

4.17 . . . the rear plane peels away to reveal a new space.

struction." Burch is far more explicit in his analysis of two other alternative practices: the "primitive" cinema that preceded the IMR and the interwar cinema of Japan.

Living Shadows and Distant Observers

In 1953 a former Los Angeles policeman named Kemp Niver started to restore thousands of old films. These "paper prints" of American films from the early silent era had been deposited at the Library of Congress. (Motion pictures were not initially protected by copyright, so submitting paper copies enabled producers to register the films as still photographs.) Using a crude rewind device, Niver transferred the images to 16mm film. A preliminary catalogue, annotated by Niver, appeared in 1967.[53] Since paper prints were in the public domain, they began to be circulated in 16mm compilations to libraries and universities.

At about the same time several archives began to expand access to pre-1920 films. Collectors turned up important but long-unseen titles such as Maurice Tourneur's *The Wishing Ring* (1914) and Raoul Walsh's *The Regeneration* (1915). One collector, Kevin Brownlow, galvanized interest in silent cinema with his vivacious book *The Parade's Gone By* (1968). His interviews with veterans of cinema's earliest days gave the era a halo of glamor and derring-do.

One of Niver's restored paper prints was *Tom, Tom, the Piper's Son,* a brief 1905 Biograph dramatizing the nursery saga of porcine larceny, chase, and capture. Ken Jacobs appropriated the movie as the basis of an avant-garde film completed in 1969. In the course of nearly ninety minutes, Jacobs' *Tom, Tom, the Piper's Son* runs the original in its entirety, slows it down, freezes it, blows up grainy patches of the image. The effect is to call attention to a world of details teeming within each shot. For instance, so much is going on in the

4.18 While the clown entertains the crowd, Tom, followed by a street urchin, dashes off with the pig.

original's crowded opening tableau that the viewer may miss Tom's theft of the pig (Fig. 4.18). Jacobs' scanning and enlargement imbue this instant with a spectral thrill. Seeking an "infinite richness," Jacobs defended the film in Greenbergian terms: "I wanted to 'bring to the surface' that multi-rhythmic collision-contesting of dark and light two-dimensional force-areas struggling edge to edge for identity of shape." He also found, in the "infinitely complex cine-tapestries" comprising the original tableaux, "the cleanest, most inspired indication of a path of cinematic development whose value has only recently been rediscovered."[54]

Jacobs' reworking of the film was as important as any archival research in suggesting that early cinema operated with a distinctive and oppositional aesthetic. That insight seemed especially persuasive to those whom Bazin and postwar modernism had taught the virtues of the crowded, "difficult" shot. Soon so-called Structural filmmakers were reworking footage from the early cinema: Peter Gidal in *Movie #2 (A Phenakistoscope Film)* (1972), Hollis Frampton in *Public Domain* (1972) and *Gloria!* (1979), Al Razutis in *Méliès Catalog* (1973), Ernie Gehr in *Eureka* (1974), and Standish Lawder in *Intolerance Abridged* (1970s). Some filmmakers sought to reshoot early film from a modernist standpoint, as in Klaus Wyborny's *The Birth of a Nation* (1973) and Malcolm LeGrice's *After Lumière—L'arroseur arrosé* (1974; Figs. 4.19, 4.20).

During the 1970s research interest in early cinema intensified in North America and the United Kingdom. Jay Leyda, in his continuing seminars at New York University, introduced Biograph films to a generation of young scholars.[55] New publications, often initiated by archivists, made pre-1915 documents available as never before.[56] Research articles, monographs, and dissertations began to appear.[57] That this inquiry had reached a critical mass was dramatically demonstrated in May 1978. Archivists and scholars gathered in Brighton, England, under the auspices of the Fédération Internationale des

4.19 One of the Lumières' early films, *Le jardinier et le petit espiègle* ("The Gardener and the Little Rascal," 1895), best known as *L'arroseur arrosé* ("Watering the Gardener").

4.20 Malcolm LeGrice's structural "remake" *After Lumière—L'arroseur arrosé.* Other shots repeat the central gag but from different angles, revising and updating the original *mise en scène.*

Archives du Film (FIAF) to watch 500 fiction films from 1900–1906. The proceedings were published in two bulky volumes.[58]

Burch's work on early film formed an important sector of this research and avant-garde appropriation.[59] He argues that there was an anti-illusionist cinema before the crest line of modernism—indeed, even before the consolidation of illusionist "film language." Burch designates as the Primitive Mode of Representation (PMR) the dominant film practice between 1894 and 1914. As an international style, it never became as thoroughly systematized as the IMR, but it did achieve a certain stability.

In the PMR, an entire episode, or indeed an entire film, usually consumed a single distant tableau. (See Fig. 1.1.) Spatial or temporal relations with earlier or later tableaux might remain unspecified. The point of view remained "external" to the characters; their interior states were displayed chiefly through behavior. The action was decidedly "nonlinear," lacking continuous development, alternations of tension and relief, and a sense of resolution or closure. The story was thus to a large extent located outside the picture, in prior cultural knowledge or in the speech of an accompanying lecturer. The PMR did employ editing, but often in ways nonstandard for the IMR.

Burch takes the Biograph *Tom, Tom, the Piper's Son* as a prototype of the PMR tableau. Until about 1908 a film's shot presented "a complex network of signifiers to be perceived and read as such, since at that stage, the screen was merely a surface to be scanned, like that of a painting."[60] Since cutting did not emphasize narrative action, the whole frame became a playing area, and key bits of business would not necessarily be centered.

Because of the nonlinear narratives and the decentered framing, a lecturer might be present to explain the action and to "harness" the spectator's eye. But

4.21 In *Play Time* Tati refuses to break down his extreme long shots into closer and clearer views. In this opening scene, characters sit on the edge of the frame and comment on the figures who pass between foreground and distant background.

then, Burch claims, the lecturer's voice further distanced the spectacle, making it impossible for the viewer to become imaginatively absorbed in the diegesis.[61] Eventually the word of the lecturer was replaced by a visual "language," that of the IMR, which created cinematic codes for guiding attention.

Many features of the PMR can be taken to anticipate the crestline "deconstructions" of illusionist codes. Early films' open and nonpsychological narratives are not focused upon the individuated human action so central to the IMR. The distant and external framings (not to mention the distracting conditions under which the films were watched) offer a quasi-Brechtian disengagement. Burch praises Bitzer's 1905 *Kentucky Feud* as prefiguring both Brecht's play *The Jungle of Cities* and Godard's *Vivre sa vie* (1962), while he argues that certain long shots in *Germinal* (1913) produce a space for reflection in the manner of the *Verfremdungseffekt*.[62] And if Pollock's Abstract Expressionism came to be called "all-over painting," we might call the PMR's use of the frame "all-over staging," since Burch considers it a protomodernist strategy. It is, he claims, revived in films like *Play Time* (1967); by salting gags throughout crammed long shots, Jacques Tati recalls the primitive cinema's tendency toward a "booby-trapped surface" (Fig. 4.21).[63]

True to Greenbergian modernism, Burch finds that the PMR also offered an interplay of surface and depth. Whereas the IMR invested its fictional space with three-dimensionality, the interior shots of primitive cinema presented comparatively flat images. Actors moved perpendicular to the camera axis, played frontally, and spread out like clothes pinned to a line. The tableaux lacked modeled lighting and utilized painted theatrical backdrops. Exterior shots, however, often presented dramatically deep space. The Lumières' *Arrivée d'un train à La Ciotat* remains for Burch (as for Sadoul) a paradigmatic example (Fig. 3.35); but so too do the chase films that staged their pursuits in

4.22 A virtually abstract backdrop, which scarcely attempts to suggest a wall, a window, and a landscape view, from *The Life of Charles Peace.*

actual locales. Consequently Burch dubs William Haggar's *Life of Charles Peace* (1905) a masterpiece because it creates a harmonious dialectic between richly perspectival exteriors and highly stylized sets (Fig. 4.22). The film presents discontinuity, collage, reflexivity, and a tension between surface and depth—in all, a panoply of protomodernist devices.[64]

According to Burch, the PMR flourished until about 1906, when it was gradually displaced by the continuity style promulgated by British and then American films. Whereas both the Standard Version and Bazin's dialectical scheme saw film style as moving from simple forms to more complex ones, Burch treats style as shifting from one fairly elaborated system, the PMR, to another one, the IMR. Aspects of the PMR lingered on, however. Feuillade and his colleagues retained many of its devices, and throughout the 1920s and even into the 1930s European films bore some traces of primitive distance, frontality, and decentering.[65] For Burch, the IMR's illusionism was obtained by deleting nonillusionistic parameters and substituting more straitened codes of filmmaking. The PMR is truly the "repressed" of the IMR, and many of its strategies return in postwar anti-illusionist modernism.

Burch attributes the rise of the IMR to the bourgeoisie's growing control of the institution. The PMR was, by contrast, "the last great Western narrative art that was at once both popular and, to a large degree, *presentational,* that is, morphologically closer to the plebeian circus and the aristocratic ballet than to the theatre of the middle classes, that *representational* art par excellence."[66] Made by bourgeois entrepreneurs for a largely untutored audience, the "primitive" cinema learned its anti-illusionism from just those forms of working-class diversion that Brecht believed would found a modern, nonalienating theater.

Brecht glimpsed other sources of epic theater in classical Chinese acting, and he was not the first modernist to look eastward for models of oppositional art.

From the Impressionists' discovery of *ukiyo-e* prints through Debussy's encounter with the Javanese gamelan and Eisenstein's interest in Kabuki and Chinese theater, up to Philip Glass's urge to master raga technique, the avant-garde has sought inspiration in Asian culture. Burch's historiographic compass swung in the same direction, not least because during the 1960s and 1970s Western film culture rediscovered Japanese film.

Film festivals brought Akira Kurosawa and Kenji Mizoguchi to international notice in the early 1950s, and they were the most prominent Japanese directors for decades. Joseph Anderson and Donald Richie's historical survey *Japanese Film: Art and Industry* (1959) whetted interest in films unknown in the West. A huge festival of Japanese cinema sponsored by the Cinémathèque Française in 1963 brought to light many new titles. At the same time, films by Nagisa Oshima, Shohei Imamura, and other directors of the "Japanese New Wave" of the late 1950s began to be seen in Europe.

A decade later a fresh tide of interest brought Yasujiro Ozu to prominence. Ozu had made more than fifty films from the 1920s until his death in 1963. In Japan he was widely considered the greatest director of his generation, but his serene domestic dramas seemed less exotic and exportable than Mizoguchi's exquisite historical tales or Kurosawa's kinetic action movies. Ozu's work was felt to be "too Japanese" to be submitted to festivals, and his studio did not aggressively pursue the Western art-house market. The Cinémathèque retrospective, however, showcased eleven of his films.

A 1972 rerelease of *Tokyo Story* (1953) won wide distribution and critical acclaim. Soon Ozu was discussed as a major director.[67] Complete career retrospectives followed in London (1975–76) and New York (1982). The rediscovery of Ozu sparked interest in other directors of *gendai-geki,* or contemporary life films, such as Mikio Naruse and Heinosuke Gosho. Screenings of Ozu's early films also hinted at the tantalizing richness of pre-1945 Japanese production. Several major Mizoguchi films, Teinosuke Kinugasa's astonishing experiment *Page of Madness* (1926), and work by other important directors came to light during the 1970s.

Burch's inquiry into the history of the Japanese cinema was far ahead of critical tastes. As early as 1969 he was ranking Ozu with Eisenstein and Renoir as a founder of new film forms.[68] While Western critics were discovering *Tokyo Story,* Burch was examining major works by Sadao Yamanaka, Hiroshi Shimizu, and other Ozu contemporaries. His 1979 book *To the Distant Observer: Form and Meaning in the Japanese Cinema* confirmed that the prewar period harbored unparalleled treasures. Polemical as always, Burch declared that this era was Japan's true "golden age" and that the postwar period, with a few exceptions, displayed a steep falling-off, even in the work of the masters.

Burch's central argument is that Japanese cinema, like "primitive" filmmaking, developed a representational system sharply different from that of the IMR. This system derived from the aesthetic which emerged from the court culture of the Heian era (794–1186) and which became the basis of Japan's traditional arts. Refusing illusionism, this aesthetic flaunted the materiality of the medium and the "play of the signifier," addressing a spectator who would not be absorbed into an imaginary world. For example, the short *tanka* poem rejects linearity in favor of polysemy.[69] In the Edo period (1603–1688), during which an urban middle class acquired power, the Heian aesthetic was recast. As in the West, the new bourgeoisie demanded greater realism in its arts. The Kabuki and Bunraku doll theater were not as abstract as the lyrical Noh theater, and the earthy, semiperspectival *ukiyo-e* woodblock prints were more realistic than Chinese-style screen painting. Nevertheless, these bourgeois entertainments never became as illusionistic as in the West. The Kabuki was far more "presentational" than Western theater; the Bunraku puppets were manipulated in highly stylized ways; and the *ukiyo-e* prints decentered their compositions and acknowledged the picture surface.[70] In Japan's premodern arts of aristocrats and merchants, Burch finds strategies that parallel Western oppositional modernism.

How could such strategies penetrate the popular art of the cinema? Unlike most of its Far Eastern neighbors, Japan did not fall victim to Western conquest and colonization in the nineteenth century. According to Burch, political isolation preserved Heian and Edo aesthetic practices until the arrival of U.S. troops at the end of World War II. Japanese cinema thus maintained the culture's anti-illusionist traditions.

When cinema came to Japan, Burch maintains, it was immediately taken as a presentational medium. The *katsuben (benshi),* a commentator in the auditorium explaining the action to the audience by reciting the titles and enacting the roles, prevented immersion in the spectacle. In the West, the lecturer vanished with the consolidation of the IMR, but the benshi were indispensable fixtures of all Japanese silent-film screenings, and they were ousted with difficulty by producers in the 1930s. According to Burch, filmmakers could leave narrative exposition to the benshi and concentrate on the elaboration of pictorial structures. Just as important, as a descendant of the chanter accompanying Kabuki or the doll theater, the benshi distanced the audience from the spectacle, producing "a *reading* of the diegesis which was thereby designated as such and which thereby ceased to function as diegesis and became what it had in fact never ceased to be, *a field of signs.*"[71] Once scanned and recounted by the benshi, any film lost its power to produce a homogeneous illusion.

Because of indigenous representational traditions and the authority of the benshi, Japanese films assimilated the IMR's codes only partially. During the

4.23 An "establishing shot" from Mikio Naruse's *Wife, Be Like a Rose!* (1935). The young woman and her boyfriend are overwhelmed by the roof edge and latticework.

1920s, American standards were introduced, but many filmmakers resisted them. Between 1930 and 1945 they continued to ignore the rules of Western découpage. They relied upon long and medium-long shots rather than the close-ups and shot/reverse-shot patterns favored by Hollywood. They decentered compositions (Fig. 4.23). They left the frame empty for prolonged periods, fastening on objects or landscapes and thereby creating "pillow-shots" (analogous to the "pillow-words," or stock adjectival epithets, in Heian verse). Directors displayed a corresponding concern for geometrical camera positions and cutting. In one scene of Yamanaka's *Humanity and Paper Balloons* (1937), for example, "each shot is at once separate from and identical to the previous shot" (Figs. 4.24–4.26).[72]

The greatest works of the 1930s and early 1940s, most notably those by Ozu and Mizoguchi, invoke Western conventions only to sabotage them. Mizoguchi mastered the IMR codes early and set about placing them within a wider system of exceptionally long takes, distant framings that present a great deal of material to be absorbed, and lateral tracking shots that create a string of precise compositions reminiscent of traditional scroll painting.[73] Ozu is said to break down diegetic space "by systematically violating the rules of eyeline-matching (the keystone of shot-reverse-shot) and raising pictorial flatness to a principle of *mise en scène*."[74] (See Figs. 4.27, 4.28.)

According to Burch, Japanese cinema's golden age was fostered by the rise of a militarist state. As the nation became more isolated and jingoistic, filmmaking practices that maintained indigenous aesthetic traditions were strengthened. The wartime films preserved their cultural uniqueness by barely characterizing men in battle, downplaying combat heroics, and assimilating the Hollywood codes "perfunctorily and superficially." But after Japan lost the

4.24 In one scene *Humanity and Paper Balloons* presents several shots down a street . . .

4.25 . . . but the consistency of angle and composition makes each one a variant of the same visual design . . .

4.26 . . . creating what Burch calls a "geometrical purity" of style.

4.27 In *Where Now Are the Dreams of Youth?* (1932) Ozu's recurrent camera height and composition allow him to mismatch shot . . .

4.28 . . . and reverse shot harmoniously. Compare the "correct" eyeline matching of Figs. 4.7 and 4.8.

war and was occupied by American forces, most filmmakers adopted the IMR. The new stage of the class struggle, in which left-wing forces gained some ground, required a more realistic system of representation. The progressive working class was committed to accepting some Western values, and this tendency fostered the arrival of illusionism within the arts. But this development was also "geared to the needs of that liberal monopoly capitalism toward which Japan was developing."[75]

In Burch's view, most postwar directors mastered the codes of the IMR; only Kurosawa and a younger avant-garde generation self-consciously contested them. Of all Japanese directors, Kurosawa has come closest to the Western crestline in transforming the normalized mode into a rigorous, original formal system. Like Eisenstein, he adheres to Western linearity while "foregrounding articulation as such," creating a "rough-hewn geometry." Burch makes Kurosawa's interplay of abstract pattern and narrative denotation as decisive a criterion as it was in *Praxis du cinéma: Ikiru* (1952) displays "a 'serial' organization of signifying elements whose place is at the same time always simultaneously determined by a wholly unambiguous narrative chain."[76]

The PMR and the Japanese aesthetic offer two significant oppositional traditions to the hegemony of the Institutional Mode. Indeed, Burch sees Japanese film practice as preserving features of the Western "primitive" mode, such as the tableau shot and the lecturer/benshi. Films of the 1920s exhibit frontal playing and flat compositions, the latter accentuated by the sliding walls and windows of domestic architecture. Even directors fully aware of the Western codes, such as Mizoguchi, Ozu, and Kurosawa, begin their deconstruction and organic restructuring from a nonillusionist heritage similar to that informing the PMR.

A man of strong opinions, Burch has not hesitated to change them. He has criticized the "'musicalist' formalism" of *Praxis du cinéma,* and he has denied feeling any nostalgia for the PMR.[77] Lengthy exposure to American television made him question his faith in Brechtian distancing.[78] Recently declaring an end to his inquiry into film form and style, he has refocused upon political content and psychoanalytic interpretation.[79] Yet his rejection of earlier views has not been wholesale. For instance, even when he repudiates his earlier belief that the primitive cinema anticipated modernism's attack on illusionism—now he finds only parallels, not prefigurations—he claims that at least some early creators sought "to deconstruct classical vision."[80] In any event, whether he currently stands by all his published works or not, they form a landmark in the oppositional research program. They typify a tendency and exert an appeal beyond the author's opinions of the moment.[81]

Burch's historical projects largely presupposed a serialist conception of film form and a "deconstructive" variant of political modernism. The result was a history of film style that set out to confute the Standard Version and the Bazinian program. *Life to Those Shadows,* he tells us, targets the belief that early cinema was naïvely theatrical and that the progress of film "language" involved a set of natural, ideologically neutral technical advances. He criticizes Bazin in turn, claiming that the idea of a universal mummy complex legitimates an attachment to the "Frankenstein dream" of recreating life. More specifically, Burch rejects Bazin's argument that 1940s deep focus was significantly different from "primitive" depth; he maintains that Feuillade, Gasnier, and others created an "extreme primitive depth" that was *re*discovered by Renoir, Welles, and Wyler.[82]

Although I have called Bazin's schema dialectical, Burch goes self-consciously further in this direction, stressing contradictions and regressions, partial and transitory syntheses. For instance, the PMR shot was not always or simply flat, as the deep perspectives of early *actualités* demonstrate. So Burch recasts the Lumière/Méliès dichotomy as an opposition between surface and depth, as if the PMR contained within itself the future tension between "primitive" flatness and Institutional depth.[83] According to Burch, the Film d'Art failed because it undertook the task of rendering middle-class theatrical representation in the primitive style. Griffith and his followers knew better: in developing the "non-theatrical," "specifically cinematic" codes of the IMR, their films achieved the involvement and identification solicited by bourgeois theater.

The search for tensions and contradictions also characterizes Burch's analyses of individual works. Again and again a particular film plunges representational tactics into conflict. Porter's *Life of an American Fireman* is said to exploit new cutting methods while clinging to the primitive tableau. Pudovkin's *Mother* (1926) exemplifies a different contradiction. In seeking to make a scene maximally "readable," Pudovkin fragments it into many discrete close-ups; but this very fragmentation works against a sense of an enveloping story space and risks disorienting the viewer.[84] The tendency to find key films exhibiting a conflictual interaction of parameters carries forward the "organic dialectics" of film form that Burch set out in *Praxis du cinéma.*

Despite his explicit desire to overturn "idealist" historiography, Burch sustains the research tradition in important ways. He accepts much of the Standard Version's periodization and many judgments about causality and influence.[85] Some passages exude orthodoxy: "The economic interests that caused the sudden emergence of the talky abruptly terminated as well a 'silent language' which was barely entering on its maturity and which we have no reason to believe was exhausted after a mere decade."[86] By and large, Burch's list of major directors and crestline works also conforms to the canon. Like

Jacobs, Sadoul, and many others he adds to the Basic Story; he nuances it; he does not demolish it.

His oppositional account also echoes Bazin's. Some of Burch's key concerns were put on the agenda by *la nouvelle critique:* the "myth of total cinema"; the importance of *profondeur de champ,* redrafted as depth versus flatness; the tactic of treating classical découpage as a comparative norm; the importance of the viewer's scanning the shot (for Bazin, in the work of deep-focus directors; for Burch, in the PMR tableau and in modernist works like *Play Time*); the tendency to treat a film's style as a systematic mixture of alternative technical choices (compare Bazin's interest in *Citizen Kane*'s "narrational dialectic"); and even perhaps the idea of classical style as "linearized."[87] Burch's detailed study of the IMR in effect picks up Astruc's hint about classical découpage: "This technique may have lacked ambition, but it was faultless and sure. It would be still interesting today to analyze its finest details."[88]

Like Bazin before him, Burch created a new standard for close analysis in stylistic history. But exactly because he works at a more fine-grained level than his predecessors, and because he mobilizes more concrete evidence, he is far more vulnerable to detailed disconfirmation. It seems clear, for instance, that some of his arguments about Japanese film style lack sufficient empirical support. Most of Japan's surviving prewar films look like ordinary Hollywood films, and the films of the war years are even more stylistically orthodox. We can explain the films' unusual moments in other ways—as the self-conscious citing of legitimating traditions or as a "decorative" approach to narration.[89] The graphic matches and "pillow-shots" in Ozu respond to demands of context and comprehension, not simply to ancient traditions of verse.[90] Burch's account of early film is open to dispute on comparable grounds.[91]

There are broader objections to be raised as well. Burch's critical vocabulary could use more refining. For example, when he employs flatness/depth as a key parameter, he treats the duality as intuitively obvious. But an image's sense of space is actually produced by many depth cues, and a more nuanced analysis would be able to examine them as distinct factors in creating the overall look of a shot. Allowing that a shot may be flat in certain respects and deep in others would allow us to show that filmmakers can produce different sorts of three-dimensional space.

By making class struggle the motor of stylistic change, Burch obliges himself to connect visual style to social interests. He does this, as we have seen, by recasting Bazin's "myth of total cinema" and identifying it not with mankind as a whole but with the European and North American bourgeoisie. Middle-class filmmakers aimed initially at a simulacrum of reality, but the result had to be properly recast for the sake of psychological identification. One could, however, object that realism was not the only style to enthrall the bourgeoisie.

From this class also came patrons of such highly stylized artistic practices as opera, ballet, and the increasingly abstract painting of post-Impressionism. It is likely that bourgeois tastes were far more pluralistic than Burch allows.

Similarly, in assuming that a class acts as a unitary force, Burch has not wholly avoided the "Hegelianism without metaphysics" that haunts this research tradition. The satisfaction of class interests now propels stylistic change. The concrete actions of historical agents, undertaken for myriad and even conflicting reasons, tend "objectively" to further the triumph of illusionism. Another Hegelian inheritance is evident in Burch's urge to find the medium's structural options played out neatly across history. The "primitive" interplay of flatness and depth, properties first appearing separately in interior tableaux and exterior filming, form a dialectical synthesis within advanced works of the PMR. The deconstructive film of the crestline tradition, both citing and criticizing the codes, may present Burch's Hegelian *Aufhebung*, the sublation that transcends illusionism and its alternatives by synthesizing them at a new level.

The Oppositional Version presumes that all "deviant" films have a naysaying relation to the mainstream; but it seems likely that many such films are just contingently different. Some directors pursue projects and problems that are utterly idiosyncratic, with no significant relation to mainstream practice. It is unlikely that Brakhage's *Fire of Waters* (1965), with its jagged bursts of light across a smoky frame, constitutes a critique of Hollywood; it seems more centrally concerned with creating a visual experience that is barely identifiable. Certainly, looking at the IMR as a unified practice and treating other types of filmmaking as rivals can be a very useful heuristic. It can alert the researcher to important stylistic differences, and it may lead to evidence of genuine commingling of traditions. But it is rash to turn this methodological hypothesis into an explanatory axiom.

It can be argued that Burch is so committed to the oppositional duality of norm and deconstruction that he maps it in fairly static fashion onto the history of the medium. Once the IMR is in place by the early 1920s, he supplies no account of change within it, apart from remarks that synchronized sound solidified it. The implication is that the IMR is a static target at which opponents in any era may fire. Similarly, Burch's crestline displays no developmental pattern of its own. Michael Fried has suggested that modernist painting has been committed to "a perpetual revolution—perpetual because bent on unceasing radical criticism of itself."[92] In such a scenario, the advanced artist works against not only "illusionist" traditions but also avant-garde experimentation. Cézanne could be considered to correct the Impressionists, while Pop Art criticizes the solemn introversion of Abstract Expressionism. Burch's crestline masters, however, avoid dialogue with their peers.[93] The camera movements in *Vampyr* (1932) bear no relation to those of *L'argent*, even though Dreyer probably knew L'Herbier's film; all that the two men share is the effort to deconstruct one illusionist code or another.

Displaying no logic of change, the crestline works get described, but their causes and conditions go unexplained. For Burch, cultural and class-based factors can account for stylistic change and stability in the IMR and other modes. Yet he seldom provides any such explanations for the crestline films of modernism. What aspects of the class struggle made works produced in such different contexts as *Caligari, Potemkin,* and *Gertrud* enlist in the same deconstructive campaign? Burch seems to assume that the avant-garde tradition itself, bent on attacking orthodoxy and discovering novelty, furnishes a sufficient impulse for change. Once the IMR was established in the late 1910s, he remarks, "successive modernist movements set about extending . . . their 'de-constructive' critiques of those representational norms to the realm of film."[94] Yet not all crestline films are allied to modernist movements in other arts; *L'argent* and *Gertrud* would seem obvious examples. Burch's research program provides a subtler account of norms and oppositions than any available from his predecessors, but the historical dynamic within the avant-garde remains elusive.

Nonetheless, like the Standard Version and the Dialectical program, Burch's work has provided robust points of departure for new research. By putting a norm-based model at the center of discussion, Burch has brought out one crucial dimension of film history. Just as important, his oppositional scheme has gained breadth and nuance by incorporating earlier insights—often tacitly, as a heritage of key works, heuristic concepts, and salient problems. Burch has participated in the tradition by studying "film language," by examining contemporary and rediscovered films in relation to the canon, by modeling cinema's development upon a notion of modernism in adjacent arts, and by organizing stylistic history according to overarching patterns of continuity and change.

chapter

5 Prospects for Progress: Recent Research Programs

The canon, the patterns of change, and the explanatory principles set out by the three research programs continue to shape readers' understanding of film history. For decades mass-market books have recycled the Standard Version.[1] More ambitious works of cultural history rely on it as well, as when one scholar finds the modern world's sense of space and simultaneity manifested in the canonical works of Porter and Griffith.[2] Tenets of the other programs have also become commonplaces. Christian Metz, probably the most influential film theorist since Bazin, formulated his view of cinematic "codes" in ways that presuppose both the Standard Version and a post-*Cahiers* conception of the evolution of "modern" film language.[3] As late as 1996, a distinguished literary essayist invoked cycles of birth, maturity, and decline in explaining how, after silent filmmaking was extinguished, film art knew a second flourishing when Neorealism ushered in the modern cinema of the 1960s and 1970s.[4]

Even the most ambitious contemporary theorists tend to assume that our historiographic tradition has adequately plotted the aesthetic history of film. Consider Gilles Deleuze's two-volume study *Cinema,* published in 1983 and 1985. Deleuze's theory relies upon a conception of cinema derived almost completely from the research programs we have been examining. Deleuze distinguishes between the "movement-image," in which movement defines time, and the "time-image," in which movement is only one consequence of temporality. Deleuze then projects this duality onto an orthodox historiography of style. The movement-image, in various forms, is typified by the silent cinema and mainstream Hollywood movies. The time-image, with its insistence on ellipses and felt duration, emerges around World War II in *Citizen Kane* and Italian Neorealism—just as Bazin argued. The time-image is further elaborated in *Voyage to Italy, Hiroshima mon amour,* and the work of Antonioni. This idea echoes Burch, Ropars, and the *Cahiers* writers, who claimed that the classical cinema was succeeded by a modern one that manipulated time in such ways.

Deleuze's unquestioning reliance upon our research tradition is further revealed in his belief that a cinematic essence unfolds across history. He follows Bazin in holding that the cinema image is inherently "automatic," recording contingent slices of time and movement.[5] Moreover, despite cinema's ability to capture motion, its basic affinity is with temporality. This became evident only with the advent of the "time-image"—or, as Bazin would put it, with Welles's "dialectical step forward in film language." In order to explain this emergence, Deleuze adopts another neo-Hegelian commonplace. "It is never at the beginning that something new, a new art, is able to reveal its essence; what it was from the outset it can reveal only after a detour in its evolution."[6]

Following Hegelian precedent, Deleuze maps philosophical distinctions onto the empirical differences constructed by our historiographic tradition. Assuming that the Soviet Montage directors all practiced "dialectical" editing, he finds that each director's oeuvre corresponds closely to one particular law of the dialectic. Likewise, the Standard Version distinction between French Impressionist cinema and German Expressionist cinema of the 1920s restates Kant's distinction between the mathematical sublime and the dynamic sublime. Within the "movement-image," two types—the "action-image" and the "emotion-image"—represent realism and idealism respectively (and Peirce's "firstness" and "secondness" as well).[7] Deleuze finds that Wölfflin's distinction between types of space in Renaissance and Baroque art lines up with Bazin's distinction between the depth of "primitive" cinema and that presented by Renoir and Welles.[8] No body of work that does not fit somewhere; no category without a historical manifestation. Orthodox historical schemes become ratified by a new teleology. Stylistic development follows not from a law of progress but from the medium's mysterious urge to fill in every square of a vast grid of conceptual possibilities.

This philosopher's foray into film theory illustrates how uncritical adherence to historiographic tradition can disable contemporary work. Instead, I suggest, we can improve our understanding of stylistic history by treating the Standard Version and its successors as research programs, chains of argumentation with distinct conceptual commitments. We should recognize these programs as offering hypotheses to be analyzed, tested, recast, or rejected.

The progress made in recent years has come from just this recognition. Since the early 1970s, scholars have greatly amplified and nuanced the history of film style. Much of this enterprise remains unknown to academic readers, as well as to writers who address a wider public. No short survey can do justice to these new departures, but in the next section I want to show how some of the presuppositions and conclusions of the three programs have been refined and contested by "revisionist" researchers.

Piecemeal History

The last major synoptic history of cinema was offered by Jean Mitry in a series of five volumes published from 1967 through 1980. In his introduction to the series, Mitry demanded that historians seek a stringent causal account of changes in film technique. He advocated centering this account not upon national spirit or upon those large-scale economic factors highlighted by Sadoul but rather upon proximate causes in the film industry and in the public's reception of films. He further insisted that the film historian had to analyze not just masterpieces but also the more ordinary works that might be influential or merely typical.[9] These points marked significant departures from Standard Version practice, and they would become axiomatic for work during the next decade. Yet Mitry remained determined to supply a broad and comparative history along the lines of Paul Rotha or Bardèche and Brasillach, arguing that the work of nations or individuals had to be understood as part of the "evolution of film language."[10]

Despite his intention to write "a history of works and styles seen in a more or less coherent manner," treated as "a temporal becoming, a living continuity," Mitry's *Histoire du cinéma* proved unequal to the task.[11] His encyclopedic knowledge was evident on every packed page, but each volume remained virtually a scrapbook. Blocks of information on biography, technique, technology, and industrial conduct squatted side by side; topics were treated in detail, but by and large they were not integrated causally. The series' continuity and coherence came principally from the Basic Story and the Standard Version. Mitry's work showed that it was not easy to give the *histoire-fleuve* a fine-grained causal texture.

In the 1970s younger historians began to doubt that one scholar could write a comprehensive history of style across the world. By concentrating more narrowly on a period, a line of development, or a single stylistic issue, they avoided the peaks-and-valleys overview and began to study continuity and change on a more minute scale. It is probably too soon to identify this revisionist enterprise as a single distinctive program, but we might provisionally call it piecemeal history.

Although they focused on narrower problems, these scholars examined more films than their predecessors had. Film archives and 16mm film circulation increased their access to films beyond the canon, and the Brighton conference of

1978 proved the value of wide and deep coverage of a single period. The Brighton tradition was carried on by the Giornate del Cinema Muto, an annual gathering in Pordenone, Italy, from 1982 onward. Its organizers arranged for dozens of films, programmed around a period or theme, to be screened under optimum conditions. The Pordenone events, and the volumes of essays and documentation that issued from them, substantially altered scholars' conceptions of silent cinema. In addition, after 1980 the variety of films available in video formats made it possible for researchers studying almost any country or period to see films that would have been otherwise inaccessible.

With increasing access to prints, problems of authentication and provenance sprang up. Archivists had long known that a film might survive in a number of variants, and that almost all the canonized classics could be found in different versions. Yet this fact had almost never been acknowledged by practicing historians.[12] The ruling assumption was that the print of *The Birth of a Nation* circulating to American film societies in the 1950s was substantially the same as that seen by original audiences. In a riposte to the younger generation, Mitry claimed that he had no need to revise his estimation of certain American films of the 1910s because he had seen them when they first came out in France. Apart from his remarkable trust in his memory (he claimed to recall films he had watched at the age of eight), Mitry ignored the touchy problem of how close those French releases were to the originals.[13] The revisionists began the serious comparison of variant copies, a process that in one case, as we shall see, had far-reaching implications for the Standard Version. The study of different versions eventually led to important debates with archivists about principles of restoration and reconstruction.[14]

The revisionists' bulk viewing also produced a much more detailed account of changes in film technique than had been available previously. For instance, by watching thousands of films, Barry Salt constructed a chronology of stylistic innovations appearing in European and American cinema from the earliest years. At a moment when film studies had just entered a stage of basic and systematic information-gathering (the most useful reference books began to appear during the 1970s), Salt's spadework proved invaluable. He also pinpointed some testable claims made by earlier writers and then sought out fresh evidence that might confute them. This strategy enabled him to reveal several predecessors of Griffith's cross-cutting, such as *The 100 to One Shot* (Vitagraph, 1906). Salt likewise disclosed patterned changes in cutting rates across films, directors, and periods. It is a significant datum of film history that the average shot length of American films has dropped quite steadily since the advent of sound; in recent years, an ordinary film may contain more than a dozen cuts per minute.[15]

Salt's work exemplifies the major conceptual advance in recent historiography of style: a greater sensitivity to collective norms. For him as for others, the most obvious norm to study was that of mainstream entertainment cinema. Where the Standard Version had seen the universal spread of devices (close-up, editing, camera movement), Astruc and Bazin saw the emergence of a distinct system of techniques. Both writers had suggested that Hollywood and its international peers could be characterized by their adherence to a particular cluster of stylistic choices. Burch and others built upon this insight, confronted as they were with a growing body of films that self-consciously pursued oppositional paths. By the late 1960s, theorists and critics had taken up the call to study "classical" cinema. Out of these activities came Burch's efforts to define the "Institutional Mode of Representation."

At this point, many people were asking how one might conceive of Hollywood's stylistic practices more precisely. One answer posed by myself and two colleagues, Janet Staiger and Kristin Thompson, was that we could consider Hollywood films to constitute a group style. In *The Classical Hollywood Cinema: Film Style and Mode of Production to 1960* we sought to spell out the principles and the range of technical choices that made this style relatively coherent. We also tried to trace the ways in which strategies of narrative construction and cinematic technique coalesced into the "standard" Hollywood film. But how to explain this consolidation? And how to explain the maintenance of this style over so many decades? One cluster of causes, we argued, could be found in the mode of film production. The studios standardized style by dividing labor quite finely and delegating tasks to particular institutions—not only to their own departments but also to trade associations and technical firms that learned to supply what filmmakers wanted.

In exploring ways in which the Hollywood style cohered and sustained itself over several decades, *The Classical Hollywood Cinema* concentrated on factors that promoted long-range stability. Some readers took this to be positing that Hollywood cinema was static and "monolithic"; but we used large-scale continuity to throw key stylistic changes into relief, analyzing change at different rates and different levels. For example, Thompson traced the emergence of a "soft" cinematography style during the 1920s, while I sought to show how, during the transition to sound, industrial conditions and a desire to maintain some editing options led studios briefly to adopt multiple-camera shooting. In such ways, the book participated in a wider effort to give a fuller sense of stylistic norms and their causal conditions than earlier historians had.

A few other national and regional film histories were written from the standpoint of style. Normally such a study mixes social and political history, descriptions of the film industry, discussions of genre, biographies of directors, and plot synopses. Burch's *To the Distant Observer* was one of the first national film histories to put stylistic matters—he would say "representational practices"—at the forefront. Later books of this sort revised orthodox histori-

5.1 *Intolerance:* The Dear One encourages the Boy in court.

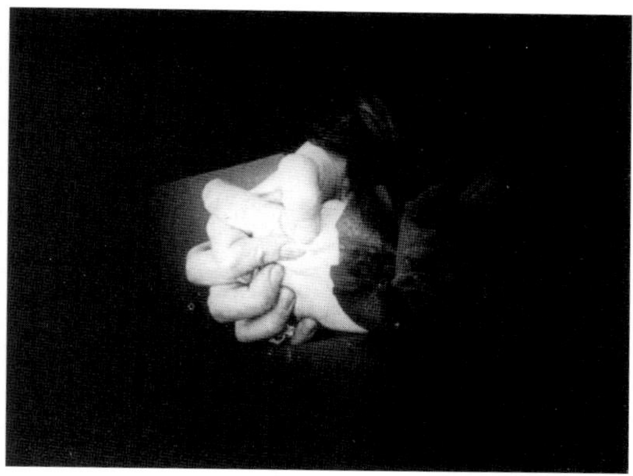

5.2 A detail shot emphasizes the Dear One's anxiety before the verdict.

orientation of the viewer. Editing might magnify a portion that was too small to be seen in the large view, but it would not be used to dissect the action into a great many shots. Only in certain circumstances, such as theater performances, hunting scenes, crowd scenes, or actions occurring in unusually large sets, would the director construct the action wholly from nearer views.

After 1912 or so, the term "close-up" seems to have come into wider use in English. Eventually it replaced the term "bust shot," but initially the new term was somewhat equivocal. Today we think of a close-up as a shot of one person, showing head and shoulders or perhaps just face, hands, or feet. In Standard Version histories, Mae Marsh's anxiety during the courtroom scene of *Intolerance* served as a vivid prototype (Figs. 5.1, 5.2). During the 1910s, however, these images might well have been considered bust shots. In the year of *Intolerance*'s release, one commentator claimed that a close-up "takes in the greater portion of the figure or figures," while the bust shot "shows only a portion of the figures."[26] In this usage, a "close-up" becomes a comparatively distant view.[27]

More than terminology is at stake here. For many practitioners the "close-up" put one or more actors in the frontmost area of a shot that might also include a lot of background. This conception ties the emergence of the close-up to staging in depth, not to the development of editing, as the Standard Version would have it. By bringing actors nearer to the camera in the course of a shot, directors may have thought that they were achieving close-ups (as distinct from bust shots, enlargements that resulted from cuts). A shot like Fig. 5.3 may have been considered a close-up in 1915 because it frames the actor from the waist up, even though it does not isolate a detail in the way our *Intolerance* prototypes do. The Standard Version historians, writing from a vantage point at which editing had come to define close-ups as enlarged,

5.3 *The Birth of a Nation:* The Little Sister in a close view as she trims her shabby dress with cotton for her brother's homecoming.

isolated details, may have projected that conception back onto the 1910s and missed the importance of depth staging during the period.

Focusing on a narrower time span, viewing films in bulk, and tracing shifts in terms and concepts allowed revisionist historians to construct fresh contexts for explaining stylistic continuity and change. One of the most important contexts was exhibition. Historians of the Standard and Dialectical Versions tended to lift the movies free from their conditions of reception, lining the films up into a procession of steps in the evolution of film art. By contrast, revisionist historians often sought causes of stylistic development in the audience and in the circumstances of projection.

For example, in a series of exacting studies Charles Musser argued that during the first five years of American film, the exhibitor was also the editor. In planning a program for a vaudeville house or museum, the exhibitor bought one-shot films from producers and arranged them in sequences that he judged would appeal to his audience. He was thus a part of a long tradition of what Musser calls "screen practice," running back to the magic lantern and shadow puppets. And there was no need to think of the film as an integral object; scenes depicting Christ's Passion or a trip to China might be interrupted by lectures or lantern slides.[28]

Around 1900 the production companies began to take control of the show, as when Edison films began to connect scenes by cuts or dissolves.[29] Soon the fictional narrative displaced documentary as the dominant mode, partly because the increasing demand for films obliged producers to turn out movies according to a standardized schedule.[30] In making longer, multiple-shot films, however, the companies faced a problem. How was a film to tell a fairly lengthy story in a comprehensible way? Musser points out that filmmakers explored several solutions. Some drew on very familiar material, including Bible tales,

5.4 *Explosion of a Motor Car:* The auto begins to explode.

5.5 After the explosion, the policeman flourishes a leg as body parts shower down on him.

illustrated songs, fairy tales, and popular verse. Another strategy was to use a lecturer to explain the action, a practice that revisionist historians have brought to light in some detail.[31] But the most common solution, particularly as films approached and then surpassed one reel in length, was to make the film as self-sufficient as possible. This was accomplished through such tactics as intertitles and editing patterns that would specify spatial and temporal connections. Like other revisionists, Musser treats the early years of cinematic storytelling as responding to concrete and contingent circumstances. Nothing inherent in the medium prevented films from remaining ingredients within ephemeral multimedia mixes varying from one venue to another.

Probably the most influential exploration of "preclassical" filmmaking was offered by Tom Gunning in his elaboration of a concept he first proposed in collaboration with André Gaudreault.[32] Gunning postulates that pre-1908 filmmaking constituted a reasonably distinct period he calls "the cinema of attractions." Standard Version historians assumed that filmmakers had from the beginning sought to tell stories, but Gunning suggests that the cinema of attractions aimed principally to present a series of views to an audience. Films drew spectators through their illusions of space and movement, abrupt presentation and withdrawal of visual effects, novel and sometimes scandalous subject matter, and startling displays of technique. In Hepworth's *Explosion of a Motor Car* (1900), for example, a tranquil outing ends brutally (Figs. 5.4, 5.5). The film aggressively confronts the spectator with a sudden shock, a grim gag, and an illusion that the auto really blew up and rained down body parts.

Early filmmakers, Gunning claims, were not groping toward our notion of a story film, a suspenseful tale populated by psychologically drawn characters acting within a coherent fictional world. By this standard, films such as Hepworth's could only be considered "primitive." Instead, the first decade of cinema traded on undeveloped incidents, surprises, transitory engagement, and a panoply of

5.6 According to the Edison catalogue, this shot could open or close *The Great Train Robbery*—evidence that it functioned not as a narrative element but as an "attraction."

stunts, gags, and tricks—just the appeals that Eisenstein later built into his "montage of attractions."[33] The emphasis on diverting momentary effects put the earliest films closer to vaudeville entertainment than to the "cinema of narrative integration" that would come to dominance after 1908. But whereas Burch tends to suggest that early film decenters attention (as do working-class entertainments like the three-ring circus), Gunning argues that an attraction powerfully commands attention, often to the exclusion of all else on screen.

This line of argument challenges some traditional conceptions of technical progress. Filmmakers did not gradually discover close-ups, camera movements, and editing; Gunning points out that all these techniques were explored in cinema's first decade. But within the cinema of attractions these devices work to accentuate the ephemeral views presented to the audience. In films devoted simply to showing facial expressions, what we now call a close-up could function as a vivid visual moment arousing curiosity or surprise. From this standpoint the shot of the bandit firing at the camera in *The Great Train Robbery* seems less a foreshadowing of close-ups in mainstream narrative cinema than an attraction capable of jolting the audience (Fig. 5.6).[34] Film technique itself might become an attraction, as in *Explosion of a Motor Car*'s stop-motion substitution of dummy limbs. Similarly, the early point-of-view shot operates not to restrict narration or to emphasize a character's state of mind, as it would within the storytelling cinema to come. Instead, the point-of-view image often serves as the basis for voyeurism, as when a peeping Tom spies on a woman undressing.[35]

These examples, Gunning argues, suggest that after 1908 Griffith and his contemporaries were not engaged in discovering cinema's unique essence. Instead they redefined films as psychological narratives and assigned fresh functions to devices earlier exploited as attractions. Not surprisingly, some techniques central to the cinema of attractions did not fit the new needs very well. Gunning points out that performers in early films commonly address the camera, turning to the viewer to register a reaction or mimic another actor. This technique suited the "exhibitionist" side of early film. With the rise of a narrative cinema, though, such asides disrupted the illusion of a self-contained story world, and so they largely disappeared.[36] Direct address would resurface at moments of comedy or musical performance—exactly those occasions that could constitute "attractions" even in a well-developed narrative context.

The idea of a cinema of attractions is, at least initially, a period-based one. According to Gunning, attractions predominated until around 1903, after which there was a transitional phase lasting until around 1908. By 1910 the cinema of narrative integration prevailed.[37] Many films before 1908 tell stories, but Gunning argues that such stories often serve simply to set off their attractions. In addition, the narrative structure tends to be profoundly unlike that of the Hollywood plot to come. In the "mischief gag" comedies, the characters are merely cogs in the gag machine; the boy who steps on the hose to block the water is only a Rascal, not a character with psychological depth (Fig. 4.19). Moreover, Gunning suggests, the temporality invoked by the cinema of attractions is inimical to the classical narratives that would come later. Based in a now-you-see-it, now-you-don't conception of display, the attraction prevents the film from developing smoothly. The spectator engages with "the unpredictability of the instant, a succession of excitements and frustrations whose order cannot be predicted by narrative logic and whose pleasures are never sure of being prolonged."[38] What follows the cinema of attractions is not merely a cinema of narrative but a cinema of narrative *integration,* which absorbs cinematic techniques and engaging moments into a self-sufficient world unified across time and space.

Dominant though it was, attraction-based filmmaking constitutes only one set of norms of the period, and so we ought to expect that some films or filmmakers will furnish in-between cases. Here Gunning echoes Burch's arguments about the Janus-faced nature of Porter and other early directors. For example, the Passion-play films moved toward linear narrative, but they also presented attraction-based tableaux.[39] In treating early films as crisscrossed by opposing tendencies, Gunning puts forth a conception of film history that breaks with the idea of an unfolding essence of the medium, a final goal for stylistic change, and a constant striving for crisp and coherent storytelling.[40]

Gunning's work exemplifies the revisionist conception of stylistic history as a dynamic of contending forces, "a jagged rhythm of competing practices . . . whose modes and models were not necessarily sketches or approximations of later cinema."[41] This idea owes a great deal to Burch's suggestion that the

"Primitive Mode of Representation" constituted a broadly unified practice. But without Bazin's positing of two rival trends running across stylistic history, it might have been more difficult to break with the unitary conception of historical development offered by the Standard Version. Like Burch, moreover, Gunning and other scholars of early cinema have been alert to the possibility of mixed or transitional bodies of work, a possibility already broached by Bazin in his discussion of "hybrid" forms such as *Citizen Kane.* To some extent as well, Musser and Gunning can be seen as exploring territory already marked out by those Standard-Version historians who denigrated a "primitive" cinema of crude tricks and gags. The revisionists do more than revise interpretations of the historical record; they also recast the conceptual schemes they inherit from their research tradition.

This process is particularly evident in the new generation's reconsideration of canonized directors. Predictably, no researcher has concluded that Méliès, Porter, and Griffith no longer matter to film history. What has changed is the nature of their significance. Instead of representing a step toward the perfection of filmic storytelling, each director now seems at once more idiosyncratic and more typical of his period than was previously thought.

Consider Méliès. For many Standard Version authors, he seemed theatrical because he minimized cutting and relied on stagy effects. But recent scholars have shown that he used editing more than was realized.[42] His famous stop-motion tricks required splicing, since he was obliged to chop out a few overexposed frames before the camera had stopped and after it was restarted.[43] (The splice marks are visible at the top of the frame in Fig. 2.4.) In some respects, furthermore, Méliès' linkage of tableaux can be considered skillful by modern standards. More than his contemporaries, he relies on consistent screen direction when characters pass from one locale to an adjacent one.[44] Méliès was even capable of fast editing; Gaudreault points out that the launch and landing of the space capsule in *A Trip to the Moon* (1902), presenting four shots in less than twenty seconds, is the most rapidly cut sequence known before 1908.[45] Again, however, these techniques are not necessarily steps toward the perfection of film narrative; storytelling was only one purpose of Méliès' *féeries,* and his editing often served to heighten legerdemain and theatrical spectacle.[46]

In 1915 Edwin S. Porter declared that he was "the first man to tell a complete story with moving pictures,"[47] and generations of film historians took him at his word. He was revered as the father of film narrative. At the hands of Musser and other revisionist historians, however, Porter became something more peculiar and interesting—again, through a more complete understanding of prevailing stylistic norms.

Musser suggests that the principal stylistic problem facing early filmmakers involved continuity of duration. Models for spatial continuity were available in lantern-slide projection, but the new medium of cinema demanded that action moving across different locales be coordinated with the time passing on the screen.[48] In *A Trip to the Moon* Méliès met the challenge with a temporal overlap: the rocket lands in extreme long shot, smacking the moon in the eye, and in the next shot on the moon's surface, the rocket is shown landing again. It seems likely that Porter borrowed this idea. In *How They Do Things on the Bowery* (1902), a bartender throws the hayseed Uncle Josh out, and the entire action is seen first from within the bar and once again from the street.[49] Odd though such repetitions look to us, this sort of cutting occurs often enough in the period to suggest that filmmakers and audiences did not find smooth durational continuity necessary.[50]

Confirmation of this tendency came in an unexpected way. Two versions of *Life of an American Firemen* (1903) survived. The one widely accepted as authentic contained a sequence of the fireman arriving at the blaze and saving first a mother and then her child. The rescues were presented in alternating shots, shifting us from outside the building to the burning bedroom, then back outside again. A second version of the film presented the action in only two shots. The first shot recorded both rescues from inside the bedroom, while the next shot repeated the entire action as seen from outside. This version, deposited for copyright, was assumed to be a rough cut, containing the two takes that would be intercut in the final film.

But archival research revealed that the two-shot copyright version was probably close to the original. It is most likely that *Life of an American Fireman* presented the rescues twice, first seen from inside the building, and then from outside.[51] How could such a peculiar film have been made? Musser argues that Porter was generalizing from his experience of magic-lantern projections, in which each image was self-contained and could be linked to the next through repeated action.[52] "Ironically," Musser writes, "the innovations that many historians have attributed to Porter based on the modernized version of *Life of an American Fireman*—parallel editing and matching action—were the very procedures that Porter had the greatest difficulty executing." Had Porter truly discovered cross-cutting and continuity editing in this film and *The Great Train Robbery*, one might expect him to have exploited these techniques when confronted with similar storytelling tasks in later works. Yet Musser points out that later Porter films continued to repeat actions across distinct scenes and shots, not adopting genuine cross-cutting until 1907, when other directors were also starting to use the device.[53]

Porter's editing was not completely anachronistic; some of the innovations credited to *Life of an American Fireman* can be found in *Jack and the Beanstalk* (1902). In *Uncle Tom's Cabin* (1903) lightning flashes are daringly simulated by alternating five or six overexposed frames with normally exposed passages of the same image. On the whole, however, revisionist historians tended to think of Porter, like Méliès, as a director who utilized techniques that seem deviant by the teleological measure of earlier accounts but that made sense in a particular production and exhibition context.

Griffith's case is more complex. We are by now familiar with the extravagant claims made for him, not least in his own self-promotion. A 1916 journalistic biography compared him to Edison, Galileo, Pasteur, Molière, and Tolstoy.[54] To this day, people otherwise unacquainted with film history believe that he invented the close-up, analytical cutting, and other devices. "Every filmmaker who has followed him," rumbled Orson Welles, "has done just that: followed him. He made the first close-up and moved the first camera."[55]

Between 1908 and 1912 the editing in Griffith's Biograph films did attract notice, but not, as Standard Version historians would have it, because of any penchant for breaking a scene into closer views. Griffith's technique was notorious for what one contemporary called "an undue amount of repetition and a bewildering number of scene shifts."[56] Griffith provided a great many "goings and comings," shots of characters hurrying down streets, bustling through hallways, bursting into parlors. Griffith apparently believed that he could hold the viewer's attention best by increasing the number of shots and constantly rushing characters to fresh locales.

Following a single character's trajectory through a flurry of shots fed into Griffith's famous fondness for "alternate scenes," the technique later called cross-cutting or parallel editing. Typically, cross-cutting alternates shots of simultaneous actions occurring some distance apart. In *The Birth of a Nation,* the Klansmen's ride to the rescue is cross-cut with shots of the whites in their besieged cabin. In American film, however, "alternate scenes" seem to have developed primarily in order to present two events taking place quite near one another, such as inside and outside a building.[57] Soon it became possible to indicate simultaneous action across greater distances. Griffith did not invent this device, which he called the "switchback," but he became famous by ringing a great many changes upon it.[58] From *The Lonely Villa* (1909) onward he linked cross-cutting to a last-minute rescue. He multiplied lines of action, chopped them into more and more shots, and devised delays that would intensify audience interest. His cuts interrupted gestures and the flow of movement. He shaped the compositions of the intercut shots to suggest converging forces, as when a son racing leftward through the countryside eventually arrives at his father's home, where the old man has all the while been gazing steadily to the right.[59] At the same time Griffith applied cross-cutting to situations not so dependent upon suspense. In films like *A Corner in Wheat* (1908) he implied moral judgments by comparing characters and situations.[60]

The revisionists' stylistic analyses refined our sense of the ways in which

5.7 *Intolerance:* The iris makes the revolver salient, even though it is filmed from fairly far back.

Griffith elaborated cross-cutting. More devastating were the results of their examining another pillar of his reputation. "My first anachronistic effort," Griffith claimed in 1916, "was what we now call the 'close-up.'"[61] Yet the close-up, as we understand the term today, is on display in the early "magnified views" in such films as *Grandma's Reading Glass* (G. A. Smith, 1900). As we have already seen, however, by the early 1910s the term was beginning to be used to describe simply bringing some characters near to the camera in the course of an ensemble scene. From quite early in his career, Griffith did move his players into the foreground, usually in medium shot (Fig. 5.3); but so did other directors during the same years. What later became the prototype of a close-up, a cut-in shot of a face or a detail (Figs. 5.1, 5.2), is not salient in his work until around 1912, and it did not become common until somewhat later.[62] The rarity of the device is underscored by a canonical example. In *The Lonedale Operator* (1911; Figs. 2.8, 2.9), Griffith's cut-in reveals that the heroine has held her attackers off with a wrench, which both the thieves and the audience have taken for a pistol. Here, the scene's surprise depends on withholding information that can be supplied only by a close-up. In films of this period, Griffith explores other ways to highlight certain elements of the shot, as when an iris masks off part of the image (Fig. 5.7). In general, his use of the cut-in close-up seems to have been more or less abreast of his peers' practice (Figs. 5.8, 5.9).[63] A tight close-up of a face or an object seems to have been quite rare in any film between 1908 and 1915 and not really frequent until the 1920s.

Apart from refining and correcting received views of what Griffith accomplished, revisionist scholarship brought to light some oddities that seem dead ends if one is tracing the "evolution of film language." For instance, Griffith had a penchant for an ambivalent form of cross-cutting. A character stands in one spot, looking in a pronounced direction. Then Griffith cuts to another character far away, also in a static pose. How do we construe the linking glance? Character

5.8 In *Le pickpocket mystifié* (1911), a detective stands examining an identification notice . . .

5.9 . . . and a cut enlarges it, along with his suspicious expression. (Compare Figs. 2.8–2.9.)

A may be thinking of character B. Or Griffith may be suggesting some likeness or affinity between them. Or there may be a quasi-supernatural sense in which A is somehow seeing B. In *A Drunkard's Reformation* (1909), the mother and child look "at" the father in a distant locale.[64] Griffith seems to have believed that this device signaled that A is thinking of B, but the power of the eyeline cues and the fact that B is usually shown in a situation that A cannot plausibly know about tend to make the cutaway seem more than merely a subjective insert. In any case, this "ruminative" eyeline cut, as Joyce Jesniowski calls it, did not become normalized within the mainstream Hollywood style.[65]

Griffith also developed a penchant for laying interior scenes out perpendicular to the camera. In his dollhouse-like sets, he would align side doors with the very edges of the shot and then fire characters across the framelines.[66] A man hurries toward a door exactly on frame left. As he crosses the threshold, Griffith cuts to the adjacent room, forcing our eye to jump back to the right edge to pick up the man's entrance. Griffith's delight in multiplying and repeating these lateral cuts, prolonging movement by lining up rooms like railroad cars, yanking characters back and forth across the viewer's sightline, was shared by few of his peers. Most directors preferred to stage interiors in depth, placing doors in the back wall and bringing the actors more sedately to the front plane.

Without losing any of his renown, then, Griffith has begun to seem atypical. Gunning has argued that he is less the creator of Hollywood's film language than a transitional director, redefining techniques created in the cinema of attractions for purposes of narrative integration.[67] By 1914 or 1915, other directors were producing films that today seem more "forward-looking" than *The Birth of a Nation.* Smoothly staged and cut, Raoul Walsh's *Regeneration,* Maurice Tourneur's *The Wishing Ring* and *Alias Jimmy Valentine,* and Cecil B. DeMille's *The Cheat* look recognizably like the Hollywood movie we know, while Griffith's masterpiece seems fairly idiosyncratic.[68]

Through such inquiries, piecemeal history-writing allowed us to grasp the origins of the Standard Version itself. Eileen Bowser has suggested that the idea that cinema might be an art arose from the development of the feature film after 1908.[69] By hiring writers and performers from the stage and by modeling shots on famous paintings and photographs, film companies sought to legitimate a mass medium. At the same time, commentators began to debate whether cinema possessed aesthetic resources different from those of theater or painting. Throughout Europe, as we saw in Chapter 2, the period from 1909 onward signals a new willingness to consider cinema a distinct form of expression. Griffith could thus step forward as film's first genuine artist; his vigorous style, as well as his flair for self-publicity, came at a moment when a public was prepared to find proof that a new art had been born.

These inquiries into early film also helped clarify the origins of what became mainstream fictional filmmaking—Bazin's and the *Cahiers*' "classical cinema," Burch's "Institutional Mode of Representation." Both the Standard Version and Bazin's dialectical account had singled out editing as the prime index of change, and with a greater understanding of "primitive" cinema historians could pinpoint changes in this technique. An example is furnished by Kristin Thompson's study of the emergence of Hollywood's continuity conventions.

According to Thompson, the components of classical Hollywood editing—analytical cutting, eyeline matching, cross-cutting, and the like—developed fairly independently of one another. They coalesced into a set of norms in the mid- to late 1910s.[70] She proposes that the demand for longer films, first consuming several shots and soon consuming several reels, encouraged filmmakers to master editing. Continuity editing could maintain a cogent, unified time and space just when narratives were becoming longer and more intricate.[71] Films by Thomas Ince, Douglas Fairbanks, and others showed how cutting could pick up the pace, imply spatial relations, and time story information quite precisely.[72] In addition, directors around 1915 began cross-cutting among different plot lines, partly because this tactic could stretch out the action to fill the allotted running time. Plots could likewise be extended by dwelling on characters' psychological states, and editing could help portray those. In the Fairbanks film *A Modern Musketeer* (1917), a sustained play of eyelines across isolated shots creates a pause in the action while allowing the spectator to register the undercurrents of the drama (Figs. 5.10–5.15).

Like Gunning, Thompson treats mainstream editing not as a replacement for "primitive" devices, as the Standard Version would have it, but as a selective blend of existing techniques within a new conception of storytelling. Directors seized upon technical options available since the first years of cinema, harnessed them to the specific purposes appropriate to the format of the longer film, and routinized them so that they yielded controlled, efficient, and

5.10 *A Modern Musketeer*: A scene begins with an extreme long shot of the tourists and their guide stopping along the river.

5.11 Chin-de-dah points out the landscape, his arm and his glance suggesting that Barris is off right.

5.12 Elsie apprehensively watches him.

5.13 Chin-de-dah shifts his glance slightly and leers at Elsie.

5.14 Elsie looks down, embarrassed.

5.15 Barris looks suspiciously at Chin-de-dah, returning the glance she avoids.

5.16 Outdoor depth staging for the Danish film *Afgrunden* (Urban Gad, 1910). (Compare Fig. 1.1.)

5.17 In the long-take tableaux of *Les vampires* (1915–16), Feuillade often presents scenes in intricate, layered depth.

standardized production. Thompson suggests that the very idea and term "continuity" came into use at this time as a recognition that film techniques should tell a visually coherent story from shot to shot.[73]

Between 1909 and 1920, most historians agree, this system of continuity editing came to dominate American cinema. But what did it displace? And what went on outside the U.S. studios? Bazin's conceptual scheme encouraged revisionist historians to plot an alternative stylistic system at work in the 1910s.

Mitry had already proposed that the editing-based cinema of America had a rival in a more "theatrical" tendency in Europe. This theatricality differed significantly from the unreflecting recording of performances characteristic of the earliest filmmaking. From 1909 onward, sets were no longer flat backdrops but more voluminous, with furniture jutting out on different planes. Actors came closer to the camera and gave more subtle performances. The camera might pan or track, and the director grew more concerned with shot composition. Mitry argued that many Italian, Scandinavian, Russian, and German directors championed this "painterly" theatricality.[74]

His insight was eventually developed with the aid of schemes derived from Bazin. In the 1980s historians began to suggest that in avoiding the continuity cutting exploited by the U.S. studios, European filmmakers' "theatrical" approach actually constituted a well-developed tradition of deep-focus, long-take filmmaking. Burch had treated the European cinema of the 1910s as an extension of the "primitive" tableau, but revisionists began to conceive it as something more complex—perhaps even a period style unto itself. At Pordenone, marathon screenings of Scandinavian films (in 1986), Russian films (1989), and German films (1990) showed that before 1920 continental filmmakers had produced a rich alternative to Hollywood continuity (Figs. 5.16, 5.17).[75]

5.18 *Ingmar's Sons:* Brita's father comes in through the door and tells her that Sven has been chosen to marry her.

5.19 She starts up from the window, looking rightward in an eyeline match.

5.22 She starts to move out frame left.

5.23 Her father and mother stride happily into the parlor.

Analyzing and explaining this tendency are on the agenda for the next chapter. Here it is enough to recall that in the 1910s Europeans recognized major differences between U.S. films and their own. Some declared the American continuity style choppy and distracting. Director Urban Gad objected that the brief flashes in American films gave no time to grasp the story, while Colette complained that cutting from face to face denied the spectator the opportunity to compare expressions within a single shot.[76] Nonetheless, European directors began to incorporate continuity devices, dissecting their tableaux into closer views and employing more cross-cutting. The eventual, if uneven and occasionally oddball, assimilation of U.S. continuity devices seems to be a pervasive tendency across the world's silent cinema.[77] It is a testimony to the powerful appeal of classical cutting that a director like Victor Sjöström, who in 1913 displayed subtle mastery of the one-take scene in depth, could half a dozen years later seize on the advantages in timing and emphasis yielded

5.20 All bluff heartiness, her father signals to her to sit down.

5.21 Sjöström cuts back to Brita, already fearing the worst; the cut has elided her lowering her eyes.

5.24 A reverse-angle cut shows them in the foreground, starting to sit down.

5.25 After the mother has cleared out of the foreground, Brita angrily confronts her father in what will be a new establishing shot, to be broken up into reverse shots.

by delicate reverse angles and eyeline matching (Figs. 5.18–5.25).[78] In 1917 another master of the tableau, Louis Feuillade, felt obscurely obliged to break a simple action into a symmetrical string of shots (Figs. 5.26–5.30). Two years before, he would undoubtedly have rendered the same action in one take.

In tracing shared assumptions and explanatory frameworks across piecemeal histories of early film, I have inevitably played down differences and disagreements. It would be worth exploring in more detail, for instance, the varying conceptions of change held by early-cinema researchers. Burch and Gunning, in differing ways, propose that one fairly distinct stylistic regime (the PMR, the cinema of attractions) was supplanted by another (the IMR, the cinema of narrative integration). By contrast, Musser and Thompson tend to hold that an initial diversity (cinema before 1917) gradually coalesced into a

5.26 In *La nouvelle mission de Judex*, Cocantin must put a letter on the study desk. He enters . . .

5.27 . . . comes to the desk . . .

5.28 . . . hesitantly sets it down . . .

5.29 . . . returns in a repetition of the second shot . . .

5.30 . . . and leaves in a repetition of the first setup, thereby completing an ABCBA pattern of cuts.

long-term, fairly stable unity. It would also be worth reviewing Musser's arguments that the cinema of attractions held sway for a much briefer period than Gunning suggests.[79] At a more local level, Salt has proposed that the repeated-action cutting that Musser attributes to Porter's contemporaries is atypical of the period.[80] Such debates are ongoing. The revisionist research program is still developing, and much of what I have surveyed will undoubtedly be recast and enriched.

Still, it is safe to say that the revisionists' efforts already mark a turning point in the historiography of style. Anyone who now retails the Méliès-Porter-Griffith line of descent or circulates the canard that Griffith invented "film language" just hasn't been paying attention. Like skillful historians in other disciplines, the revisionists have built fine-grained explanations of local phenomena. They have gathered and organized fresh and probitive data. They have avoided the teleological commitments of the Standard and Dialectical Versions, and their scrutiny of diverse practices has produced more varied and nuanced accounts than Burch's broad, class-determination explanation yielded. The revisionists have richly elaborated Bazin's insight into what German art historians call the "non-contemporaneity of the contemporaneous"—the fact that very different stylistic tendencies coexist at any moment.

Perhaps most important, the 1970s generation acknowledged the conceptual frameworks governing any research program. In survey articles they laid bare key assumptions of their predecessors.[81] The revisionists treated the Basic Story as an obligatory point of departure, to be analyzed and criticized. They set out to test and refine and refute the ideas they had inherited. The study of film's stylistic history became a sophisticated conversation within a community of resourceful, self-conscious scholars.

Culture, Vision, and the Perpetually New

Each of the research programs I've been considering was shaped by its intellectual milieu. The Standard Version won authority in the 1920s and early 1930s, when intellectuals were trying to show that cinema could be a distinct art form. Bazin's dialectical variant emerged during the 1940s and 1950s, a period in which the French intelligentsia fell under the sway of Hegelian modes of thinking.[82] Burch's oppositional program came to prominence in the 1960s and 1970s, when left-wing writers embraced notions of "counter-cinema" and sought to chart the range of films' ideological effects.[83] Still later, the expansion of cinema studies in the university provided the time and funds for more specialized inquiry. Revisionism is a product of the professionalization of film research.

Just as important, revisionist historiography developed in a context dominated by wide-ranging theories of film. Since the 1970s, the encounter of revisionist research with what we might call Grand Theory has had important consequences for the study of style. Most relevant to our purposes are the efforts mounted by several theorists to explain stylistic qualities largely by appeal to a cultural "history of vision." In this section I trace how history-of-vision accounts have sought to explain changes in film style within modern and postmodern culture. Although this research program is still forming, I shall suggest that it already faces some significant difficulties.

Film theory has existed since the 1910s, when thinkers began to ask about the nature and artistic functions of the medium. Theoretical speculation of this sort informed the Standard Version, the work of Bazin and his peers, and Burch's earliest writings. In the academic setting of the 1970s, and with the crucial influence of French Structuralism and Poststructuralism, film theory became Theory. Here was a comprehensive account of representation in which film took its place as one signifying system among many. Unlike classical film theory, Grand Theory constituted a large-scale account of how signifying systems constructed subjectivity within society. Ideas drawn from semiotics, feminism, Marxism, and Freudian and Lacanian versions of psychoanalysis coalesced into the view that social ideology and the dynamics of the unconscious "position" individuals as ostensibly volitional, self-aware agents.

This mixture of ideas came to be regarded as the most advanced framework for academic discussion of cinema.[84] Still, although Burch eventually incorporated some subject-position ideas into his account of early film, few revisionist historians drew upon the new trend. Most researchers contented themselves with the sort of empirical, fallibilist explanations that would be familiar to historians in fields as yet untouched by Grand Theory. On the other side, subscribers to Grand Theory were sometimes inclined to dismiss revisionist history as "positivist" and "empiricist."

But times changed. Subject-position theory imploded. Internal contradictions, persistent criticism by skeptics, and the predictability of the textual readings that the theory encouraged all hastened its demise.[85] So did the impressive arguments of revisionist historians. History had come to be more intriguing than the minuet of Grand Theory. In the mid-1980s one began to hear that Grand Theory was ahistorical and had to be "historicized." When adherents of feminism, Marxism, and psychoanalysis began to show up for obscure silent movies at the Pordenone festival, one sensed that history had arrived on theorists' agenda. By the early 1990s, the most prominent Parisian film theorists formed the Collège d'Histoire de l'Art Cinématographique, holding weekly lectures and discussions under the aegis of the Cinémathèque Française.

Film academics who began purging their shelves of Althusser and Lacan did not all hurry to the library to crank through microfilm. The empty shelf space was quickly packed with works by Foucault and the Frankfurt School. History, many theorists believed, was too important to be left to historians. If Grand Theory had to be historicized, much historical research seemed embarrassingly under-Theorized. The result was an a priori, "top-down" commentary on film history, whereby theoretical conclusions came to be illustrated by colorful historical examples. The revisionist historians had built their cases inductively, proposing generalizations only after trawling through many documents and films. By contrast, top-down arguments tended to skim off key films isolated by piecemeal historians and then interpret them in the manner popularized by subject-position theory.[86]

Although much of this top-down history took no interest in style, some theorists granted that recent research into early cinema and the classical Hollywood cinema had made matters of technique inescapable. They suggested, however, that the proper way to understand style was not to limit one's understanding to the films, the makers, the technology, and the institutions of filmmaking and exhibition. The best explanations, many began to argue in the 1980s, would give primacy to the broader culture in which films were made and used. As "cultural studies" was coming to replace subject-position theory in academic circles, various versions of "culturalism" formed a new Grand Theory in cinema studies as well.[87] Culturalism in turn underwrote a particularly popular research program, which I am calling the "history of vision" approach.

The reasoning runs something like this. We cannot explain stylistic patterns just by appeal to activities in the artistic sphere. Style is produced and sustained by the culture in which it functions. But often the stylistic features of artworks have no evident connection with culture. A painting's subject and theme derive pretty obviously from social sources; but how can its use of pigment, its composition, its play with perspective be connected to cultural processes? One answer was to argue that culture affected technique by way of influencing human perception. The enabling assumption, deriving from an art-historical tradition usually traced to Aloïs Riegl, was phrased pointedly by Walter Benjamin: "The mode of human sense perception changes with humanity's entire mode of existence."[88] Consequently, the "collective perception" dominating a place or epoch could be reflected, expressed, or otherwise embodied in style. This deeply Hegelian idea turns up even in the arch-formalist Heinrich Wölfflin's admonition that "vision itself has a history."[89] The history of style in a pictorial art, many scholars came to believe, could be explained by conceiving the history of vision as at least partly social.

More specifically, and more relevantly to the history of cinema, one could postulate that at some point between 1850 and 1920, perception within European societies changed. Reflecting on the work of art in the era of mechanical reproduction, Benjamin maintained that the expansion of industrial capitalism trained the human "sensorium" to internalize the shocks of urban life. People developed a "distracted" apprehension of the environment, a skittish and absent-minded attention.[90] The experience of the capitalist city—its velocities and jolts, its ephemeral stimuli, its fragmentation of experience—created a new perceptual "mode" specific to modernity.[91]

The assumptions of the history-of-vision doctrine warrant more critical attention than they have received. We might start by asking what is meant by "perception" or "vision." If such terms are shorthand for "thought" or "experience," the position becomes vague, if not commonplace. But advocates of the position certainly talk as if there is not only a history of ideas, beliefs, opinions, attitudes, tastes, and the like but also a history of how people take in the world through their senses.

This claim makes the position more interesting, but also more troublesome. In what sense can we talk about short-term changes in perception, that intricate mesh of hard-wired anatomical, physiological, optical, and psychological mechanisms produced by millions of years of biological selection? If vision has adapted itself in a few decades to collective experience and the urban environment, we have a case of Lamarckian evolution.[92] Since this conclusion is highly implausible, should we not rather speak of changes in *habits and skills,* of cognitively monitored ways of noticing or contextualizing information available in new surroundings? The woman next to me in the subway might be superbly trained in detecting cancer cells under a microscope, whereas I may be better at spotting violations of continuity editing. Both of us have focused our mature perceptual mechanisms upon certain informational domains. But the mechanisms themselves have not been altered.

If habits and skills are what are at stake, social circumstances probably don't recast perception all the way down. Even if both the oncologist and I share the experience of urban life, we need not have had our perceptual apparatus fundamentally recast. True, we have both become adept at glimpsing indications that our subway stop is coming up next and then edging through the crush toward the door. The peasant used to leaning dreamily over his plow might have trouble dodging swiftly through crowds in the train station. Yet it still seems more plausible to hold that he could adjust to the new environment with some practice, and this is because such skills involve acquired knowhow rather than some fundamental reorganization of perception.

A proponent of the history-of-vision thesis might admit that perception in a strong sense is not at issue and that habits and skills are indeed what constitute a culture's "mode of perception." This is, however, a big concession. For the habits and skills demanded by modern urban vision will be like other habits and skills in important respects. They are distributed unevenly across a population. They are intermittent, specialized, and transitory. They can be picked up and cast off; they can thrive or wither. If acquired habits and skills are the most pertinent and plausible sources of changes in visual experience within culture, we need not posit a pervasive, entrenched, and uniform "way of seeing." It is very likely that a wide variety of perceptual abilities is at work in any given period, and this state of affairs casts doubt on the initial assumption that a single "mode of perception" rules an epoch. The fact that we can mount persuasive accounts of pictorial style by appeal to variations in a culture's visual practices suggests that we oversimplify things by postulating one "way of seeing" per period.[93]

Nonetheless, film scholars have found Benjamin's claims attractive, perhaps because he declares that cinema was the medium most in tune with the new mode of perception. Film reflects modernity, Benjamin believes, by being inherently an art of abruptness. A film produces "changes of place and focus which periodically assail the spectator . . . No sooner has his eye grasped a scene than it is already changed. It cannot be arrested."[94] In manifesting the culture of distraction, cinema maintains the city's sensuous barrage; presumably the sensorium's training is reinforced every time the spectator visits a movie theater.

Benjamin, writing in the late 1930s, is not seeking to produce a stylistic history of films. Yet he inherits important assumptions from some of the historians we have surveyed. Although Benjamin challenges the Standard Version's conception of film as a high art, he does endorse that research program's candidate for the supremely cinematic technique—the instantaneous shifts in time and space provided by cutting. Many recent writers who have been inspired by Benjamin characterize the medium in similarly traditional ways. The idea that cinema created a modern "mobile gaze," for instance, seems to presuppose the spatiotemporal freedom supplied by editing.[95] Another writer in this vein notes: "With its dialectic of continuity and discontinuity, with the rapid succession and tactile thrust of its sounds and images, film rehearses in the realm of reception what the conveyor belt imposes upon human beings in the realm of production."[96] In arguing that film cutting reflects a culture of splintered experience, theorists have preserved the 1920s tendency to treat editing as central to cinema's essence. This seems a curious commitment to maintain, since many films made in the first fifteen years of cinema rely little upon editing, and thousands of the films that purportedly exemplify modern vision consist only of one shot.

More damagingly, this version of the modernity thesis holds that editing as such, not just in this film or that tradition, reflects the fragmentation of urban life. This is a baggy explanation. It accounts in the same way for all films using editing, including those made in regions less urbanized and industrialized than Europe or North America. This explanation also fails to discriminate among exactly those manifold differences in editing technique that revisionist historians like Musser, Salt, Thompson, and Gaudreault have painstakingly brought to light. We don't really want to know why all films have editing; this may not even be an answerable question. We want to know why a body of films employs editing of particular sorts. On this the modernity theorists have largely been silent.

Largely, but not entirely. One revisionist historian has proposed a fairly tight fit between Benjaminian modernity and stylistic history. Tom Gunning suggests that many tactics of the "cinema of attractions" reflect culturally determined modes of experience at the turn of the century. He adduces examples of an "aesthetic of astonishment"—locomotives hurtling to the viewer, early audiences' wonder at magical transformations, the charm of the very illusion of motion. The attraction, Gunning claims, at once epitomizes the fragmentation of modern experience and responds to alienation under capitalism.[97] It reflects the atomized environment of urban experience and the new culture of consumption; like an advertisement, the movie's isolated gag or trick tries to grab attention. The now-you-see-it-now-you-don't aspect of attractions makes them emblematic of the ephemeral appeals of the city. In such ways, the attraction played a role in creating characteristically modern conceptions of time and space, sometimes—as in those shots taken from trains plunging into tunnels—even pushing human perception to new limits.[98] "The cinema of attractions," Gunning writes, "not only exemplifies a particularly modern form of aesthetics but also responds to the specifics of modern and especially urban life, what Benjamin and Kracauer understood as the drying up of experience and its replacement by a culture of distraction."[99]

The more exactly Gunning ties modernity to this phase of stylistic history, though, the more problematic the case seems to become.[100] Gunning initially proposes the idea of a cinema of attractions as a way of characterizing a major trend in the films made during a period; he grants that many films made before 1908 do not rely on the attraction. But why not? If there was indeed a radical and pervasive change in ways of seeing, should not all early films bear traces of it? Like other citizens, filmmakers presumably underwent the perceptual transformations wrought by modernity, and these ought to be reflected in their films. How could filmmakers, after fifty years of adjusting to the perceptual mode specific to urban capitalism, fail to exploit the attraction?

Gunning might reply that the spread of the new perceptual mode was gradual and uneven, and many filmmakers clung to older experiential modes. But, as I've already suggested, it is axiomatic in the history-of-vision account that railroads, boulevards, the assembly line, and the like have overhauled humans' experiential equipment. Benjamin begins his most famous essay with a quotation from Valéry: "For the last twenty years neither matter nor space nor time has been what it was from time immemorial."[101] Benjamin did not add "at least sometimes" or "more often than not" or "for a certain sector of the population." According to proponents of this framework, film viewers and filmmakers (who are themselves film viewers) had been internalizing the conditions of modernity since at least 1850. Given the social determination of perception, there would seem to be no voluntary going back.[102] If people can slip out of synchronization with the new mode of seeing or slide back to earlier modes, the history-of-vision account loses a good deal of its explanatory power.

Some vision-in-modernity theorists may nonetheless argue for plural and uneven development. But to accept this view we would need a more refined historical account than we have yet seen. How did very sweeping economic and social changes create different ways of seeing among various groups? Did the clerks and shopgirls who flocked to the cinema possess a different mode of perceiving the world than blue-collar workers who stepped in fresh from the assembly line? Middle-class citizens were exposed to advertising, traffic, and sidewalk crowds; shouldn't they have developed the same distracted perception as other classes? Note too that writers trying to demonstrate a diversity of perceptual modes within the modern era cannot, on pain of circularity, point to academic painting or bourgeois theater as proof that some groups failed to assimilate the new way of seeing. For it is exactly such disparities among representational practices that the history-of-vision culturalist is now obliged to explain.

It seems, then, that Gunning would face problems in claiming that some filmmakers ignored attractions and clung to more old-fashioned modes of representation. Moreover, he asserts with good reason that the cinema of narrative integration largely displaced the cinema of attractions. How can we explain this shift toward coherence if we hold that attractions were adapted to the distracting, fugitive conditions of urban modernity? Presumably the culturally determined mode of vision did not mutate radically around 1910. Certainly industrial capitalism, urban development, and mass consumption did not halt when D. W. Griffith and his contemporaries began to develop more integrated storytelling.

This seems to me to create two parallel difficulties. First, by Gunning's account spectators had adapted over decades to a distraction and fragmentation determined by massive social forces. How then could viewers adjust so quickly to the more concentrated, unified film style that became dominant by 1920? If, as most revisionist historians believe, we need to posit some transitional stylistic period between 1908 and 1915 or so, we would also need to show a comparable transition in the culture's mode of perception, its sense of time and space, and the like.[103] Second, the attraction, according to Gunning, provides "one of [modernity's] specific methods." Attractions are "small doses of scopic pleasure adapted to the nervous rhythm of modern urban reality."[104] If one assumes that modernity and its mode of perception did not cease around 1910, why was the cinema of attractions displaced at all? And by something closer to traditional, even "bourgeois," modes of storytelling at that?[105]

In sum, we do not have good reasons to believe that particular changes in film style can be traced to a new way of seeing produced by modernity. Perhaps future research and reflection will enable scholars to mount a firmer case along these lines. The prospects, however, do not strike me as encouraging.

A comparable set of difficulties arises when we examine the less well-developed but more widely publicized argument that we live in a postmodern era. Some theorists have claimed that wrenching changes in culture, economic activity, and social organization have altered our experience—that is, our perception—in ways that affect film form and technique.

This view needs to be distinguished from the view that the contemporary art world has created a distinct style, Postmodernism, with its own conventions. Thus *Blade Runner, True Stories,* and *Wings of Desire* can be seen as Postmodernist films. Postmodernist style is purportedly distinguished by fragmentation, nostalgia, pastiche, a dwelling on "surfaces," a "technological sublime," and other strategies.[106] In my view, these qualities are so loosely characterized that, guided by intuition, association of ideas, and urgent rhetoric, the critic may fit many features of many artworks to them. In any event, the existence of a Postmodernist style would not establish the major point: that social life within postmodernity creates a distinct mode of perception that leaves its traces in artworks. How, the historian asks, may we trace stylistic qualities of many sorts of films to a postmodern way of seeing?

Postmodernism, Fredric Jameson tells us, offers "a whole new type of commercial film," "a whole new culture of the image," "a whole new type of emotional ground tone," "a whole new technology," "a whole new economic world system," and "a whole new Utopian realm of the senses."[107] Despite such claims that the phenomenon is radically novel, theories of postmodernity restate themes already articulated by the Frankfurt School and its disciples. Like the theorist of modernity, the analyst of postmodernity posits a fundamental rupture, marking what went before as relatively unified, what followed as radically fragmented. If we are to believe both camps, we have lost many things twice: both in modernity and postmodernity there vanished a sense of history, a belief in realistic representation, the tie of sign to referent.

And, like the theorists of modernity, advocates of postmodernist theory subscribe to versions of the history-of-vision thesis. Some writers find contemporary perceptual experience to be fully reflected in the floating fragments of representation. Others suggest that our senses have actually lagged behind the development of postmodern culture. Writing of the Westin Bonaventura Hotel, Jameson suggests that "we do not yet possess the perceptual equipment to match this new hyperspace." He claims that the most characteristic works of our era present "something like an imperative to grow new organs"—a striking articulation of the Lamarckian tendency which haunts efforts to show that culture determines perception.[108]

As in the modernity case, the correspondences between cinema and culture posited in most postmodernity arguments turn out to be quite broad and loose. There has been little effort to explain stylistic continuity or change in the light of postmodernity. Still, the flavor of the tendency can be caught by examining one of the few books that discuss film history from this perspective. Régis Debray launches *Vie et mort de l'image,* a study in the "*a priori*s of the occidental eye," with a bold statement of the strong history-of-vision thesis: "This book has then for its subject the invisible codes of the visible, which define very transparently and for each epoch a certain state of the world; that is, a culture. Or: how the world gives itself to be seen to those who see it without thinking it."[109] Cinema will have a privileged place in this account, Debray claims, because each epoch has not only its "visual unconscious" but also its dominant art, and cinema has in recent times played this role. Technology also shapes the history of perception because every prosthetic extension of the human faculties modifies the nature of perception: "Each new technique creates a new subject while renewing its objects. Photography has changed our perception of space, and the cinema our perception of time (via montage. . .)."[110]

Debray's account is massively epochal. He postulates three great "ages of the look": the age of the idol (when the image was tied to magical and religious practices, up to the mid-fifteenth century); the age of art (the period of a search for illusionist representation, from the Renaissance to the mid-nineteenth century); and the age of simulation (the century and a half from photography through cinema to video). By neat analogy, the epochs also correspond to Peirce's three conceptions of the sign—index, icon, and symbol.[111] And these phases, in the wheels-within-wheels fashion common to such neo-Hegelian models of history, manifest themselves at a lower level as well. Even though the cinema as a whole is within the age of simulation, and hence under the aegis of the arbitrary symbol, the medium's true identity emerges gradually. According to Debray the development of film recapitulates the universal history of art. Lumière and his contemporaries treat the cinema as index, an imprint of raw reality; sound cinema of the 1930s exemplifies film as icon, recreating an illusion of reality within the studio; only then came the ciné-symbol, with the *caméra-stylo* in the hands of the postwar auteurs.[112]

In postmodernity, however, video becomes the dominant art, and its simulation of reality has radical consequences. Unlike those writers who argue that cinema is the apogee of modernity because it reflects and reinforces the urban fragmentation of experience, Debray sees the film image as offering a totalizing coherence of time and meaning. For true fragmentation, one must turn to television, the ultimate vehicle of distracted, atomized perception.[113]

Debray's historical argument trades upon a highly selective use of examples. He ignores the extent to which Renaissance painting was religious; he assumes that all post-Renaissance art sought illusion and no prior art did. He makes Lumière stand in for all early cinema, puts aside the documentary impulses of the 1930s, forgets that studio-based moviemaking is not specific to the 1930s, and takes broadcast television to define all video imagery. Conceptually, the problems are numerous as well. Debray replays familiar Hegelian schemes: categories derived from prior theoretical systems tidily manifest themselves in empirical historical events; just one collective perception rules an epoch; a medium's essence unfolds only in the fullness of time. Again, the sweeping tale told by the postmodernist somehow escapes the postmodern skepticism about grand narratives.[114]

Debray's account illuminates another difficulty in the culturalist position. When discussing either modernity or postmodernity, culturalist historians have largely taken for granted traditional periodization, movements, canons, and masters. Debray accepts the Lumière/Méliès split, the concepts of the *nouvelle vague* and *cinéma-vérité,* and the golden age of the studios as unquestioningly as Benjamin accepts the idea that montage defines film art. Yet epochal culturalist history ought to redraw the map of the territory in major respects. According to most postmodernist theorists, our received categories, the commonplaces of a discipline, purportedly derive from inadequate beliefs: that history progresses, that individuals matter, that patterns of change and stability can be grasped as intelligible wholes. How can such outmoded concepts produce findings that radical theory can accept unquestioningly? Worse, postmodernists tend to accept a thoroughgoing constructivism, according to which the very idea of intersubjective evidence is suspect. How can traditional historians who have "constructed" their data according to a "grand narrative" be taken on trust by postmodern skeptics? A true postmodern history of film would, I submit, have to start *ab ovo;* the historian would have to build up a case from scratch. None has. Like Deleuze, Debray has simply seized upon the findings of traditional historians and reinterpreted them according to a preferred Grand Theory.

Once more, we can see that contemporary ideas shape historiographic impulses. The search for cultural sources of film style grew keener after revisionist scholars had unearthed a great many fresh findings. When academics who retained a faith in the social construction of virtually everything were dismissing ideological determination as too rigid, many found that the idea of culture offered a more flexible top-down explanation of stylistic change. For the most part, though, the ideas of modernity, postmodernity, and the history of vision have informed the historiography of film style in vague and problematic ways.

My criticisms of history-of-vision accounts do not show that cultural explanations cannot supply persuasive answers to some questions. I simply suggest that the lines of investigation pursued to date are not up to the task of rethinking *stylistic* history. How might we reconsider the history of film style—its causes and convolutions, its patterns of change and stability—after the work of the revisionists? And what roles does culture have to play in this explanatory enterprise?

Problems and Solutions

You know which way the men are going to come in, and then you experiment and see where you're going to have Wayne sitting at a table, and then you see where the girl sits, and then in a few minutes you've got it all worked out, and it's perfectly simple, as far as I am concerned.

Howard Hawks, 1976

In Truffaut's *La nuit américaine* (1973), the movie director Ferrand is beset all day by turn-on-a-dime decisions. Is this wig too light? What camera position do you prefer? Which gun is best for the final scene? Ricocheting from one decision to another, Ferrand reflects that a director is "someone who's constantly asked questions about everything."

Filmmaking is an avalanche of such minute choices. Fortunately, the questions do not bury the director. As Ferrand adds, "He even knows some of the answers." Most demands are not unique; something like these options have been seen before. The filmmaker can adapt successful decisions to the task at hand. In making her choices, the filmmaker is guided by the craft she has mastered, the models she knows, the trials and errors and habits of experience. After a little tinkering, Hawks suggests, a professional can adjust to the new situation, perhaps even capitalize on it.

These commonplaces of practical filmmaking offer important leads for studying the history of style. Indeed, it seems evident that they underpin the most promising recent work. The revisionist scholars of early cinema assumed that filmmakers pursued goals and employed practical reasoning, aided by trial and error, to achieve them. Let us try to generalize this assumption. As a first approximation, imagine reconstructing the history of film style, its patterns of continuity and change, as a network of problems and solutions.

At first glance, "problems" might only seem to be technological obstacles: sound and widescreen created difficulties in staging, cutting, and so on. Actually, as Ferrand's musing reminds us, problems crop up at every moment, and they can be conceived in many ways. David Fincher, director of *Alien 3* (1992) and *Seven* (1995), remarks: "Staging to me is everything. That's the whole game—where do you place the window?"[115] Godard broods over another question: "The only great problem with cinema seems to me more and more with each film when and why to start a shot and when and why to end it."[116]

Explaining artistic continuity and change through a rhythm of problem and solution has a long lineage, running back at least to Vasari's account of the mastery of realism during the Italian Renaissance.[117] The idea has been recast and nuanced by E. H. Gombrich in the course of a scintillating career. It has been criticized as well, perhaps most cogently by James Ackerman.[118] It is not the only explanatory tool available, but I want to try it out as a way of clarifying not just the sort of narrow, in-depth questions posed by revisionists but broader stylistic trends as well.

Some advantages of the problem/solution model are immediately apparent. It allows us to focus on particular aspects of film style—certain problems rather than all of them—while still acknowledging that patterns of problem and solution can intersect with one another or with other factors (technological, economic, or cultural). The model also breaks with overarching teleologies. Just because a filmmaker formulates a goal, there is no reason to believe that it is somehow foreordained by the ontology of the medium. In addition, the problem/solution framework leaves room for the possibility that varying tendencies can coexist within the same period, as filmmakers conceive their problems and solutions along competing lines.

During the 1970s Grand Theorists took individual agency out of film history; since then they have been struggling to put it back. The problem/solution model faces no such difficulty. It invites us to reconstruct decisions made by active agents, and it treats persons as concrete forces for stability or change (or both). *Contra* Panofsky's suggestion that the medium gradually became aware of its distinctive features, a problem-based account holds that the medium does nothing. The history of style will be the history of practitioners' choices, as concretely manifested within films. By granting a role to the artist's grasp of the task and of her own talents, the problem/solution framework acknowledges various reasons for the agent to act. The job need not be imposed from without; as Gombrich points out, innovation often springs from an artist's urge to be different, to compete with others, to savor the exercise of skill, or to seek new challenges. Nor does this frame of inquiry obliterate the possibility of errors, accidents (happy or unhappy), unintended consequences, spontaneous and undeliberated actions, and decisions made for reasons not wholly evident to the agents.

Even as it centers upon choices made by social agents, the problem/solution model recognizes that individual action takes place within a social situation with its own demands. The artist's choices are informed and constrained by the rules and roles of artmaking. The artistic institution formulates tasks, puts problems on the agenda, and rewards effective solutions. Gombrich points out that even that precious resource individuality can be achieved only when the artist asks "What is there for me to do?" within the artistic institution and the larger culture.[119] Standard Version historians were right: individual initiative matters. Bazin and Burch were right: group norms matter too.

Problems stand out against a horizon of purpose and function. Once films are supposed to tell stories, filmmakers must try out ways to tell them clearly. How do you ensure that viewers recognize the main characters on each appearance? How do you delineate cause and effect in unambiguous ways? How do you portray psychological states that propel the action? How do you draw the viewer's attention to the most important events in a shot or scene? From a goal-oriented perspective, for instance, some of the "exhibitionism" that Gunning highlights in the "cinema of attractions" derives from the urge to make explicit the rudimentary situations that harbor gags or stunts. A mischievous boy who looks at the camera not only acknowledges the viewer's presence but also makes his own reaction hard to miss. Later solutions to the problem of clarity, such as cutting in to a closer view, will yield different benefits (as well as different costs).

Conceived as a response to a task, function can be studied from several angles. There is the broad purpose assigned to any film in a particular tradition, such as the demand for storytelling in the Hollywood cinema. There is also functionality within the constraints laid down by the particular task. For example, purely physical constraints of length often shape how form and style are deployed. The cinema of attractions has a fleeting, now-you-see-it quality partly because the movies ran only a minute or two. Once feature films came to dominate production, more elaborated storytelling offered a plausible way to fill out the format.

Functionality also bears upon the work's internal patterning. A stylistic device plays a role in the formal development of the film as a whole. Instead of picking out a technique and locating an inventor of it, the historian of style can be alert to changing functions of the device across a film. Bazin, Burch, and the revisionists who followed were exemplary in discussing style as an integral part of complete works. In this spirit the next chapter will suggest, for example, that some of the deep-focus devices that Bazin praised in Wyler's films systematically underscore dramatic motifs or participate in a larger audiovisual unity.

The filmmaker pursues goals; stylistic choices help achieve them. But no filmmaker comes innocent to the job. Task and functions are, more often than not, supplied by tradition. For any given stylistic decision, the artist can draw

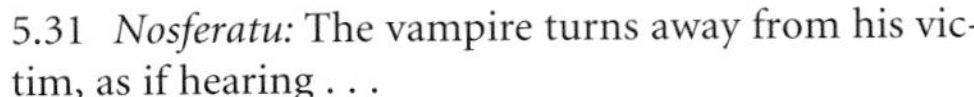

5.31 *Nosferatu:* The vampire turns away from his victim, as if hearing . . .

5.32 . . . the desperate cries of Ellen in a faraway city.

on the solutions bequeathed by predecessors. Most minimally, as Noël Carroll has suggested, the artist can just replicate devices that have proved successful.[120] The formulaic shot/reverse-shot handling of dialogue is an example. Gombrich calls such ready-to-hand formulas *schemas.*[121] Schemas are barebone, routinized devices that solve perennial problems. Experienced artists can apply them quickly to new situations, trusting that they will serve as they have served before. Practitioners prize their schemas partly because they represent sophisticated craft knowledge, partly because they have been won through long trial and error.

Isolating schemas and their replications leads us away from the canonized turning points toward ordinary works, those films which testify to the stubborn persistence of tradition. The ordinary film is an ideal place to study the stylistic choices that have been proved to work reasonably well. The artist will always feel this tug of tradition, the temptation simply to stick with what has succeeded before. And replicating a schema is not as easy as it might seem. Old hands accustomed to earlier solutions may adjust to a new trend with difficulty. Feuillade's uneasy assimilation of intrascene cutting (Figs. 5.26–5.30) suggests an uncertainty in handling an emerging device. Gombrich points out that artists can also revamp schemas to suit new purposes. In *Nosferatu* Murnau combines the prototypical compositions of shot/reverse-shot with the principle of cross-cutting. Without any of the ambivalence of Griffith's ruminative cuts, the editing suggests that Ellen Hutter can somehow halt Count Orlok's attack on her husband hundreds of miles away (Figs. 5.31, 5.32). On a broader scale, we can see that a 1910s depth formula—foreground desk or table, background door (Fig. 5.33)—was recruited to serve as an establishing shot in later cinema (Fig. 5.34). There the shot would give way to closer views and shot/reverse-shot cutting. For purposes of greater intensity,

5.33 In a prototypical 1910s setting (deep room, door in the background, desk in the foreground), Yevgeni Bauer arranges his characters diagonally (*Daydreams,* 1915).

5.34 A similar compositional schema, refunctionalized as an establishing shot for an edited sequence (*Only Angels Have Wings,* 1939).

5.35 A lower, closer camera position revises the depth schema for greater dramatic intensity (*Stagecoach,* 1939).

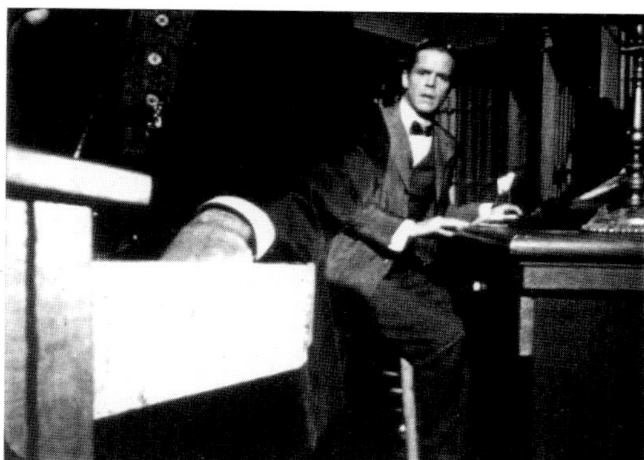

5.36 A still closer foreground creates a looming composition (*The Little Foxes,* 1941).

some directors tightened up this composition (Fig. 5.35). The innovations of Welles and Wyler become intelligible as revisions of this revision (Fig. 5.36). What Bazin viewed as an ineluctable dialectic is more plausibly seen as one stage in the successive recastings of a long-lived compositional schema.

Carroll calls the process of revision "amplification" because in adjusting a device to fresh functions, the filmmaker widens its range of application. This is what happened with the depth schema. With Welles and Wyler, the composition could provide a close-up of one figure or another, and thus it became not only an establishing framing but also a detail within analytical découpage. Once the Welles/Wyler revision proved successful, their choice could be replicated by all the "deep-focus" directors of the 1940s and 1950s. In the course of time, directors might also innovate by synthesizing familiar schemas in

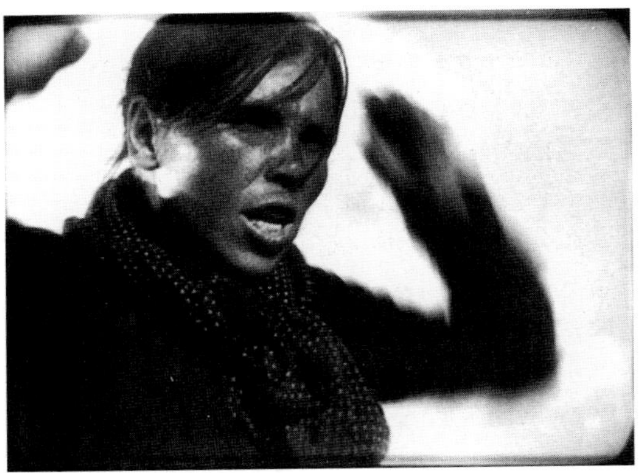

5.37 The peasant Marfa, driven to fury, pounds her fist in the field . . .

5.38 . . . and her gesture is continued in the next scene, a peasants' meeting.

fresh ways. As we shall see, other directors exploring unusually deep compositions in the 1920s and 1930s had already experimented with combining aggressive foregrounds with standard continuity cutting. Similarly, the contemporary stylistic pluralism pointed out by advocates of postmodernism marks a period in which some filmmakers seek to distinguish their work by synthesizing a variety of techniques (slow motion, handheld camerawork, expressionistic performance styles) drawn from earlier periods of film history.

Instead of replicating, amplifying, or synthesizing schemas, the filmmaker can turn away from common practice more sharply. A director may reject an accepted device, a function, or an entire stylistic tradition. Trained in the czarist cinema, Lev Kuleshov learned long takes, depth composition, and nuanced psychological acting. But after 1917 he turned toward violent stunts, chases, and fistfights, all rendered in a rapid editing derived from American films. He repudiated stylistic schemas cultivated in his milieu for the sake of creating a modern popular cinema for the new Soviet state.

Like Kuleshov, filmmakers who repudiate one tradition often draw upon another, which in turn supplies new schemas. Even the most intransigent artist seldom starts from scratch. The avant-garde has its own conventions of form and style. Many "modernist" films share principles of storytelling and stylistic patterning.[122] The "impossible" continuity of the tramp taking off his hat in two different rooms (Figs. 1.8–1.10) replays a device employed in *Un chien andalou* (1928) and *The General Line* (1929; Figs. 5.37, 5.38) and revived in *L'année dernière à Marienbad* (1961).[123]

Replication, revision, synthesis, rejection: these possibilities allow us to plot the dynamic of stability and change across the history of style. For example, since every film demands a multitude of technical choices, we should expect that most choices will replicate or synthesize traditional schemas. Revising or rejecting an inherited schema always demands fresh decisions, and unforeseen problems can swiftly proliferate. Since the virtues of a new schema can be discovered only through trial and error, the strategic filmmaker will innovate in controlled doses, setting the novel element in a familiar context that can accustom the viewer to the device's functions. For such reasons, in any film very few schemas are likely to be revised or rejected. (No wonder Godard seems very adventurous; he revises or repudiates different schemas in almost every scene.)

We thus return to a point broached by Burch and explored by the revisionists: that in cinema's earliest years an "advance" on one front is often accompanied by a "retreat" on another. From the standpoint of problem and solution, it is not surprising that a filmmaker who innovates with respect to one schema may prove conservative with respect to others. The boldness and vigor of Griffith's editing may have encouraged him to treat depth in simpler ways than his contemporaries did. Burch called Porter "Janus-faced," a term picked up by Gunning in describing Griffith; but probably most innovative filmmakers face at once back toward tradition and toward a future (unknown to them, of course) opened up by their recasting or rejection of particular schemas.

Once we recognize as well that alternative devices are available—there is always another way to do anything—we can see that schemas often compete with one another. They will be judged by their ease, their comparative production economy, and their ability to fulfill functions deemed important to the task at hand. Over time one set of schemas can beat its rivals and win a prime place. Such was the status of that combination of cutting devices which around 1917 formed mainstream or "classical" continuity and which remains with us today. If we cannot imagine a widely accessible filmmaking practice that does not utilize this set of norms, it may be because it has proved itself well suited to telling moderately complicated stories in ways that are comprehensible to audiences around the world.

Problems and solutions do not respect borders. In 1902 filmmakers in several countries had to convey continuous duration across cuts. By identifying this shared problem we can make sense of Musser's hypothesis that Porter chose to replicate Méliès's solution: repeating the action in both shots. Confronted with the task of filling the multireel format with a sustained story, directors in Europe and in some American studios plumped for one solution (lengthy scenes relying on nuanced performances) while some American directors opted for another (rapid cutting that expanded and prolonged the action and spread it across many locales). Trends in the contemporary humanities discourage us from seeking out commonalities across periods and cultures, but in order to do justice to the dynamic of continuity and change, the historian of style should be alert for shared problems and parallel or linked solutions.

That dynamic, Gombrich reminds us, may be prolonged indefinitely. A successful solution can pose new problems. The new realists of fifteenth-century European painting conquered the storytelling problem, but the result threatened to make compositions discordant and unreadable, especially at a distance. Painters like Raphael and Van der Weyden found ways to retain detail and realistic figure placement within a harmonious composition.[124] In 1910s cinema, the adoption of editing did not dispel all difficulties of pacing and clear storytelling. Indeed, Thompson suggests, editing was a risky strategy, for in the hands of the inexpert it could confuse rather than clarify. Through experiment filmmakers had to devise fine-grained schemas for matching movements, glances, body positions, lighting, and angle across a cut. Today, as rapid cutting attempts to quicken viewer interest, cinematographers are obliged to compose images that are legible at a glance.[125]

So the history of a technique is not likely to consist of one problem and one solution; often, a problem links to a solution and thence to a new problem. For the same reason, the problem/solution model does not commit itself to a neat outline of overarching change. There is no guarantee of a rise and fall, a birth or maturity or decline. A simple solution can persist for decades, consistently outlasting more complex ones; shot/reverse shot would seem to be such a hardy survivor. Similarly, the dynamic of problem and solution can lead to quite diverse, competing outcomes, all coexisting at the same moment, none of them emerging as the preferred solution.

The task facing the student of style, then, is one of reconstruction. On the basis of surviving films and other documents, the historian reconstructs a choice situation. This becomes a node within a hypothetical network of purposes and functions, problems and solutions and new problems, schemas and revisions and rejections. Central to this task, as Astruc, Bazin, Burch, and their successors have shown, and as I have argued elsewhere, is the labor of spelling out the reigning norms of a period.[126] To study norms is not necessarily to embrace a simple norm/deviation conception of style, still less to believe that bold films "deconstruct" a norm. Nor is it to reduce the complexity of a tradition to a unitary, one-size-fits-all algorithm. A stylistic norm can be reconstructed as a coherent set of alternatives, weighted choices, preferred schemas that can be replicated or modified in fresh situations. The norms we build are idealizations, but not in a bad sense: they are empirical generalizations founded upon the examination of films. And each of those films is in turn the deposit of thousands of concrete choices, traces of all the questions asked of hundreds of filmmakers like Truffaut's Ferrand.

My summary of this way of thinking is itself fairly schematic; the case studies in the next chapter should put more flesh on the bones. But it should already be evident that this approach contrasts sharply with current models of ideology and culture. They project their preferred theoretical conclusions down to the data, treating selected stylistic devices as embodying the class struggle or urban modernity. The model I propose seeks to be more delicate, building from patterns of task-governed decision-making to schemas and thence to norms and their open-ended dynamic across time.

This approach does not seal film off from social processes. Tasks, problems, solutions, and schemas can issue from any domain in the filmmaker's community. Nonetheless, the historian is not obliged to assign a technique a purely local origin or use. Culture or social context will not be the source of every plausible explanation for a stylistic choice. It is perfectly possible that the distinctive qualities of French or Swedish society leave no trace on, say, the staging practices of Feuillade or Sjöström. It is more likely that, as directors who were asked questions all day, they hit upon sound answers through craft wisdom, trial and error, and a sensitivity to some of the transcultural appeals that shape viewers' experience of cinema.

chapter

6 Exceptionally Exact Perceptions: On Staging in Depth

When we frame a research question, we often start from vivid examples. For Standard Version historians, *The Birth of a Nation* was the prime instance of American editing, while the Odessa Steps sequence epitomized Soviet Montage. It is worth remembering, though, that a striking prototype remains one node in a network of historical processes. In some ways Griffith and Eisenstein typify larger trends in the history of editing, but in other ways they do not. If we want to trace a broad pattern of continuity and change, we should guard against reifying a single case.

For Bazin and many critics who followed, *Citizen Kane* was the paradigm case of *profondeur de champ.* From that prototype Bazin moved backward to "primitive" depth and the 1930s Renoir, and forward to the later works of Wyler and others, tracing a line of succession in which *Kane* constituted "a dialectical step forward in film language." Yet if we make some distinctions—such as that between depth of *staging* and depth of *field,* or focus—and examine a wide body of films, *Kane* comes to seem less a monument than an intersection of forces. Moreover, in the history of Western cinematic depth *Kane* represents a somewhat eccentric extreme; it may not be a good prototype if we want to understand the norms governing depth staging.

This chapter sketches an alternative account. What principal norms of depth staging have emerged within fictional filmmaking? What directorial strategies have shaped them? What functions has the technique fulfilled? How have the norms been altered or maintained across history? What factors have promoted stability as well as change? In trying to answer these questions, I trace the interplay between idiosyncratic choice and collective standards. I assume that filmmakers strive to fulfill particular tasks and to solve stylistic problems by replicating, revising, synthesizing, or rejecting schemas already in circulation. My scope is transnational, since filmmakers around the world faced comparable problems of depth staging. At certain points, however, I try to indicate how local factors—technological, institutional, cultural—favored certain options rather than others. My survey cannot be definitive, of course; I aim to do no more than open up this area for further investigation.

Conveniently, studying the history of depth also allows us to distinguish the problem/solution model from one of its top-down rivals. I therefore start by glancing at the most influential argument that cinematic depth has been determined by large-scale social factors.

Ideology and Depth

In the early 1970s, as part of his call for a "materialist" film history, Jean-Louis Comolli proposed that we could best explain the history of depth by appeal to the general notion of ideology. Comolli argues that previous historians have taken the technology and technique of the cinema to be ideologically neutral. By contrast, the "materialist" historian would be sensitive to the economic and ideological forces that govern cinematic representation. *Profondeur de champ* (by which Comolli seems to mean depth of field, not just deep staging regardless of focus) is governed in just this way. At the most basic level, the motion picture camera "inscribes" Renaissance perspective into every film image. Images with strong depth of field exemplify this tendency most powerfully. Comolli considers two phases in the history of depth of field: early cinema and talking pictures.

Early film images had a great deal of depth of field. Why? The historian who is fixated on technique answers that early lenses, often 35mm and 50mm, yielded images of robust depth. But why were these lenses used? Because, Comolli suggests, they were felt to correspond to "normal vision." And according to this conception of ordinary vision, cinema was obliged to obey codes of realism. Moreover, Comolli indicates that the impression of reality was itself codified by representational media preceding the cinema—not only the codes of Renaissance perspective but also those of the theater. In an argument that Burch will develop, Comolli concludes that primitive depth of field represented not a neutral, natural reality but the conception of reality with which the bourgeoisie at the turn of the century was most comfortable.[1]

From 1925 to about 1940, Comolli claims, *profondeur de champ* fell into almost complete disuse. A purely technical history will say that this occurred because panchromatic film stock was incapable of focusing in great depth. But then we must ask why filmmakers adopted this stock. And why should we assume that an industry capable of perfecting panchromatic emulsions in a few years could not have restored depth of field with the new stock if filmmakers had demanded it? There was no demand, Comolli claims, because depth of field was sacrificed to the new "ideology of shooting in the studio," and this procedure in turn yielded better sound reproduction, an increased impression of reality on another front. Comolli hints at several "realistic" possibilities of panchromatic stock, but he explicitly argues that the increased auditory realism of sound permitted a reduction of hard-edged visual depth. Programmed by "the ideology of resemblance," filmmakers aimed primarily to capture movement, perspectival depth, color, and now synchronized sound.[2] Comolli thus turns Bazin on his head: the "asymptotic" progress toward a total cinema is actually a bourgeois dream of presenting a certain conception of reality. Again, Burch will refine this aspect of Comolli's argument.

Comolli's series of articles ceased before he considered *Kane* in detail, but there are hints as to how he would rebut Bazin's account of the film. In captions for photographs running alongside his texts, Comolli indicates that in the films of Lumière and Renoir, depth of field's debt to perspective serves to "center" the viewer, fixing her or him at a point of illusory coherence.[3] By contrast, Comolli construes some images as "subverting" naturalistic depth.[4] In *Lady from Shanghai*, "the underlining of the perspective code denaturalizes the scene; the code is given to be read, it functions as a reading [*lecture*] and not, as in the Primitives, as nature."[5] Had Comolli continued the series, he would undoubtedly have argued that some films, in a self-conscious, perhaps even Brechtian way, "bare the device" of depth of field and thereby cloud the technique's ideological transparency. In any event, Comolli urges that we not treat *profondeur de champ* or any other technical device as simply given, to be identified in a body of films. We must understand it in relation to the "textual systems" of particular films and the conditions that shape the technique's relation to noncinematic codes derived from photography, painting, theater, or other signifying practices.[6]

This last point is unexceptionable. Overall, however, Comolli's case seems weakened by empirical inaccuracies and conceptual shortcomings. For instance, he believes depth of field to be governed only by the lens and the film stock; but of course lighting, shutter speed, and diaphragm settings are just as important. (He is here isolating technical devices in a fashion that he criticizes elsewhere.) Moreover, like Bazin, he does not distinguish depth staging from depth of focus, and this conflation particularly vitiates his claims about Renoir (who frequently stages in depth but does not sustain focus on all planes). More generally, by positing a link between Hegel's lectures on aesthetics, the invention of photography, and experimental research into seeing, Comolli provides a skewed account of the history of empirical theories of vision. Scientific inquiry into vision was well under way before photography; and it was not, as Comolli charges, Descartes who confounded seeing and knowing. Descartes in fact put the problem of reconciling the two on the philosophical and scientific agenda.[7]

Comolli's invective against historical research into technology forms a *summa* of 1970s theoretical correctness:

> If there was ever a discourse that deserves to be called disordered and confused, anchored in the "middle way" and "common sense," proceeding not from historical or dialectical materialism but from an empiricism that is totally blind to the ideology that it speaks, it is that . . . which is the discourse-of-the-technicians, pure positivism and objectivism.[8]

Such passages set a style in theoretical debate, but Comolli's substantive claims betray an odd indebtedness to the tradition he excoriates. Comolli has undertaken no research himself, so he must rely on evidence mounted by the very historians he criticizes. Hence the curious sense of reading Mitry's and Bazin's work in a distorting mirror: the canonized concepts and examples recur, but now each one somehow expresses bourgeois ideology. The difficulty with Comolli's invocation of these ideas is that they have been initiated by scholars purportedly in the grip of "empiricism." How do we know that his predecessors did not, because of their ideological shortcomings, overlook or suppress data relevant to Comolli's case for the ideological determination of style? Can we be confident that the evidence they choose to exhibit is not distorted by their blind adherence to common sense? Comolli cannot satisfy us on these scores without indulging in that positivism he rejects—that is, by digging up some new information.

Consequently, Comolli must often rest his claims on appeal to authority; he bolsters his points by quoting at length from Althusser, Kristeva, and the like. When he offers conclusions, his generalizations tend to be sweeping. He suggests that during the 1930s "the hard, high-contrast image of the first years of cinema no longer satisfied the codes of photographic realism developed and refined by the diffusion of photography [among the public, presumably]."[9] He offers no warrant for this remarkably broad claim. Seen in proper prints, early images are rich in low-contrast textures; and Comolli supplies no evidence that the public changed its taste in photographic reproduction. Comolli's concept of ideology is correspondingly vague. In one passage, ideology is the basis of bourgeois representation at a particular epoch; at another it assures the very sense of a coherent spectator across many epochs; at another it is merely the practice of shooting in the studio.

Generalizations of this sort damage Comolli's central argument. Consider the "code" of Renaissance perspective. Put aside the fact that several distinct perspective systems were devised from the 1300s to the 1600s, and they often varied between northern and southern Europe. What does Comolli mean by

"Renaissance perspective"? It is, he says, that signifying practice which yields "a two-dimensional space that creates the *illusion* of the third dimension (depth) from the fact that objects regularly diminish in size (smaller to the extent that they are felt to be farther off)."[10] This definition ignores a crucial feature of monocular perspective: that the space is organized in relation to a tacit viewpoint of the observer. Many pictures in non-Renaissance traditions render distant objects as consistently smaller than closer ones without implying a unified viewing point.[11]

However we conceive of linear perspective, we can go on to ask what *alternative* system of representation the camera could have produced. It is one thing to say that orthodox cinema reproduces only one conception of reality; it is something else to show that there are other realities to which cinema, or other media, could give access. True, there are many pictorial schemes that do not rest on perspective construction, such as the "split-form" portrayal of animals seen in Northwest American Indian art.[12] But how could these have been reproduced in photographed motion pictures?[13] Comolli mentions wide-angle and telephoto lenses as yielding contrary pictorial systems, but although such lenses may occasionally violate certain linear perspective cues, they provide a great deal of standard information about depth; and bourgeois cinema, as we shall see, has not been shy about using such lenses.[14]

For a system bent on representing the world in circumscribed ways, Comolli's ideology of appearances seems oddly capricious. If the image's "impression of reality" lessened during the 1930s, it did so because another factor, sound, emerged to carry it; but if bourgeois ideology sought to ensnare audiences, why would it slacken on any front? The impression of reality, vague enough to start with, turns *ad hoc* as the argument demands.

Most crucially for our purposes here, we can ask exactly *how* an ideology of "the impression of reality" could have governed the concrete decisions around depth staging. Stated starkly, the ideological demand that an image must exhibit depth carries no instructions about how to stage or shoot or light a shot, since there are many ways of doing these things that will create a sense of depth. The individuals who worked in specific institutions—all the directors, cinematographers, set designers, and the like—had still to find ways to realize the depth principle through each of the multifarious choices that faced them during filmmaking. Moreover, strategies of depth staging changed significantly across the history of fiction filmmaking (and did not, as Comolli suggests, die out between 1925 and 1940). Since all of these strategies can be construed as affirming "the impression of reality"—because all represent depth—the explanatory principle that Comolli invokes cannot capture the finer-grained differences we want to understand. Historians are not really asking why film images have depth, but rather why certain images represent depth in certain ways at certain times.

We will need, then, both a richer conception of how depth can be represented in cinema and a more nuanced framework within which to plot stylistic stability and change. As a start, we can grant that the "optical pyramid" of Renaissance perspective is quite important for cinematic staging, but we shall see that it has implications quite different from those that Comolli ascribes to it. Moreover, the sense of depth yielded by the movie image is not traceable only to perspective. *Linear* perspective, the organization of orthogonal planes and foreshortening according to an observer's station point, is only one cue for depth. Some shots display linear perspective, but many do not. More important are the cues for overlap (the plane that overlaps another is closer), a rough diminution of size with distance, familiar size of people and things, shadows and shading, texture gradients (the hazier or grainier a plane, the more likely it is to be distant), and the "kinetic depth effect" (a moving overlap, whereby we see closer objects as shearing across more distant planes). Lenses and film can capture all these sources of information about the three-dimensional world, so we ought to expect that motion pictures will coordinate them to supply a display that preserves some qualities of actual depth.

Given that cinema has such powers, how might we better understand the history of staging in depth? As a point of departure, assume that the "impression of reality," whether in the hands of Bazin or Comolli, will not be an illuminating guide to every matter of style we might want to study. Taking depth as a tool for achieving a variety of ends brings us closer to a precise account of continuity and change. Further assume that directors have since the beginning of cinema sought to direct viewers' attention to significant aspects of the visual display. Simple and obvious as it sounds, this presupposition can do a lot of work in explaining why images in fictional filmmaking have taken the shapes they have.

Making the Image Intelligible

Before directors wish to convey ideas or moods, evoke emotion or themes, transmit ideology or cultural values, they must take care of some mundane business. They must make their images intelligible. If a viewer just can't discern what's happening, the story and its implications are lost. Perhaps this is why early writers in trade journals praised clarity of photography: in mainstream cinema, a well-defined image is a precondition for more complicated effects.

More specifically, the director directs not just actors and crew but also the viewer's attention. This rudimentary fact was acknowledged by the three major research programs we have examined. The Standard Version emphasized that editing developed as a way to concentrate attention. Bazin believed that Welles distracted our eye during the kitchen scene of *The Magnificent Ambersons* and Wyler frustrated our attention by the out-of-focus staircase in *The Little Foxes.* For Burch, the Primitive Mode of Representation was notable for its centrifugal dispersal of attention across the frame. Suitably recast, the idea of attention still offers a powerful way to explain certain patterns of stability and change across the history of film style.

People scan pictures, pausing on areas of high information content.[15] They tend to fasten on particular items, such as faces, eyes, and hands; on vivid, prominent compositional features, such as areas where light values contrast or vectors cross; and on movement. A large part of the film director's craft consists of an intuitive understanding of how to induce viewers to look at certain parts of the frame at certain moments. The director learns that, all other things being equal, the viewer will tend to watch the actor's face, especially the eyes and mouth.[16] The director also learns that an immobile, silent, watching figure can call our attention to another character. This is in fact the basis of the "pretext action" in the *Ambersons* kitchen scene: the anxious but quiet Fanny steers our attention to Georgie's inconsequential chewing.

Someone might object that appealing to attentional processes commits us to the dubious view that compositions compel an audience to look only at one part of the frame, and in unison as well. But we need not treat attention as being so regimented. The viewer can of course resist the pull of the image, obstinately staring at areas that are not salient. The best the filmmaker can do is create a composition that offers a line of least resistance, coaxing the viewer to attend to certain components more or less involuntarily.[17] And all spectators need not see the important material at exactly the same moment. Duration can be the director's ally; the actor can hold a pose or move slowly so that many viewers have time to pick out the salient information.

Our capacity to shift visual attention in this way is a robust example of a transcultural regularity with which any filmmaker must work.[18] Moreover, phenomena such as fast movements, facial displays, and the direction of other people's gazes are virtually universal triggers for attention. A sensitivity to such environmental features has bestowed great evolutionary benefits on primates like us. Culture-specific factors can teach people to attend to certain things, but we may plausibly think of such learned skills as "constructed" out of given biological capacities and matured perceptual abilities.[19]

For the historian of style, asking how filmmakers exploited such perceptual constants can help unravel riddles of continuity and change. Filmmakers faced

6.1 In *The Man with the Rubber Head* (1902), Méliès not only centers the inflatable head but also frames it in an archway.

a concrete problem: how to direct attention? We can examine the history of depth staging as a series of answers that craft practice has proposed to this question.

From the very earliest films, scenes were arranged so as to make certain aspects of the image salient for viewers. The Lumière brothers themselves are on record as indicating that in a good composition in still photography, "The eye must be struck by a salient principal object on which interest will fall immediately; the eye must then be guided gradually across all the portions of the picture."[20] Not surprisingly, the pre-1908 era presented some schemas of shot design that have remained in force ever since.

Putting the major elements in the geometrical center of the composition is perhaps the simplest option, and it is quite common throughout the first fifteen years of film history (Fig. 6.1; see also Fig. 1.1). This strategy should not startle us. Centering an element in the composition is the easiest way to balance the frame and attract the viewer's attention, and filmmakers, especially those with experience in other visual media, would have understood this fact. Although early documentaries are often quite jammed with detail, camera placement often centers the major elements, as in Lumière's famous shot of the train arriving at La Ciotat station (Fig. 2.1).

In assuming that pre-1908 filmmakers sought to direct the viewer's attention, I run counter to a long-standing view about "primitive" cinema. Proponents of the Standard Version argued that cutting up the scene into closer views was effective partly because it guided the viewer to the salient dramatic elements. This view is surely sound. But many historians thereby presumed that the earlier *lack* of editing had led to inherently *un*guided shot designs. Bazin likewise noted that only after Griffith had discovered how to direct attention with cutting could Welles and Toland shape viewers' understanding of deep-space long takes. This assumes that before Griffith, whatever *profondeur de champ* might be found in "primitive" cinema was not precisely organized for the viewer's comprehension.

Burch takes over these presuppositions in his celebration of the "acentric" or "centrifugal" compositions of the Primitive Mode of Representation. Like Bazin, he reverses the value judgments implicit in the Standard Version, finding virtues in "theatrical" cinema and drawbacks in the supposedly progressive technique of editing. He also makes explicit Bazin's tacit belief that early film was less concerned to guide the viewer's attention. In many films before 1914, Burch claims, the viewer is obliged to take in the shot through "a reading that could gather all signs from all corners of the screen in their quasi-simultaneity, often without very clear or distinctive indices immediately appearing to hierarchise them, to bring to the fore 'what counts'; to relegate to the background 'what doesn't count.'"[21] Editing, along with sound, color, and other technical devices, created this hierarchy, but before this happened, the spectator was confronted with a notably more unguided display.

Yet this traditional line of argument does not acknowledge the extent to which unedited scenes were organized to solicit and sustain the viewer's attention. Burch's analysis, the most explicit and detailed in this respect, exaggerates the "acentric" qualities of the primitive shot. Not even his prototypes of this tendency, the Lumières' films, fit the description very well. We shall see shortly that when a Lumière cameraman staged the action, he tended to place it at frame center. Burch's other paradigm case, *Tom, Tom, the Piper's Son* (American Mutoscope & Biograph, 1905), is at best equivocal. The opening tableau is, as Burch says, crammed and confused (Fig. 4.18). Although the action is roughly centered, most viewers today miss Tom's theft of the pig. (I suspect that the antics of the more centrally placed clown distract us.) But the subsequent tableaux depicting the chase and punishment of Tom are far more intelligible (Fig. 6.2).[22] In light of the later shots, the opening may testify only that the filmmakers were unable to solve the problem of staging a scene packed with so much activity. The script for *Tom, Tom* indicates that the filmmakers intended to make the theft the primary action of the shot.[23] We have other early instances of "illegible" staging that are plainly errors. In *The Pickpocket—A Chase through London* (dir. Alfred Collins, British Gaumont, 1903), a policeman's tussle with a crook on the street is inadvertently blocked by a woman passing in the foreground. She turns to the camera and then, evidently responding to a shout from offscreen, moves aside.[24]

What does "decentering" mean for Burch? At times it seems to imply that the action does not take place at the geometrical center of the frame. In fact, however, early directors were often very literal in their sense of centering. They put the heads about halfway up the frame, providing what looks to us to be too

6.2 Legible action in the final tableau of *Tom, Tom:* the townsfolk prepare to dunk Tom in a well.

6.3 The long shots of G. A. Smith's *Mary Jane's Mishap* (1903) place the maid's head midway down the picture format, as was common in the period.

much space in the top of the picture (Fig. 6.3). This principle appears to be still in force today: in distant framings, a lot of empty space may be left above the figures. Perhaps too directors wished to steer attention to the most informative part of the body, the face. In the absence of cutting and close-ups, it is not unreasonable to put actors' expressions at the geometrical center of the format.

Furthermore, the fact that an action does not occur at the center of the picture format does not mean that it does not become *a* center of attention. In general, image makers can decenter the primary object and rely on many other devices for molding attention. Many medium shots and close-ups in current movies avoid framing actors dead-center, but these shots are not disorienting or difficult to grasp, largely because the human figure tends to be salient in any composition. In most images in Western culture since the Renaissance, some decentering is perfectly acceptable. Often, the more distant the framing, the more off-center the key components can be. We see this in the self-conscious tucking of figures into one corner of a landscape, or in the tendency to seat a person at one end of a park bench in order to make the figure look more isolated. Moreover, in a time-based art like cinema, the composition may start off uncentered but move toward greater centering as it unfolds.

So treating "decentering" as an off-center composition is fairly problematic if we want to describe early film images. At other moments, though, Burch wants decentering to mean that the shot in the Primitive Mode of Representation is overstuffed. There are, he says, too many "signs" soliciting our attention all at once, with little "hierarchization" among them. Now the earliest films do occasionally present confusing and distractingly busy compositions, such as the opening of *Tom, Tom;* but these do not seem to constitute the norm. Moreover, we should expect some uncertainties of composition in the first decade of an art form that poses many challenges of visual design and

6.4 Two major planes of arrangement seen when Bluebeard's new wife opens the wrong cupboard (*Barbe bleu,* 1907).

movement over time.[25] We might rather be surprised that the period of trial and error was so short.

We cannot do without some notion of centering if we want to analyze shot design, but it is probably best considered a part of visual balance. Centering, that is, involves not just placement in the picture format but also the dynamic among masses, sizes, textures, movements, and the kinds of objects presented (especially faces). Many "decentered" shots in early film create adequate visual balance, what Rudolf Arnheim calls "a hierarchy of centers, some more weighty than others."[26] Furthermore, even off-center or busy compositions can guide the viewer. While the early long-shot aesthetic naturally absorbed a great deal of material into the frame, filmmakers used several means to bring certain elements to notice and let others become subsidiary. In many fiction films made before 1908, filmmakers were already trying out fairly complex ways in which schemas of visual design could shape attention.

Given the dominance of the long shot and the impulse to guide the viewer's attention, how can any filmmaker stage the interplay of characters? Only two options seem feasible. The director can spread the performers out like clothes on a line, along a single plane or in several parallel planes. Alternatively, the director can arrange the figures diagonally, along axes that are oblique to the camera's lens.

The first choice, that of lateral staging perpendicular to the lens, was very common in early film, particularly in interiors. Such shots presented depth, not only because the row of figures stood rigidly out against the set, but also because the actors could be arranged in what Wölfflin calls "planimetric" patterns.[27] In such compositions each layer lies parallel to the picture plane and often to background planes as well (Figs. 1.1, 6.4). A sense of depth is conveyed primarily through comparative size and overlapping edges.

6.5 Porter's composition puts two heads high on frame left and two low on frame right; the sloping white mass of Eva's bedclothes connects them (*Uncle Tom's Cabin; or, Slavery Days,* 1903).

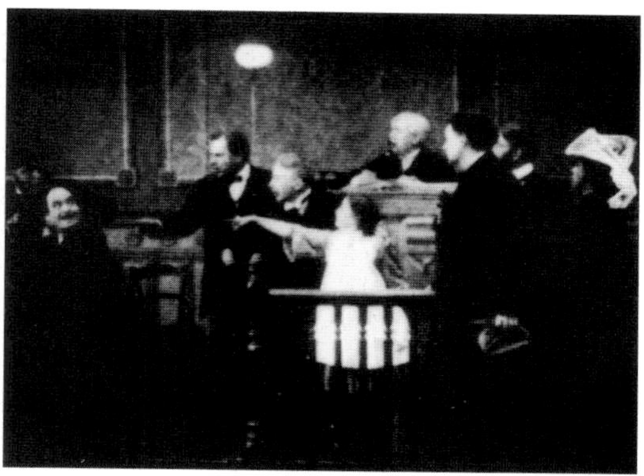

6.6 Guided scanning in *The Skyscrapers:* As in the tableau of *Uncle Tom's Cabin,* a central action is counterweighted by vectors converging on an off-center one.

But lateral staging poses a problem of visual balance. Only one character can stand at frame center. In spreading characters out, the filmmaker will need to highlight important elements lying outside the geometrical center of the format. Early directors experimented with cues that would steer attention across the figures. They soon discovered that movement, glances, compositional trajectories, sustained poses, and other elements could guide the scanning of the shot. In Porter's *Uncle Tom's Cabin* (Edison, 1903), the death of Little Eva presents a strongly centered movement—the angel lifting her soul to heaven—but the shot design encourages us also to register the characters mourning on frame right (Fig. 6.5). When the foreman's little girl denounces Dago Pete in *The Skyscrapers* (Biograph, 1906), a string of accusing looks follows her centrally highlighted finger, pointing to him at the left side of the frame (Fig. 6.6).

The contrast between such comparatively "flat" interiors and "deep" action in exteriors is one of the most striking features of early cinema. Since walls were framed in straight-on views, interior staging tended to be very planimetric (Fig. 6.4). Characters entered from left or right and arranged themselves in friezelike patterns. By contrast, the daylight available from open-air shooting, combined with the relatively sharp lenses in general use, enabled directors to film exteriors in greater depth.[28] Directors accordingly staged outdoor action in ways that Wölfflin calls "recessional."[29] Here at least some planes cut obliquely into the picture plane. Now the background is no longer a perpendicular surface, and the characters stand or move along diagonals. Striking examples of recessional staging can be found in the chase films that became internationally popular around 1904. Typically the pursuit traces a diagonal path from the background, passing through frame center to leave the frame in the right or left foreground.[30] Moreover, buildings, streets, walls, and other architectural features create angu-

6.7 *The Suburbanite* (1905): As the truckers smash the family's belongings in the foreground, the husband protests in the middle ground and the wife expostulates in the rear.

6.8 *L'Affaire Dreyfus* (1899): After listening to the testimony . . .

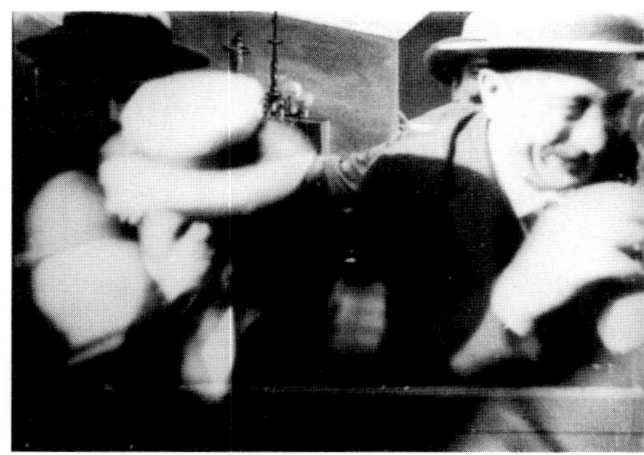

6.9 . . . reporters bustle out of a courtroom right to the camera. Presumably this unusual staging was partly motivated by the bizarre "low angle" view painted on the backdrop.

lar perspectives (Figs. 4.9–4.11). Occasionally, films that don't utilize the chase structure also employ recessional staging in exteriors (Fig. 6.7). This sort of composition was well established in nineteenth-century painting and photography; the Lumières' manual for amateur photographers recommended recessional composition as an antidote to the "boring" straight-on views.[31]

Some early films, while still presenting rear walls as perpendicular to the viewer, include corners and oblique walls. And occasionally figures in interior settings break out of lateral patterns; a striking example occurs in Méliès' dramatization of the Dreyfus affair (Figs. 6.8, 6.9). On the whole, though, it was not until around 1906 that many filmmakers created recessional studio settings and moved figures diagonally within them. In the biblical stories, dense compositions within complex sets lined up figures in parallel layers,

6.10 *La Vie du Christ* (Gaumont, 1906): The Magdalene washes Jesus' feet in a planimetric, painterly composition, but the watching women on the left occupy a recessional diagonal that ends on the principal plane of activity.

6.11 In *Foul Play* (1907), a courtroom scene is staged in a corner, creating many recessional planes. Compare the courtroom in Fig. 6.6.

while touches of recession coaxed the eye to the important material (Fig. 6.10). Danish films began to use corners, rear doors, and entrances and exits close to the camera.[32] Jon Gartenberg has shown that by 1907 directors at the Vitagraph studio had created a sharper sense of depth in interiors (Fig. 6.11).[33]

Well before 1906, however, filmmakers had explored yet another powerful recessional schema. Movement between background and foreground, exploited in the chase genre as well as in such rare cases as the scramble of Méliès' journalists (Figs. 6.8, 6.9), proved to be a simple way of guiding attention. Making action thrust diagonally to the foreground is a very old principle in painting, but moving pictures gave it a new force. From Lumière's train onward, depth-through-movement characteristically presented action coming from back to front, and this proved a very advantageous schema. Movement toward the camera is perceptually salient simply as movement. It also tends to present the front surfaces of people and things, and frontality is another attention-getter. A figure moving forward may occupy the center of the frame, and even if it pursues a diagonal trajectory it is likely to pass through the central area. To-camera movement also gives the shot an internal trajectory, with the gradual enlargement of key elements attracting and holding the eye. Directors eventually discovered that this arc toward greater visibility could be complemented by a movement from the foreground to the background, the diminishing figure that signals the end of a shot, a scene, or an entire film.

Within narrative cinema, forward movement gives us more time to identify the participants in the action than lateral movement does.[34] In chase films, the diagonal staging allows us to see several participants clearly in three-quarter views for a sustained period—something not possible if they were to run straight from left to right. Forward movement also accentuates narrative de-

6.12 *The Skyscrapers:* After leaving his construction workers . . .

6.13 . . . the foreman discovers that his purse has been stolen.

6.14 The passenger is slain in *The Great Train Robbery.*

6.15 The climax of *Bataille de neige* (1896).

velopment. Just taking one step toward the viewer can give a character greater significance. In *The Skyscrapers,* when the foreman leaves his workers, he strides toward the camera and then stops as he checks his pockets; this pause underscores his realization that he has been robbed (Figs. 6.12, 6.13). As in our earlier example from *Explosion of a Motorcar* (Figs. 5.4, 5.5), the arrival at the frontmost plane can give the shot a climax. *The Eviction* (Alfred Collins, British Gaumont, 1904) shows householders scuffling with police in a field; as the battle grows more intense, the struggles move ever nearer to the camera. The murder in Porter's *Great Train Robbery* (1903) is staged so that the man who starts to flee is shot down in the center foreground (Fig. 6.14).

This arc of shot interest already governs several of the staged Lumière films. In *Bataille de neige* (1896), the viewer has time to watch a snowball fight in the foreground while also registering the approach, from the distance, of a hapless cyclist. As the cyclist arrives at frame center, he is caught in the crossfire and knocked down (Fig. 6.15). He rapidly rights himself and pedals back in the

6.16 *Arroseur et arrosé:* The boy steps on the hose in the right middle ground and douses the gardener.

6.17 The boy flees into the distance before being caught.

6.18 The gardener brings the boy back to the front for the inevitable reprisal.

6.19 After being hosed, the boy runs into the distance again, the gardener still spraying after him.

direction from which he came.[35] Similarly, the "remake" of *Le jardinier et le petit espiègle* identified as *Arroseur et arrosé* (1896 or 1897) begins with a deeper staging than its predecessor (Fig. 6.16; compare Fig. 4.19). After the hosing, the chase leads into the far left background (Fig. 6.17). Then the gardener drags the boy back to the right front area for his punishment (Fig. 6.18). This phase of the shot ends with the boy scrambling off into the distance, sprayed by the gardener (Fig. 6.19). As an epilogue, the gardener placidly returns to the key patch of foreground to resume his sprinkling. The shot has three high points, each played in the foreground and linked by actions that depart from and return to the key dramatic site.

Despite their lack of finesse, such early films indicate that very soon filmmakers were trying out rough schemas for directing attention not through planimetric arrangement but through frontward movement. But the new

6.20 In *Une dame vraiment bien* (1908), the setup for the gag depends on the painter in the foreground appreciating the beautiful woman approaching in the distance.

devices came with a price; a solution, Gombrich reminds us, may bring new problems.

For one thing, recessional staging creates compositional difficulties. Bring one actor diagonally forward and you may unbalance the frame, since he or she will probably loom larger than the other players. You will therefore need something to give the distant figures more visual weight. A simple expedient is to have the nearest figure turn from the camera; the lack of frontality, aided by the act of looking, can steer our attention to the distant plane. If the director wishes to deepen the space and activate many zones of the frame, however, all the cues available will have to be carefully choreographed. In Fig. 6.20, the woman's centrality in the frame, the perspective cues (including the wonderful ladder), and the orientation of the painter's body all offset his foreground placement.

Deep staging also poses problems of visibility. The closer actors come to the camera, the more frame area they occupy and the more they block action behind them. Another Lumière garden-hose film illustrates the difficulty. Two card players start to quarrel, and in the background a passerby directs the gardener to cool them off. But the wrestling men in the foreground block our view of the gardener spraying them (Fig. 6.21). The passerby and the gardener must step to our left to become visible again (Fig. 6.22). This seems a spur-of-the-moment decision, but ambitious directors eventually realized that blotting out background action was a positive advantage. Momentary concealment could be controlled to shift attention to other regions of the image. Filmmakers also discovered that they could refine such simple schemas by exploiting certain optical peculiarities of cinema.

6.21 *Joueurs de cartes arrosés* (1896): The quarrelers block the gardener.

6.22 The gardener obligingly makes himself and his hose visible.

Dumb Giants

The years 1909–1920 constitute a golden age of depth staging. Interior settings became far more varied and voluminous, and directors devised fresh ways of arranging actors in the frame. Exteriors, which had already provided deep playing spaces, were handled in ever subtler ways. The result was a *mise en scène* whose richness is only now coming to be appreciated.

During these years directors fully mastered the task of balancing the frame around the central axes. They induced actors to move in tight synchronization, hit and hold poses on cue, and modulate their movements so as not to deflect attention from key events elsewhere in the frame. Urban Gad's *Afgrunden* (1910) offers an instructive case. The fallen woman has reunited with her former fiancé; at a sofa on frame left he consoles her (Fig. 6.23). But when her brutal lover bursts in (Fig. 6.24), Gad obliges the timid fiancé to take two long steps rightward and closer to the camera, turning from the confrontation as he does so (Fig. 6.25). This movement highlights the major conflict between the woman and her lover while also suggesting the fiancé's cowardice. The thug then takes one step leftward to occupy the central zone, and at the same moment the fiancé takes one unobtrusive step rightward and into depth. The result is a cogent, triangulated composition (Fig. 6.26). When the lover lunges leftward to grab the woman, the fiancé's awkward reluctance to intervene is expressed by his taking two halting steps to the left (Fig. 6.27). Throughout the sequence, the thug has the initiative; each of his aggressive movements is feebly echoed by slight, compensating shifts in the fiancé's position. The composition retains an overall poise while still concentrating attention on the jealous lover's disruption of the reconciliation.

The *Afgrunden* scene suggests that as directors modified compositional

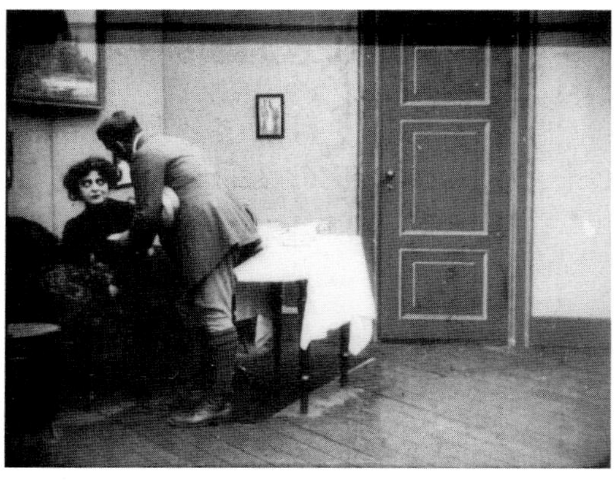

6.23 *Afgrunden:* The lovers reunite in a temporarily unbalanced composition.

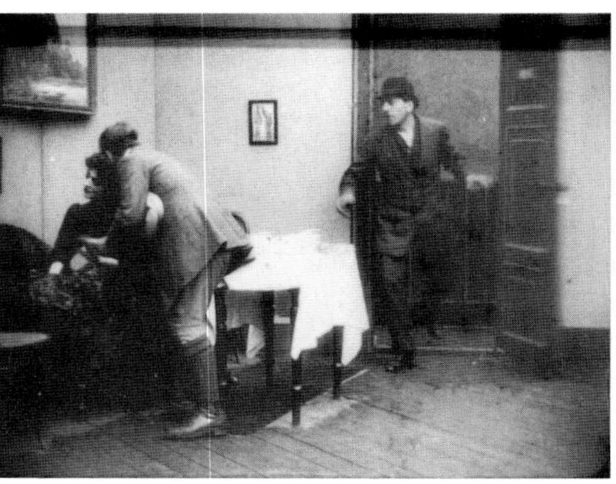

6.24 The lovers are disturbed; the heroine's face is blocked just as a new center of interest appears on the right.

6.25 The fiancé recoils from the couple, edging rightward and forward but always with his back to the camera.

6.26 The thug conveniently occludes the potentially distracting picture hanging in the upper center of the shot.

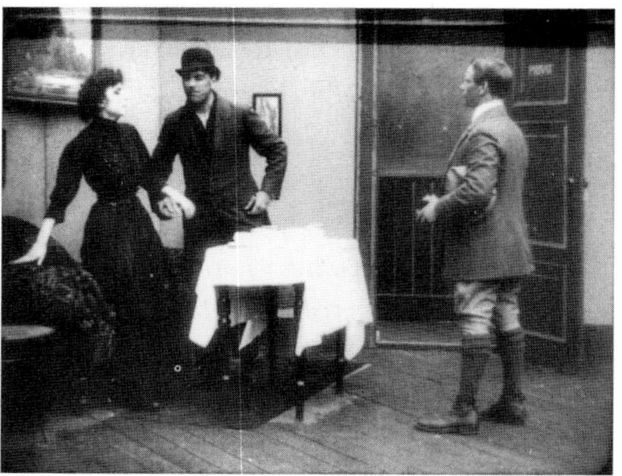

6.27 The lover shifts ineffectually as the thug seizes the heroine.

6.28 *L'assassinat de Duc de Guise:* The low camera height accentuates the foreground figures.

balance they began to experiment with letting the flow of depth patterns highlight first one action, then another. Alongside these developments in staging came strategies of camera placement that deepened the space. Most early cinematographers put their cameras four to five feet above the ground, but Ben Brewster has noted that *L'assassinat de Duc de Guise* (1908) seems to have popularized a waist-level camera height. This choice, which became standard practice at the Pathé and American Vitagraph studios, probably arose from a desire to bring figures forward while keeping both head and feet in the frame. In strengthening the impression of depth, the lower camera position reweighted the shot: foreground figures loomed larger, and characters dropped quickly in importance as they moved back into the set (Fig. 6.28).[36] The device thus provided a useful tool for directing attention.

Whether they put the camera low or high, 1910s directors were committed to extending depth through creating closer foregrounds. Brewster has suggested that as film exhibition moved from vaudeville houses and music halls to smaller venues like nickelodeons, the shrinking of screens encouraged filmmakers to bring the action nearer to the camera. This tactic retained the "life-size" scale of figures that audiences had come to expect.[37] Here is an excellent example of filmmakers innovating a stylistic solution to a problem of visibility. In addition, as we have seen, greater depth allowed the director to concentrate attention by virtue of the larger size of foreground elements and the eye-catching quality of movement toward the camera. Both features are seen to amusing expressive effect in Pathé's *Le Petit Poucet* (1909), where the low-positioned camera creates a giant (Figs. 6.29, 6.30).

The joke in *Le Petit Poucet* depends partly on a cunning floor, which appears flat but actually makes the giant stride slightly uphill so that he towers over us. In such ways set construction could enhance depth. After 1906, angled wings began to replace backdrops, and soon longer side walls came into use. Interest-

6.29 *Le Petit Poucet:* The giant enters his home in the distance . . .

6.30 . . . and stalks to the camera with a flourish.

ingly, the side walls of sets seem to have seldom stood at ninety-degree angles to the back. A favorite configuration was a back wall more or less perpendicular to the camera, flanked by a side wall shooting off at an improbably obtuse angle, as if to suggest enclosure but also to maximize the playing area (Fig. 6.11).

Across these years, Kristin Thompson points out, sets expanded "from back to front," closing the gap between the foreground plane and the camera.[38] In the earliest films movement to the camera was often unmotivated, as when Lumière's card players come grappling toward us (Fig. 6.21). Now a foreground desk or chair could justify the characters' approach.

With deeper sets, however, a new problem arose. If a man walked into the shot from the side of the frame, the audience might wonder if he had already been in the room for some time, but offscreen. So directors increasingly placed doors in the back wall, as in the *Petit Poucet* instance. The rear doorway proved an economical way to specify how and when a character enters the scene's action.[39]

The sets of the 1910s also became more recessional. Now furniture stood at more oblique angles to the background, and the rear surfaces might not be perpendicular to the lens axis. Figures began crossing rooms from the rear to the front in the diagonal trajectory common in outdoor locales. It may be that directors beyond the West were handling the same problems in comparable ways. For example, what little Japanese footage survives from the 1910s suggests that deeper sets, recessional blocking, and diagonal movement were becoming normative there as well (Fig. 6.31).

As directors exploited more recessional staging, they faced a new decision. Should everything be in focus? The fine-grained focus of the earliest films seems to have encouraged cameramen of the 1910s to render all planes as sharply as possible. So too did the desire to capture the expressions of actors placed far from the camera.[40] Under ordinary shooting conditions, with the standard

6.31 In this scene from *Chushingura* (1913 or 1917), Shozo Makino stages the hero's approach to the villain's entourage along a deep diagonal.

6.32 An outrageously close foreground in *Mabel's Awful Mistake* (1913); both face and background are in remarkably good focus.

6.33 The astonishing three-roomed set for *Love Everlasting* (Mario Caserini, 1913).

50mm lens and the diaphragm opened as wide as f/8, the cinematographer could achieve a depth of field—that is, an area of acceptably sharp focus—from about ten feet to thirty feet or more.[41] Using higher levels of illumination or lenses of short focal length (40mm, 35mm, even 25mm) allowed the cameraman to stop down the lens diaphragm and bring a much nearer foreground plane into focus. Usually the crisp medium-shot foreground with an in-focus background marked the limit of conventional practice, but some shots survive which show that startling depth of field was attainable (Fig. 6.32).

By filming in studio sets or outdoor locations, assisted by a cinematographer prepared to provide, as one cameraman put it, "as deep a stage as possible within a given lens aperture," the director of the 1910s could lay out the action in considerable depth.[42] In a vast set (some were sixty feet front to back), the playing areas might be multiplied, with distinct zones activated in the course of a scene (Fig. 6.33). The cameraman might also focus on different planes in the

6.34 *The Black Ball* (Franz Hofer, 1913): Early in the vaudeville scene, the foreground box area is out of focus, concentrating our attention on the audience and the stage in the distance.

6.35 Later, when the conversation of the men in the foreground is paramount, the background regions are cast out of focus.

6.36 The mirror, abetted by Asta Nielsen's eyeline, carries our attention to the dancers in offscreen depth (*Weisse Rosen*, Urban Gad, 1914).

6.37 In Evgeni Bauer's *Child of the Big City* (1914), the heroine tangos with her beau, framed by a curtain, as her maid hesitates outside.

course of a scene (Figs. 6.34, 6.35). Mirrors could open up the playing spaces and channel the viewer's attention (Fig. 6.36).[43] Doorways, windows, and curtains could serve as slots framing a character or gesture (Fig. 6.37). This practice, which we might call "aperture framing," became quite subtle, often relying on centering or movement to draw the eye to the merest sliver of space (Fig. 6.38).

In particular, a close foreground made action clearer and permitted the actor to work with small gestures and slight changes of facial expression. Urban Gad pointed out that the camera gives sharper pictures at shorter distances, so the director should place primary action in the foreground, even if focusing for that might blur the sets somewhat.[44] And, as the early chase films showed, movement through depth allowed the director to create a rhythmic curve of interest from background entry to foreground activity.

6.38 Within a teeming shot of a crowd's reception, Léonce Perret frames the officers at the base of a central, cleared vertical and within a carriage window (*L'enfant de Paris,* 1913).

6.39 The visual pyramid at work: Because onscreen space tapers toward the lens, the foreground figures fill up more of a plane than do the background ones (*Quo Vadis?* Enrico Grazzoni, 1913).

Depth offered the director a fine-grained scale of emphasis, a way of raising or lowering an actor's significance from moment to moment as other performers were brought into play. To exploit this orchestration of figure movement, however, the director had to master some other problems inherent in cinematic space.

Looking at the people and things on the screen, we tend to see them as occupying a cubical area. In interiors, for instance, we easily assume that the frontmost playing area is as wide as what we see of the set's back wall. This is an illusion. Kuleshov, in his 1929 monograph *The Art of the Cinema,* reminds us that the area visible within the frame has the shape of a sidelong pyramid, with the tip resting on the lens (Fig. 6.39).[45] This tapering of space toward the lens is not so much ideological (*pace* Comolli) as inevitable, at least in photography-based forms of cinema. Regularities in the behavior of light were not constructed by Renaissance humanism or bourgeois ideology; they were discovered by artists, artisans, and scientists. Geometrical optics describes certain of those regularities, and photography exploits them to project the layout of a space onto a frame of film. The lens's sampling of that layout systematically excludes information about what lies outside the converging light rays. Photographic lenses can defeat some depth cues offered by linear perspective, but they cannot abolish the optical pyramid itself. Indeed, some version of the optical pyramid would seem to be necessary for any representation of depth in a moving image. Although animated films could invoke other representational systems, nearly all in practice imitate monocular geometrical projection (Fig. 6.40). Programs for computer animation make the visual pyramid the basis of calculating the spatial array (Fig. 6.41).

Like the "visual triangle" described by Alberti in his treatise on painting, cinema's optical pyramid presupposes a monocular viewing point.[46] And this

6.40 The visual pyramid mimicked in a cartoon: A depth shot from the Japanese animated feature *Silent Moebius* (1991).

6.41 The visual pyramid replicated in computer animation (*Toy Story,* 1995).

monocular projection is what film scholars commonly consider film's debt to "Renaissance perspective." But by treating perspective as solely a way of representing what happens in the distance—dwindling figures and vanishing points—we have tended to miss what Kuleshov and his contemporaries found so important about lens optics. Where Comolli and other advocates of the ideological determination of technique see only the Western tradition of pictorial illusionism, filmmakers of the 1910s saw an opportunity for shaping the audience's attention in a way not possible in theater.

On a stage the performers are watched from all over the auditorium, so the action must be visible from a wide range of positions. In cinema, however, the action is relayed to every member of the audience from exactly the same point—the lens. "The thousands of spectator eyes," Gad remarks, "are compressed into the camera's narrow peephole."[47] Since the only view that matters is that of the lens, Kuleshov says, cinema provides an "exceptionally exact perception" of a gesture or movement.[48] Aperture framing and mirrors in the set succeed only thanks to the camera's cyclopean vision; on the stage they would fail utterly, since the correct alignment of elements would be visible to only a few spectators.

Furthermore, the field of view afforded by cinema's optical pyramid was much narrower than that available to the human eye. A dozen years before he wrote *The Art of the Cinema,* Kuleshov pointed out that the set designer's canvas was not the rectangle of the studio's shooting area but rather "the camera's thirty-five-degree angle of vision."[49] And even this angle, that afforded by a 40mm lens, was wider than that provided in most filmed scenes. The standard lens of the silent era, the 50mm or two-inch lens, yields about 28 degrees of horizontal coverage—as compared with the 200-degree field available to two-eyed humans. No wonder that the earliest filmmakers set the action at a fair distance; only near the base of the visual pyramid (against a rear wall, say) could one be sure of keeping all the players in frame.

For such reasons, many practitioners believed that the wedge-shaped acting arena made cinema a unique form of spectacle.[50] Although Standard Version historians later criticized films of the 1910s as "theatrical," many contemporary commentators presumed that cinema's playing space differed radically from that of theater. One writer marked the difference vividly:

> Fundamentally, the stage and screen angles are absolutely reversed. In the playhouse, the farther the actor comes down stage the wider it [the "angle," or playing area] becomes, until, in the immensity of the proscenium arch, the contrast with his environment is tremendously exaggerated . . . The stage angle in the playhouse might be likened to a fan whose handle is way up stage and the ribs of which point toward the eyes of a thousand spectators distributed around the arc of a circular balcony. In the camera, however, this angle is reversed. There is but a single eye to behold the picture, and the handle of the fan would be in the lens with the ribs pointing out from it within an angle of about twenty or thirty degrees. Thus it is, as the performer comes forward, his stage becomes narrower, until, in the semi-close-ups, instead of having the full width of the proscenium he must confine his action to perhaps eight or ten feet.[51]

Accordingly, as Ben Brewster and Lea Jacobs have shown, filmmakers designed the film set to be narrow and deep.[52] At the same time, the fan-shaped playing area made the actors loom larger as they approached the camera. In 1915 Vachel Lindsay complained that "the little far-away people" on a stage seemed merely scraps of cardboard compared to the "high sculptural relief" of the "dumb giants" in photoplay foregrounds.[53]

Since the lens could not focus on action that was too close, directors treated the visual pyramid as a truncated one. The playing space was bounded by a "front line" perpendicular to the camera; actors could not step across it without going out of focus. In studio practice, the front line and sidelines were marked by tape, chalk marks, stretched ropes, the edges of carpets, or strips of wood.

This trapezoidal playing space constrained the actors. Sjöström recalled that at the time of filming *Ingeborg Holm* (1913) three strips of wood tacked to the floor marked the area in which the actors would stay in frame. "This restricted area constituted the biggest headache for stage actors working in film."[54] In particular, the front line often squeezed actors together unnaturally. With a 50mm lens and the camera ten feet away, the front line became only five feet across. A French commentator complained that close foreground players made the image seem cramped; even in a crowd scene, he noted, a few characters close to the camera tended to obscure everyone behind them.[55]

6.42 The "French foreground" in *Sur les rails* (Léonce Perret? 1912).

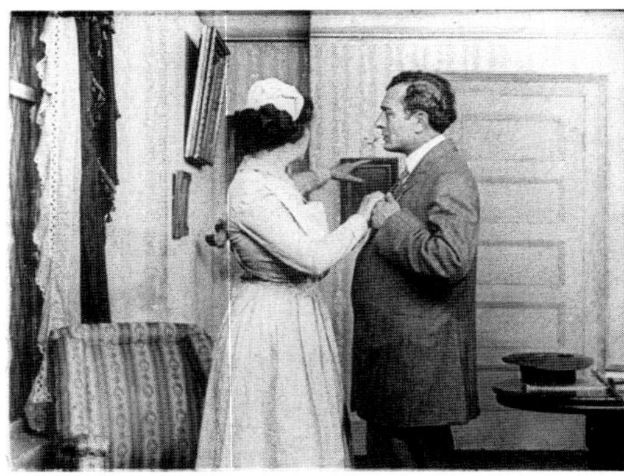

6.43 The Vitagraph nine-foot line creates a large foreground (*The Inherited Taint,* 1911).

Often, noted Lindsay, "the only definite people are the hero and heroine in the foreground, and maybe one other."[56] The increasing use of lenses of short focal length, such as the 40mm one referred to by Kuleshov, may have resulted from directors' efforts to widen the front playing space.[57]

Perhaps in response to the crowding of the foreground, directors often decided on camera distance by determining the best width for the front line.[58] Early in the 1910s, European and Russian filmmakers often used quite distant front lines, showing the entirety of the nearest figures (Figs. 6.23–6.27). One common arrangement was called by Americans the "French foreground"; the camera was set about twelve feet back and the actors were cut off around the shins (Fig. 6.42). Some directors in the United States presented closer framings.[59] In 1909 Vitagraph and other studios began to place the camera nine feet from the foreground plane; this yielded a front line only four and a half feet across.[60] The result could cut the actors off at midthigh or at the waist. It became known in France as the *plan américain,* and in the United States as the "American foreground" (Fig. 6.43; see also Fig. 1.2).[61]

Fairly close front lines, of course, fulfill a significant task in making it easier for the viewer to notice important aspects of the actors' performance. In innovating nearer foregrounds, wrote a commentator in 1912, "The American producers were the first to see the advantage of concentrating the spectators' attention on the face of the actor. In this way the subtler points of the picture-play are conveyed by facial expression and by actually speaking the dialogue written or suggested by the author."[62]

Despite their advantages, close foregrounds posed new difficulties. For once a legend holds good: between 1909 and 1913, several American commentators did complain when Griffith and other directors cut off characters' feet.[63] Perhaps critics were also disturbed by the fact that the close foregrounds often wiped out the ground plane, obliterating the cues showing that the furniture and the people rested upon the same surface. Still, viewers seem to have accepted the new schema fairly readily, for many U.S. directors adopted the Vitagraph "American foreground."

The more serious problem for composition runs back to the Lumière films we have already examined. The closer the foreground figures come, the bigger they get, and thus the more they block the rear areas. How, directors had to ask themselves, could one exploit foreground elements without losing the possibility of putting action in the distance as well?

The primary solution had been bequeathed by earlier filmmakers. They had moved characters around the frame so as to highlight salient action, using glances and composition to funnel attention. Gad's *Afgrunden* illustrates that by 1910 this option was well developed. Of course the task became notably harder when the foreground action was played closer to the lens than Gad had attempted, but the rewards in clarity and emphasis were also greater. The directors of the 1910s, often with no more than a few jottings in hand, perhaps signaling performers with a conductor's baton (Jakov Protazanov) or a whistle (Louis Feuillade), smoothly choreographed the brief glances and shifts of position, the outstretched arms and slightly swiveled bodies, the occluding of a background detail until the drama necessitated that it be apparent to all. Out of the resources of set design, aperture framing, and figure movement directors in many countries distilled highly functional staging patterns. It is a tribute to their subtle efficiency that these elaborations of earlier schemas, discovered by intuition and perfected by practice, have gone almost completely unnoticed by film historians.

Nothing, for example, might seem easier to stage than a scene in which a woman seduces a man. Sit her down in the foreground and show him pulled toward her until she captures him. But in *Red and White Roses* (1913), a Vitagraph director turns the scene into a *pas de deux* of temptation, hesitation, and acquiescence (Figs. 6.44–6.52). Here the "American foreground" never blots out key scenic elements in the rear, partly because of the slightly high angle of view but chiefly thanks to the constantly changing character positions. Like other American filmmakers, our director achieves his effects within a playing space that is not only narrow at the front line but fairly shallow as well. In American films the principal zone seems to have run four to six feet back from the front line; here, insisted a 1913 commentator, "all of the important action must occur so that the figures may be large and the expressions distinct."[64]

European directors were slower to adopt such close foregrounds, but the choreography was if anything even more nuanced. Consider the ubiquitous rear door. If someone is going to appear there, we need an unimpeded view of it. But when other actions are more important, the director should draw our

6.44 *Red and White Roses:* The errant husband, Andrews, enters from the rear, with the maid going off with his hat.

6.45 The maid could easily have continued out right, leaving the stage to the two main players; but she departs by moving back leftward, hitting frame center as Andrews opens the letter.

6.46 Once the maid is gone, Andrews comes to the center in an "American foreground."

6.47 But soon he steps back and into shadow, allowing Lida to take his place . . .

6.48 . . . and pass to the left edge of the front line, where she sniffs a rose. Here, as elsewhere, he pivots slightly to accommodate her.

6.49 After Lida has pulled Andrews a bit from the camera, she retreats to the central table, where she stands posed: "I am a red rose—glowing and made for love."

6.50 Lida comes forward, and he embraces her.

6.51 Again she withdraws to the right foreground, and Andrews starts away, determined to resist. She halts him with a call.

6.52 Andrews comes diagonally forward and falls to kissing her.

eye away from the door. Kuleshov's mentor Yevgeni Bauer finds an elegant expedient in *The Dying Swan* (1917): the foreground player simply blocks the door (Figs. 6.53–6.55). Bauer superimposes the composition's two nodes of activity, face and door, a tactic yielding the extra advantage that the doorway neatly frames the ballerina's head. After she moves to a mirror to check her tiara, Bauer needs to prepare the viewer for a new character's entrance, so he cuts in to a closer view and repeats the process in reverse, letting her reveal the door just as someone enters (Figs. 6.56, 6.57).

Feuillade extends this strategy in the astonishingly fluid opening scene of *Les vampires* (1915). In a "French foreground" Philippe the journalist discovers that someone has stolen his dossier. His wringing a confession from the clerk Mazamette is played out as a flow of bodies obscuring and then framing background action, while heads and doorways constantly create apertures (Figs. 6.58–6.67). The scene is completely unnaturalistic (why do the two

6.53 *The Dying Swan:* When the maid comes in, the ballerina is seated so as to make the entrance wholly visible.

6.54 While the maid departs in the rear, her mistress opens the chest.

6.55 She moves slightly to the left as she takes out the tiara, and now she blocks the doorway.

6.56 Before the mirror, the ballerina shifts rightward, revealing the door panel behind.

6.57 As she lowers her arm, she opens up the doorway space for the entrance of her father, who will come to the foreground.

6.58 *Les Vampires:* Philippe enters the press office, framed in the doorway.

6.59 After greeting his colleagues in the middle ground. . .

6.60 . . . he comes to his desk. His act of bending over blocks one reporter but gives us a glimpse of Mazamette on the left, turning face front.

6.61 When Philippe discovers his dossier rifled, he rises—and Mazamette does as well.

6.62 As Philippe questions his colleagues, Mazamette slinks away in the distance, through the center of the frame.

6.63 He almost makes it out the door before Philippe halts him—the distant reporter turning away from us as Mazamette becomes frontal, framed precisely in the doorway.

6.64 Brought back downstage, Mazamette is questioned. At first, the background men are framed by him and Philippe . . .

6.65 . . . but Philippe's act of discovering the stolen document takes center stage when his seizing of Mazamette blocks the onlookers.

6.66 Feuillade highlights the rear door again when one reporter leaves to call the police and Mazamette calls after him. (Compare Figs. 6.58 and 6.63.)

6.67 The remaining reporter turns obligingly away to pace as Mazamette starts to explain that he stole the document to get money to support his child.

journalists accept such a poor view of Mazamette? why not surround the culprit?), but it is so smoothly executed that the viewer is scarcely aware of how the stylized ensemble movement has directed attention.

The ballet of blocking and revealing can offer premonitions too, as Feuillade demonstrates in a restaurant scene in *Fantômas* (1913). A violinist strolls down the aisle on the left center and serenades Josephine, seated on frame right (Fig. 6.68). His fiddling directs our attention to this area of the shot, so that when he moves aside, he reveals Juve and Fandor entering the restaurant in the background (Fig. 6.69). As the violinist departs, they move to the center aisle (Fig. 6.70). The violin player, an extra, has been a spatial pretext, a mere pointer marking a zone for the major characters to occupy.[65]

Dozens of films made between 1912 and 1918 could illustrate how directors

6.68 *Fantômas.*

6.69 *Fantômas.*

6.70 *Fantômas.*

refined schemas of staging in depth, but I conclude this cavalcade of examples with Sjöström's *Ingeborg Holm,* one of the finest works of the *annus mirabilis* 1913. It demonstrates the emotional effects that the *mise en scène* of the period could wring from a subtle direction of the viewer's attention.

Business reversals and the death of her husband have driven Ingeborg into the poorhouse. Her children must be boarded out to other families. In a single shot lasting nearly three minutes, she brings her son and daughter into the superintendent's office and bids them goodbye. Ingeborg's face becomes the emotional and pictorial fulcrum of the scene, but Sjöström also uses foreground blockage and aperture framing to guide us to the proper area at the right moment.

Ingeborg's entry with her children from the rear doorway establishes the trajectory that will be followed during the scene as foster mothers come in and take away the children (Fig. 6.71). (Again, the scene is built around move-

6.71 *Ingeborg Holm.*

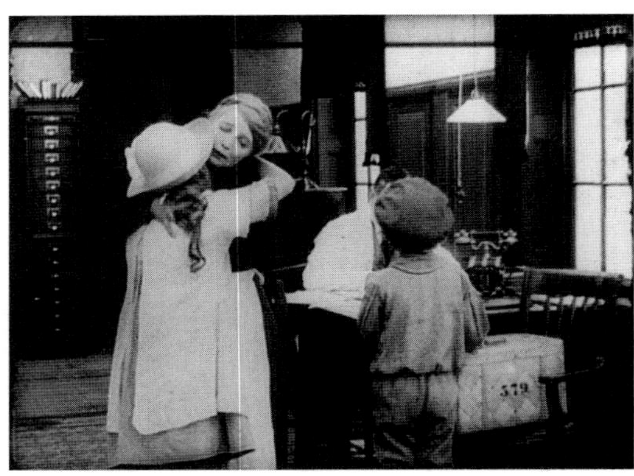
6.72 *Ingeborg Holm.*

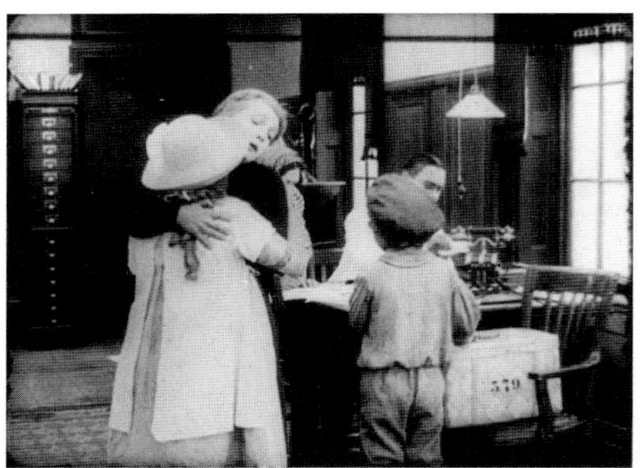
6.75 *Ingeborg Holm.*

6.76 *Ingeborg Holm.*

ments toward and away from the camera.) In a brilliant stroke, Sjöström immediately plants the young son in the foreground, back to us. The boy will stand there immobile for this first phase of the scene, occasionally serving to block the superintendent, as in Fig. 6.72. Ingeborg buries her face in her daughter's shoulder at the precise moment the foster mother enters from the rear left (Fig. 6.73). She passes behind Ingeborg, and as she is momentarily blocked, the superintendent twitches into visibility, handing the woman a document to sign (Fig. 6.74). During the signing, when the woman is briefly obscured, the superintendent shifts position again and Ingeborg lifts her face once more (Fig. 6.75). Ingeborg and the daughter move slightly leftward as the foster mother comes forward (Fig. 6.76). This phase of the scene concludes with the departure of the daughter (Fig. 6.77) and the embrace of Ingeborg and her son in the foreground, once more concealing the superintendent (Fig. 6.78).

6.73 *Ingeborg Holm.*

6.74 *Ingeborg Holm.*

6.77 *Ingeborg Holm.*

6.78 *Ingeborg Holm.*

As mother and son turn to the camera, a guard announces the next mother (Fig. 6.79). He then leaves. As the new mother enters, Ingeborg takes one step leftward to disclose the superintendent (Fig. 6.80). She continues to move left, freeing the central middle ground as her son's new mother comes forward (Fig. 6.81). This is a more expansive replay of the staging of the entry of the first mother (Figs. 6.73–6.76). The foster mother leaves with the boy, retiring to the door in the distance as Ingeborg stands crushed, back to us, screen center (Fig. 6.82). After a final embrace, Ingeborg is permitted to follow them out to watch them leave (Fig. 6.83). The scene ends as it has begun, with the superintendent working coolly at his desk (Fig. 6.84).[66]

The *mise en scène* of *Ingeborg Holm,* John Fullerton tells us, derives from efforts in Swedish theater to create deep and oblique playing spaces.[67] Yet even the most intimate chamber theater could not duplicate the nuances of staging in this remarkable shot. Minute shifts of character position—a shoulder

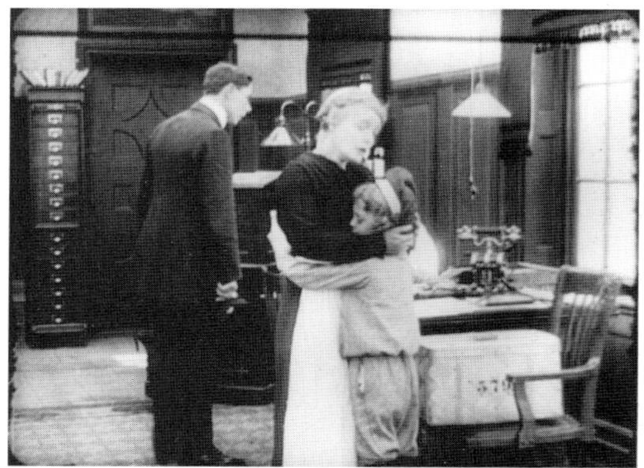

6.79 *Ingeborg Holm.*

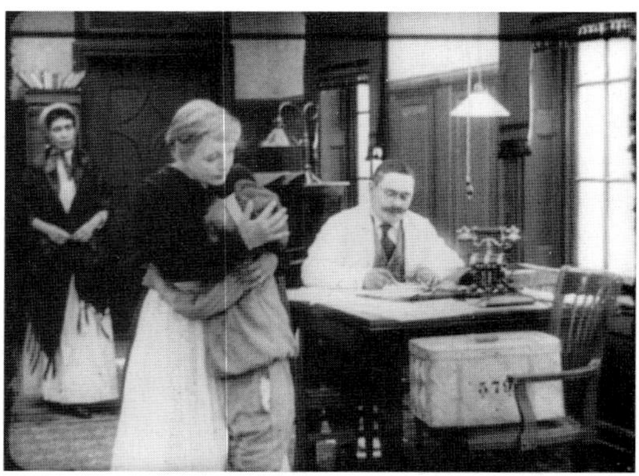

6.80 *Ingeborg Holm.*

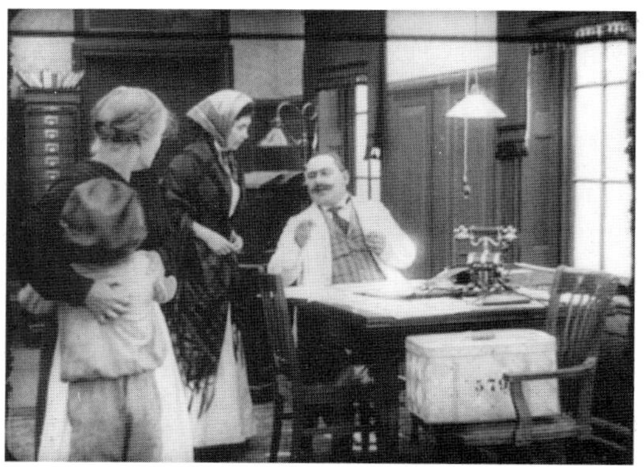

6.81 *Ingeborg Holm.*

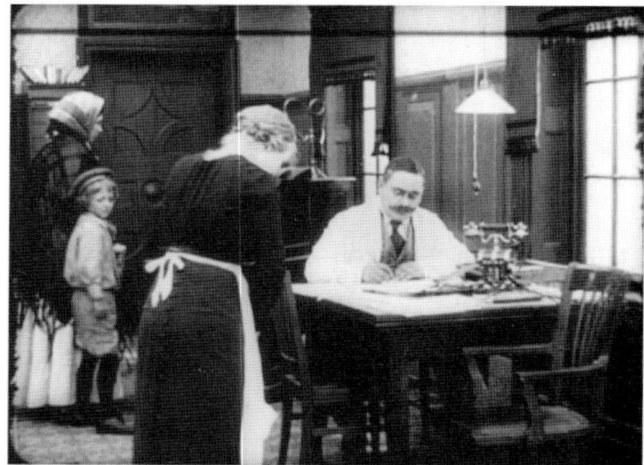

6.82 *Ingeborg Holm.*

6.83 *Ingeborg Holm.*

6.84 *Ingeborg Holm.*

6.85 A "1913" staging, complete with door and partially blocked faces: Ilya Repin's painting *They Did Not Expect Him* (1888).

turned, a neck lifted or lowered, a half-step more or less—glide our attention from one area to another, often to a mere crevice of space adjacent to the first (Figs. 6.72–6.75). This nuanced concealing and revealing cannot be accomplished on any stage: at any point, audience members in certain seats would see a new slice of space, but spectators sitting elsewhere in the theater would find their views still blocked. Here is Gad's peephole principle at work.

Nor would most of the compositions illustrated on these pages make sense as paintings. Undoubtedly film directors' concern for centering and counterweighting the composition and for using contours and glances to guide the viewer's attention are indebted to age-old principles of visual design. And certainly the *mise en scène* of 1910s cinema owes a good deal to the realist and narrative paintings of the previous century (Fig. 6.85). But cinema's movement over time allows the director to shift action around a central zone and to balance a shot by means of a succession of poses, as in *Afgrunden* and *Red and White Roses.* The visual harmonies that are present all at once in a painting are sounded sequentially in cinema. Kuleshov was right: the exceptionally exact perceptions unfolded moment by moment in these films are as "specifically cinematic" as any editing choices.

In this story Griffith no longer holds the starring role. Historians are now well aware of his lingering commitment to shots in which characters plunge across the frame edges. One scholar suggests that Griffith believed that elaborations of diagonal movement slowed down the shot.[68] Still, he occasionally

6.86 *A Corner in Wheat* (1908): The Wheat King toasts his entourage after his success.

6.87 *Musketeers of Pig Alley* (1912): The young couple prepare for the husband's departure. When they turn from the camera . . .

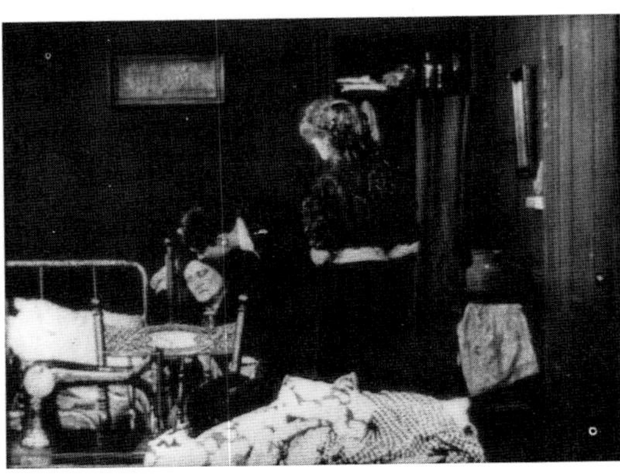

6.88 . . . and go to the rear, his sick mother is now revealed.

staged in depth (Fig. 6.86).[69] The Biograph camera yielded very high-resolution images, and these could create quite close foregrounds.[70] Griffith sometimes flaunts foreground blockage, particularly in his late Biograph efforts (Figs. 6.87, 6.88). Yet usually such shots provide brief pauses in what is essentially an editing-dominated approach; Griffith seems to have had little recourse to the fine-grained intrashot choreography developed by his contemporaries.

In other directors' films of the 1910s, staging achieves a compositional intricacy and emotional density unseen only a few years before. Scholars have begun to show that these staging techniques could be extended to create motifs across entire films.[71] Yet even without examining the roles played by my sample shots within the films' overall development, we can see rich "subthematic" processes at work. Feuillade's brisk juggling of figures suits an intrigue full of twists, while the solemn delicacy of Sjöström's staging dignifies Ingeborg's desperation as she strains against the stolid institution to which she is abandoned. Clearly, Standard Version writers erred in identifying the artistic resources of cinema almost wholly with the "antitheatrical" possibilities of editing. By taking their prototype of closer views to be cut-in close-ups, they failed to see the virtuosity of directors who incorporated large foregrounds into an expressive rhythm that could guide attention even as it organized the frame.

In parallel fashion, Burch seems too quick to assume that "petty-bourgeois" directors such as Feuillade adhered to the "primitive" tableau.[72] Like the orthodox position, his account ignores how the closer foregrounds of post-1909 films shape viewer activity. Instead, a significant continuity in staging practices runs from Lumière's doused card players (Fig. 6.22) through the fleeing passenger's bolt for freedom in *The Great Train Robbery* (Fig. 6.14) and the deliberately advancing giant of *Le Petit Poucet* (Fig. 6.30) up to the seduction scene of *Red and White Roses* (Fig. 6.46). By treating this continuity as a process of schema and revision, we can recognize how directors of the 1910s refined and sharpened earlier staging tactics.

I have already indicated some proximate causes for this pattern of change—principally, an urge to clarify narrative actions and to guide the spectator's attention to the proper aspect of the shot. But these impulses were aroused by a task set from without. In the years 1907–1914, films became "feature-length," and plots became more complicated. Continuity editing of various sorts was one response to this demand, as many researchers have shown.[73] Cross-cutting allowed several intrigues to be developed. Eyeline editing and cut-in close-ups permitted the director to build dramas around what characters saw and felt, and these stylistic innovations in turn sustained a more psychologically based plotting. It seems plausible that the *mise-en-scène* strategies of this era were also driven by a concern for more cogent storytelling. The closer foregrounds, the dynamic movement of figures in depth and across the lateral stretch, and the rapid alternation of attention from one face to another in *Ingeborg Holm* and *Les vampires* can be seen as responding to a demand for a more subtle and intricate dramaturgy.

Looking back from 1925 two French observers noted that Feuillade, Perret, and Jasset had mastered a style capable of "narrating actions as clearly as possible."[74] Some directors were learning to guide attention within the shot at exactly the same period that others were learning to guide attention among shots. Functionally, there is an affinity between developing the plastic possibilities of staging and exploiting the strategies of continuity: both guide the viewer in following a fairly complicated narrative and responding to its emotional dynamics. If filmmakers on both continents were working along parallel lines in their efforts to master storytelling, the duality between a pre-1918 cinema of tableaux and a subsequent cinema of classical découpage no longer looks so sharp.

Clarity, emphasis, and moment-by-moment switches of attention were not the only aims of the new staging in depth. Several commentators applauded the depth uniquely available in films of the 1910s, with one claiming that characters coming forward "showed that the set had depth, the illusion being so perfect that many of the audience believed that they were watching a person in a real room."[75] Nevertheless, the idea that depth staging is wholly propelled by a principle of realism—Comolli's "impression of reality," Burch's "haptic space"—seems inadequate to explain the particular changes we have plotted. Realism, of whatever sorts, had to be reconciled with increasing pressures to steer spectators to salient story material within the optical constraints afforded by cinema's visual pyramid and front line. Depth staging of the 1910s answered to the need, common among artists of all places and traditions, to shape the material for specific effects on the perceiver. In the absence of cutting-based stylistic norms, imaginative filmmakers took rough schemas from early film and developed them into a *mise en scène* displaying a range of emphasis, dynamism, and refinement suitable to the new complexities of longer films. Scarcely acknowledged at the time or since, these nuanced tactics of directing the audience's attention became permanent additions to the filmmaker's repertoire.

Depth, Découpage, and Camera Movement

If the long-take, "scenic" method of the early to mid-1910s was so elegant, why did it give way to editing-based norms in only a few years? One reason was probably the success of American films with international audiences. Continuity-based storytelling seemed to be the wave of the future, and a younger generation of directors took it up eagerly, perhaps partly as the sort of rebellion against the elders which Kuleshov records in his attacks on tsarist cinema's one-shot scenes.[76]

Another reason why Hollywood's editing conventions swept the world so quickly reminds us that even successful solutions can produce new problems. With the rise of feature-length films, production became more routinized. Sustained takes required lengthy rehearsal, and if someone made a mistake during filming, the entire cast and crew would have to start all over again. From the standpoint of industrial organization, it is reasonable to break the scene into shorter, simpler shots that can be taken separately, many of which need occupy only a single player and a few staff. The American studios showed that if the filmmakers were willing to prepare the film on paper, in the format of a continuity script, editing could make filmmaking more efficient and predictable.[77]

This circumstance may not fully explain the emergence of analytical cutting, since with skilful professionals long-take filming can be as efficient as découpage-based production. Richard Abel has shown that French filmmakers easily adjusted to the coming of features and the demand for more footage.[78] Editing did, however, give producers more latitude in adjusting the film's pace and in omitting and rearranging shots. An advantage during production, continuity cutting allowed the film to be fine-tuned in postproduction as well.

The most commonly voiced rationale for chopping a scene into several shots, as we might expect, was that it guaranteed that the audience's attention would fasten on the proper piece of action. One can see the lengthy, deep-space shot breaking down in a 1916 U.S. manual which notes that important expressions and gestures would be lost "if the camera held on the front line." The author advises directors to start by showing the locale in a "big scene" before starting "to pick the action apart and assign each important action to its respective stage."[79] (Still gripped by the idea of the playing space as the decisive factor, the writer can conceive a closer view only as a smaller "stage.") Mastering découpage made it easier for less skilled directors to get the story across.

Standard Version historians, as well as many writers of the period, identified cutting-based norms principally with the films of Griffith and other American directors. More recent researchers into silent film have tended to counterpose editing (the American approach) to depth staging (the European tendency).[80] Certainly many contemporaries recognized differences between European and American film styles.[81] Varying modes of film production may have affected the stylistic paths that were taken. Whereas American producers controlled the preproduction phase (scripting and centralized planning of projects) and postproduction (editing), European directors conceived *mise en scène* as the central act of filmmaking.[82] Not surprisingly, they concentrated their authority by creating scenes that were often improvised and that could not be cut up afterward.

Still, to distinguish too sharply between American cutting and European depth risks simply projecting back onto history the split between the Standard Version's aesthetic and Bazin's Dialectical account. Although analytical cutting and lengthy takes can be seen as logical alternatives, historically they often functioned as flexible, nonexclusive options. Many directors synthesized the schemas available from continuity editing and from depth staging. Sjöström's *Ingmar's Sons* (1919) employs both finely broken-down découpage (Figs. 5.18–5.25) and a self-consciously "archaic" depth (Fig. 6.89). Cutting and deep space could complement one another within a given scene as well. Depth

6.89 *Ingmar's Sons:* Ingmar and Brita's father leave the parson, their carriage occupying the background. (Compare the detailed découpage of an earlier scene, Figs. 5.18–5.25.)

6.90 Harold sprays his tormenters in *An Eastern Westerner* (1920).

6.91 *Our Hospitality:* Willie sits on a ledge as water sluices over a cliff.

6.92 Just as a sheet of water covers Willie, the brothers who are stalking him step into the foreground.

could enhance a cutting-based approach, while editing could extend the depth aesthetic in new directions. Our example from Bauer's *The Dying Swan* shows that a cut to a medium shot (Figs. 6.55, 6.56) can peel away one foreground layer only to establish a new one (Fig. 6.57).

Reciprocally, within an editing-based aesthetic directors sustained depth compositions for various ends. American comedies often played out the entire dynamics of a gag in deep space. Harold Lloyd is usually identified as an editing-heavy director, but nearly every one of his films contains at least one scene of comically developed depth (Fig. 6.90). Buster Keaton's mammoth gags involving hurricanes, runaway locomotives, stranded steamships, and burst dams all utilized remarkable depth staging (Figs. 6.91, 6.92).[83] Noël Carroll has shown that depth composition allows Keaton to show both cause and effect and to render work processes visually intelligible.[84]

6.93 In *The Last of the Mohicans* (1920), a foreground interior frames the action, serving to establish the characters in the scene.

Bazin assumed that the rise of analytical editing discouraged the exploration of deep space (thereby allowing Wellesian *profondeur de champ* to emerge as a kind of découpage within the individual shot). But it seems evident now that as a découpage-based style came to dominate American films, depth staging was mobilized for particular functions within that. Most commonly, the depth composition functioned as an establishing shot. Maurice Tourneur distinguished himself by using long shots with strong foregrounds to frame a scene before analytical editing dissected the action (Fig. 6.93). In the hilarious restaurant scene of Chaplin's *The Immigrant* (1917), patterns of blocking and disclosure in the broader shots serve to execute comic bits of business, while cut-in closer views, with little or no change of angle, emphasize character reactions (Figs. 6.94–6.96). Similarly, somewhat deep medium shots could aid redundancy, reiterating the proximity of two characters (Figs. 6.97, 6.98).

European directors likewise absorbed the deep-space shot into classical continuity sequences. In Murnau's *Der brennende Acker* (1922), a character enters in the rear doorway of a fairly packed long shot of the farmhouse dining room (Fig. 6.99). A 1913 film would move away the secondary character and allow the newcomer to advance to the foreground. Murnau, however, immediately cuts in to emphasize the main conflict; this allows him to keep the visitor in the background as a secondary presence in a later shot (Figs. 6.100–6.102). Yet, like his American and European counterparts, Murnau could use depth for more directly expressive purposes as well. *Nosferatu* (1922), while displaying a mastery of classical continuity, also presents long-shot depth compositions that reiterate the graphic motif of the arch (Fig. 6.103).

Throughout the 1910s directors usually strove for sharp focus on all planes, but continuity editing posed problems for this hard-edge aesthetic. It was easy

6.94 *The Immigrant:* In the foreground two waiters discover that a patron cannot pay the bill.

6.95 In a larger view at the same angle, they thrash him. The scuffle all but hides the reaction of Charlie, sitting at the rear table.

6.96 A cut to a medium shot shows Charlie and Edna startled; later Charlie will find that he can't pay either.

6.97 A moderately deep two-shot from *Manhattan Madness* (1916) establishes Doug Fairbanks at his club, other members visible behind him . . .

6.98 . . . before a cut isolates him. A slight iris effect on the frame edges keeps attention from straying to background areas.

6.99 Murnau's *Der brennende Acker* (1922): In the establishing shot, Maria rises and partially blocks Johann's rear entrance.

6.100 Murnau immediately cuts to a shot of Peter . . .

6.101 . . . and a shot of Johann standing in the doorway.

6.102 Later, depth is used to segregate Johann from the others.

6.103 *Nosferatu:* The arch motif creates whorls around the innocent Harker and the vampire who awaits him.

6.104 The faces are heightened not only by the close framing but also by the out-of-focus background (*The Four Horsemen of the Apocalypse,* 1921).

6.105 The shallow-focus facial shot has remained a mainstay of international film style (*Yaaba,* Idrissa Ouedraogo, 1989).

to preserve focus in long shots and *plans américains,* but what to do about framings that cut the figure off at the waist, bust, or neck? Given a lot of light and small apertures, it was technically possible to keep reasonable focus from somewhat close foregrounds to quite far back, as we have already seen (Figs. 6.32, 6.46). Still, as Bazin pointed out, editing encouraged directors to use shallow focus for close-ups. "If at a given moment in the action the director . . . goes to a close-up of a bowl of fruit, it follows naturally that he also isolates it in space through the focusing of the lens. The soft focus of the background therefore confirms the effect of editing [*montage*]."[85]

Many filmmakers began to control attention within the closer framing. An iris might mask off distracting backgrounds (Fig. 6.98), but more often, as Bazin noted, the cameraman would emphasize the main figure by throwing the background out of focus (Fig. 6.104). Such selective focus was usually accomplished by employing wider diaphragm openings and by filming with longer lenses.[86] (By the mid-1920s close-ups were commonly taken with a 75mm or 100mm lens.) The shallow-focus close-up became a staple of filmmaking, still widely used today (Fig. 6.105). Even with selective focus, however, the interplay of foreground and background so salient in the 1910s was not completely forgotten. For example, Kozintsev and Trauberg's *The New Babylon* (1929), combining sharp foregrounds with blurred or misted background elements, creates a planimetric frontality—a laminated space to suggest that during the Paris Commune bourgeois spectacle spills out of the theaters into the streets (Fig. 6.106).[87]

At the same time that directors began to exploit selective focus, some American cinematographers created a "soft style" that made all planes of the image somewhat hazy. Gentle lighting, wide-open apertures, and heavy filters and scrims glamorized stars and lyricized landscapes. The results were often

6.106 *The New Babylon:* Rain blurs the background figures whom the officer is about to execute.

self-conscious imitations of "artistic" photography at the turn of the century.[88] The consequences of the soft style for depth staging can be seen in Frank Borzage's poignant pastoral *Lazybones* (1925). The arrival of Elmer Ballister in his carriage opens up a new strip of action between the foreground figures and the background figure, and the cutting isolates Lazybones while arranging the other characters in lustrous layers (Figs. 6.107–6.110).[89] Such scenes remind us that depth staging is perfectly possible without "deep focus," and they indicate that the shallow panchromatic images which Comolli took as characteristic of the sound era were in fact modifications of the "soft style" of mid-1920s silent film.

One beneficiary of Borzage's explorations was Yasujiro Ozu, a director who has seldom attracted notice for his use of depth. Despite Burch's claim that Ozu's shots are supremely flat, Ozu's low camera position often juxtaposes middle-ground action with props or items of landscape in the foreground (Fig. 6.111). He also sets important elements in the distance and then subtly grades planes by the degree to which they are out of focus. As in *Lazybones,* movement or centrality will then draw our eye away from the most sharply focused region (Fig. 6.112). Ozu's cuts play on the same principle as they sidle us through a locale: a significant element out of focus within the first shot will be in focus in the next, but then a new out-of-focus element draws our attention.[90]

By contrast, some directors pushed for greater sharpness in their depth compositions. They began to explore the possibility that a lens of short focal length (35mm or less), stopped down to small apertures, could hold a reasonable focus on both a fairly close foreground and important background material. It is as if the viewer has been brought a great deal nearer those "tableaux" of the 1910s, with the foreground correspondingly enlarged. Now the director could keep action and reaction or character and object in the same shot,

6.107 *Lazybones:* As the hero watches secretly . . .

6.108 . . . his sweetheart and her mother in the foreground, along with his own mother in the background, watch Elmer drive up.

6.109 Elmer's carriage arrives in the middle ground, blocking the mother . . .

6.110 . . . before a new shot restores soft-focus depth, revealing Lazybones' mother.

presenting them in a more compact and vigorous design while still reaping the advantages of continuity editing.

Stroheim's *Greed* (1924), one of the earliest films to emphasize the aggressive foreground consistently, experiments with the new depth possibilities. Here the wide-angle lens not only enhances Stroheim's vaunted naturalism but also creates disturbing juxtapositions.[91] It yields bulging establishing shots (Fig. 6.113), closer views with unusually crisp backgrounds (Fig. 6.114), and steep diagonals (Fig. 6.115). Such depth shots seldom had recourse to the delicate masking and revelation seen in the work of Feuillade or Sjöström. In being revised, the 1910s schema had become simplified. Stroheim's film may also have reinforced the association of aggressive foregrounds with the histrionic intensification demanded by serious drama. In a reversion to the early

6.111 Multiplanar composition for a gag: In *I Was Born, But . . .* (1932), the office worker exercises while shirts, outstretched like his arms, dry in the breeze.

6.112 In *Where Now Are the Dreams of Youth?* (1932), Ozu's characteristic interest in peripheral objects is manifested through highly selective focus.

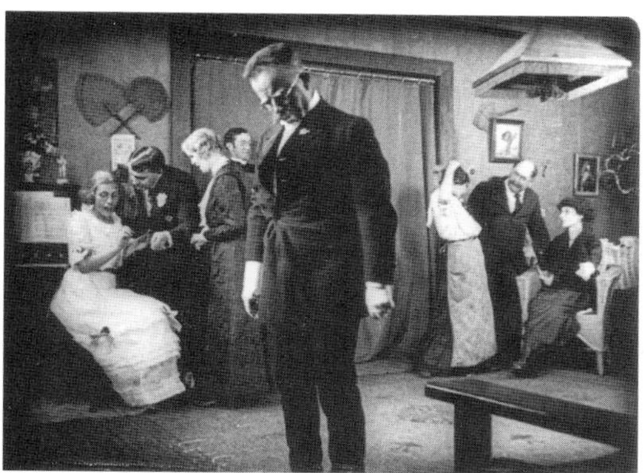

6.113 An establishing shot with the wide-angle lens from *Greed.*

6.114 A closer view with sharply focused background and foreground.

6.115 A famous depth shot from *Greed;* unlike the sunlit passersby behind McTeague in 6.114, Trina is not quite in focus.

6.116 *Wings* (William Wellman, 1927): Depth for a composition in a shot/reverse-shot passage.

6.117 The distorted foreground yielded by the wide-angle lens (*A Woman of Affairs*, 1929).

years' segregation of techniques by genres, the close-up foreground would in the decades to come seldom be systematically used in comedies.

Greed's images sometimes center the foreground element and reveal background elements flanking it (Figs. 6.113, 6.114), but the most striking depth shots of the 1920s would counterpose only two dramatically significant planes, a close-up foreground on the left or right and a strong second plane (middle ground or background) set in the center or on the opposite side of the frame. This stripped-down "biplanar" composition proved advantageous to an editing-based aesthetic. The aggressive foregrounds—fairly close to the camera, more or less in focus, shot with wide-angle distortion—could be incorporated into shot/reverse-shot patterns and expressive or decorative sequences (Figs. 6.116, 6.117). Perhaps such instances were what Adrian Brunel had in mind when he deplored the 1920s fashion for "clever angles" that showed "a foreground of the hero's ear as we see a close-up of the heroine."[92]

Off-center foregrounds set against striking depth created pictorial dynamism and emphasized the simultaneous presence of key narrative elements, but they also presented problems of balance. Centering and other devices of emphasis could call attention to the distant element, but there was inevitably a strain. This quality might be intensified through the choice of a high or low angle, which tended to create stronger perspective diminution. The pictorial tension created by a big foreground could be contained by alternating editing: an overstressed foreground in one shot could become the background of another, as in shot/reverse-shot combinations. Alternatively, the imbalance of the aggressive foreground could be exploited for dramatic tension or for frankly stylized ends (Fig. 6.118). Dreyer's *La Passion de Jeanne d'Arc* (1928)

6.118 L'Herbier's *Don Juan and Faust* presents an almost abstract composition of a man on a tower looking at another on the ground far below.

6.119 In *La Passion de Jeanne d'Arc,* the camera angle cuts figures' faces free of their surroundings, while foreground bits of scenery become looming abstract shapes.

6.120 An imperialist rendered both sinister and cartoonish by the wide-angle lens (*Blue Express,* Ilya Trauberg, 1929).

6.121 The tractor as a hulking beast, defeating the driver's efforts to repair it (*The General Line,* Eisenstein, 1929).

absorbed such compositions into an idiosyncratic montage construction, using them to provide bizarre variants of traditional establishing shots (Fig. 6.119).

Comolli has suggested that *profondeur de champ* is inherently tied to bourgeois ideology, yet from the 1920s onward it emerged vividly in the cinema of the USSR as well. In the Montage period, the aggressive foreground was largely a tool of satiric and grotesque caricature (Fig. 6.120). Eisenstein praised the 28mm lens for its ability to yield "Gogolian hyperbole" (Fig. 6.121).[93]

In sum, the close foreground with strikingly sharp depth was well suited for an editing-based aesthetic, either Soviet Montage or Hollywood découpage. During the late silent era directors tended to handle such shots as static compositions or to deploy very limited patterns of movement within them—

6.122 George Burns and Gracie Allen in a telephoto medium shot in *Lambchops* (1929). (Compare the greater sense of depth revealed in Fig. 6.46.)

certainly nothing so elaborate as was seen in the more distant views of the 1910s. The optical pyramid once more dictated certain choices: the bigger the foreground, the less of the frame was available for intricate *mise en scène.* For decades after aggressive foregrounds appeared, filmmakers assumed that the bigger the frontmost element, the simpler the staging would be and the more editing would come into play.

By the late 1920s, filmmakers had built up an array of distinct options for handling depth. In medium shots or close-ups, selective focus could highlight the important action. Significant elements in two planes could be emphasized by putting one somewhat out of focus, as Borzage did. In wider framings, depth staging remained possible even in the soft style of cinematography. Most of these alternatives would continue to be viable after the arrival of talking pictures.

The coming of sound, despite all the technical problems it raised, did offer one powerful new cue for directing the viewer's attention. During dialogue scenes, all other things being equal, the spectator would tend to watch the character who was speaking. This probably seemed to simplify the task of staging and shooting. In addition, early problems with cutting sound encouraged the unambitious director simply to film a continuous scene with several cameras equipped with very long ("telephoto") lenses (Fig. 6.122). The practice yielded a straightforward editing schema: an establishing shot followed by a closer view or by shot/reverse-shot cutting that simply obeyed the flow of the dialogue. In these early multiple-camera productions, directors tended to mobilize fewer planes of depth.

Directors soon returned to a single camera and the flexibility afforded by varying setups and lens lengths. But now they faced a new problem. Henceforth dialogue would occupy a large part of most films. How could the

6.123 In *The Party Card* (1938), the wife is writing a note to denounce her husband as he comes in at the rear.

filmmaker dramatize speech and retain visual interest without falling back into the static recording associated with the early talkies?

Several solutions seem to have emerged. Some directors intensified cutting, perhaps expecting that it would supply visual variety as it had during the silent years. Since rapid editing of synchronized dialogue scenes was technically difficult during the earliest years of sound, only a few directors, such as Lewis Milestone in *The Front Page* (1931), pursued this practice systematically. It would, however, become an important option many decades later; from the 1970s onward, many directors began to cut as rapidly as their U.S. predecessors had in the 1910s and 1920s.

During the 1930s, a more common strategy for providing visual interest involved camera movement. A dialogue scene, many directors believed, could be enlivened by propelling the players through the set and panning or tracking to follow them, with continuity editing highlighting major turning points of the action. At times a camera movement could substitute for a cut, enabling the director to move from long shot to close-up or vice versa without breaking "the flow of story movement."[94]

Within the international framework of classical découpage enhanced by camera movement, depth staging did not die out. In fact certain conventional schemas appeared. A director in any country might emphasize depth by framing action in a doorway (Fig. 6.123) or window (especially the window of a car or a train compartment). The director could move figures up and down corridors, shoot beyond one person looking into a distant space, or film a cluster of seated characters at an angle that heightened the distinct planes they occupied (Fig. 6.124). Establishing shots might be framed by a picturesque detail (Fig. 6.125).

6.124 In the Mexican film *Enemigos* (1933), Chano Urueta utilizes the receding ellipses of the sombreros to frame the central drama.

6.125 The characteristic low angle of decorative depth in the 1930s (*The Scarlet Pimpernel,* Harold Young, 1938).

6.126 *The Bartered Bride* (Max Ophuls, 1932): A rack focus from a pair in the foreground . . .

6.127 . . . to the new character arriving in the background; space is cleared so that he is centered as well.

Another way of suggesting depth was to change the plane of focus in the course of the shot. By racking focus, the director could draw attention from point to point at dramatic moments (Figs. 6.126, 6.127). Though sometimes used in the silent period, rack focus became a principal tool in the director's kit during the sound era, and it would later help solve some problems posed by color and widescreen.

The international continuity style of the 1930s integrated such depth-enhancing devices with fluid camera movement. One scene in Michael Curtiz's *The Charge of the Light Brigade* (1936) begins with a close view of Geoffrey's hands packing his bag (Fig. 6.128). As Elsa enters to him, the camera swings up and racks focus to frame her coming in through a door in the rear, veiled by a curtain (Fig. 6.129). Geoffrey turns from the camera and steps toward her

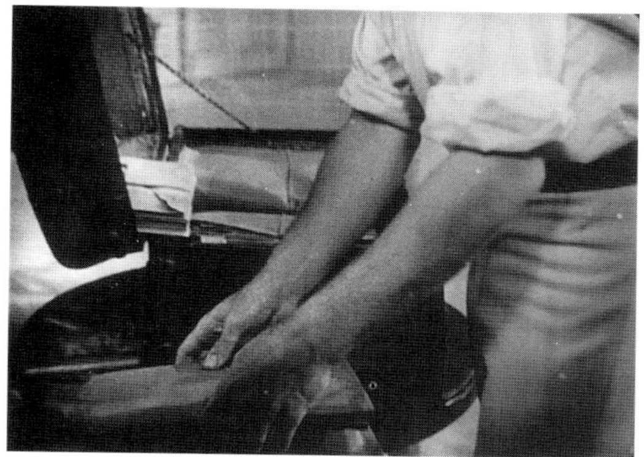

6.128 *The Charge of the Light Brigade.*

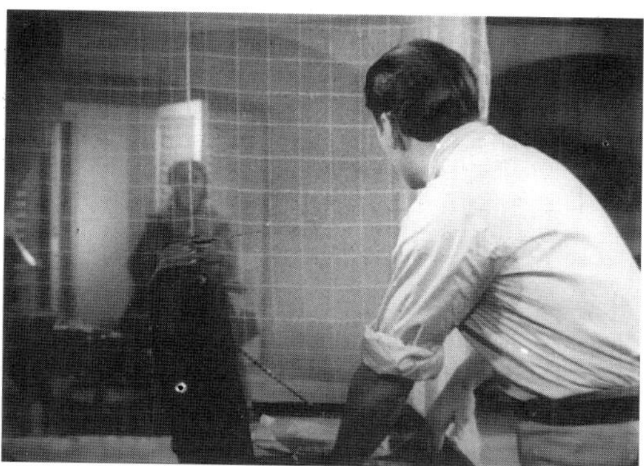

6.129 *The Charge of the Light Brigade.*

6.130 *The Charge of the Light Brigade.*

6.131 *The Charge of the Light Brigade.*

while the camera glides forward and to the right, making her the center of attention (Fig. 6.130). The shot ends with the two characters facing each other in profile (Fig. 6.131). Curtiz now begins to cover their conversation with shot/reverse-shot editing of shallow-focus closer views.

If this scene had been staged in a 1913 long take, Geoffrey's suitcase might well remain distractingly evident in the foreground for the duration of the shot, but Curtiz's diagonal pan takes it out of frame very easily. This more "open" approach to cinematic space, seen in many countries at the period, served as the basis of Jean Renoir's style. Instead of treating his 1930s work as a harbinger of Welles and Wyler, we might better view Renoir as a director who built a supple and distinctive style out of newly emerging 1930s staging tactics.

Renoir synthesizes and refines many devices available at his moment. Staging action in depth, he occasionally presents close front planes while avoiding the exaggerated foregrounds of Stroheim or Eisenstein. More commonly,

6.132 From across the courtyard, the little laundress is brought to the invalided boy in *The Crime of M. Lange* (1935).

Renoir prefers to sustain camera movement and figure movement within shots, even if that leads to surprisingly awkward compositions and jerky reframings. He guides the viewer in depth through apertures, rack focus, and centered distant planes (Fig. 6.132). He also multiplies the number of playing areas within the shot's space, counterweighting them by, say, putting a large foreground element out of focus and moving it slowly while endowing a distant figure with clarity and rapid movement (Fig. 3.10). All these choices serve to create the sense that his characters inhabit a vivacious, bustling world.

Instead of slavishly exploiting these techniques in every scene, Renoir typically alternates passages of standard continuity editing with sequences that explore many distinct sorts of depth. In *La Marseillaise* (1936) solemn long takes and measured tracking shots characterize the declining classes, whereas a more orthodox découpage and a freewheeling camera portray the revolutionaries. *La règle du jeu* presents an even more extreme range of stylistic alternatives. Renoir reserves cross-cutting and oddly geometrical shot/reverse-shot cutting for the early portions of the film, when the various plot lines are running in parallel in different locales. As romantic intrigues interweave in the Marquis's chateau, Renoir starts to employ mercurial depth staging, full of rapid panning movements and character bustle. The film's virtuosic party sequence displays rapid shifts from one line of action to another, usually facilitated by sound cues, a roving camera, characters twisting toward and away from us, and the use of doorways for aperture framing (Figs. 3.31–3.33). Here the choreographic density of 1910s fixed-camera *mise en scène* is recaptured in crowded tracking shots.

Remarkable as Renoir's accomplishments are, they drew upon tendencies already common in the 1930s. We can observe the same process at work when we look beyond Bazin's canon. For instance, Renoir's contemporary Kenji

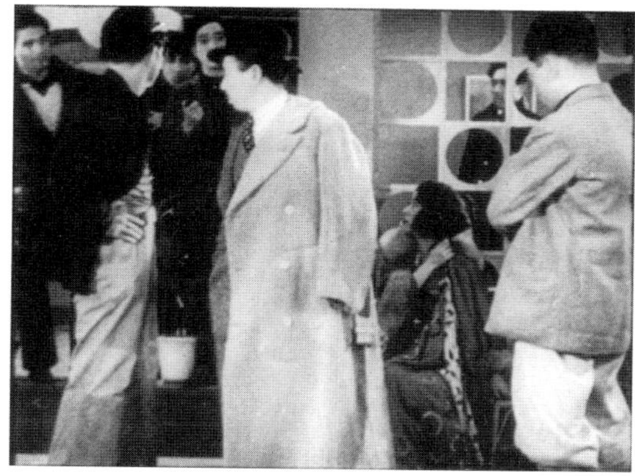

6.133 A game of visual hide-and-seek in Yasujiro Shimazu's *First Steps Ashore* (1932): The key reaction, that of the young man, is tucked into the northeast square.

6.134 A Toland-like foreground in *Naniwa Elegy* (1936).

Mizoguchi also extended the depth practices of the early sound era—and he did it well before those postwar films so admired by the young *Cahiers* critics. During the 1930s Mizoguchi's milieu encouraged deep staging, oblique compositions, and aperture framings. This trend probably owes a good deal to directors' desire to cite pictorial traditions that were considered "distinctively Japanese." In any event, these filmmakers' vigorous exploitation of honeycombed depth makes Wyler's long-distance phone booth in *The Best Years of Our Lives* (Fig. 3.23) look positively legible (Fig. 6.133). Mizoguchi distinguished his work by making current devices functional in fresh ways.

Apart from an occasional shot that is Wellesian well before Welles (Fig. 6.134), Mizoguchi's films of the 1930s and the early 1940s seldom rely on aggressive foregrounds. Instead, his images, dark or light, near or far, with or without camera movement, tend to strip the foregrounds of detail, set the nearest planes in the middle ground, and present only a few zones of narrative interest. The rest of the frame is taken up by walls, ceilings, or expanses of floor—empty areas whose diagonal vectors pick out the main points of attention. But then, almost perversely, Mizoguchi makes those points illegible in various ways. His early 1930s films occasionally present a shot that impedes our sight of characters, particularly of their faces. A scene sometimes arranges the figures so that camera distance, posture, lighting, and architectural features such as walls and doorways cooperate to create distant, opaque depth (Fig. 6.135).

In his work from 1936 onward, Mizoguchi seized upon the long take as a way to stretch and intensify the audience's concentration upon such highly impeded images. The long take permits him to exploit camera movements and to make the illegible action far more prominent. A climactic scene in *Naniwa*

6.135 Decentered and opaque depth in *The Downfall of Osen* (1935).

6.136 *Naniwa Elegy.*

6.137 *Naniwa Elegy.*

Elegy presents Ayako's shamefaced confession to Fujino as a series of retreats from the camera, so that much of the scene is played with both figures, seen in long shot, turned from the viewer (Fig. 6.136). When Ayako goes into the next room, instead of cutting in to a revelatory close-up Mizoguchi simply moves Fujino rearward to the doorway, cuts to a new angle, and starts Ayako's retreat all over again there—indeed, pushing her to the very farthest corner of the room (Fig. 6.137).[95]

This "dorsality" strategy, inverting the advance-to-the-camera schema directors had utilized since the very beginning of cinema, is a brilliant innovation. It focuses attention on Ayako's words, it powerfully expresses her sense of shame, and it creates suspense by hiding Fujino's reactions. And here the absence of character frontality is not merely a tantalizing moment of concealment that will give way to a nearer, clearer view. By comparison with Welles or Wyler, Mizoguchi puts his camera at exactly the wrong spot; the most informative vantage point would be 180 degrees opposite the point that the

6.138 A brooding foreground dominates a cluster of heads (*The Great Citizen*).

camera occupies. It is as if Mizoguchi anticipated and negated in advance the frontality and proximity of the foregrounds in *Citizen Kane* or *Best Years.*

Renoir and Mizoguchi are only two examples of the great resourcefulness we can find in 1930s depth staging. Even the relentlessly didactic cinema of Soviet Socialist Realism displays surprising ingenuity on this front. Ironically, the closest kin to that conception of depth which Bazin admired in Welles and Wyler are the Stalinist films he so despised.[96] Fig. 6.138 irresistibly recalls *Citizen Kane,* but it comes from Fridrikh Ermler's *The Great Citizen* (released in two parts, in 1938 and 1939), made well before Welles walked into RKO. It is worth pausing on Socialist Realist cinema, since some of its filmmakers explicitly discussed problems of depth staging, and it illustrates ways in which the problem of dynamizing dialogue scenes revised thinking about *mise en scène.*

As a young set designer Kuleshov had suggested that Russian directors sought to increase depth, either through exaggeratedly deep sets or by means of an "eye-catcher" *(dikovinka)* in the foreground, some piece of furniture that would provide a center of interest.[97] In the 1920s, when most commentators were preoccupied with montage, Kuleshov paid attention to *mise en scène* as well, elaborating the idea of the visual pyramid as a network projecting out from the lens. He argued that conceiving this as a gridwork of proportional units allowed the director to calculate all staging in advance.[98] Kuleshov understood that the optical pyramid was essentially a geometric projection system that could specify a shot's three-dimensional layout; his "metric spatial web" anticipates the grids used in computer-generated imagery today.

During the 1930s the cameraman Vladimir Nilsen set forth less stringent proposals. His book, *The Cinema as a Graphic Art,* maintained that "intra-shot dynamism," neglected during the 1920s montage craze, could benefit from staging in depth. Nilsen argues that the filmmaker can push key elements to the foreground or make an actor near the camera turn away to stress a distant item. He urges that emphasis and expressiveness be intensified by recessional staging ("foreshortening"), rack focus, and wide-angle lenses; his draft of a hypothetical sequence heightens tension by progressing from the soft, flattish space of a long lens to the perspectival disproportions of a 25mm one. Nilsen partially anticipates Bazin's dissection of Horace's heart attack in *The Little Foxes,* pointing out that movement in an out-of-focus background can deflect the eye from a focused but static foreground plane.[99]

Nilsen, who perished in Stalin's Terror of the late 1930s, took part in Eisenstein's courses at the film school VGIK, and many of his ideas were streamlined reworkings of his mentor's evolving theory of direction. Historians from the Standard Version onward have thought of Eisenstein's style principally in terms of editing, but from the late 1920s onward he was no less concerned—one might say obsessed—with staging in depth.

Eisenstein declared in 1929 that foreground/background interactions could create a form of "montage within the shot," and during the 1930s and 1940s he elaborated a theory of direction predicated on depth staging. He took *mise en scène* to be the initial organization of dramatic and emotional material; framing and editing would transform that into something characteristically cinematic. He taught that *mise en cadre,* or framing, combined with staging to create a continuous dynamism that heightened the drama. He also introduced the idea of "montage units," clusters of shots taken from approximately the same vantage point that would build to miniclimaxes in the course of a scene.[100]

Eisenstein believed that a shot's compositional contours lead the spectator's eye to points of interest, so he treated two-dimensional design as the foundation of three-dimensional *mise en scène.* Further, long before Bazin had elaborated his conception of the long take in depth, Eisenstein asked his students to depict the *Crime and Punishment* murder episode in a single shot using outrageously close foregrounds. His aborted projects of the 1930s—*Qué viva Mexico!, The Glass House,* and *Bezhin Meadow*—were all virtually mannerist exercises in deep staging and depth of field (Figs. 6.139, 6.140). Eisenstein taught his students to develop a scene as a thrust to the foreground, a process that would make the action seem to envelop the spectator.[101]

The writings of these Soviet filmmakers thus made explicit several schemas that had been developed for depth staging. Kuleshov was applying the 1910s notion of the truncated triangle to problems of performance in the late silent film. Nilsen sought to show how depth could serve expressive purposes. Eisenstein's staging precepts imaginatively extended the aggressive-foreground schemas of the 1920s and the movement-to-camera schema we have traced back as far as Lumière. Undoubtedly all these thinkers had some influence, but

6.139 The mourning that opens *Qué viva Mexico!*

6.140 From the banned *Bezhin Meadow:* The father has killed his son.

their ideas became diluted in mainstream practice. Most Soviet directors of the sound era gravitated toward a ponderous academic style that treated depth in a calculatedly overwhelming way.

Obliged by official policy to reject the extreme montage tactics of the silent era and to adopt a more Hollywoodian style, Soviet filmmakers of the 1930s often used long takes with moderate depth and camera movement (Fig. 6.123). But when directors were charged with glorifying the accomplishments of the Party and its leaders, this solemn style swelled to monumental proportions. In keeping with that "gigantomania" seen throughout high Stalinist culture, the new depth films aggrandized their subjects.[102] As Soviet directors cast off the abrasive discontinuities of Montage editing, they also surrendered the caricatural deformations of the wide-angle image. In a manner consistent with Socialist Realism's appropriation of avant-garde techniques, the satirically grotesque image was revised to amplify the heroic side of the stories told.[103]

Soviet Montage had been well suited to portraying mass movements sweeping through cities and continents. The new depth style could focus on individual characters while also inflating them and their enterprises. Within gigantic sets, towering figures play out momentous dramas of treachery and loyalty, sacrifice and betrayal. In *The Great Citizen,* a looming foreground at the dining table and two distant backgrounds stake out three playing areas; Ermler stages Maxim's visit as a symmetrical advance to and retreat from the camera, with editing punctuating emotional moments and revealing more deep space (Figs. 6.141–6.145).

The aggressive foregrounds of the Soviet directors have their counterparts in other national cinemas. Malraux's *Espoir* (1939) occasionally displays the same tendency (Fig. 3.1). In particular, the cinematographers and directors of

6.141 *The Great Citizen:* The old woman is at the table when Maxim enters in the right rear . . .

6.142 . . . and comes to the foreground for their conversation in medium shot.

6.143 At a key moment there is a cut to her in close-up.

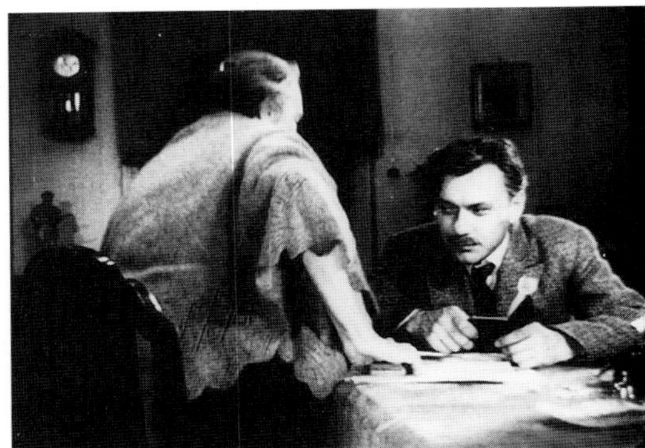

6.144 After a return to the medium shot of the two of them, there is a cut to another angle as the old woman rises. This shot serves to emphasize the depth veering off into the left rear.

6.145 She goes into the depths of the next room as they continue to speak.

Hollywood sought to master such effects. These efforts form the most proximate context for understanding the distinctive visual design of *Citizen Kane.*

Redefining Mise en Scène

Because any norm can be considered a bundle of options, we cannot say that there was an inexorable progress toward *Citizen Kane.* Several strategies of handling depth developed over the silent and early sound eras. One director might avoid staging in much depth, relying almost wholly upon a shallow playing space and selective focus. Another might reserve marked depth for conventional situations, such as views through doorways or windows or angles upon courtroom scenes (Fig. 6.146). During the late 1930s and early 1940s, many directors across the world pursued a third option, that of consistently exploiting greater depth. In Hollywood, concrete conditions, both individual and institutional, fostered this more acute deep staging and depth of field.[104]

During the early sound era, U.S. filmmaking moved almost completely indoors, where dialogue recording could be controlled for maximum audibility. The introduction of incandescent lighting and panchromatic film stock, along with a propensity for cameramen to use wider apertures for comfort in the studios, encouraged filmmakers to continue the fairly soft look of many silent films. Yet Hollywood also encouraged its workers to innovate, and during the 1930s many directors and cinematographers cultivated techniques for staging in greater and harder-edged depth.

Take just two examples. William Cameron Menzies, an art director and occasional director who would eventually win fame as production designer for *Gone with the Wind* (1939), developed a Gothic-Baroque style of set design. From the early 1920s onward, in designs for films of fantasy, mystery, and adventure, Menzies created atmospheric Expressionistic effects through deep compositions of almost comic-book exaggeration (Fig. 6.147). John Ford's films of the era explore depth in more sober ways. Sometimes with Toland as cinematographer, more often without, Ford mastered two-plane and three-plane compositions, often holding quite sharp focus throughout (Fig. 6.148). *Stagecoach* (Fig. 5.35) was supposedly the film that Welles studied most closely before making *Kane.*[105] Roger Leenhardt might have been less quick to cry "À bas Ford! Vive Wyler!" if he had recognized Ford's contributions to 1930s depth staging.

What encouraged this trend? Depth compositions still functioned within analytical editing, and their roles remained stable—to provide an establishing shot laying out the playing space, or to stress the simultaneity of two actions. Sound promoted the latter option, since the director could count on the viewer's attention shifting from speaker to speaker.[106] Vivid depth shots could

6.146 In *No Other Woman* (1933), the director puts the court stenographer in the foreground, plaintiff's counsel in frame center, and the brooding husband within the arch of a gooseneck lamp.

6.147 As Drummond looks down at the mysterious laboratory, a skewed window adds a touch of Expressionist depth (*Bulldog Drummond,* 1929).

6.148 *How Green Was My Valley* (1941): Huw and his father discuss his future as he overhears Bron telling of missing her dead husband.

also display virtuosity, a quality that had value within the craft culture of the studios. In addition, some cinematographers sought to distinguish themselves by posing technical problems and solving them in institutionally approved ways. A cameraman who could capture a significant range of focus would add importantly to the filmmaker's creative choices.

A drive to expand the array of stylistic options, and thus to distinguish one's own work, led many cinematographers to seek greater depth of field for interior filming. Gregg Toland was the most famous exponent of this strategy. Working with Ford and Wyler in the 1930s, Toland soon centered his energies on solving the problem of rendering depth. Probably he was spurred on by competition with other cameramen; as Gombrich remarks, the desire to surpass one's peers often prods artists to innovate.[107]

6.149 Zigzag three-plane depth arrangement in Wyler's *These Three* (1936), filmed by Toland.

6.150 *The Long Voyage Home* (1940): A close foreground yields a comparatively shallow playing space.

6.151 *Our Town* (1940): The wide-angle lens swells a humble New England kitchen.

6.152 A three-layer depth shot facilitated by the low angle (*The Maltese Falcon*).

Toland constantly experimented with depth, but like his colleagues he hit a limit imposed by current technical standards, most importantly the low light levels customary on sets. When Toland deepened the playing space, the foreground could be no closer than medium shot and often could not sustain focus (Fig. 6.149). At other times Toland strove for very aggressive foregrounds, but then there was noticeable distortion, focus fell off quickly, and the playing space could not be very deep (Fig. 6.150).

Toland was not alone in his efforts. In the early 1940s several American dramas displayed a penchant for depth staging and deep-focus imagery. *Our Town* (1940), directed by Sam Wood and designed by Menzies, turned Thornton Wilder's stripped-down play into an orgy of depth effects (Fig. 6.151). John Huston's *The Maltese Falcon* (1941) made daring use of multiple planes and wide-angle lenses (Fig. 6.152). At RKO Boris Ingster's *Stranger on the Third Floor* (1940) and William Dieterle's *The Devil and Daniel Webster* (aka

6.153 Kane finishes Leland's review; Welles types against back-projected footage of Joseph Cotten and Everett Sloane.

All That Money Can Buy, 1941) displayed brooding, sometimes expressionistically distorted depth. In these works and others, filmmakers strove for close foregrounds and quite distant backgrounds, usually at the cost of crisp focus in one or the other.

Kane, released in spring of 1941, represented a striking solution to this problem. Replacing incandescent illumination with the hard light of arc lamps (reintroduced in the mid-1930s for Technicolor) and using faster film stock and coated lenses with increased light-gathering power, Toland was able to generate shots with foregrounds in close-up and background planes very distant, all the while holding several planes in focus. As we have seen, he announced this as "pan-focus," a range of sharpness supposedly closer to that available to the eye.

What Toland did not acknowledge so freely was that many "pan-focus" shots were optical tricks, exploiting matte work, double exposure, and other special effects (Fig. 6.153).[108] Susan's famous suicide scene (Fig. 3.21), the lynchpin of Bazin's arguments about *Kane*'s depth, was an in-camera superimposition. The bottle and glass were filmed in sharp focus against a darkened background. Then the foreground was darkened, the entire set lit, and the film wound back in the camera. The scene was reshot with the lens refocused to show Susan in bed in the middle ground and Kane bursting through the door in the background. (Even so, Susan is still too close to be in crisp focus.) RKO's skilled effects department, which had put a leopard in a car with Cary Grant and Katharine Hepburn for *Bringing Up Baby* (1938), rigged many of the film's most impressive feats of *profondeur de champ.* Welles called his film a "big fake": "There were so many trick shots . . . full of hanging miniatures and glass shots and everything. There was very little [set] construction."[109]

Bazin believed that Welles's shots displayed a respect for recording an integral time and space within the continuum of phenomenal reality. In many of these shots, though, there was no coherent phenomenal reality to be recorded: the space we see is closer to the artificiality of an animated cartoon. Even so, with or without special effects, one consequence of this flamboyant imagery was to bring the quest for "pan-focus" to critical notice. What had been discussed in the pages of professional journals became the stuff of magazine picture spreads.[110] As the responses of Bazin and his contemporaries indicate, the press campaign for *Kane* made critics aware of a technique that had been a staple of filmmaking practice since the beginning.

Like other 1930s amplifications of the 1920s "biplanar" schema, *Kane*'s compositions spread several significant areas into depth (for example, Fig. 3.11). Just as important, *Kane* flaunted its innovations by uncoupling depth staging from camera movement and continuity editing. "Welles' technique of visual simplification," Toland explained, "might combine what would conventionally be made as two separate shots—a close-up and an insert—in a single, non-dollying shot."[111] Virtually no deep images in *Kane* used camera movement, often because even a pan would have spoiled the special effects. Although Toland's fixed long-take shots called attention to technique in a way that many film professionals found objectionable, the film's emphatic deep-focus look undoubtedly promoted the style.[112] Far from being a prototype of depth staging, *Kane* is an anomaly. If it had not been made, many Hollywood directors would have continued to combine occasional, moderate depth with cutting and camera movement. But *Kane* probably did more than any other film to persuade directors that inflated foregrounds and great depth of focus could intensify a scene's drama.

Toland's work after *Kane* would never rely on so many fixed single-shot scenes. In the films he shot for William Wyler, we see a very skilful director adapting Toland's innovations to the demands of more orthodox découpage. In Wyler's films before and after *Kane* (and with or without Toland), the director usually seeks not to create *tour de force* long takes with extremely close foregrounds but rather to treat deep space as part of a broader audiovisual pattern-making.

The Little Foxes, for instance, uses depth to conceal as well as to reveal: when Oscar overhears Birdie criticizing him, his face and shoulders are hidden by a curtain (Fig. 6.154). A parallel effect obtains during the scene of Horace's heart attack, when Wyler holds the staircase out of focus (Figs. 3.25–3.29).[113] *The Little Foxes* further exploits depth by unfolding Lillian Hellman's play across distinct acting spaces. As the drama intensifies, the arena of action gets pushed back through the parlor to the threshold and then into the hallway and up the staircase. Similarly, the breathtaking phone-booth shot of *The Best Years of Our Lives* (Fig. 3.23) has been prepared for by a series of earlier scenes in Butch's tavern that orient us to views

6.154 As Birdie prattles on, Oscar stands listening just outside the parlor, masked by a curtain.

6.155 *The Best Years of Our Lives:* Butch greets his nephew Homer in a setup that prefigures the famous telephone-booth shot (Fig. 3.23).

6.156 Later in the same scene, a setup that emphasizes the piano playing primes us for the shot that will eventually include the phone booth.

6.157 The scene of Fred and Al's confrontation establishes the phone booth in the tavern; this shot, which shows Homer arriving at the bar, is one of several showing Fred in the phone booth before we see the most famous setup (Fig. 3.23).

stretching down the bar (Fig. 6.155) and repeatedly establish Fred making the call, well before we arrive at the famous framing (Figs. 6.156, 6.157). It is partly this "priming" of the background area that allows Wyler to invert the traditional hierarchy of significance which favors the plane closest to the camera.

In addition, Wyler coordinates depth with cutting in order to stress parallels among the characters. In *The Little Foxes,* segregating a powerless character in depth becomes a dramatic motif (Figs. 6.158–6.160). During *Best Years'* wedding ceremony, a depth shot shows all three couples, paralleling marriages in the past, present, and future (Fig. 6.161). But then, while the minister recites Homer and Wilma's vows, the editing picks out Peggy and Fred, creating a

6.158 Early in *The Little Foxes* Birdie is shut out of the family's debates, and so Wyler puts her in the background (but near the center).

6.159 A cut in to Birdie while the others talk emphasizes her isolation while quietly stressing the hallway chair in the background; Zan will settle there in the climactic scene.

6.160 In an earlier scene, Birdie has predicted that her niece will become just like her. Here, at the climax, Regina spars with her rapacious brother in the central hall, while Zan sits behind them as Birdie had before, morose (and centered).

6.161 After this master shot of the wedding party, shots of Peggy and Fred punctuate the scene, accompanied by the recitation of the couple's vows.

virtual double wedding (Figs. 6.162, 6.163), crowned by a variant of the establishing shot that emphasizes the new couple (Fig. 6.164). We might consider this scene a riposte to the Standard Version critics who resisted talkies; here depth composition, editing, and dialogue create an integrated style suitable for the sound cinema.

Wyler did not regard a cut as violating the purity of the long take in depth; his 1940s work displays the advantages of integrating robust depth staging with orthodox analytical editing. Other U.S. directors adopted this strategy. Now that Toland had made bigger foregrounds possible, they could be adapted to normal purposes. As film speeds and lighting levels increased, both interiors and exteriors could be rendered with noticeable depth of field. And

6.162 From offscreen, Homer repeats: "For better, for worse; for richer, for poorer."

6.163 From offscreen, the minister says: "In sickness and in health, to love and to cherish till death us do part."

6.164 A reestablishing shot uses blockage of the foreground to single out the next couple to be formed.

6.165 Hollywood action director Samuel Fuller often uses depth compositions of a "Wellesian" cast in his gritty crime films (*Underworld USA,* 1961).

filmmakers realized that even if several characters were jammed into the frame on different planes, attention could be directed by cues of centering, lighting, frontality, and dialogue. All things being equal, the viewer was still likely to concentrate on the person who was talking, especially if the other players kept still and fastened their eyes on the speaker.

Selective focus on single figures in medium shots and close-ups was certainly not abandoned, but from the 1940s well into the 1960s, quite sharp-focus depth shots with close foregrounds became a common stylistic option for black-and-white dramas (Fig. 6.165). Like Welles in *Kane,* directors used matte shots and other special effects to conjure up deep images (Fig. 6.166)—a tactic that has continued into our era of computer-generated imagery (6.167). Close foregrounds became staples for decades in every filmmaking country,

6.166 Hitchcock employs a matte shot to create a very close foreground (*Stage Fright,* 1950).

6.167 Through digital compositing, two versions of one actor become elements of a depth array (*City of Lost Children,* Jeunet and Caro, 1995).

6.168 In Andrzej Munk's *The Man on the Tracks* (1956), a critique of socialist bureaucracy, aggressive foregrounds heroicize the engineer who is wrongly charged with malfeasance.

across Europe (Fig. 6.168) and into the Third World (Figs. 6.169–6.171). Olivier insisted on shooting *Hamlet* (1948) deep and crisp: "There I am in a great big head in the foreground, and she is right down at the other end of the stage and very sharp."[114] Sidney Lumet, who has claimed that lens length is the director's most fundamental camera choice, planned the scenes of *The Hill* (1965) to progress from 24mm to 21mm to 18mm lenses, intensifying the close-up foregrounds as the film unfolded.[115] In the same year, Bergman's very deep-focus *Persona* employed depth to convey the theme of psychological disintegration (Fig. 6.172).

Nearly all such shots achieved their effects within continuity editing patterns, not by means of static long takes as in *Kane.* Even Welles gave way: beyond an occasional deep-space long take (particularly in *Touch of Evil,* 1958,

6.169 In the Egyptian melodrama *This Was My Father's Crime* (1945), a birthday party for a dissipated young man is staged in robust depth.

6.170 Satayajit Ray, India's most famous director, cultivated a deep-focus look in his earliest films (*The World of Apu,* 1959).

6.171 The close foregrounds of Ruy Guerra's *Os Fuzis* (1964) portray the listless soldiers brought in to subdue a rebellious town.

6.172 Bergman utilizes deep focus from his earliest films onward, but in *Persona* it often creates floating, indeterminate spaces reminiscent of Dreyer's *La Passion de Jeanne d'Arc.*

and *Chimes at Midnight,* 1966), his late films rely on cutting while still exploiting grotesquely exaggerated depth.[116] He distinguished his late style by canted low angles, sinuous camera movements, and spasmodic cuts that are at times closer to Pudovkin than to Hollywood continuity principles. *Othello* (1952), for example, reminds us that very deep space and constructive editing are not incompatible (Figs. 6.173, 6.174).

Like Welles, several directors reworked depth norms to create individual styles. In France, Bresson's early features turned deep-focus close-ups into abstract images reminiscent of silent art cinema (Fig. 6.175), while Tati's long shots brought foreground objects or bystanders into quietly enigmatic relations with gags occurring elsewhere in the frame (Fig. 6.176). In Mexico, Emilio Fernández won fame for a wide-angle depth that recasts imagery from

6.173 With Desdemona at his side, Othello congratulates his men for defeating the Turks.

6.174 In the absence of an establishing shot, the foreground helmets suggest a continuous space linking the trumpeters to the previous shot.

6.175 Robes and wimples create masses of black, white, and gray, which Bresson deploys in depth (*Les anges du péché*, 1943).

6.176 In *Les vacances de M. Hulot* (1953), card players in the foreground are oblivious to Hulot's unique Ping-Pong style.

Eisenstein, Hollywood, and earlier Mexican cinema (Fig. 6.177).[117] Even avant-gardists like Maya Deren and Stan Brakhage explored the new schema (Fig. 6.178).

The depth that Bazin praised in such Neorealist efforts as *La terra trema* (Fig. 3.30) was thus a worldwide trend, running across the ideological spectrum. At Mosfilm and Lenfilm, directors seemed to compete to push depth of field to new limits, creating grandiose effects that would inflate the Great Helmsmen and lesser heroes of the people (Fig. 6.179). Even after Stalin's death, such wide-angle imagery pervaded films coming out of the USSR (Fig. 6.180). Here as elsewhere, bulging foregrounds had become a standard way in which shots were thought to achieve dramatic force. Much as Welles distinguished his later work by exaggerating the depth schemas he had popularized, Eisenstein took academic depth staging to outlandish extremes

6.177 The idealistic schoolteacher Rosaura unpacks her gift—a pistol—as her tormenter, Don Regino, walks off in the distance (*Rio Escondido,* 1947).

6.178 Lenses on 16mm amateur cameras allowed for even greater depth of field than did those for 35mm, a fact exploited by experimentalist Stan Brakhage in *Reflections on Black* (1955).

6.179 Patiently packing their fixed frames with looming, frontally placed figures, Soviet directors often created very aggressive foregrounds, as here in *The Vow* (Mikhail Chiaureli, 1946).

6.180 Though innovative in other respects, Mikhail Kalatozov's *The Cranes Are Flying* (1957) remains committed to the monumentalizing wide-angle compositions canonized in the 1940s.

in *Ivan the Terrible;* in Part II (1946/1958), Baroque foregrounds become climaxes of movement boldly punching out at the viewer (Fig. 6.181).[118]

As well as being absorbed into editing constructions, the new depth compositions could be blended with the lengthy tracking shots normalized in the 1930s. (Oddly enough, Renoir did not take the lead; one of the great mysteries of stylistic history is why, when robust depth and free-ranging tracking shots were coming into use everywhere, the director of *La règle du jeu* gave up both for a more placid, editing-based style.) As in the 1930s, filmmakers found ways to integrate closer foregrounds and camera movements in order to direct the viewer's attention smoothly and efficiently. Two instances will illustrate.

6.181 *Ivan the Terrible:* Pyotr, the avenging angel, hurls himself toward the camera to leave, while Ivan yanks him back by his robe.

Preminger's *Fallen Angel* (1945): A small-town waitress has been murdered, and a retired New York policeman takes it on himself to investigate. He drags along a drifter who has been trying to seduce the woman. They stride into her apartment (Fig. 6.182), and Preminger's camera follows them around the cramped parlor as they move from witnesses and suspects (Figs. 6.183, 6.184) to the local police chief (Fig. 6.185), then back to the witnesses (Figs. 6.186–6.188), before the detective finally ushers the lubricious salesman out for the third degree (Figs. 6.189, 6.190). More crisply focused and virtuosic than Curtiz's brief set-up in *The Charge of the Light Brigade* (Figs. 6.128–6.131), Preminger's four-and-a-half-minute *plan séquence* needs no shot/reverse shot. Characters take turns assuming an over-the-shoulder stance with utter naturalness, and the tightly confined camera movements present constantly changing foregrounds that hold or deflect our attention.

Ten years later, a scene from Antonioni's *Le amiche* (1955): Rosetta has just agreed to break off her affair with the painter Lorenzo so that his wife, Nene, may keep him. After a quarrel with an architect in a café, Lorenzo storms out. Rosetta looks after him as her friend Clelia leaves frame right (Fig. 6.191). Cut to a shot showing Franco the architect in the foreground, nursing his wound. Clelia enters and pauses at the door, while Nene in the middle-ground center shamefacedly hesitates to follow the man she supposedly loves (Fig. 6.192). As Rosetta comes into the shot from the left, the camera arcs slightly leftward (Fig. 6.193) to lose Franco. Clelia shifts leftward one step, like Asta Nielsen's fiancé in *Afgrunden,* allowing Rosetta in frame center to turn accusingly to Nene just as Clelia's reaction becomes visible (Fig. 6.194). After Clelia comes forward two more steps, Rosetta is framed between her two friends and a path is cleared, enabling her to rush out after Lorenzo (Fig. 6.195). As in many

6.182 *Fallen Angel:* Eric, on left, has followed Inspector Judd into the room; the despairing Pop, who adored the dead waitress, sits in the window seat.

6.183 Judd strolls rightward to question Stella's neighbor and then to Atkins, framing the woman in the background.

6.186 Judd turns back to the suspects, and the camera follows him . . .

6.187 . . . as he returns to the suspects . . .

6.190 . . . past the chief and into the next room.

6.184 Eric leaves Judd as the inspector comes forward, camera tracking back . . .

6.185 . . . to stop before the police chief, who tells him that the killer dropped a watch.

6.188 . . . dismisses Pop . . .

6.189 . . . and leads Atkins away . . .

Antonioni scenes, it is as if Renoir's camera choreography in the party episode of *La règle du jeu* had been slowed down for a sober scrutiny of characters' lingering reactions to an event.

What is *mise en scène?* asked Alexandre Astruc in 1959, summing up the decade-long preoccupation of his *Cahiers* confrères. The sequences by Preminger and Antonioni suggest an answer. In many national cinemas between 1930 and 1960, *mise en scène* was a demonstration of pacing and poise, a sustained choreography of vivid foregrounds, apposite and neatly timed background action, precisely synchronized camera movements, and discreet découpage, the whole leading the viewer gracefully and unobtrusively from one point of interest to another. No wonder that Astruc spoke of the director writing fluently with the camera-pen. Still, these close foregrounds and subtle camera movements simplified or elaborated long-standing strategies of balance and decentering and recentering, blocking and revealing, aperture fram-

6.191 *Le amiche:* In the trattoria.

6.192 *Le amiche.*

6.193 *Le amiche.*

6.194 *Le amiche.*

6.195 *Le amiche.*

ing and diagonal thrusts to the foreground—in short, schemas elaborated since the very first years of cinema.

Expanding the Image and Compressing Depth

Wouldn't great *mise en scène,* like great painting, be flat, hinting at depth through slits rather than gaps?

Jacques Rivette

The close foreground juxtaposed to a fairly sharp middle or background plane remained a major staging schema after the 1940s. In black-and-white and nonanamorphic filming, it remained a common stylistic option. But as studio film production increased the use of color and introduced anamorphic widescreen formats, filmmakers were handed new problems. Those problems, and the solutions that were developed, remain with us in the films released today.

Color filming became dominant around the world in the 1960s and 1970s, but it posed difficulties for the representation of depth.[119] Color film stocks were, and still are, much less sensitive to light than the "fastest" black-and-white emulsions. Color could not therefore sustain as great a depth of field as black-and-white afforded. In 1948 one cinematographer acknowledged that he had to shoot Technicolor at f/2, a very wide aperture that precluded deep focus.[120] Even with improvements in sensitivity, most color stocks could produce sharply focused depth only if the light levels were raised steeply. Hence the tendency for deep-focus color shots to be almost exclusively exteriors, where sunlight permitted stopping down the aperture. In the studio, cinematographers usually chose not to create great depth of field for color shooting, especially if the director wanted a scene to contain significant patches of shadow.

Obliged to use significantly less depth of field, directors working in color tended to stage the action more shallowly. It was as if the "pan-focus" trend of the 1940s discouraged directors from using shots that put significant information out of focus, as Borzage had in *Lazybones.* Rack focus was still an option, but with color even that technique could not be employed over a very deep playing space. More generally, many deep-focus directors reverted to a safer, long-distance staging and shallow-focus close-ups (Fig. 6.196).

The trend was intensified by the emergence of widescreen formats. These set filmmakers a new task. Anamorphic lenses yielded "wide-angle" coverage but no compensating depth of field. The standard 50mm CinemaScope lens provided 46 degrees of horizontal view, widening the apex of the visual triangle about as much as a 30mm lens had in the normal format. But anamorphic lenses have effectively longer focal lengths than nonanamorphic ones, so they provide less depth of field. Moreover, the most prestigious widescreen films were made in color, and color required more light.

As a result, CinemaScope initially forced filmmakers back to the knees- and waist-up foreground figures of the 1910s. In that era, however, sharp

6.196 Anthony Mann, proponent of deep space par excellence in the 1940s, turns shallow in color for *The Glenn Miller Story* (1954).

focus had extended very far back. Now, even quite near middle-ground planes passed drastically out of focus. Shooting the second CinemaScope release, *How to Marry a Millionaire* (1953), the cinematographer complained that the biggest problem was "proper staging for depth of focus."[121] Shooting at f/2.8, a common aperture setting in the early years of widescreen, and setting focus at ten feet, the cinematographer could obtain a well-focused playing space starting eight feet from the camera and halting a mere four feet beyond that. To secure sharp focus on background objects, the frontmost focal plane would have to be set further back, often at least fifteen feet from the lens. In shooting a facial close-up at standard diaphragm settings, the CinemaScope filmmaker had an acceptably focused playing zone only two feet deep. This constraint ruled out big foregrounds with well-focused rear action, the biplanar "deep-focus" image popular in current nonanamorphic cinematography.

Other 1950s widescreen processes were no more flexible. The 65mm Todd-AO, used for *Oklahoma!* (1955), could cover up to 128 degrees horizontally, but it yielded very little depth of field. The wider the film gauge, in fact, the less depth of field it provided.

By the mid-1950s, cinematographers working with color widescreen processes had largely resigned themselves to out-of-focus backgrounds on close-ups and medium shots.[122] The technical improvements introduced by the Panavision company at the end of the decade increased sharpness somewhat, partly through the introduction of lenses of shorter focal length.[123] Yet today's cinematographers still struggle to obtain crisp rendition of deep planes and close foregrounds in anamorphic formats (Fig. 6.197). Director John Cameron remarks of contemporary Panavision work: "I look at these films and see half the movie's out of focus."[124]

6.197 The drastically limited focus of anamorphic color films: As in Fig. 6.196, the protagonist's eyes constitute the only plane in focus (*Speed,* 1994).

The problem was vividly apparent as early as *A Star Is Born* (1954). George Cukor discovered that the playing zone of CinemaScope was quite shallow. "If someone were too much upstage," he complained, "they would be out of focus."[125] Cukor tried for a modicum of depth staging, even though middle-ground characters become notably indistinct when moving only a step forward or back (Figs. 6.198, 6.199).

The simplest solution was to stage action laterally, reverting somewhat to pre-1910 planimetric principles. CinemaScope, Elia Kazan remarked, called for a more "relaxed" arrangement of figures—"more like a stage—more 'across.'"[126] "The greatest kick I get," Darryl F. Zanuck confessed in a memo, "is when one person talks across the room to another person and when both of them are in the scene [shot] and near enough to be seen without getting a head closeup."[127] Many early CinemaScope films subscribe to this "clothes-line" staging principle (Fig. 6.200).

Cukor lost patience. "I don't know how the hell to direct people in a row. Nobody stands in rows."[128] Yet Jacques Rivette, fresh from screenings of the first CinemaScope film, *The Robe* (1953), suggested in the pages of *Cahiers du cinéma* that lateral staging might actually be the culmination of the history of *mise en scène.* He argued that acute depth staging had been haunted by disproportion, imbalance, and an inclination to the Baroque; confrontations became confused and imprecise when staged in several oblique planes. By contrast, all great directors, from Griffith and Murnau to Renoir and Lang, harbored an urge toward horizontality, spreading out characters and blank spaces in "a perfect perpendicular in relation to the spectator's look."[129] CinemaScope, Rivette argued, would finally make cinema an art of *mise en scène,* not only by minimizing cutting but also through achieving a classical, friezelike serenity.

6.198 *A Star Is Born:* Vicky does a comic dance for Norman, and when she starts out both are in focus.

6.199 But after a few steps forward and a slight camera track backward, he has gone out of focus.

6.200 Lateral staging in one of the earliest CinemaScope productions, *How to Marry a Millionaire.*

6.201 *Bigger than Life.*

6.202 *Bigger than Life.*

This line of argument enabled the Young Turks of *Cahiers* to differentiate their views from the *profondeur de champ* aesthetic of Bazin's generation. But the point goes beyond polemic. What Rivette had in mind is, I think, exemplified by a scene from *Bigger than Life* (1956). Ed, about to leave the hospital, thanks his doctors for the treatment. The pink bottle of pills (out of which the rest of the drama will issue) glows quietly on the far right table at the foot of the bed until, as Ed is about to leave, a doctor reaches over and fetches it (Figs. 6.201, 6.202). For Susan's aborted suicide in *Kane,* Welles thrusts the bottle and glass to us (Fig. 3.21), but here Nicholas Ray strings out all the relevant elements of the scene horizontally, adding the bottle of pills as an end-stop, the point of the shot. Such a diagrammatic spread would be the hallmark of that "age of *metteurs en scène*" which Rivette prophesied.

6.203 *The Cobweb:* As Stevie visits Mrs. Rinehart's office, the initial framing allows us to see her in the foreground, him in the doorway, and people in the craft shop behind them.

Directors who pull our attention across the horizontal expanse still rely upon cues explored in the early silent film—lines of force, glances, counter-weighted composition. One tactic more specific to CinemaScope was the effort to block off sides of the image with props or patches of darkness. Another was to use what Kazan called "inner frames," which broke the picture format into chunks that were more readily grasped.[130]

Depth staging did not altogether vanish with the wide screen. If the director was willing to set the frontmost plane quite far off, an intriguing play with crisp backgrounds could be maintained in CinemaScope. The cabin scenes of Preminger's *River of No Return* (1954) make brilliant use of aperture framing and background details.[131] In *The Cobweb* (1955), a triumph of ingenious horizontal staging, Minnelli employs foreground/background manipulations that recall strategies of the 1910s (Figs. 6.203–6.205). Moreover, directors occasionally continued to tuck moderately significant elements into out-of-focus planes, not worrying about perfect legibility.

Closer foregrounds could be achieved under certain conditions. Brightly sunlit exteriors posed less of a problem for depth of field in color and wide-screen; in the same year as *A Star Is Born, Rebel without a Cause* (1954) could create striking big-foreground compositions in its scene outside the Los Angeles planetarium (Fig. 6.206). For similar reasons, black-and-white anamorphic processes permitted somewhat greater depth (Fig. 6.207). Occasionally directors also used split-field diopters. These are lens attachments that allow the filmmaker to focus on a very close foreground plane on one side of the image and a distant plane on the other edge, while losing focus on objects between those two zones (Figs. 6.208, 6.209). Finally, rack focus always remained an option. In extensive use since the 1930s, it had proved handy in the early days

6.204 After Stevie has come forward and begun to ask about her past, his body blocks the doorway, and nothing distracts from his dialogue.

6.205 For the bulk of the scene, as Stevie tells of his past, he moves aside to allow a clear view of Sue centered in the background; Sue will eventually fall in love with him.

of CinemaScope (Figs. 6.198, 6.199), to adjust for camera movement or changes of character position.

If widescreen ratios of the 1950s pressed directors to stage in less robust depth than they had in nonanamorphic shots, another technical innovation reinforced this tendency. In the opening shot of *A Hard Day's Night* (1963; Fig. 6.210), three of the Beatles flee a horde of screaming fans. They run not diagonally toward the front, as in the earliest chase films, but straight along the lens axis. Moreover, the space between the figures appears very compressed; bodies lack volume, and the crowd seems very close to catching the boys. Perhaps most oddly, as the figures run toward us they do not get significantly larger.

6.206 An almost academically symmetrical shot from Nicholas Ray's *Rebel without a Cause.*

6.207 Depth of field in the Senate chambers, with heads dotted about the screen (*Advise and Consent,* Otto Preminger, 1962).

These anomalies are created by a lens of very long focal length. This so-called telephoto lens furnishes a "flatter" image, as if we were watching the action through binoculars or a telescope. The lens "squeezes" space by subtracting some familiar cues for volume, but the shot still represents depth because it retains other cues—overlap, kinetic shear, familiar size of figures, systematic (if very gradual) diminution of figures with distance, loss of definition on faraway planes.

When *A Hard Day's Night* was made, a common telephoto lens might be 100mm, 150mm, or 250mm; today directors frequently employ telephoto lenses of 400mm or more. Unlike the wide-angle lenses exploited by cine-

6.208 Split-field diopter work in *King of Kings* (1961).

6.209 Brian DePalma flaunted the use of diopters in his anamorphic films of the 1970s and 1980s (*Blow-Out,* 1981).

matographers since the 1910s and made famous by Toland, telephoto lenses radically narrow the angle at the apex of the optical pyramid. In nonanamorphic formats they yield as little as one or two degrees of horizontal coverage. With such lenses it is not feasible to spread several figures in a zigzagging depth array. A figure in foreground medium shot will fill most of the frame. Just as markedly, the long lens shrinks depth of field. At twenty feet from the subject, a 150mm telephoto typically yields a sharply focused playing area just three feet deep, while a 400mm lens at fifty feet will provide, under normal shooting conditions, a well-focused zone of only sixteen inches. "Blocking with long lenses," remarks one director, "forces actors to stop on millimeter-sharp cue-marks."[132] When filming motion to or from the lens,

6.210 *A Hard Day's Night:* The opening image, filmed with a long lens.

like that in our *Hard Day's Night* example, the camera operator must "follow focus" constantly.

Long lenses have been used since the 1910s, chiefly for reportage and exploration. During the 1920s they were commonly employed to shoot close-ups of stars; their flattening and blurring proved compatible with the fashion for a soft look. Telephoto lenses might also film explosions, chases, and stunts at a safe distance. When sound arrived, long lenses were put to use in multiple-camera shooting, with results we have already seen (Fig. 6.122).

It is possible that the 1950s films of Kurosawa spurred directors to exploit the long lens; he experimented with multiple-camera shooting in the battle scenes of *The Seven Samurai* (1954) and in the drama *I Live in Fear* (1955; Fig. 6.211).[133] Another factor that popularized the device was the increased use of the "zoom" lens, which allows the filmmaker to alter focal length from a wide-angle setting of 25mm or so to a telephoto setting of 250mm or more. Moreover, the filmmaker can vary focal length while shooting, thus creating that recognizable effect of "zooming in" on a detail (that is, magnifying and flattening it as a telephoto does) or "zooming back" from it (that is, demagnifying it and giving the space more volume).[134]

The zoom lens was available in rudimentary form at the end of the 1920s, and over the next two decades, directors occasionally zoomed during filming, often to enlarge a detail for a shock effect.[135] In the 1940s the lens was improved for television and used for covering sports events. As filmmakers began to shoot on location more frequently during the 1950s and 1960s, the zoom proved very handy. By setting the lens at the extreme telephoto range, cinematographers could shoot from a great distance, allowing actors to mingle with crowds while still keeping attention on the main figure via centering, frontality, and focus. That cliché of television news—the telephoto shot of citizens on

6.211 The long lens observes a family gathered to determine the sanity of their patriarch (*I Live in Fear*).

6.212 István Szabó's *The Age of Daydreaming* (1966): The hero adrift among the urban masses.

the street, jammed together and stalking to and from the camera—has its source in early 1960s films aiming at greater naturalism (Fig. 6.212).

Shooting with a long lens could be comparatively simple and cheap, requiring uncomplicated lighting and staging. The new gadget was hurriedly embraced by the many "Young Cinemas" that sprang up in the 1960s. Soon long lenses and zooms became staples of shooting in the studio as well as on location (Figs. 6.213–6.215). Crowd scenes, such as the party in Milos Forman's *Fireman's Ball* (1967), could play "in the round" and be filmed from many points outside the action, with long lenses supplying shot/reverse-shot setups. Zooms while shooting, common throughout *A Hard Day's Night* and other films of the early 1960s, could dynamize a sequence. Ng See-Yuen, director of Hong Kong martial-arts films, claims to have innovated the use of the rhythmic zoom-out to intensify fight scenes: "When it comes to the fist, the 50mm lens shot lacks impact."[136]

Comolli argued that the long lens yields a "non-Renaissance" perspectival code, but he never explained why such a lens became commonplace in Hollywood, bastion of bourgeois ideology. In fact, commercial directors competed to flaunt their virtuosity with the new device. An early example is John Frankenheimer's *The Train* (1964), with its audacious 10-to-1 zooms. Francis Ford Coppola's *The Conversation* (1973) opens with a relentless and oddly untargeted zoom shot, while Antonioni's *The Passenger* (1975) concludes with an elaborate zoom during which the camera passes through a barred window. After *Kane*, most directors assumed that the *plan séquence* would be a wide-angle shot in aggressive depth, as in our excerpt from *Fallen Angel* (Figs. 6.182–6.190). By 1967, though, a single-take scene in *Bonnie and Clyde* used a 400mm lens to squash its figures into drifting apparitions (Fig. 6.216).[137]

Since the telephoto image tends to turn surroundings into ribbons and figures into cardboard cutouts, it offers possibilities for pictorial abstraction

6.213 *Das Maedchen Rosemarie* (Rolf Thiele, 1958): As the prostitute enters the hotel lobby, the camera slowly zooms back.

6.214 Panning leftward with her, the zoom ends to show the clerk in the foreground.

6.215 He turns to notice Rosemarie, and the camera zooms in on his back.

6.216 Mr. Moss walks outside the ice cream parlor after betraying Bonnie and Clyde.

(Fig. 2.217). Filmmakers quickly realized that the lens not only flattens planes but also blurs and brightens them. When he began to use the 250mm lens habitually, Andrejz Wajda noted: "The background, dotted with secondary elements, loses its aggressiveness. The image softens, the medley of colors melts into flat tints of color . . . The foreground, however, is transformed into a colored haze that seems to float."[138] Probably Claude Lelouche's *Un homme et une femme* (1966) popularized the romantic connotations of misty blobs of color swarming around the characters (Fig. 6.218). Wajda and his cameraman called the fuzzy foreground shapes "lelouches." Antonioni had already put lelouches to rigorous use in *Red Desert* (1964), an antilyrical melodrama that thematically contrasts the thin, dingy planes of an industrial wasteland with the sparkling depths of an imaginary island.

The long lens, combined with zooming or rack focus, offered various staging options. A director could simply let the lens yield the standard range of

6.217 Under a Hong Kong bridge, the boy and girl of Clara Law's *Autumn Moon* (1992) become part of the pattern created by rippling water and the telephoto lens.

6.218 Bunches of pink and red flowers, out of focus, surround the heroine of *Un homme et une femme.*

6.219 In *Doña Herlinda and Her Son* (1986), two mothers converse in the foreground while their sons flirt in the distance, all framed in a doorway by the long lens.

shot scales from long shot to close-up, and cut the images together according to conventional schemes. Or the director might squeeze significant foreground and background actions within the telephoto's narrow angle of view (Fig. 6.219). Alternatively, many directors began covering scenes in long takes structured by panning and zooming. From a wide-angle view of the setting the filmmaker might zoom in and pan with the actors as they played out the scene; still tighter zooms would be reserved for moments of crucial drama. This "searching and revealing" approach, allowing the camera to scan the action and overtly pick out key details, became a significant norm of the 1960s and 1970s.[139] It was elaborated by such newcomers as Aleksandar Petrović (*I Even Met Happy Gypsies,* 1967) and Robert Altman (*M*A*S*H,* 1970) as well as by veterans like Visconti, Fellini, Bergman, and most notably Rossellini (Figs.

6.220 *The Rise to Power of Louis XIV* (1966): A long lens picks out the doctors entering the bedroom of the dying Cardinal Mazarin.

6.221 As they move leftward the camera zooms back and pans . . .

6.222 . . . to end in a full establishing shot of them approaching the Cardinal's bed.

6.220–6.222). Alan Rudolph (*The Moderns,* 1988) and Patrice Chéreau (*La reine Margot,* 1994) have continued to exploit this option.

Although the pan-and-zoom approach sometimes became identified with low-budget shooting, it offered some fresh staging opportunities. New camera viewfinders allowed the cinematographer to see exactly what the camera was filming, so directors could combine zooming with very precise rack focus or tracking movements. In *The Long Goodbye* (1973), Altman's obsessive forward zooms are mitigated by a rightward drift of the camera, which seems to be edging uneasily away from the action even as the lens is centering and enlarging it. A comparable technique appears in Claude Chabrol's *Que la bête meure* (1969), but here the sidelong camera movement allows foreground foliage to become a lelouche masking out one character at a climactic moment of dialogue (Figs. 6.223–6.225). Miklós Jancsó's films combine zooms, pans, and elaborate lateral tracking with dancelike character movement (choreographed

6.223 In *Que la bête meure* Charles sits in the park with Philippe, the son of the odious man he plans to kill.

6.224 As the camera arcs leftward and zooms in on them, Philippe asks, "Why don't you kill the bastard?"

6.225 Branches and leaves glide by; the boy says that he himself would do it.

in circles or spirals) to make space plastically malleable, squashed or stretched on a moment's notice. When Jancsó packs a great many characters into the frame, he often revives the slit-staging principles of the 1910s, combining slight figure movement with the minute changes of scale or focus made possible by the long lens (Figs. 6.226–6.228).[140]

Even in such idiosyncratic shots, the new techniques of the 1960s served to guide the spectator in picking up salient information. The telephoto image offers a great deal of help about what to watch. Within what is often a very planimetric space, the standard principles—centering, frontality, foreground action, and focus—persist. In fact many of these new devices offer even more guidance than was common earlier. The deep-focus norms of the 1940s aimed at keeping two or more planes before the viewer at once. In contrast, by racking focus or by zooming while panning, the filmmaker gives us each patch of the shot at the exact moment desired, making it difficult or impossible to see action on other planes. Thus even an array of unmoving figures may be unfolded gradually; layers of depth in the shot are revealed at the pace determined by the filmmaker.

6.226 In *The Confrontation* (1969) a constant, scarcely noticeable rack focus picks characters out of a packed frame . . .

6.227 . . . by conjuring up new and unexpected layers of space . . .

6.228 . . . through which schemas of frontality and centering still guide the eye.

6.229 Vacationers arrive at Amity Island in telephoto shots (*Jaws*).

Eclecticism and Archaism

Most postwar directors, modernist or mainstream, cannot be distinguished by their commitment to a distinctive aesthetic of depth. Bresson, Tati, and a few others developed idiosyncratic personal styles, but Bergman, Fellini, Antonioni, Buñuel, Satayajit Ray, and other renowned masters of the "art cinema" did not repudiate prevailing depth norms. Neither did most of the younger generation, including the various New Waves in Europe and the Third World. Virtually all of *Cahiers'* canonized "modern" directors shot with deep focus in the 1940s and 1950s and shifted to telephoto lenses and zooms during the 1960s and 1970s. They quickly adapted the new techniques to their aims of more self-consciously realistic, reflexive, and ambiguous storytelling.

In spite of the technical and stylistic innovations, distinct options remained available. Even when telephoto compositions were the rage, wide-angle depth continued to be important as well. During the 1960s and 1970s, some Hollywood directors emphasized one look over another, but most mixed options quite freely. We can watch the process at work in two key films.

Steven Spielberg's *Jaws* (1975) reserves certain stylistic options for specific sorts of situations. By 1975 the anamorphic format could yield telephoto shots, and Spielberg occasionally uses the long lens in standardized ways (Fig. 6.229). But throughout the film Spielberg relies primarily on wide-angle staging in depth. Indoors, with low light levels, deep-space stagings are presented through rack focus. Outdoors, with the reflected light available from ocean and sand, Spielberg can lay out a low-angle long take reminiscent of the 1940s (Figs. 6.230–6.235). As if paying homage to this tradition, when the shark expert Hooper snaps a photo on the *Orca* he asks Sheriff Brody to step out on the prow: "I need to have something in the foreground to give it some scale."

6.230 Hooper and Brody argue with the Mayor in front of the defaced billboard.

6.231 Hooper retreats to the rear, letting the Mayor and Brody's quarrel occupy the front line.

6.232 Coming forward, Hooper tells Brody that he will leave town.

6.233 As the Mayor moves still farther into the foreground, steepening the camera angle, Brody pursues Hooper into the distance to persuade him to stay . . .

6.234 . . . before the two men come forward, blocking out the billboard in a final effort to convince the Mayor.

6.235 Hooper reminds the Mayor of the shark's proportions, in a blocked arrangement that highlights the threat captured in the drawing. (Compare Fig. 6.230.)

6.236 *The Godfather:* The viewer is assaulted as Carlo helplessly kicks through the windshield.

6.237 Like most exterior scenes in *The Godfather,* the wedding is dominated by telephoto images.

Coppola tries for a somewhat different mix of depth options in *The Godfather* (1972). Although at least once a wide-angle lens dynamizes a burst of violence (Fig. 6.236), most outdoor scenes, whether involving ensembles or couples, are filmed with quite long lenses (Fig. 6.237). In interiors Coppola stages in more depth, but the dark sets and the middle-range lenses yield very shallow planes of focus. Like Borzage, he does not hesitate to put key background elements out of focus (Fig. 6.238). Such layering allows depth patterns to serve as motifs. When Michael comes forward to fetch a cigarette from a pack sitting innocuously on the blotter (Figs. 6.239, 6.240), he starts to take his father's place at the desk, the seat of family power established in the opening shot (Fig. 6.241).

Since the early 1970s a few directors have favored a narrower set of visual devices. Tony Scott (*The Last Boy Scout,* 1991; *Crimson Tide,* 1995) prefers very long lenses that blur nearly every plane, even in close-ups (a softening that he heightens by smoke and atmospheric haze). But overt, hyperbolic zooms have become relatively rare in Hollywood and elsewhere; they are perhaps most often used to build tension by slowly enlarging characters in a shot/reverse-shot exchange. Mainstream directors now storyboard most sequences, and this practice may encourage them to elaborate the individual composition in greater depth than in the 1970s. Since *Jaws* Spielberg has relied heavily on depth staging, shooting with short focal-length lenses and exploiting Panavision's "slant-focus" lens to create aggressive foregrounds in color (Fig. 6.242).[141] In 1980s and 1990s films, looming foregrounds often impart caricatural distortion, as in Spike Lee's *Do The Right Thing* (1989; Fig. 6.243) and in the films of Joel and Ethan Coen (*Raising Arizona,* 1987; *The*

6.238 As the Don congratulates Johnny Fontaine for being a good father, Sonny in the background reacts to the Don's oblique criticism of his promiscuity.

6.239 During the Corleone brothers' battle plans, a prominent empty foreground . . .

6.240 . . . brings Michael forward to his father's desk, prefiguring his ascent in the family business.

6.241 At his desk Don Vito Corleone becomes a shadowy foreground shape in the opening shot of *The Godfather.*

Hudsucker Proxy, 1994).[142] Scorsese predicts that wider television formats will favor "the use of a close-up in the foreground and a figure in the background, whether it is all in focus or it is slightly off on one character or another—it all emphasizes things in a different way."[143]

Scorsese's mention of focus that is "slightly off" points to one of the most common compromises in depth staging to emerge since the 1970s. Directors have faced the need to work with the restricted depth of field presented by color film stock and anamorphic lenses. They have also accepted fairly low light levels on sets for the sake of a wider range of shadows and greater comfort for the players. Yet producers and directors also want actors' faces in close foregrounds, chiefly because most films will eventually be shown on the television screen. At

6.242 Vigorous 1940s-style depth composition in *Jurassic Park* (1993).

6.243 *Do the Right Thing:* Grotesque distortion of head and hand thanks to the wide-angle lens.

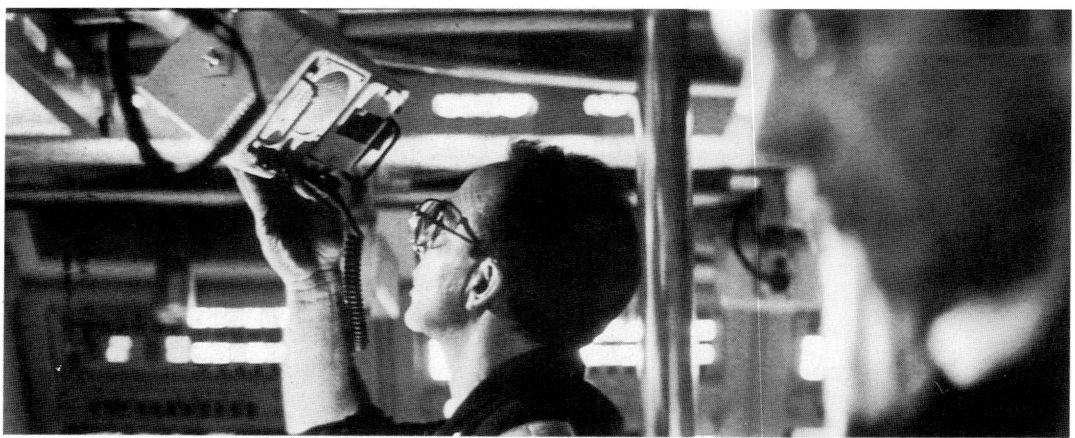

6.244 *The Hunt for Red October:* One shot presents three zones of depth successively. First we see a technician in the left middle ground, while the captain stands out of focus in the right foreground.

the same time, clothesline staging in the early CinemaScope manner is generally to be avoided, so some degree of deep staging is considered desirable. One synthetic solution has been to present widescreen depth by panning from one close-up foreground to another, reinforcing the points of interest by racking focus. In *The Hunt for Red October* (1990), this tactic allows John McTiernan to evoke many layers of space within confined submarine settings, while the abrupt changes of composition and framing set up a strong dramatic pulse (Figs. 6.244–6.246).[144] Such sequences remind us again that editing and depth staging are not absolute alternatives; in McTiernan's deep-space shots, each swivel of the camera and snap of focus has the abruptness of a cut.

6.245 The camera pans right and racks focus to another technician in the background, who speaks his line.

6.246 The camera now pans left, racking focus to a tight close-up of the captain in the foreground. The rapid changes of image underscore the dialogue somewhat as cuts to each man would.

This sort of compromise between deep space and selective focus typifies mainstream style today. The eclecticism introduced at the end of the 1960s and canonized in such films as *Jaws* and *The Godfather* seems to have become the dominant tendency of popular filmmaking around the world. Long lenses for picturesque landscapes, for traffic and urban crowds, for stunts, for chases, for point-of-view shots of distant events, for inserted close-ups of hands and other details; wide-angle lenses for interior dialogue scenes, staged in moderate depth and often with racking focus; camera movements that plunge into crowds and arc around central elements to establish depth; everything held

6.247 In *Fong Sai-Yuk* (Yuen Kwai, 1993), editing, depth staging, and selective focus cooperate to indicate layers of space: The hero's father calls out from the foreground . . .

6.248 . . . before a cut enlarges the hero as he turns to the villain in the rear plane.

together by rapid cutting—if there is a current professional norm of 35mm commercial film style around the world, this synthesis is probably it (Figs. 6.247, 6.248).

The precise grasp of dramatic detail that Kuleshov found available in cinema has been enhanced by filmmakers' discovery of new means of guiding the eye. Apparently producers believe that shallow-focused, rapidly cut close-ups make a film more video-friendly, and so these shots have become prevalent. At the limit, these simplified images may seem to pull us through a strict itinerary. Vilmos Zsigmond claims: "When a shot is only going to be on screen for three seconds that composition and lighting has to be very good to allow the viewer's eye to see what you want them to. There's no time to decide what is important, so you have to direct their eye, *force* it."[145] Does this mean that the programming of vision which Burch attributed to the Institutional Mode of Representation has reached its culmination? Before we decide, we ought to remember how often historians in our research tradition have envisioned their moment as the climax of tendencies they have picked out. In 1926, when most films utilized very rapid cutting, who would have predicted that only a few years later a more leisurely *profondeur de champ* staging would have spread scenic elements out, letting composition and dialogue shape the viewer's attention? As I write this, a prominent manufacturer announces a lens that holds focus from the lens surface to infinity. If the device proves feasible, might it lead enterprising directors to revive longer takes and shots of greater density?[146]

Part of what I've been calling the problem of the present is that current developments become fully intelligible only in hindsight. The tendency toward rapid cutting over the last two decades, coupled with revised schemas of staging in depth, may be part of a larger dynamic of change and stability not yet evident to us. A technique does not rise and fall, reach fruition or decay. There are only prevalent and secondary norms, preferred and unlikely options, rival alternatives, provisional syntheses, overlapping tendencies, factors

6.249 *One from the Heart:* The foreground action takes place miles away from the background one, but depth staging makes them adjacent.

promoting both stability and change. We find innovations and replications, consolidations and revisions. Loose schemas may be tightened up; long-lived ones may be streamlined, roughened, or combined. All these stylistic phenomena are driven by human aims and ingenuity. Within institutional imperatives, agents understand their purposes and problems in certain ways, settling on ends and seeking alternate means of achieving them. There are no laws of stylistic history, no grand narratives unfolding according to a single principle; but that does not prevent us from proposing explanations for long-term, middle-level trends of continuity and change.

Who, for instance, could have predicted that Coppola, don of the New Hollywood, would have explored depth compositions that openly falsified narrative space? In *One from the Heart* (1982), Hank has broken up with Franny, but Coppola violates realism to keep them bound together, making far-flung locales adjacent through depth compositions. When Franny tries to call Hank from her friend's apartment, an impossible framing reveals her in medium shot and Hank in depth, even though he is across town in a distant apartment (Fig. 6.249). Similarly, in *Tucker: The Man and His Dream* (1988), the hero's wife standing in the foreground receives a call from him, standing at a phone booth in the background. If Welles revised schemas developed by Ford and others, Coppola here revises Welles.

Such experiments remind us that one way to seem new is to be old, and some of the most original handlings of depth over the last thirty years appear to be deliberately archaic strategies. We can conclude this sketch of the history of staging by looking at two striking secondary norms that reject contemporary eclecticism.

The first tendency might be called the mug-shot option. Here the action is staged frontally or in profile, with clothesline figure arrangement and a camera

6.250 A mug-shot prototype (*All the Vermeers in New York,* Jon Jost, 1990).

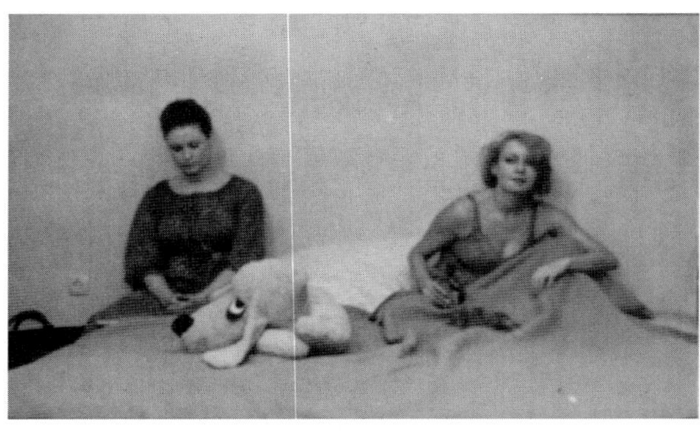

6.251 An early instance of what would become a common schema (*Everything for Sale*).

6.252 The small-town loafers in *Katzelmacher.*

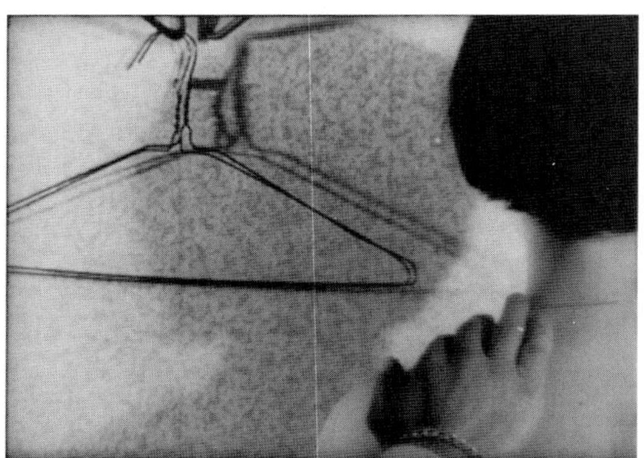

6.253 The abstracted perpendicular shot in Godard's *Vivre sa vie* (1962).

position at ninety degrees to the background (Fig. 6.250). This new tableau image probably constitutes a revision of the flattened perspectives and spread-out staging schemas that became salient with widescreen formats and the long lens. It is a short step from our *Hard Day's Night* opening (Fig. 6.210) and the flat-on establishing shot in Wajda's *Everything for Sale* (1968; Fig. 6.251) to the tableaux of the wastrels in Fassbinder's *Katzelmacher* (1969; Fig. 6.252). Certainly, too, Godard's "blackboard" compositions (Fig. 6.253) provided another prototype that could be modified in this direction.

While signalling the resolutely nonmainstream film, the perpendicular schema suits a dedramatized narrative. Resisting camera movement and scaling down figure action, such shots can create a scene of stillness, even serenity. Abbas Kiarostami seems to be gently mocking this minimalism in *Through the Olive Trees* (1994), in which the angular depth and offscreen

6.254 In *Through the Olive Trees,* Kiarostami stages his film-within-a-film as static perpendicular long takes that the amateur actors, overwhelmed by real-life passions, keep spoiling.

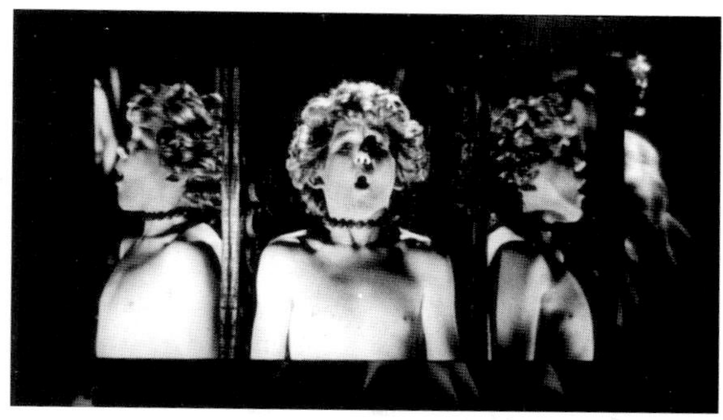

6.255 Puck plays out three variants of the mug-shot composition in *Prospero's Books* (1991).

space activated in most shots throw into relief the static, planimetric images in the film that the characters are shooting (Fig. 6.254). When stripped down to a few starkly outlined elements, the mug-shot staging can repudiate the busy *mise en scène* of Hollywood in the name of simplicity; when crammed with detail, as a shot by Greenaway often is, it scatters the major points of interest (Fig. 6.255).

The perpendicular composition can be used sporadically, as an establishing shot or as a moment of punctuated stasis (Fig. 6.256). As such it has became something of a cliché since the 1970s. But it can also serve as a break with the naturalistic tenor of the action, and so it is tailored to the art cinema's questioning of narrative reality (Fig. 6.257). Or it can generate the visual design of an entire film. Georgy Shengelaya's *Pirosmani* (1971), the biography of a Georgian painter, relies almost wholly upon the mug-shot principle (Fig. 1.11), as do Serge Paradzhanov's pseudofolktales (Fig. 6.258). Terence Davies builds *Distant Voices, Still Lives* (1988) out of such frontal and profiled shots, creating "family portraits" over years of anguish (Fig. 6.259).

During the 1970s and 1980s, norms of faster cutting and more fluid, close-up camera movement made complex staging within the shot a rare choice. In a sense, the mug-shot solution reinforced that tendency, reducing staging to an even more simplified lateral arrangement than was seen in the early widescreen films. The most intriguing recent efforts toward sustained depth staging are to be found in the work of a handful of directors who repudiate both rapid editing and the flatness of perpendicular staging. They pursue an alternative that in some ways recalls the dynamics of *Ingeborg Holm* and other films of the 1910s.

Here is an example. Spiros, an elderly socialist, returns to Greece after decades of exile. He visits a village where he once lived, and his wife and son follow him. She goes into a cottage to fetch him. We can see her open the gate

6.256 *Buffet froid* (Bernard Blier, 1979): The perpendicular shot as a dramatic punctuation.

6.257 A stylized theatrical grouping of the hero and SS men interrupts the action of *Your Unknown Brother* (Ulrich Weiss, 1981).

6.258 *The Legend of Suram Fortress* (1984): An echo of folk-art design in the rectilinear tableau.

6.259 Brother and sister confront each other before the photograph of their dead father (*Distant Voices, Still Lives*).

(Fig. 6.260), but instead of cutting or tracking in to their meeting, the director keeps the camera planted obstinately at a distance. Beyond the spindly gate, we can barely see the old couple reunite (Fig. 6.261). Slowly they make their way back toward us (Fig. 6.262).

This scene, from Theo Angelopoulos' *Voyage to Cythera* (1984), harks back to the 1910s: the retreat and advance from the camera, the drama of blockage and revelation, the tactic of placing distant elements in the central zone to compensate for their shrinking. But few directors of an earlier era would have built up to the salient event by moving the action into the distance. In 1984, moreover, the indirect handling gains even greater force: Angelopoulos refuses the cuts that would underline the important elements. As with Bazin's example of Horace's heart attack in the out-of-focus background, we strain to see the key story event, all the while knowing that the filmmaker could have brought it closer.

6.260 *Voyage to Cythera.*

6.261 *Voyage to Cythera.*

6.262 *Voyage to Cythera.*

Angelopoulos has declared himself influenced by Antonioni, and there are traces of the elder director in this "dedramatized" shot; but Antonioni's 1950s films depend on closer foregrounds, and he seldom employs such slowly paced long takes. Angelopoulos perpetuates the 1970s tendency toward lengthy shots framed at a distance and subordinating the actor to landscape or decor.[147] Sometimes he has recourse to perpendicular staging. But just as often the camera angle is oblique, and the result is a composition with far more recessional depth than we find in the mug-shot option. Like Mizoguchi during the 1930s, Angelopoulos turns the drama from us, pushes it into the background, slips it into niches of the set, or slices it off by walls or doorways.

The strategy of oblique staging can be manifested in closer views as well. Instead of persisting in his often-imitated posterlike shots, Godard's 1980s films complicate our grasp of a scene by handling continuity découpage elliptically and by staging action in oblique, often opaque ways. In *Je vous salue Marie* (1985), Joseph reaches to touch Marie's belly; but Godard sets a chair

6.263 Aperture framing reminiscent of the 1910s (Fig. 6.38) in Godard's *Je vous salue Marie.*

6.264 *India Song:* With the parlor dominated by the immense mirror, Duras splits her scene into recessive slabs of space recalling those of *Love Everlasting* (Fig. 6.33).

in the foreground, out of focus but squarely commanding the center, so that Joseph's upright palm hovers within a slot (Fig. 6.263).

Like the perpendicular option, the recessional strategy can be exploited in widely different circumstances. Marguerite Duras makes extensive use of it in the parlor shots of *India Song* (1975; Fig. 6.264). More recently, the Taiwanese director Hou Hsiao-Hsien has explored a variety of oblique staging devices. Filming in takes that average half a minute or more, he often stages outdoor action with deep perspectival space and sharp focus but setting the foreground plane quite far off. As a consequence, entire scenes may be played out in views more distant than many directors' establishing shots. Hou puts the foreground somewhat closer in interiors, but then he complicates the staging by zigzagging the action along aisles and apertures (Fig. 6.265).

These examples make it doubtful that alternative manners of handling depth are wholly explicable in terms of an overarching "resistance to bourgeois ideology." For filmmakers have bent these two staging schemas to significantly different purposes. Paradzhanov's tableaux echo folk painting and, in presenting mysterious, often fanciful ceremonies, celebrate unofficial spirituality in non-Russian republics. Davies' family-portrait compositions in *Distant Voices* intensify the painful story of a family ruled by a demented father. Angelopoulos tells us that he developed his long-shot technique under the influence of Brecht, whereas Hou Hsiao-Hsien insists that he keeps his distance so as not to frighten his inexperienced actors. "It has nothing to do with resisting Hollywood conventions or consciously trying to evolve a 'Chinese' style."[148] As a pair of international norms, the perpendicular option and the oblique strategy answer to the transcultural and nonideological purpose of directing or deflecting attention within the image, while also serving specific formal and expressive ends in particular films.

6.265 *Dust in the Wind:* The hero's apartment shot in a long take, with faces blocking and revealing a central doorway. (Compare Figs. 6.54, 6.55.)

Once more, problem links to solution and thence to new problems. The mug-shot schema and the oblique recessional schema tap well-established cues for guiding our attention, but in ways that differentiate the filmmakers' work from the mainstream. This is an important benefit for directors working in independent or "art" cinema. At the same time, managing these schemas poses the filmmaker new challenges. How to maintain interest through a static planimetric image? How to concentrate attention within a distant, obliquely framed array? Artists in any medium will compete with their predecessors and peers by setting themselves tasks that call out for novel, even virtuosic, solutions. Once the problem is conquered, however, the solution becomes available to everyone. In recent years, as these two stylistic approaches have become fairly familiar, many of their difficulties have been mastered. To make a mark, some ambitious filmmakers of the future may find engaging ways in which to revise or reject these schemas.[149]

Even if other avenues get explored, however, successful solutions can stretch our sense of the possibilities of cinema. In the age of Steadicam, tracking characters strolling through a locale is almost criminally easy. The filmmakers I have just discussed remind us of the cost of such flash and fluency. Speed hurtles past nuance; exhilaration in sheer motion misses minute gestures. In modifying the schemas available from earlier periods, Angelopoulos, Davies, Hou, and other directors remind us that the viewer can be deeply engaged by exceptionally exact perceptions of bodies shifting delicately through space and light before a fixed camera.

I have told a story of continuity and change across a hundred years of cinema. But it has not been a grand tour. I have offered a middle-level history of a single technique, taken as one strand in a network of stylistic processes. Someone could undertake a much finer-grained history of this technique, or indeed of any stretch within the century I have surveyed. I would expect that such an enterprise would refine and correct my account. Note, though, that just by expanding my purview I have not proposed anything monolithic. I have sketched out competing alternatives, conflicting demands, divergences, detours, and unexpected returns. Nor has my narrative reified a split between high art and popular art; our specimens have been both canonized masterworks and marginal, sometimes forgotten films.

This middle-level enterprise has cut across accepted period boundaries. If we are concentrating on staging and its corollary problems of directing attention, we may not need to distinguish between the "cinema of attractions" and what followed. The men who staged the Lumières' short films had to direct the viewer's eye, and that obligation persisted into the era of more elaborate storytelling. Likewise, *Citizen Kane* starts to seem less a watershed or a "dialectical step forward in film language" than a revision of schemas that circulated in many countries during the 1920s and 1930s.

My research questions, focusing on the elaboration of norms, have led me to stress continuity. The lesson of this is quite general. Modernism's promoters asked us to expect constant turnover, virtually seasonal breakthroughs in style. In most artworks, however, novel devices of style or structure or theme stand out against a backdrop of norm-abiding processes. Most films will be bound to tradition in more ways than not; we should find many more stylistic replications and revisions than rejections. Especially in a mass medium, we ought to expect replication and minor modifications, not thoroughgoing repudiation. We must always be alert for innovation, but students of style will more often encounter stability and gradual change.

One surprising consequence of an emphasis on continuity is to rehabilitate the idea of progress. A tradition can set goals that artists can collectively and systematically strive to meet. For some stretches of time, filmmakers can focus on overcoming shared difficulties—staging complex actions in long shot during the 1910s, directing attention within the widescreen format. Recognizing this process does not pledge us to canonizing particular works simply because they present successful solutions to particular problems. (For my money, *The Birth of a Nation* is a great film and *Red and White Roses* is a good one, even though the latter poses and solves more intricate staging problems.) Nor does a belief in focused and short-span progress, agents' purposeful attempts to fit means to ends, commit us to a teleology arching across the history of the medium. The problem/solution model simply proposes that along one dimension or another artists can enrich the body of techniques they inherit.

Where does middle-level history leave "top-down" historiography? Before I answer, let us acknowledge exactly what questions we are trying to answer. Certain questions about film's technology or its social significance or economic practices do not require us to talk about style at all. Many matters of reception or cultural effects do not hinge on details of staging or fine points of editing. But when our questions center upon the look and sound of films, style cannot be ignored.

In tracing one course of stylistic events, the changing and constant norms of depth staging, we have seen this strand in our network tie in with others. The history of depth staging intersects with histories of technology (lenses, film stock, camera carriages, lighting equipment) and of production practice (decisions about efficiency in the U.S. studios of the 1910s, a proclivity for low-budget location shooting in the 1960s). The historical questions we ask will lead us outside the films to neighboring causal domains that we hypothesize to be pertinent.

Undoubtedly culture and ideology play important roles as well. At the least, they often set a task. Longer running times, synchronized-sound movies, and widescreen technology arose in response to extrastylistic demands, from the social milieu and production companies' conception of how to hold or expand a market. And certainly culture can constrain the range of particular solutions to problems. Censorship is one obvious example. So too is the way in which Stalinist "gigantomania" or Japan's self-conscious celebration of distinctive traditions appears to have shaped filmmakers' stylistic decisions. Cinematic style is not a closed world of films and technical devices. One advantage of the problem/solution model is that it presses our explanations to account for the concrete decisions of individuals acting within institutions. Those decisions, like any human action, are open to influence from an indefinitely large array of social factors.

Nonetheless, cultural and ideological factors are often molded, deflected, or weighted by norms, those prevailing clusters of available schemas, the inherited problems and solutions. Once feature-length films, sound, color, and widescreen became obligatory, any pervasive impression of reality or any effect of modernity that we might postulate still could not determine the finer-grained choices that filmmakers made. Craft traditions and problem-solving logic intervened to test competing stylistic means. Ideology or culture cannot prepare every detail in advance, and style is a matter of details. The filmmaker, like Ferrand in *La nuit américaine,* must always reply to hundreds of fine-grained questions to which culture or ideology offers no ready-made answer.

Our case study allows us go farther and float a more unfashionable suggestion. Particular cultural forms probably do not shape every film technique we can discern. Some stylistic factors will be *cross*-cultural, trading on the biological or psychological or social factors shared among filmmakers and their audiences. A movie is a bundle of appeals, some narrow, some fairly broad, and some universal.[150] Movies are intelligible across barriers of time and nation, and this intelligibility requires zones of transcultural convergence.[151]

The historian ought therefore to expect some stylistic problems to be cross-cultural too. Guiding the viewer's attention constitutes a challenge that any narrative filmmaker anywhere must face. Not every stylistic problem will be on every filmmaker's agenda, but it is perfectly reasonable to expect that some will crop up in many places.

This case study could not have been undertaken outside the ambit of the research tradition plotted in this book. My depth-staging history is a response to the Basic Story, as well as to the canon, the periods, and the explanations supplied by the three research programs and the revisionist developments of the last twenty years. The conceptual frameworks developed by Brasillach and Bardèche, Bazin, and Burch have been recast by later historians, in somewhat the way that filmmakers have revised what they have inherited from their predecessors. Which is to say there is an interplay of schema and revision not only in film history but also in film historiography.

Such considerations ought to help dissolve theorists' doubts about the intellectual virtues of stylistic history. Writers under the sway of the doctrines of Post-Structuralism and postmodernism have too quickly embraced an easy skepticism about the validity of historical narratives, the solidity of evidence, even the significance of human agency. From our perspective, we can see this reaction as the Problem of the Present in yet another guise: How are we to write a history that incorporates our sense of contemporary experience?

At this point it is useful to recall that both Standard Version historians and Bazin were trumped by stylistic changes that did not fulfill their broad scenarios. One lesson of these research programs is that we should try not to act as if history stops with us. For centuries each generation has felt that it lived in a special time, the culmination of all that came before. This "presentism" has been a recurring theme through the history of the arts. We have been told that the orchestra was exhausted as a musical resource, that the novel was dead, that figurative painting had reached a blind alley, that theater no longer spoke to its moment. Aristotle, Pliny, Vasari, Hegel, and many modernists have all taken their present as an end of historical development: works would continue to be produced, but significant aesthetic change had ceased. All of these great thinkers were wrong. It is likely that the postmodernists are too. I know that it seems we are radically different. When music videos mimic famous experimental films it is tempting to believe that an era has ended.[152] Yet, although history is invariably written from the standpoint of the present, to use moods of the moment as coordinates for plotting epochal change will incline us to treat our world as the climax, crisis, or aftermath of all that has gone before.

A good cure for Post- pessimism is to acknowledge the intellectual gains we have made. Stylistic history of film produces worthwhile knowledge that is available no other way. It traffics in truth claims and it captures realities. There are people who can look at a film and say with good accuracy when and where it was made. This simple fact suggests that there is something real and rich to be learned about movies. Admittedly, the rewards of stylistic history come hard. It is never likely to be as popular a vein of film scholarship as criticism or theory. But its difficulty helps make it deeply interesting. Unlike most interpretive criticism or top-down theorizing, this enterprise keeps you guessing. You never know your conclusions in advance.

The historiography of style is one of the strongest justifications for film studies as a humanistic discipline. Historians of style have produced substantive knowledge and invigorating ideas. Through schema and revision, conjecture and correction, they have forged an honorable tradition of scholarly research. They have taught us to pay attention to qualities that make movies engaging. Above all, they have started to make the history of the twentieth century's most influential art intelligible as a creative human endeavor.

NOTES

1. THE WAY MOVIES LOOK

Studies of film historiography particularly relevant to this book are Robert C. Allen and Douglas Gomery, *Film History: Theory and Practice* (New York: Random House, 1985); and Paolo Cherchi Usai, *Burning Passions: An Introduction to the Study of Silent Cinema,* trans. Elizabeth Sansone (London: British Film Institute, 1994). Articles on the subject are collected in *Les cahiers de la Cinémathèque* no. 10–11 (Summer–Autumn 1973); *Cinématographe* no. 60 (September 1980); Jacques Aumont, André Gaudreault, and Michel Marie, eds., *Histoire du cinéma: Nouvelles approches* (Paris: Publications de la Sorbonne, 1989); and *Film History* 6, no. 1 (Spring 1994). See also Kristin Thompson and David Bordwell, *Film History: An Introduction* (New York: McGraw-Hill, 1994), pp. xxv–xlii.

1. An example of this criticism can be found in Patrice Petro, "Feminism and Film History," *Camera Obscura* no. 22 (January 1990): 9–26.

2. See Allen and Gomery, *Film History: Theory and Practice,* pp. 67–76.

3. I try to inventory these in *Making Meaning: Inference and Rhetoric in the Interpretation of Cinema* (Cambridge: Harvard University Press, 1989).

4. For a discussion of the relations between research traditions and research programs, see Larry Laudan, *Progress and Its Problems: Towards a Theory of Scientific Growth* (Berkeley: University of California Press, 1977), chap. 3.

5. Early examples are Francesco Pasinetti, *Storia del cinema dalle origini a oggi* (Rome: Bianco e Nero, 1939); and Ove Brusendorff, *Filmen: Dens navne og historie,* 3 vols. (Copenhagen: Universal-Forlaget, 1939–1940).

6. This problem is discussed briefly by a roundtable of scholars in Daan Hertogs and Nico de Klerk, eds., *Nonfiction from the Teens: The 1994 Amsterdam Workshop* (Amsterdam: Netherlands Film Museum, 1994), pp. 32–35, 64.

7. See, for example, Rick Altman, ed., *Sound Theory Sound Practice* (New York: Routledge, 1992); Michel Chion, *Audio-Vision,* trans. Claudia Gorbman (New York: Columbia University Press, 1994); Kathryn Kalinak, *Settling the Score: Music and the Classical Hollywood Film* (Madison: University of Wisconsin Press, 1992); Royal S. Brown, *Overtones and Undertones: Reading Film Music* (Berkeley: University of California Press, 1994).

The period of film history considered in this chapter is surveyed in Kristin Thompson and David Bordwell, *Film History: An Introduction* (New York: McGraw-Hill, 1994), chaps. 1–9.

On French film culture of the post–World War I era, see Richard Abel, ed., *French Film Theory and Criticism, 1907–1939: A History/Anthology* (Princeton: Princeton University Press, 1988). See also Vincent Pinel, *Introduction au ciné-club: Histoire, théorie et pratique du ciné-club en France* (Paris: Editions Ouvrières, 1964); and Georges Sadoul, "Les ciné-clubs en France et dans le monde," *Synthèses* no. 2 (1947): 155–161. German film culture and film theory are surveyed in Sabine Hake, *The Cinema's Third Machine: Writing on Film in Germany, 1907–1933* (Lincoln: University of Nebraska Press, 1993).

Myron Lounsbury's *The Origins of American Film Criticism: 1909–1939* (New York: Arno Press, 1973) provides a fine analysis of American writing about film before World War II. Two useful anthologies are Stanley Kauffmann and Bruce Henstell, eds., *American Film Criticism: From the Beginnings to Citizen Kane* (New York: Liveright, 1972); and Stanley Hochman, ed., *From Quasimodo to Scarlett O'Hara: A National Board of Review Anthology, 1920–1940* (New York: Ungar, 1982). In addition, there is the indispensible George C. Pratt collection, *Spellbound in Darkness: A History of the Silent Film* (Greenwich, Conn.: New York Graphic Society, 1973). For discussions of this tradition, see Myron O. Lounsbury, "'The Gathered Light': History, Criticism, and *The Rise of the American Film*," *Quarterly Review of Film Studies* 5, no. 1 (Winter 1980): 49–85; and Robert C. Allen and Douglas Gomery, *Film History: Theory and Practice* (New York: Random House, 1985), pp. 51–62.

Janet Staiger discusses the creation of the repertoire of classics in "The Politics of Film Canons," *Cinema Journal* 24, no. 3 (Spring 1985): 4–23.

The literature on the development of modernism is enormous. A thoughtful overview is Christopher Butler, *Early Modernism: Literature, Music and Painting in Europe 1900–1916* (Oxford: Oxford University Press, 1994). Robert Hughes's *The Shock of the New* (New York: Knopf, 1981) is an incisive popular survey. *Peinture cinéma peinture* (Paris: Hazan, 1989), a stunning exhibition catalogue, contains important essays on the relations between film and modernism in the visual arts.

On the history of film archives see Penelope Houston, *Keepers of the Frame: The Film Archives* (London: British Film Institute, 1994); and Raymond Borde, *Les cinémathèques* (Lausanne: L'Age d'Homme, 1983). More specific studies are Anthony Slide, *Nitrate Won't Wait: Film Preservation in the United States* (Jefferson, N.C.: McFarland, 1992); Ivan Butler, *To Encourage the Art of the Film: The Story of the British Film Institute* (London: Hale, 1971); Anne Head, ed., *A True Love for Cinema: Jacques Ledoux, 1921–1988* (The Hague: Universitaire Pers Rotterdam, 1988); and "Jacques Ledoux, L'éclaireur," special issue of *La revue belge du cinéma* no. 40 (November 1995). The history of MOMA's Film Department is traced by Russell Lynes in *Good Old Modern: An Intimate Portrait of the Museum of Modern Art* (New York: Atheneum, 1973) and by Mary Lea Bandy and Eileen Bowser in "Film," in *The Museum of Modern Art, New York: The History and the Collection* (New York: Abrams, 1984), pp. 527–530. See also John E. Abbott and Iris Barry, "An Outline of a Project for Founding the Film Library of the Museum of Modern Art," *Film History* 7, no. 3 (1995): 325–335. A major contemporary statement of the film archive's mission is Catherine A. Surowiec, ed.,

The Lumière Project: The European Film Archives at the Crossroads (Paris: Projecto Lumière, 1996).

On Henri Langlois see Richard Roud, *A Passion for Films: Henri Langlois and the Cinémathèque Française* (New York: Viking, 1983); and Georges P. Langlois and Glenn Myrent, *Henri Langlois: Premier citoyen du cinéma* (Paris: Denoël, 1986). Langlois's own writings, gathered in *Trois cents ans de cinéma* (Paris: Cahiers du Cinéma, 1986), rely upon the Basic Story and, in somewhat skeletal form, invoke the Standard Version's explanations.

On Gilbert Seldes, see Michael Kammen's biography *The Lively Arts: Gilbert Seldes and the Transformation of Cultural Criticism in the United States* (New York: Oxford University Press, 1996), particularly chap. 6. A useful introduction to Robert Brasillach's career is William R. Tucker, *The Fascist Ego: A Political Biography of Robert Brasillach* (Berkeley: University of California Press, 1975). Three revealing 1930 essays by Brasillach on sound cinema have been reprinted in "Cinéma par Robert Brasillach," *Cahiers de la Cinémathèque* no. 10–11 (Summer–Fall 1973): 85–89. On the political context of the Bardèche/Brasillach *Histoire,* see Alice Yaeger Kaplan, *Reproductions of Banality: Fascism, Literature, and French Intellectual Life* (Minneapolis: University of Minnesota Press, 1986).

Georges Sadoul was probably the most methodologically self-conscious of Standard Version historians. He contributed to the Encyclopédie de la Pléiade volume *L'histoire et ses méthodes,* ed. Charles Samaran (Paris: Gallimard, 1961): "Photographie et cinématographie," pp. 771–782; "Cinémathèques et photothèques," pp. 1167–78; and "Témoignages photographiques et cinématographiques," pp. 1390–1410. See also his posthumously published 1964 lecture "Matériaux, méthodes et problèmes de l'histoire du cinéma," *La nouvelle critique* no. 228 (October–November 1971): 65–75.

Some of the most vocal proponents of the Basic Story and the Standard Version have been unabashed fans of the silent screen. Examples are Edward Wagenknecht, *The Movies in the Age of Innocence* (Norman: University of Oklahoma Press, 1961); and James Card, *Seductive Cinema: The Art of Silent Film* (New York: Knopf, 1994), in which one finds such claims as "There has never been a great film without close-ups" (p. 22). Connoisseurship can also create fresh appraisals and divergences from orthodoxy, as in William K. Everson's *American Silent Film* (New York: Oxford University Press, 1978).

For a defense of the Standard Version against charges that it is teleological, see Jean Mitry, "De quelques problèmes d'histoire et d'esthétique du cinéma," *Cahiers de la Cinémathèque* no. 10–11 (Summer–Autumn 1973): 112–141. Mitry took up some of these themes again in "L'ancien et le nouveau," in *Histoire du cinéma: Nouvelles approches,* ed. Jacques Aumont, André Gaudreault, and Michel Marie (Paris: Publications de la Sorbonne, 1989), pp. 199–205.

The chapter epigraph on page 12 is from René Clair, *Cinema Yesterday and Today,* ed. R. C. Dale, trans. Stanley Applebaum (New York: Dover, 1972), p. 23. The quotation from Kuleshov on page 27 comes from Lev Kuleshov, "The Art of Creating with Light (Foundations of Thought)," in *Fifty Years in Films: Selected Works,* trans. Dmitri Agrachev and Nina Belenkaya (Moscow: Raduga, 1987), p. 35.

1. René Jeanne, "Evolution artistique du cinématographie," in *Le cinéma: Des origines à nos jours,* ed. Jean-Georges Auriol (Paris: Editions du Cygne, 1932), pp. 169–248.

2. Guido Adler, one of the founders of modern musicology, wrote in his *Der Stil*

in der Musik (1911), "In the course of the origin, flowering, or decline of a style, the intermediate period invariably serves as the principal basis of comparison. Stylistic criteria are drawn from this middle period"; quoted in Karl Dahlhaus, *Foundations of Music History,* trans. J. B. Robinson (Cambridge: Cambridge University Press, 1983), p. 15.

3. I describe this tendency as neo-Hegelian because it reflects that "Hegelianism without metaphysics" which E. H. Gombrich has traced through cultural historiography of the late nineteenth and early twentieth centuries. See Gombrich, "In Search of Cultural History," in *Ideals and Idols: Essays on Values in History and in Art* (Oxford: Phaidon, 1979), pp. 24–59.

4. Some examples are Ettore Margadonna, *Cinema: Ieri e oggi* (Milan: Domus, 1932); Carl Vincent, *Histoire de l'art cinématographique* (Brussels: Trident, 1939); Pietro Bianchi and Franco Berutto, *Storia del cinema* (Milan: Garzanti, 1957); Lino Lionello Ghirardini, *Storia generale del cinema (1895–1959)* (Milan: Marzorati, 1959); Ulrich Gregor and Enno Patalas, *Geschichte des Films* (Gütersloh: Sigbert Mohn, 1962); and Octavio de Faria, *Pequena introdução a história do cinema* (Sao Paulo: Martins, 1964).

5. Victorin Jasset, "Etude sur le mise-en-scène en cinématographie" (1911), reprinted in Marcel Lapierre, ed., *Anthologie du cinéma* (Paris: La Nouvelle Edition, 1946), pp. 83–98.

6. An entertaining book-length example is *Film-Photos wie noch nie* (Cologne: König, 1929), in which texts and photographs identify not only major stars but also major directors.

7. Jeanne, "Evolution artistique."

8. Iris Barry, *Let's Go the Movies* (New York: Payson and Clarke, 1926), p. 197.

9. Paul Rotha, *The Film till Now: A Survey of the Cinema* (London: Cape and Harrison, 1930), p. 99.

10. The phrase is Harold Rosenberg's; see *The Tradition of the New* (Chicago: University of Chicago Press, 1982), p. 9.

11. *New York Dramatic Mirror* no. 1823 (26 November 1913): 26.

12. Cited in Pratt, *Spellbound in Darkness,* p. 205.

13. "Die entfesselte Kamera," *Ufa-Magazin* 2, no. 13 (25–31 March 1927): n.p.

14. On *Close-Up,* see Anne Friedberg, "Writing about Cinema: *Close-Up* 1927–1933" (Ph.D. diss., New York University, 1983).

15. For a detailed study of these groups, see Denise Hartsough, "Soviet Film Distribution and Exhibition in Germany, 1921–1933," *Historical Journal of Film, Radio and Television* 5, no. 2 (1985): 131–148.

16. See Jan Heijs, ed., *Filmliga: 1927–1931* (Nijmegen: Socialistiese Uitgeverij, 1982).

17. "Eröffnung der 'Kamera,'" *Licht-Bild-Bühne* 21, no. 62 (12 March 1928): n.p.

18. For a discussion and review, see Kristin Thompson, "Early Film Exhibitions and the 1920s European Avant-Garde Cinema," in *Künstlerischer Austausch/Artistic Exchange: Akten des XXVIII. Internationalen Kongresses für Kunstgeschichte, Berlin 15–20 Juli 1992,* ed. Thomas W. Gaehtgens (Berlin: Akademie Verlag, 1993), pp. 141–152.

19. Henri Langlois, "Histoire de la Cinémathèque," *Cahiers du cinéma* no. 200–201 (April–May 1968): 63.

20. Borde, *Les cinémathèques*, pp. 79–80.

21. Roud, *A Passion for Films*, p. 19.

22. Butler, *To Encourage the Art of the Film*, p. 57.

23. Barr quoted in Roud, *A Passion for Films*, p. 33.

24. Iris Barry, "The Film Library and How It Grew," *Film Quarterly* 22, no. 4 (Summer 1969): 26.

25. Iris Barry, "A Review of Film History in a Cycle of 70 Films," in *Art in Our Time: An Exhibition to Celebrate the Tenth Anniversary of the Museum of Modern Art and the Opening of Its New Building Held at the Time of the New York World's Fair* (New York: Museum of Modern Art, 1939), p. 335.

26. Barry, *Let's Go to the Movies*, p. 224.

27. Iris Barry, *D. W. Griffith: American Film Master* (1940; reprint, New York: Museum of Modern Art, 1965), p. 13.

28. Richard Griffith, ibid., p. 5.

29. Barry, "The Film Library," p. 21.

30. Quoted in Slide, *Nitrate Won't Wait*, p. 21.

31. As late as the 1960s, the published program notes of the Wisconsin Film Society, one of the country's oldest, centered almost completely upon the MOMA canon. See Arthur Lennig, ed., *Film Notes* (Madison: Wisconsin Film Society, 1960) and *Classics of the Film* (Madison: Wisconsin Film Society Press, 1965).

32. Arthur Knight, *The Liveliest Art* (New York: Macmillan, 1957), p. vii. Knight may also have exercised an influence on academic film teaching through his article "An Approach to Film History," in *Film Study in Higher Education*, ed. David C. Stewart (Washington, D.C.: American Council on Education, 1966), pp. 52–67. There Knight outlines the Basic Story for aspirant film teachers, with topics keyed principally to the MOMA canon.

33. For indications of the role played by other archives, see National Film Library, *Forty Years of Film History: 1895–1935: Notes on the Films* (London: British Film Institute, 1951); and Musée d'Art Moderne, *60 ans de cinéma; 300 années de cinématographie* (Paris: Cinémathèque Française, 1955). These publications offer versions of the Basic Story very similar to that promulgated by MOMA.

34. Erwin Panofsky, "Style and Medium in the Moving Pictures," *Transition* no. 26 (Winter 1937): 128. A later version of the essay is available in Panofsky, *Three Essays on Style*, ed. Irving Lavin (Cambridge: MIT Press, 1995), pp. 91–125. For a discussion of Panofsky's treatment of film see Thomas Y. Levin, "Iconology at the Movies: Panofsky's Film Theory," in *Meaning in the Visual Arts: Views from the Outside: A Centennial Commemoration of Erwin Panofsky (1892–1968)*, ed. Irving Lavin (Princeton: Institute for Advanced Studies, 1995), pp. 313–333.

35. Paul Souday, "Bergsonisme et cinéma," *Le Film* no. 83 (15 October 1917): 10. For similar comments, see Vladimir Mayakovsky, "The Relationship between Contemporary Theatre and Cinema and Art [1913]," in *The Film Factory: Russian and Soviet Cinema in Documents, 1896–1939*, ed. Richard Taylor and Ian Christie (Cambridge, Mass.: Harvard University Press, 1988), pp. 36–37.

36. For a discussion of the theoretical implications of this line of argument, see Noël Carroll, *Philosophical Problems of Classical Film Theory* (Princeton: Princeton University Press, 1988), pp. 20–29.

37. See Moishe Barash, *Theories of Art from Plato to Winckelmann* (New York: New York University Press, 1985), pp. 168–169.

38. For an argument that this conception of art is a misapplication of Kant's ideas on "free beauty," see Noël Carroll, "Beauty and the Genealogy of Art Theory," *Philosophical Forum* 22, no. 4 (Summer 1971): 307–334.

39. Lazarus quoted in Edward Lippman, *A History of Western Musical Aesthetics* (Lincoln: University of Nebraska Press, 1992), p. 302.

40. Maurice Denis, "Définition du néotraditionnism," in *Théories: 1890–1910: Du Symbolisme et de Gauguin vers un nouvel ordre classique,* 2nd ed. (Paris: Bibliothèque de l'Occident, 1912), p. 1.

41. Alexander Kruchenykh and V. Khlebnikov, "From *The Word as Such,*" in *Russian Futurism through Its Manifestoes, 1912–1928,* ed. Anna Lawton (Ithaca: Cornell University Press, 1988), pp. 60–61.

42. Roger Fry, "Some Questions of Esthetics," in *Transformations* (Garden City, N.Y.: Doubleday, 1956), p. 35.

43. Rollin Summers, "The Moving Picture Drama and the Acted Drama: Some Points of Comparison," *Moving Picture World* (19 September 1908), reprinted in Kauffmann and Henstell, *American Film Criticism,* p. 10.

44. Ibid., pp. 10–13.

45. Riccioto Canudo, "The Birth of a Sixth Art," in Abel, *French Film Theory and Criticism,* p. 59.

46. Alexander Bakshy, "The Cinematograph as Art," *The Drama* no. 22 (May 1916): 284.

47. Hugo Münsterberg, *The Film: A Psychological Study* (1916; reprint, New York: Dover, 1970), p. 17.

48. Riccioto Canudo, *L'usine des images* (Geneva: Office Centrale d'Edition, 1927), p. 19. For a similar view see William Morgan Hannon, *The Photodrama: Its Place among the Fine Arts* (New Orleans: Ruskin Press, 1915), pp. 21–27.

49. Victor Oscar Freeburg, *The Art of Photoplay Making* (New York: Macmillan, 1918), pp. 1–4.

50. For an example, see Seymour Stern, "An Analysis of Motion," *Greenwich Village Quill* no. 19 (November 1926): 40–44; 20 (December 1926): 33–35.

51. Leonid Andreyev, "Second Letter on Theatre [Extract]," in Taylor and Christie, *The Film Factory,* p. 38.

52. Georg Lukács, "Thoughts on an Aesthetic for the Cinema," *Framework* no. 14 (1981): 3.

53. Henry MacMahon, "*The Birth of a Nation,*" *New York Times* (6 June 1915), reprinted in Kauffmann and Henstell, *American Film Criticism,* p. 93.

54. Iris Barry, "The Cinema: Hope Fulfilled [1924]," in Pratt, *Spellbound in Darkness,* p. 316.

55. Barnet G. Braver-Mann, "The Modern Spirit in Films," *Experimental Cinema* no. 1 (February 1930): 11.

56. Rudolf Arnheim, *Film,* trans. L. M. Sieveking and Ian F. D. Morrow (London: Faber and Faber, 1933), pp. 41–115.

57. Aristotle, *The Poetics: Translation and Commentary,* trans. and ed. Stephen Halliwell (Chapel Hill: University of North Carolina Press, 1987), p. 35.

58. Léon Moussinac, *Naissance du cinéma* (Paris: Povolosky, 1925), p. 32.

59. C. A. Lejeune, *Cinema* (London: Alexander Maclehose, 1931), p. 170.

60. Georges Charensol, *Panorama du cinéma* (Paris: Kra, 1930), p. 149.

61. See V. F. Perkins, *Film as Film: Understanding and Judging Movies* (New York:

Penguin, 1972), pp. 9–39; and Carroll, *Philosophical Problems of Classical Film Theory,* chaps. 1 and 2.

62. Anonymous, in *Exceptional Photoplays* (March 1921), reprinted in Kauffmann and Henstell, *American Film Criticism,* p. 124.

63. Arnheim, *Film,* pp. 185–186.

64. Jeanne, "Evolution artistique," p. 240.

65. Terry Ramsaye, "The Motion Picture," *Annals of the American Academy of Political and Social Science* 128 (November 1926): 12.

66. See V. I. Pudovkin, *Film Technique and Film Acting,* trans. and ed. Ivor Montagu (New York: Grove Press, 1960), p. 88.

67. See *Kuleshov on Film: Writings of Lev Kuleshov,* trans. and ed. Ronald Levaco (Berkeley: University of California Press, 1974), p. 54. Portions of this experiment have been unearthed; see "The Rediscovery of a Kuleshov Experiment: A Dossier," trans. and ed. Yuri Tsivian, with a contribution by Ekaterina Khokhlova and an introduction by Kristin Thompson, *Film History* 8, no. 3 (1996): 357–367.

68. *Kuleshov on Film,* p. 54.

69. *Naissance du cinéma,* called by Sadoul "the first historical study of cinema for the 1914–1924 years," was soon followed by Moussinac's study of the Soviet cinema and his discussion of films that had appeared since the first volume. See *Le cinéma soviétique* (Paris: Gallimard, 1928) and *Panoramique du cinéma* (Paris: Sans Pareil, 1929). These volumes, along with *Naissance du cinéma,* are collected in condensed form in *L'âge ingrat du cinéma* (Paris: Sagittaire, 1946). The quotation from Sadoul comes from his introduction to the 1967 edition of this collection (Paris: Editeurs Français Réunis), p. 12.

70. Moussinac, *Le cinéma soviétique,* pp. 169–170.

71. Raymond Spottiswoode, *A Grammar of the Film: An Analysis of Film Techniques* (1935; reprint, Berkeley: University of California Press, 1950), p. 84.

72. Sergei Eisenstein, Vsevolod Pudovkin, and Grigori Alexandrov, "Statement on Sound [1928]," in Taylor and Christie, *The Film Factory,* p. 234.

73. Arnheim, *Film,* pp. 283–290.

74. Gilbert Seldes, *The Seven Lively Arts* (1924; reprint, New York: Sagamore Press, 1957), p. 276.

75. Gilbert Seldes, *An Hour with the Movies and the Talkies* (Philadelphia: Lippincott, 1929), p. 76.

76. Gilbert Seldes, "The Movies Commit Suicide," *Harper's* 157 (November 1928): 706.

77. Gilbert Seldes, "The Talkies' Progress," *Harper's* 159 (September 1929): 454–458.

78. Gilbert Seldes, "The Movies in Peril," *Scribner's* 97 (February 1935): 85–86. Not until twenty years later did Seldes grant that "the essence of the moving picture—its movement—survived the coming of sound"; *The Public Arts* (New York: Simon and Schuster, 1956), p. 23.

79. For discussions of their research method, see Robert Brasillach, *Notre avant-guerre* (1941), in *Oeuvres complètes de Robert Brasillach,* ann. Maurice Bardèche, vol. 6 (Paris: Club de l'Honnête Homme, 1955), pp. 145–150; and Maurice Bardèche, preface to *Histoire du cinéma,* in *Oeuvres complètes,* vol. 10 (Paris: Club de l'Honnête Homme, 1964), pp. 3–9. In the latter, Bardèche claims that virtually all of the *Histoire* is Brasillach's work (pp. 7–8). In *Brasillach . . . le maudit* (Paris: Denoël, 1989), Pierre

Pellissier reports that Charensol's competing 1935 updating of *Panoramique du cinéma* bore a wrapper declaring: "By a critic who has seen all the films he talks about" (p. 159). Yet cf. the remark of Henri Langlois: "Up to 1934 a young man of twenty living in Paris could have seen almost all the great films that had ever been made"; quoted in Roud, *Passion for Films*, p. 65.

80. For a discussion of nationalism in the *Histoire*, see Mary Jane Green, "Fascists on Film: The Brasillach and Bardèche *Histoire du cinéma*," in *Fascism, Aesthetics, and Culture*, ed. Richard J. Golsan (Hanover, N.H.: University Press of New England, 1992), pp. 164–178. Green argues that the *Histoire*'s claims that art reflects national character, that silent film was superior to talkies, that Hollywood exhibited unbounded rapacity, and that French production had fallen from glory all reflect the authors' fascism. Her argument is weakened by the fact that many of these views were common in contemporary film culture and were held by people of quite divergent political views. Bardèche and Brasillach mobilize these widespread *topoi* in the service of a fascist aesthetic, a process that seems only slightly visible in the 1935 *Histoire* but quite evident in the 1943 edition.

81. This emphasis, predictably, is even more central to the Occupation revision of the *Histoire*. For a discussion of the authors' conception of national culture, see Kaplan, *Reproductions of Banality*, pp. 144–158.

82. Maurice Bardèche and Robert Brasillach, *Histoire du cinéma* (Paris: Denoël & Steele, 1935), p. 235.

83. Ibid., p. 311.

84. Significant examples would be Charensol, *Panorama du cinéma* (1930); and Rotha, *The Film till Now*.

85. Maurice Bardèche and Robert Brasillach, *Histoire du cinéma: Edition définitive illustrée de soixante et une photographies hors-texte* (Paris: Denoël, 1943), p. 174. Although this sentence does not appear in the 1935 edition, it is in keeping with the position articulated there.

86. See René Clair, "Brasillach et le cinéma," in *Oeuvres complètes de Robert Brasillach*, vol. 10, pp. xi–xvi.

87. Bardèche and Brasillach, *Histoire du cinéma*, 1935 ed., p. 312.

88. So far as I know, the *Histoire* has been translated only into English, by Iris Barry under the title *The History of Motion Pictures* (New York: Norton, 1938). Barry excised a few portions of the French edition and wrote a postscript.

89. Most of this material is deleted from the 1948 edition, though some anti-Semitic asides remain. For a discussion of the fascist aspects of the first two editions of the *Histoire*, as well as an intriguing 1982 interview with Bardèche, see Kaplan, *Reproductions of Banality*, pp. 142–188.

A work contemporary with Brasillach's offers an instructive comparison. Lucien Rebatet's *Les tribus du cinéma et du théâtre* (Paris: Nouvelles Editions Françaises, 1941) names and excoriates Jews in the French film industry. "Rebatet" was the pen name of François Vinneuil.

90. Bardèche adhered to the Standard Version for decades; see his essay "Le cinéma muet," *Le Crapouillot* no. 59 (January 1963): 22–39.

91. John E. Abbott, "Foreword," in Bardèche and Brasillach, *The History of Motion Pictures*, trans. Barry, p. xi.

92. Georges Sadoul, *Histoire d'un art: Le cinéma des origines à nos jours* (Paris: Flammarion, 1949), p. 448.

93. See Georges Sadoul, *Histoire générale du cinéma,* vol. 3: *Le cinéma devient un art: 1909–1920,* part 2: *La première guerre mondiale* (Paris: Denoël, 1952), pp. 451–454.

94. See Sadoul, *Histoire d'un art,* p. 6. The periodization outlined here and elaborated in subsequent editions is somewhat at variance with the periods as delineated in the published volumes of his *Histoire générale du cinéma* (Paris: Denoël, 1946–1975), but the congruences are close enough. Bardèche and Brasillach identify "Film's First Steps" as the period 1895–1908; Sadoul's *Histoire générale* finds the "pioneering" period to lie in the years 1897–1909. Bardèche and Brasillach mark off a "prewar" period of 1908–1914, very close to Sadoul's (1909–1914). Both sources agree that the war years 1914–1918 constitute yet another period. Both also agree that 1919–1929 defines the era of the "silent art," with Bardèche and Brasillach further subdividing the decade into two phases.

95. Georges Sadoul, *Histoire générale du cinéma,* vol. 3: *Le cinéma devient un art 1909–1920,* part 1, *L'avant-guerre,* rev. ed. (Paris: Denoël, 1973), p. 73.

96. Georges Sadoul, *British Creators of Film Technique* (London: British Film Institute, 1948), p. 10.

97. Sadoul also produced popularizations and condensed versions of his major works, for example the abbreviated *Histoire du cinéma* (Paris: Flammarion, 1961) and *Conquête du cinéma* (Paris: Geldage, 1960), a book for young readers.

98. Jean Mitry's 3-volume *Histoire du cinéma* (Paris: Editions Universitaires, 1968–1973) varies scarcely at all from the periodization offered by his predecessors. He even follows Bardèche and Brasillach in marking the postwar period into two phases, 1919–1923 and 1923–1929. And, like Bardèche and Brasillach, Mitry argues that cinema became a "language" *(langage)* before it was used as a means of artistic expression.

99. See Antonio del Amo, *Historia universal del cine* (Madrid: Plus-Ultra, 1945); and Angel Zuñia, *Una historia del cine* (Barcelona: Destino, 1948). More specifically, many historians follow Bardèche/Brasillach and Sadoul in breaking periods around 1908 and 1918. Carlos Fernandez Cuenca, for example, ends the first volume of his *Historia del cine* (Madrid: Afrodisio Aguardo, 1948) with a consideration of "The Struggle for [Cinematic] Expression (1900–1908)." The 1918 period boundary is also common, since the war is often believed to have signaled the American ascendancy and the beginning of distinctive national schools in France and Germany. See, for example, René Jeanne and Charles Ford, *Histoire illustré du cinéma,* vol. 1: *Le cinéma muet* (Paris: Marabout, 1966).

100. François Truffaut, review of *Histoire du cinéma, Cahiers du cinéma* no. 32 (February 1954): 59.

101. See Gombrich, "In Search of Cultural History."

3. Against the Seventh Art

The period considered in this chapter is surveyed in Kristin Thompson and David Bordwell, *Film History: An Introduction* (New York: McGraw-Hill, 1994), chaps. 9–19.

The interwar movement toward realism in the visual arts is comprehensively discussed in the excellent catalogue *Les réalismes, 1919–1939* (Paris: Pompidou Center, 1980). On the French context specifically, see Fernand Léger et al., *La querelle du réalisme* (Paris: Diagonales, 1987); *Paris 1937–Paris 1957* (Paris: Pompidou Center, 1981); Kenneth E. Silver, *Esprit de Corps: The Art of the Parisian Avant-Garde and the First World War, 1914–1925* (Princeton: Princeton University Press, 1989); and Romy

Golan, *Modernity and Nostalgia: Art and Politics in France between the Wars* (New Haven: Yale University Press, 1995).

Dudley Andrew traces Bazin's life in *André Bazin* (New York: Oxford, 1978). Andrew's "Realism and Reality in Cinema: The Film Theory of André Bazin and Its Sources in Recent French Thought" (Ph.D. diss., University of Iowa, 1972) dissects Bazin's theory and includes a comprehensive bibliography. See also the special Bazin number of *Cahiers du cinéma* (no. 91, January 1959) and of *Wide Angle* 9, no. 4 (1987), as well as Richard Roud's "Face to Face: André Bazin," *Sight and Sound* 28, no. 3–4 (Summer–Autumn 1959): 176–179. Janet Staiger's essay, "*Theorist,* Yes, but What *of?* Bazin and History," *Iris* 2, no. 2 (1984): 99–109, argues that Bazin's progress-based account of stylistic history is heavily indebted to Personalism and the philosophy of Merleau-Ponty.

Roger Leenhardt reviews his life in *Les yeux ouverts: Entretiens avec Jean Lacouture* (Paris: Seuil, 1979). On Astruc's early career see Raymond Bellour, *Alexandre Astruc* (Paris: Seghers, 1963).

Background information on major Parisian journals of the period can be found in Olivier Barrot, *L'écran français 1943–1952: Histoire d'un journal et d'un époque* (Paris: Les Editeurs Français Réunis, 1979); and in Antoine de Baecque's engrossing *Les cahiers du cinéma: Histoire d'un revue,* vol. 1: *À l'assaut du cinéma* (Paris: Cahiers du Cinéma, 1991). Samples of Young Turk criticism, with particular emphasis on Nicholas Ray and widescreen cinema, can be found in Jim Hillier's well-annotated anthology *Cahiers du cinéma: The 1950s: Neo-Realism, Hollywood, New Wave* (Cambridge, Mass.: Harvard University Press, 1985).

Another 1940s effort to counter the dominance of the silent-film aesthetic is Jean A. Keim, *Un nouvel art: Le cinéma sonore* (Paris: Albin Michel, 1947). Written in a prison camp in Germany, Keim's book offers a more traditional defense of the sound cinema than that of *la nouvelle critique,* relying as it does on such early sound classics as *The Blue Angel* and the films of Clair.

The writing of Marcel Pagnol on sound film is voluminous and repetitious. Apart from the four issues of his journal *Les cahiers du film* (1933–1934), a synthesis of his views is presented in the miscellany *Cinématurgie de Paris* (Monte Carlo: Pastorelly, 1980). See also *Les années Pagnol,* ed. Pierre Lagnan (Renens: 5 Continents, 1989). On Sacha Guitry see not only his *Le cinéma et moi,* ed. André Bernard and Claude Gauteur, 2nd ed. (Paris: Ramsay, 1984), but also *Sacha Guitry, cinéaste,* ed. Philippe Arnaud (Brussels: Yellow Now, 1993).

Denis Marion's *André Malraux* (Paris: Seghers, 1970) recounts Malraux's foray into filmmaking. The novel upon which *Espoir* was based is layered with cinematic references; one of the protagonists is a film sound recordist. The English version is *Days of Hope,* trans. Stuart Gilbert and Alastair MacDonald (London: Routledge, 1938).

Sartre's essay on *Citizen Kane* first appeared in *L'écran français* no. 5 (3 August 1945): 2–3, 15. It is available in English in *Post Script* 7, no. 1 (Fall 1987): 60–65. For a background study, see Dana Polan, "Sartre and Cinema," *Post Script* 7, no. 1 (Fall 1987): 66–87.

Somewhat parallel to *La revue du cinéma, Gazette du cinéma,* and *Cahiers du cinéma* was Britain's *Sequence* (published 1946–1952). An essay relevant to this chapter is Karel Reisz, "The Later Films of William Wyler," *Sequence* no. 13 (New Year, 1951): 19–30.

Of all the *Cahiers* critics, Eric Rohmer came closest to offering an extensive theoretical rationale for *mise-en-scène* criticism. Many of his writings of the period are collected in *Le goût de la beauté* (Paris: Editions de l'Etoile, 1984). The English version, not always felicitously rendered, is *The Taste for Beauty*, trans. Carol Volk (Cambridge: Cambridge University Press, 1989). Another important document is Rohmer's serialized essay arguing for a cinematic classicism in terms that recall the "synthetic" approach to defining film's essence we find in silent-era polemics. See "Le celluloïd et le marbre," *Cahiers du cinéma* no. 44 (February 1955): 32–37; no. 49 (July 1955): 10–15; no. 51 (October 1955): 2–9; no. 52 (November 1955): 23–29; no. 53 (December 1955): 22–30.

For further argument that the writers around *Cahiers* and *Movie* drastically revised Bazin's theory of cinema, see David Bordwell, "Widescreen Aesthetics and Mise-en-Scène Criticism," *Velvet Light Trap* no. 21 (Summer 1985): 18–25. The same issue of this journal contains translations of articles by Bazin on CinemaScope and Cinerama. The most important essay on widescreen film produced within a *mise-en-scène* perspective is Charles Barr's "CinemaScope: Before and After," *Film Quarterly* 16, no. 4 (Summer 1963): 4–24. A vigorous response to the widescreen aesthetic promulgated by *Cahiers* and *Movie* is Gavin Millar's chapter (Section 4) of his and Karel Reisz's *Technique of Film Editing*, 2nd ed. (London: Focal Press, 1968), a book largely informed by the Standard Version.

The Astruc epigraph on page 46 comes from "Prisonniers du passé," in *Du stylo à la caméra . . . et de la caméra au stylo: Ecrits (1942–1984)* (Paris: L'Archipel, 1992), p. 269. The epigraph on page 75 is from a 1988 interview, "Godard Makes (Hi)stories: Interview with Serge Daney," in Raymond Bellour and Mary Lea Bandy, eds., *Jean-Luc Godard: Son and Image, 1974–1991* (New York: MOMA, 1992), pp. 159–160.

1. "The Evolution of the Language of Cinema" (available in English in André Bazin, *What Is Cinema?* ed. Hugh Gray [Berkeley: University of California Press, 1967], pp. 23–40) was assembled by Bazin from three earlier essays: "Pour en finir avec la profondeur de champ," *Cahiers du cinéma* no. 1 (April 1951): 17–23; "Montage," in *Twenty Years of Cinema in Venice* (Rome: Edizioni dell'Ateneo, 1952), pp. 359–377; and "Le découpage et son évolution," *L'âge nouveau* no. 93 (July 1955): 54–61. I shall refer to these when they contain remarks not included in the later synthesis.

2. Maurice Bardèche and Robert Brasillach, *Histoire du cinéma*, 2nd ed. (Paris: Denoël, 1943), p. 369.

3. Colin Crisp provides a careful discussion of their ideas and context in *The Classic French Cinema, 1930–1960* (Bloomington: Indiana University Press, 1993), pp. 284–293.

4. Marcel Pagnol, "Dramaturgie de Paris," *Cahiers du film* no. 1 (15 December 1933): 8.

5. Reported by François Truffaut, "Sacha Guitry, cinéaste," in Guitry, *Le cinéma et moi*, p. 16.

6. André Malraux, "Outline of a Psychology of the Cinema," *Verve* 8, no. 2 (1940): 69–73; reprinted in Susanne K. Langer, ed., *Reflections on Art: A Source Book of Writings by Artists, Critics, and Philosophers* (New York: Oxford University Press, 1961), pp. 317–327. The essay was republished after the war as a pamphlet, *Esquisse d'une psychologie du cinéma* (Paris: Gallimard, 1946).

7. André Malraux, *Psychologie de l'art: Le musée imaginaire* (Geneva: Skira, 1947), pp. 114–117.

8. Alexandre Astruc, "Prisonniers du passé," in *Du stylo à la caméra*, pp. 269–270.

9. The famous expression of this view is Alexandre Astruc, "La caméra-stylo," first published in 1948. It is translated in English as "The Birth of a New Avant-Garde: *La Caméra-Stylo,*" in *The New Wave,* ed. Peter Graham (Garden City, N.Y.: Doubleday, 1968), pp. 17–23. It is possible that Astruc was picking up on a suggestion made by Bazin in an earlier essay, where he had argued that the cinema had achieved aesthetic maturity and that the director now possessed a means of expression "as obedient [*docile*] as the pen" ("Le cinéma est-il majeur?" *L'écran français* no. 60 [1946]: 12).

10. Alexandre Astruc, "L'avenir du cinéma," in *Du stylo à la caméra,* p. 330.

11. See Lev Kuleshov, "Principles of Montage," in *Kuleshov on Film,* ed. Ronald Levaco (Berkeley: University of California Press, 1974), p. 183; Sergei M. Eisenstein, "Film Form: New Problems," in *Film Form and The Film Sense,* trans. and ed. Jay Leyda (New York: World, 1957), pp. 122–149.

12. Roger Leenhardt, "Les temps du film," in *Chroniques de cinéma* (Paris: Editions de l'Etoile, 1986), p. 145.

13. André Bazin, "À la recherche d'une nouvelle avant-garde," in *Almanach du théâtre et du cinéma 1950,* ed. Jean Vagne (Paris: Editions de Flore, 1949), pp. 146–150.

14. Malraux, "Outline of a Psychology," p. 71.

15. See, for example, Roger Leenhardt, "Réflexions sur les limites plastiques du cinéma," in *Chroniques,* p. 172.

16. Leenhardt interpreted Malraux's *Verve* essay as pointing out "the fundamentally realist aesthetic of the cinema" ("Malraux et le cinéma," in *Chroniques,* p. 96). Astruc likewise insisted that the cinema's power lay in its concrete realism; see, for example, "Dialectique et cinéma," in *Du stylo à la caméra,* p. 338.

17. It seems likely that Malraux's relativizing of modernism in *Le musée imaginaire* owes something to the resurgence of realism in the most prominent art of the previous two decades.

18. As when Sadoul writes that in *Grandma's Reading Glass* "the alternation of close-up and long shots in the same scene is the principle of the *découpage.* Smith thereby created the first true editing [*montage*]"; Georges Sadoul, *Histoire de l'art du cinéma des origines à nos jours* (Paris: Flammarion, 1949), p. 40.

19. The French rendering of a V. I. Pudovkin essay, "Le montage et le son," *Le magasin du spectacle* no. 1 (April 1946): 8–20, employs this distinction.

20. Malraux, *Esquisse,* n.p.; Bardèche and Brasillach, *Histoire du cinéma,* p. 87.

21. Alexandre Astruc, "Notes sur Orson Welles," in *Du stylo à la caméra,* p. 322.

22. Claude-Edmonde Magny, *The Age of the American Novel: The Film Aesthetic of Fiction between the Two Wars,* trans. Eleanor Hochman (New York: Ungar, 1972), pp. 21–23.

23. André Bazin et al., "Six Characters in Search of *Auteurs,*" in Hillier, *Cahiers du cinéma: The 1950s,* p. 39.

24. See, for instance, Bazin's essay "On *L'Espoir,* or Style in the Cinema," in *French Cinema of the Occupation and Resistance: The Birth of a Critical Esthetic,* ed. François Truffaut, trans. Stanley Hochman (New York: Ungar, 1981), pp. 145–146.

25. Bazin, "Le cinéma est-il majeure?" p. 5.

26. Leenhardt, "Les temps du film," p. 146.

27. Astruc, "Notes sur Orson Welles," p. 322.

28. "If the scene were played on a stage and seen from a seat in the orchestra, it would have the same meaning. The changes of point of view provided by the camera would add nothing"; Bazin, "Evolution of the Language of Cinema," p. 32.

29. André Bazin, "Le cas Pagnol," in *Qu'est-ce que le cinéma?* vol. 2: *Le cinéma et les autres arts* (Paris: Cerf, 1969), pp. 119–125.

30. André Bazin, "Theatre and Cinema," in *What Is Cinema?* pp. 76–124.

31. Roger Leenhardt, "Le cinéma impur," in *Chroniques,* pp. 28–29.

32. Bazin, "À la recherche," pp. 151–152.

33. Alexandre Astruc, "L'évolution du cinéma américain," in *Du stylo à la caméra,* p. 291.

34. Roger Leenhardt, "Continuité du cinéma français," in *Chroniques,* p. 133.

35. Bazin, "À la recherche," pp. 151–152.

36. The campaign promoting the film's self-conscious use of depth is traced in David Bordwell, "Film Style and Technology, 1930–1960," in Bordwell, Janet Staiger, and Kristin Thompson, *The Classical Hollywood Cinema: Film Style and Mode of Production to 1960* (New York: Columbia University Press, 1985), pp. 346–349.

37. Gregg Toland, "The Motion Picture Cameraman," *Theatre Arts* 25, no. 9 (September 1941): 652–653.

38. Gregg Toland, "Realism for 'Citizen Kane,'" *American Cinematographer* 22, no. 2 (February 1941): 80. This essay is reprinted in *American Cinematographer* 72, no. 8 (August 1991): 37–42.

39. Jean-Paul Sartre, "Quand Hollywood veut faire penser: 'Citizen Kane,' film d'Orson Welles," *L'écran français* no. 5 (1 August 1945): 3–5, 15.

40. See *La revue du cinéma* no. 1 (October 1946) and no. 3 (December 1946), as well as Toland, "L'opérateur de prise de vues," *La revue du cinéma* no. 4 (January 1947): 16–24, a translation of Toland, "Motion Picture Cameraman."

41. Jean Vidal, "L'art du cinéma et sa technique," in *Almanach du théâtre et du cinéma 1949,* ed. Jean Vagne (Paris: Editions de Flore, 1948), pp. 156–158.

42. See Roger Leenhardt, "*Citizen Kane,*" in *Chroniques,* p. 118; Astruc, "Notes sur Orson Welles," p. 323.

43. André Bazin, "La technique du *Citizen Kane,*" *Les temps modernes* 2, no. 17 (1947): 945–947.

44. Roger Leenhardt, "À bas Ford! Vive Wyler!" in *Chroniques,* p. 158; the italicized words are rendered in English in the original. A relevant Sadoul essay is "John Ford, inégal et brillant," *L'écran français* no. 14 (3 October 1945): 8–9, 15.

45. Astruc, "Notes sur Orson Welles," p. 322. See also Magny, *Age of the American Novel,* pp. 27–28.

46. William Wyler, "No Magic Wand," *Screen Writer* 2, no. 9 (February 1947): 10. It seems likely that Bazin saw this article before writing his essay on Wyler, published in February 1948.

47. See, for example, Roger-Marc Théroud and Jean-Charles Tacchella, "Hitchcock se confie," *L'écran français* no. 187 (25 January 1949): 3–4.

48. André Bazin, "Let's Rediscover Cinema!" in Truffaut, *French Cinema of the Occupation and Resistance,* p. 26.

49. André Bazin, "For a Realistic Aesthetic," ibid., p. 36.

50. Bazin, "Let's Rediscover Cinema!" p. 27.

51. Bazin, "Evolution of the Language of Cinema," p. 24.

52. Bazin, "Montage," p. 376.

53. Bazin, "Evolution of the Language of Cinema," p. 35.

54. Georges Sadoul, "Hypertrophie du cerveau," *Les lettres françaises* (5 July 1946): 9.

55. Bazin, "Le découpage et son évolution," p. 58.

56. André Bazin, *Orson Welles: A Critical View,* trans. Jonathan Rosenbaum (New York: Harper and Row, 1978), pp. 81–82. This is a translation of the 1972 French edition (Paris: Cerf), which is a revised version of the original edition (Paris: Chavane, 1950).

57. Bazin, "Montage," p. 373.

58. André Bazin, "William Wyler ou le janséniste de la mise en scène," in *Qu'est-ce que le cinéma?* vol. 1: *Ontologie et langage* (Paris: Cerf, 1969), pp. 166–169.

59. Bazin, *Orson Welles,* pp. 72–73.

60. Bazin, "William Wyler," p. 163.

61. Bazin, "Evolution of the Language of Cinema," p. 39.

62. Bazin, "William Wyler," p. 165. Wyler remarked: "I wanted audiences to feel they were seeing something they were not supposed to see. Seeing the husband in the background made you squint, but what you *were* seeing was her face"; Axel Madsen, *William Wyler* (New York: Crowell, 1973), p. 209.

63. André Bazin, "*La terre tremble,*" in *Qu'est-ce que le cinéma?* vol. 4: *Une esthétique de la réalité: Le néo-réalisme* (Paris: Cerf, 1962), pp. 40–41.

64. Bazin, "Evolution of the Language of Cinema," p. 38.

65. André Bazin, *Jean Renoir,* trans. W. W. Halsey II and William H. Simon (New York: Simon and Schuster, 1973), p. 89. In 1948 Astruc had anticipated this idea; see "L'avenir du cinéma," p. 334.

66. Bazin, *Jean Renoir,* p. 90.

67. Bazin, *Orson Welles,* pp. 15–18.

68. See Robert L. Carringer, *The Making of Citizen Kane* (Berkeley: University of California Press, 1985), pp. 117–120.

69. Roger Leenhardt, "*La Marseillaise,*" in *Chroniques,* p. 79.

70. André Bazin, "The Myth of Total Cinema," in *What Is Cinema?* pp. 20, 21.

71. André Bazin, "The Ontology of the Photographic Image," ibid., p. 15.

72. Bardèche and Brasillach, *Histoire du cinéma,* p. 394.

73. For a detailed critique along these lines, see Noël Carroll, *Philosophical Problems of Classical Film Theory* (Princeton: Princeton University Press, 1988), pp. 94–171.

74. This pattern is discussed by Kristin Thompson in "An Aesthetic of Discrepancy: *The Rules of the Game,*" in *Breaking the Glass Armor: Neoformalist Film Analysis* (Princeton: Princeton University Press, 1988), pp. 230–243.

75. Sadoul, *Histoire de l'art du cinéma,* pp. 20, 270, 327.

76. Bardèche and Brasillach, *Histoire du cinéma* (Paris: André Martel, 1948), pp. 437–438.

77. Renoir, for instance, suggested in 1939 that after an era dominated by the star and a subsequent "age of the director," a new period was beginning, "that of *auteurs;* henceforth it will be the scenarist who makes a film"; quoted in Bernard Chardère et al., *Jean Renoir, Premier plan* no. 22–24 (1962): 278.

78. For an informative account, see Crisp, *Classic French Cinema,* pp. 307–323.

79. Cited in Barrot, *L'écran français,* p. 153.

80. See Maurice Schérer [Eric Rohmer], "Etude technique de 'La corde,'" *Gazette du cinéma* no. 1 (1950): 1, 4.

81. Jean-Luc Godard, "Defense and Illustration of Classical Construction [*Découpage*]," in *Godard on Godard: Critical Writings by Jean-Luc Godard,* ed. Jean Narboni and Tom Milne (New York: Viking, 1972), pp. 26–30.

82. Jacques Rivette, "Letter on Rossellini," in Hillier, *Cahiers du cinéma: The 1950s,* pp. 202–203.

83. Eric Rohmer, "Le cinéma, l'art de l'espace," in *Le goût de la beauté* (Paris: Editions de l'Etoile, 1984), pp. 27–35.

84. Astruc, "Birth of a New Avant-Garde," p. 20.

85. Three decades later Truffaut offered a comparable definition: "In the earliest days, at the beginnings of the cinema, *mise en scène* designated the arrangement of visual material *in front of* the camera . . . Only the initiates knew that the term instead designated all the decisions taken by the director: camera position, angle, the duration of the shot, an actor's gesture; and those initiates therefore knew that *mise en scène* is at once the story that is told and manner in which it is told"; "Sacha Guitry, cinéaste," p. 14.

86. Jean-Luc Godard, "Montage My Fine Care," in Narboni and Milne, *Godard on Godard,* p. 40.

87. Schérer, "Etude technique de 'La corde,'" p. 1.

88. Philippe Demonsablon, "Qui nâquit à Newgate . . . ," *Cahiers du cinéma* no. 33 (March 1954): 59–60.

89. Luc Moullet, "*Les contes de la lune vague,*" *Cahiers du cinéma* no. 95 (May 1959): 22.

90. Jacques Rivette, "Mizoguchi vu d'ici," *Cahiers du cinéma* no. 81 (March 1958): 28.

91. Alexandre Astruc, "Le feu et la glace," in *Du stylo à la caméra,* p. 365.

92. Charles Bitsch, "Naissance du CinémaScope," *Cahiers du cinéma* no. 48 (June 1955): 41–42.

93. André Bazin, "La politique des auteurs," in Graham, *New Wave,* pp. 37–155.

94. Jean-Luc Godard, "*No Sad Songs for Me,*" in Narboni and Milne, *Godard on Godard,* p. 21.

95. See David Bordwell, *Making Meaning: Inference and Rhetoric in the Interpretation of Cinema* (Cambridge, Mass.: Harvard University Press, 1989), pp. 44–48.

96. Moullet, "*Contes de la lune vague,*" p. 22.

97. Godard acknowledged as much in a tribute to Langlois: "We now know, too, that Alain Resnais and Otto Preminger have not progressed beyond Lumière, Griffith, and Dreyer, any more than Cézanne and Braque progressed beyond David and Chardin: they did something different . . . Henri Langlois has given each twenty-fourth of a second of his life to rescue all these voices from their silent obscurity and to project them on the white sky of the only museum where the real and the imaginary meet at last"; "Speech Delivered at the Cinémathèque Française on the Occasion of the Louis Lumière Retrospective in January 1966: Thanks to Henri Langlois," in Narboni and Milne, *Godard on Godard,* p. 236.

4. The Return of Modernism

The periods considered in this chapter are surveyed in Kristin Thompson and David Bordwell, *Film History: An Introduction* (New York: McGraw-Hill, 1994), chaps. 1–3, 11, and 20–24.

Useful synoptic histories of postwar modernism include Katherine Hoffman, *Explorations: The Visual Arts since 1945* (New York: HarperCollins, 1991); Serge Guilbaut, *Reconstructing Modernism: Art in New York, Paris, and Montreal, 1945–1964* (Cambridge: MIT Press, 1990); Pontus Hulten, ed., *Paris—New York* (Paris: Centre National d'Art et de Culture Georges Pompidou, 1977); Dominique and Jean-Yves Bosseur, *Révolutions musicales: La musique contemporaine depuis 1945,* 4th ed. (Paris: Minerve, 1993); and Elliott Schwartz and Daniel Godfrey, *Music since 1945: Issues, Materials, Literature* (New York: Schirmer, 1993).

On the aesthetics of total serialism, see, besides the writings of Boulez himself, Peter F. Stacey, *Boulez and the Modern Concept* (Lincoln: University of Nebraska Press, 1987). Hans Werner Henze nursed bitter memories of Darmstadt School days. "Discipline was the order of the day. Through discipline it was going to be possible to get music back on its feet again, though nobody asked what for. Discipline enabled form to come about; there were rules and parameters for everything . . . The audience, at whom our music was supposed to be directed, would be made up of experts. The public would be excused from attending our concerts; in other words, our public would be the press and our protectors" (*Music and Politics: Collected Writings, 1953–1981,* trans. Peter Labanyi [London: Faber and Faber, 1982], p. 40). Benoît Duteurtre's *Requiem pour une avant-garde* (Paris: Laffont, 1995) offers an acerbic history of this ascetic modernism, which came to dominate musical culture in France and thus turned into that familiar anomaly: an antibourgeois modernism financed by the state.

We still lack a thoroughgoing history of postwar modernism in the European cinema. Discussions of particular films and directors are to be found in Roy Armes, *The Ambiguous Image* (London: Secker and Warburg, 1976); Robert Phillip Kolker, *The Altering Eye: Contemporary International Cinema* (New York: Oxford University Press, 1983); and John Orr, *Cinema and Modernity* (Cambridge: Polity, 1993).

The authoritative history of the vicissitudes of *cahiers du cinéma* during the 1960s and 1970s is Antoine de Baecque's *Les cahiers du cinéma: Histoire d'un revue,* vol. II: *Cinéma, tours détours* (Paris: Cahiers du Cinéma, 1991). Two anthologies offer samples of the writing: Jim Hillier, ed., *Cahiers du cinéma: The 1960s: New Wave, New Cinema, Reevaluating Hollywood* (Cambridge, Mass.: Harvard University Press, 1986), which contains editorial annotations and supplementary material; and Nick Browne, ed., *Cahiers du Cinéma: 1969–1972: The Politics of Representation* (Cambridge, Mass.: Harvard University Press, 1990).

"Political modernism" can be seen as an outgrowth of the reflections of the Frankfurt School and the Parisian journal *Tel quel.* On parallel developments in film theory, see D. N. Rodowick, *The Crisis of Political Modernism* (California: University of California Press, 1995). Annette Michelson, who argued for the potential political radicality of avant-garde art, pleaded the case in several important essays, notably her review of Bazin's *What Is Cinema?* in *Artforum* 6, no. 10 (Summer 1968): 67–71; "Screen/Surface: The Politics of Illusionism," *Artforum* 11, no. 1 (September 1972): 58–62; and "Camera Lucida/ Camera Obscura," *Artforum* 11, no. 5 (January 1973): 30–37, which develops the argument that Eisenstein and Brakhage define the most important issues facing film theory. Soon Michelson was to participate in the founding of *October,* a journal that blazons on its cover "Art/Theory/Criticism/Politics."

On the relation of experimental to primitive film, see the exhibition catalogue *The Avant-Garde and Primitive Cinema* (Toronto: Funnel Film Centre, 1985). Bart Testa's *Back and Forth: Early Cinema and the Avant-Garde* (Toronto: Art Gallery of Ontario, 1992) treats several historians of early film. Burch's own films on early cinema include the Brechtian pedagogical exercises *Correction Please; or, How We Got into Pictures*

(1979) and *The Year of the Bodyguard* (1981), as well as a more conventional series of television programs *What Do Those Old Films Mean?* (1987). The historiographic implications of Burch's films are examined by Michelle Lagny in *De l'histoire du cinéma: Méthode historique et histoire du cinéma* (Paris: Colin, 1992), pp. 265–273.

The most thorough discussion of Burch's study of Japanese cinema is Donald Kirihara, "Critical Polarities and the Study of Japanese Film Style," *Journal of Film and Video* 39, no. 1 (Winter 1987): 17–26. See also Kirihara's "Reconstructing Japanese Film," in *Post-Theory: Reconstructing Film Studies,* ed. David Bordwell and Noël Carroll (Madison: University of Wisconsin Press, 1996), pp. 501–519.

The epigraph on page 83 is drawn from a roundtable discussion, "Hiroshima notre amour," in *Cahiers du cinéma: The 1950s: Neo-Realism, Hollywood, New Wave,* ed. Jim Hillier (Cambridge, Mass.: Harvard University Press, 1985), p. 61. I have borrowed the Picasso remark (page 84) from Serge Guilbaut's essay "Postwar Painting Games: The Rough and the Slick," in his anthology *Reconstructing Modernism: Art in New York, Paris, and Montreal, 1945–1964* (Cambridge: MIT Press, 1990). The epigraph from Godard (page 95) comes from "Premiers 'sons anglais,'" *Cinéthique* no. 5 (September–October 1969): 14.

1. Pierre Boulez, "Olivier Messaien," in *Orientations: Collected Writings,* trans. Martin Cooper, ed. Jacques Nattiez (Cambridge, Mass.: Harvard University Press, 1986), p. 413.

2. Clement Greenberg, "Modernist Painting," in *The Collected Essays and Criticism,* ed. John O'Brian, vol. 4 (Chicago: University of Chicago Press, 1993), p. 86.

3. Ibid., p. 85.

4. Clement Greenberg, "Towards a Newer Laocoon," in *The Collected Essays and Criticism,* ed. John O'Brian, vol. 1 (Chicago: University of Chicago Press, 1986), p. 35.

5. Some examples are Arthur L. Gaskill and David A. Englander, *Pictorial Continuity: How to Shoot a Movie Story* (New York: Duell, Sloan and Pearce, 1947); Renato May, *Il linguaggio del film* (Milan: Poligono, 1947), especially the section "Montaggio continuo," pp. 78–133; Emil E. Brodbeck, *Handbook of Basic Motion-Picture Techniques* (New York: McGraw-Hill, 1950), pp. 90–157, 181–214; Karel Reisz, *The Technique of Film Editing* (London: Focal Press, 1953); and Don Livingston, *Film and the Director* (New York: Macmillan, 1953), pp. 15–46.

6. P. Adams Sitney, "'Anticipation of the Night' and 'Prelude,'" *Film Culture* no. 26 (Fall 1962): 55.

7. A detailed discussion of this critical schema may be found in James Peterson, *Dreams of Chaos, Visions of Order: Understanding the American Avant-Garde Cinema* (Detroit: Wayne State University Press, 1994), pp. 85–90.

8. P. Adams Sitney, "Structural Film," in *The Film Culture Reader,* ed. Sitney (New York: Praeger, 1970), p. 339.

9. André Bazin, "The Evolution of the Language of Cinema," in *What Is Cinema?* trans. and ed. Hugh Gray (Berkeley: University of California Press, 1967), p. 36.

10. Jean Domarchi et al., "Hiroshima notre amour," in Hillier, *Cahiers du cinéma: The 1950s,* pp. 60–61.

11. Michel Delahaye, "D'un jeunesse à l'autre: Classement élémentaire de quelques notions et jalons," *Cahiers du cinéma* no. 197 (Christmas 1966/January 1967): 78–81.

12. Ropars-Wuilleumier's writings of the period are gathered in *L'écran de la mémoire: Essais de lecture cinématographique* (Paris: Seuil, 1970).

13. See Marie-Claire Ropars-Wuilleumier, *De la littérature au cinéma* (Paris: Colin, 1970), pp. 116–142.

14. Raymond Durgnat, "Images of the Mind, Part 2: Ebb and Flow," *Films and Filming* 14, no. 11 (August 1968): 15; "Images of the Mind, Part 3: The Impossible Takes a Little Longer," *Films and Filming* 14, no. 12 (September 1968): 14–15.

15. André Hodeir, *Since Debussy: A View of Contemporary Music* (New York: Grove Press, 1961); idem, *Toward Jazz* (New York: Grove Press, 1962); idem, *The Worlds of Jazz* (New York: Grove Press, 1972).

16. Noël Burch, "Qu'est-ce que la nouvelle vague?" *Film Quarterly* 13, no. 2 (Winter 1959): 26.

17. Ibid., p. 29.

18. Noël Burch, *Praxis du cinéma* (Paris: Gallimard, 1969), p. 29. A somewhat different translation of this passage is to be found in the English version, *Theory of Film Practice,* trans. Helen R. Lane (New York: Praeger, 1973), p. 15. The French and English versions of this work sometimes differ significantly, partly because of translation and partly because of authorial revision. When the difference matters to my point, I supply page references for both versions.

19. Burch, *Praxis,* p. 23; *Film Practice,* p. 11. "From a formal point of view, a film is a succession of slices of time and slices of space . . . Two partial *découpages* (in space and time) are joined in a single *Découpage*" (my translation, *Praxis,* pp. 12–13; *Film Practice,* p. 4).

20. A precedent, and possible inspiration, for Burch's argument here is Roger Leenardt's 1964 suggestion that in an era in which the narrative film must subordinate visual form to meaning, it is rare to find "a fiction film in which the 'facture' is as important as the message"; *Chroniques de cinéma* (Paris: Editions de l'Etoile, 1986), p. 208.

21. Burch, *Praxis,* p. 24; *Film Practice,* p. 12. See Pierre Schaeffer, *Traité des objets musicaux: Essais interdisciplines* (Paris: Seuil, 1966).

22. Jacques Rivette, "L'art du présent," *Cahiers du cinéma* no. 132 (June 1962): 37.

23. Indeed, Kubelka explicitly compared his frame-units to Schoenbergian tone-rows; see the discussion in Peter Weibel, "The Viennese Formal Film," in *Film as Film: Formal Experiment in Film, 1910–1975,* ed. Philip Drummond (London: Arts Council of Great Britain, 1979), pp. 108–111. On Kren see Malcolm Le Grice, *Abstract Film and Beyond* (Cambridge, Mass.: MIT Press, 1977), pp. 96–102.

24. Burch criticizes Pollet's film for its lack of an "organic" structuring principle; see *Film Practice,* pp. 71–74.

25. Burch's conception of parametric cinema is invoked in several papers in a 1977 colloquium, Dominique Chateau, ed., *Cinémas de la modernité: Films, théories* (Paris: Klincksieck, 1981). In my own *Narration in the Fiction Film* (Madison: University of Wisconsin Press, 1985), I argue that Burch's theory helps us identify an important option in the history of cinematic narration (pp. 274–310).

26. The most famous example is Brakhage's comment on the sort of film he tried to create: "Imagine an eye unruled by man-made laws of perspective, an eye unprejudiced by compositional logic, an eye which does not respond to the name of everything but which must know each object encountered in life through an adventure of perception"; Stan Brakhage, *Metaphors on Vision,* ed. P. Adams Sitney (New York: Film Culture, 1963), n.p.

27. Christian Metz, *Langage et cinéma* (Paris: Larousse, 1971) and "Au-delà de

l'analogie, l'image" (1970), in *Essais sur la signification au cinéma* (Paris: Klincksieck, 1972), pp. 151–162.

28. See in particular P. Adams Sitney, *Visionary Film: The American Avant-Garde, 1943–1978* (New York: Oxford University Press, 1979). See also Noël Burch, *In and Out of Synch: The Awakening of a Ciné-Dreamer* (Aldershot: Scolar Press, 1991), p. 186.

29. Probably the most influential formulation was that of Marcelin Pleynet, in "Economique, ideologique, formel," *Cinéthique* no. 3 (1969): 10.

30. Annette Michelson, "Film and the Radical Aspiration," *Film Culture* no. 42 (Fall 1966): 39.

31. Jean-Louis Comolli, "Technique et idéologie: Caméra, perspective, profondeur du champ," *Cahiers du cinéma* no. 229 (May 1971): 5–21; no. 230 (July 1971): 51–57; no. 231 (August–September 1971): 42–49; no. 233 (November 1971): 39–45; no. 241 (September–October 1972): 20–24. Portions of this series have been published in English: part 1 appears in *Film Reader* no. 2 (1977): 128–140, parts 3 and 4 in Philip Rosen, ed., *Narrative, Apparatus, Ideology: A Film Theory Reader* (New York: Columbia University Press, 1986), pp. 412–443.

32. Burch, *Film Practice,* p. xix.

33. Burch, *In and Out of Synch,* pp. vii–viii.

34. For instance, in 1976 John Hanhardt counterposed "the narrative model of traditional literary forms" to such avant-garde tendencies as Soviet cinema of the 1920s and modern film; the latter "subverts the dominant codes which assume linearity and spatio-temporal cohesiveness and traditional narrative structures"; "The Medium Viewed: The American Avant-Garde Film," in *A History of the American Avant-Garde Cinema,* ed. Marilyn Singer (New York: American Federation of the Arts, 1976), pp. 27, 29.

35. Jean-Louis Comolli and Jean Narboni, "Cinema/Ideology/Criticism (1)," in *Screen Reader* (London: Society for Education in Film and Television, 1977), pp. 5–8.

36. See Claudine Eizykman, *La jouissance-cinéma* (Paris: Union Générale d'Editions, 1976), p. 10.

37. Burch, *Praxis,* p. 243; *Film Practice,* p. xix.

38. Burch, *In and Out of Synch,* p. 98.

39. Noël Burch, *Life to Those Shadows,* trans. and ed. Ben Brewster (Berkeley: University of California Press, 1990), pp. 6–7.

40. Noël Burch, *To the Distant Observer: Form and Meaning in the Japanese Cinema* (Berkeley: University of California Press, 1979), p. 69. In France this view was articulated by Aragon; see his 1936 contribution to *La querelle du réalisme* (Paris: Diagonales, 1987), p. 85.

41. Burch also hints that the drive toward such illusionism is part of the Western psyche, and that its logic can be elucidated only by psychoanalysis; *Life to Those Shadows,* pp. 267, 273.

42. Ibid., p. 202.

43. Burch, *Correction Please,* p. 8.

44. Burch, *Life to Those Shadows,* pp. 244, 264n.

45. Burch, *In and Out of Synch,* pp. 3–9.

46. Burch, *Life to Those Shadows,* pp. 143–147.

47. Noël Burch and Jorge Dana, "Propositions," *Afterimage* no. 5 (Spring 1974): 42.

48. Burch, *Life to Those Shadows,* pp. 182–184.

49. Noël Burch, "Revoir 'L'argent,'" *Cahiers du cinéma* no. 202 (June–July 1968): 47.

50. Noël Burch, *Marcel L'Herbier* (Paris: Seghers, 1973), pp. 134–157.

51. Noël Burch, *In and Out of Synch,* p. 73.

52. Quoted in Roger Shattuck, *The Banquet Years: The Origins of the Avant-Garde in France, 1885 to World War I,* rev. ed. (New York: Vintage, 1968), p. 146.

53. Kemp R. Niver, ed., *Motion Pictures from the Library of Congress Paper Print Collection, 1894–1912* (Berkeley: University of California Press, 1967). See also Kemp R. Niver, *The First Twenty Years: A Segment of Film History* (Los Angeles: Locare Research Group, 1968) and *D. W. Griffith: His Biograph Films in Perspective* (Los Angeles: Locare Research Group, 1974).

54. Ken Jacobs, "*Tom, Tom, the Piper's Son,*" *Film-Makers' Cooperative Catalogue* no. 5 (New York: Filmmakers' Cooperative, 1971), p. 167.

55. See, for example, the work of Tom Gunning, Charles Musser, Steven Higgins, and Roberta Pearson. See also Cooper C. Graham et al., *D. W. Griffith and the Biograph Company* (Metuchen, N.J.: Scarecrow Press, 1985).

56. George C. Pratt, Associate Curator of Motion Pictures at the George Eastman House, assembled an anthology of early material in *Spellbound in Darkness: A History of the Silent Film* (Greenwich, Conn.: New York Graphic Society, 1973). Eileen Bowser, Associate Curator at the Museum of Modern Art Film Library, oversaw the facsimile reprinting of the 1908–1912 volume of *Biograph Bulletins* (New York: Farrar, Straus and Giroux, 1973). The previous volume (Los Angeles: Locare Research Group, 1971) was edited by Kemp Niver.

57. Russell Merritt, "Nickelodeon Theatres: Building an Audience for the Movies," *American Film Institute Report* 4, no. 2 (May 1973): 4–8; Gordon Hendricks, *Eadweard Muybridge: The Father of the Motion Picture* (New York: Grossman, 1975); Richard Koszarski, ed., *The Rivals of D. W. Griffith* (Minneapolis: Walker Art Center, 1976); Paul Spehr, *The Movies Begin: Making Movies in New Jersey 1887–1920* (Newark: Newark Museum, 1977); and Robert C. Allen, *Vaudeville and Film, 1895–1915: A Study in Media Interaction* (New York: Arno Press, 1980).

58. Roger Holman, ed., *Cinema 1900–1906: An Analytical Study by the National Film Archive (London) and the International Federation of Film Archives,* 2 vols. (Brussels: FIAF, 1982). See also Jon Gartenberg, "The Brighton Project: The Archives and Research," *Iris* 2, no. 1 (1984): 5–16.

59. The fruits of his efforts include a series of articles and the book *Life to Those Shadows,* which Burch claims was largely written in the late 1970s and early 1980s. He also made several films relating to early cinema; see the bibliographical note preceding the notes for this chapter.

60. Burch and Dana, "Propositions," p. 63. See also Burch, *Life to Those Shadows,* p. 152.

61. Burch, *Life to Those Shadows,* pp. 154–155.

62. Burch, *In and Out of Synch,* p. 97; "*Germinal:* Avant le sujet ubiquitaire," *1895,* special issue: "L'année 1913 en France" (1993): 22.

63. Burch, *Life to Those Shadows,* p. 155.

64. Ibid., pp. 173–176.

65. Ibid., pp. 74, 186.

66. Ibid., p. 241.

67. Paul Schrader, *Transcendental Style in Film: Ozu, Bresson, Dreyer* (Berkeley:

University of California Press, 1972); Donald Richie, *Ozu* (Berkeley: University of California Press, 1974).

68. Burch, *Praxis,* p. 245.

69. Burch, *Distant Observer,* p. 47.

70. Ibid., pp. 69–72, 91–92.

71. Ibid., p. 79.

72. Ibid., p. 195.

73. Ibid., pp. 224–229.

74. Burch, *In and Out of Synch,* p. 97.

75. Burch, *Distant Observer,* pp. 264, 274.

76. Ibid., pp. 299, 297, 301.

77. Burch asserts that although the PMR produced "minor masterpieces," the emergence of the IMR was "an objective advance" in the history of film style; *Life to Those Shadows,* pp. 1, 198.

78. Ibid., p. 263.

79. See his (undated) pamphlet for his television series, *What Do Those Old Films Mean?;* his preface to his edited volume *Revoir Hollywood: La nouvelle critique anglo-américaine* (Paris: Nathan, 1993); his psychoanalytic interpretation, in collaboration with Geneviève Seller, of Guitry's *Donne-moi tes yeux* in Arnaud, *Sacha Guitry, cinéaste,* ed. Philippe Arnaud (Brussels: Yellow Now, 1993), pp. 206–207; and his *Les communistes de Hollywood: Autre chose que des martyrs* (Paris: Presses de la Sorbonne Nouvelle, 1994).

80. Burch, *Life to Those Shadows,* p. 198.

81. Significantly, Burch has not tried to exclude his earlier views from discussion: he has continually republished writings from all phases of his career.

82. Burch, *Life to Those Shadows,* pp. 1–3, 22, 173. See also idem, *In and Out of Synch,* p. 120; and Burch and Dana, "Propositions," p. 52.

83. Burch, *Life to Those Shadows,* p. 173.

84. Noël Burch, "Film's Institutional Mode of Representation," in *In and Out of Synch,* pp. 122–127.

85. The French title of *Life to Those Shadows* is *La lucarne de l'infini: Naissance du langage cinématographique* (Paris: Nathan, 1991). The subtitle, perhaps ironically, recapitulates both the "birth of cinema" metaphor and the idea of "film language" found in the Standard Version.

86. Burch, *Life to Those Shadows,* p. 241. See also Noël Burch, "Japon: D'une parole à l'autre," in *Conférence du Collège d'Histoire de l'Art Cinématographique,* ed. Jacques Aumont, vol. 1 (Paris: Cinémathèque Française, 1992), p. 159.

87. In 1947 Bazin described classical construction in language close to Burch's: "The plot [*récit*] thus analyzed is recomposed on the screen according to a visual melodic line that joins all the twists of the action . . . O minotaur, here is Ariadne's thread: *découpage*"; "La technique de *Citizen Kane,*" *Les temps modernes* 2, no. 17 (1947): 945.

88. Alexandre Astruc, "L'évolution du cinéma américain," in *Du stylo à la caméra . . . et de la caméra au stylo: Ecrits (1942–1984)* (Paris: L'Archipel, 1992), p. 291.

89. See David Bordwell, "A Cinema of Flourishes: Japanese Decorative Classicism of the Prewar Era," in *Reframing Japanese Cinema,* ed. David Desser and Arthur Noletti (Bloomington: Indiana University Press, 1992), pp. 327–345; and idem, "Visual Style in Japanese Cinema, 1925–1945," *Film History* 7, no. 1 (Spring 1995): 5–31.

90. See David Bordwell, *Ozu and the Poetics of Cinema* (Princeton: Princeton University Press, 1988), pp. 74–118, 143–159.

91. See David Bordwell and Kristin Thompson, "Linearity, Materialism, and the Study of the Early American Cinema," *Wide Angle* 5, no. 3 (Spring 1983): 4–15.

92. Michael Fried, "From *Three American Painters*," in Harrison and Wood, *Art Theory 1900–1990*, p. 772.

93. On this point it is worth contrasting Burch's project with that of P. Adams Sitney. Sitney's history of the American avant-garde film traces the transformation of formal problems from one period or group to another. In *Visionary Film* he argues that an effort to render states of mind propels the American avant-garde through the psychodramas of the 1940s, the lyric film developed by Brakhage, the "mythopeic and picaresque" epics, all eventually challenged by a more minimalist conception of cinematic subjectivity, Structural film. With each tendency complementing, correcting, or contesting the image of mind put forth by its predecessors, this scheme exemplifies the "perpetual revolution" within modernism that Fried posits. This point is particularly explicit in Sitney's "The Idea of Morphology: The First of Four Lectures on Film Theory," *Film Culture* no. 53–55 (Spring 1972): 1–24.

94. Burch, *In and Out of Synch*, p. 160.

5. Prospects for Progress

In the enormous literature on early film history, the most useful anthology is Thomas Elsaesser, ed., *Early Cinema: Space, Frame, Narrative* (London: British Film Institute, 1990). See also John Fell, ed., *Film before Griffith* (Berkeley: University of California Press, 1983); and the invaluable volumes issuing from the Giornate del Cinema Muto held at Pordenone, notably Yuri Tsivian, ed., *Silent Witnesses: Russian Films, 1908–1919* (Pordenone: Biblioteca dell'Immagine, 1989); and Paolo Cherchi Usai and Lorenzo Codelli, eds., *Before Caligari: German Cinema, 1895–1920* (Pordenone: Biblioteca dell'Immagine, 1990).

DOMITOR, the international association for the study of silent cinema, was founded in 1985 at a Pordenone gathering. Under the group's auspices Elena Dagrada has published a basic guide to research on early film, *Bibliographie internationale du cinéma des premiers temps/International Bibliography on Early Cinema*, 2nd ed. (Madison, Wis.: DOMITOR, 1995).

Tom Gunning's hypothesis that the "cinema of attractions" characterizes the dominant trend in pre-1904 cinema is partly indebted to André Gaudreault's explorations into the narrative organization of early films. Gaudreault and Gunning's article "Le cinéma des premiers temps: Un défi à l'histoire du cinéma?" in *L'histoire du cinéma: Nouvelles approches*, ed. Jacques Aumont, André Gaudreault, and Michel Marie (Paris: Publications de la Sorbonne, 1989), pp. 49–63, was originally presented as a joint paper in August 1985. See also Gaudreault, "Narration et monstration au cinéma," *Hors cadre* no. 2 (Spring 1984): 87–98; and his book with François Jost, *Le récit cinématographique* (Paris: Nathan, 1990). Donald Crafton develops some similar points in "Pie and Chase: Gag, Spectacle and Narrative in Slapstick Comedy," in *The Slapstick Symposium: May 2 and 3, 1985: Museum of Modern Art, New York: 41st FIAF Congress* (Brussels: FIAF, 1988), pp. 49–59.

On the development of the "history of vision" argument in art historiography, see Part Two of Michael Podro, *The Critical Historians of Art* (New Haven: Yale University

Press, 1982). Ernst Gombrich offers a cogent critique of the tradition, particularly in its appeal to cultural determination of style, in the introductory chapter of *Art and Illusion: A Study in the Psychology of Pictorial Representation* (Princeton: Princeton University Press, 1961), pp. 11–24. Gombrich's remarks incline me to think that the "culture of modernity" strain in current Frankfurt School film theory is replaying preoccupations of nineteenth-century Viennese art history. For an account arguing that this art-historical tradition is itself symptomatic of modernity, see Antonia Lant, "Haptical Cinema," *October* no. 74 (Fall 1995): 45–73.

This chapter's criticisms of the modernity thesis do not concentrate on technology; obviously, many of cinema's basic features, such as the display of moving images in rapid succession, have their sources in "modernizing" forces in the nineteenth century. Ian Christie's *The Last Machine: Early Cinema and the Birth of the Modern World* (London: BBC, 1994) offers an entertaining popular introduction to this area. Similar issues are taken up in the essays collected in Leo Charney and Vanessa R. Schwartz, eds., *Cinema and the Invention of Modern Life* (Berkeley: University of California Press, 1995). Neither volume tackles the question of how features of modernity might explain stylistic continuity and change in filmmaking practice.

R. S. Crane outlines a type of history close to the one I am suggesting here; Crane, "Critical and Historical Principles of Literary History," in *The Idea of the Humanities and Other Essays Critical and Historical*, vol. 2 (Chicago: University of Chicago Press, 1967), pp. 45–156. Crane's critique of a priori history-writing closely parallels my objections to "top-down" histories of cinema. Just as important is Crane's insistence that historical research pivots upon precise and open-ended *questions* rather than a prior commitment to an overarching scheme of historical change (such as, in my line of argument, a cultural shift into modernity or postmodernity).

The epigraph on page 149 comes from an interview with Howard Hawks in Eric Sherman, *Directing the Film: Film Directors on Their Art* (Boston: Little, Brown, 1976), p. 99.

1. Recent examples are Geoffrey O'Brien, *The Phantom Empire* (New York: Norton, 1993); David Parkinson, *History of Film* (London: Thames and Hudson, 1995); David Robinson, *From Peep Show to Palace: The Birth of American Film* (New York: Columbia University Press, 1996).

2. Stephen Kern, *The Culture of Time and Space, 1880–1918* (Cambridge, Mass.: Harvard University Press, 1983), pp. 71–88, 218–219.

3. See David Bordwell, "Textual Analysis, Etc.," *Enclitic* 5, no. 2/6, no. 1 (Fall 1981/Spring 1982): 125–136.

4. Susan Sontag, "The Decay of Cinema," *New York Times Magazine* (25 February 1996): 60–61.

5. Gilles Deleuze, *Cinema 1: The Movement-Image*, trans. Hugh Tomlinson and Barbara Habberjam (Minneapolis: University of Minnesota Press, 1986), p. ix.

6. Gilles Deleuze, *Cinema 2: The Time-Image*, trans. Hugh Tomlinson and Robert Galeta (Minneapolis: University of Minnesota Press, 1989), p. 43.

7. Deleuze, *Cinema 1*, pp. 37–40, 48–53, 123.

8. Deleuze, *Cinema 2*, p. 221. For what I take to be a more nuanced and faithful use of Wölfflin's distinction, see Chapter 6.

9. Jean Mitry, *Histoire du cinéma*, vol. 1: *1895–1914* (Paris: Editions Universitaires, 1967), pp. 11–18.

10. Jean Mitry, "De quelques problèmes d'histoire et d'esthétique du cinéma," *Cahiers de la Cinémathèque* no. 10–11 (Summer–Autumn 1973): 113.

11. Mitry, *Histoire du cinéma,* 1: 12.

12. Sadoul was almost alone among Standard-Version historians in his acknowledgment of the difficulties posed by different versions. See his "Matériaux, méthodes et problèmes de l'histoire du cinéma," *La nouvelle critique* no. 228 (October–November 1971): 69–73.

13. Jean Mitry, "L'ancien et le nouveau," in *Histoire du cinéma: Nouvelles approches,* ed. Jacques Aumont, André Gaudreault, and Michel Marie (Paris: Publications de la Sorbonne, 1989), pp. 200–201.

14. The case of *Intolerance* is exemplary in this regard. See Gillian Anderson, "'No Music Until Cue': The Reconstruction of D. W. Griffith's *Intolerance,*" *Griffithiana* no. 38/39 (October 1990): 158–169; Eileen Bowser, "Some Principles of Film Restoration," ibid., pp. 172–173; and Russell Merritt, "D. W. Griffith's *Intolerance:* Reconstructing an Unattainable Text," *Film History* 4, no. 4 (1990): 337–375.

15. Barry Salt, *Film Style and Technology: History and Analysis,* 2nd ed. (London: Starword, 1992), pp. 265–266, 283, 296.

16. Richard Abel, *French Cinema: The First Wave, 1915–1929* (Princeton: Princeton University Press, 1984), pp. 286–289.

17. Teshome H. Gabriel, *Third Cinema in the Third World: The Aesthetics of Liberation* (Ann Arbor: UMI Research Press, 1979); Michèle Lagny, Marie-Claire Ropars, and Pierre Sorlin, *Générique des années 30* (Paris: Presses Universitaires de Vincennes, 1986).

18. See Katherine Singer Kovács, "Georges Méliès and the *Féerie,*" in Fell, *Film before Griffith,* pp. 244–257.

19. See Eileen Bowser, "Preparation for Brighton: The American Contribution," in *Cinema 1900–1906: An Analytical Study by the National Film Archive (London) and the International Federation of Film Archives,* ed. Roger Holman, vol. 1 (Brussels: FIAF, 1982), pp. 8–9.

20. Richard Abel, *The Ciné Goes to Town: French Cinema, 1896–1914* (Berkeley: University of California Press, 1994), pp. 183, 246.

21. Stephen Bottomore, "Shots in the Dark: The Real Origins of Film Editing," in Elsaesser, *Early Cinema,* pp. 104–110.

22. Ben Brewster, "Frammenti Vitagraph alla Library of Congress," in *Vitagraph Co. of America: Il Cinema prima di Hollywood,* ed. Paolo Cherchi Usai (Pordenone: Studio Tesi, 1987), pp. 279–321.

23. Meyer Schapiro, *Words and Pictures* (The Hague: Mouton, 1973), p. 38.

24. In 1913 a scene was defined as "all of the action of a play that is taken in one spot at one time without stopping of the camera" (Epes Winthrop Sargent, *Technique of the Photoplay,* 2nd ed. [New York: Moving Picture World, 1913], p. 164). Henri Diamant-Berger referred to a tableau as "a view taken by the camera from a constant angle" (*Le cinéma* [Paris: Renaissance du Livre, 1919], p. 154). I am grateful for many discussions with Ben Brewster, Lea Jacobs, and Kristin Thompson on this matter.

25. See J. Berg Esenwein and Arthur Leeds, *Writing the Photoplay* (Springfield, Mass.: Home Correspondence School, 1913), p. 201; Epes Winthrop Sargent, *The Technique of the Photoplay,* 3d ed. (New York: Moving Picture World, 1916), pp. 148–149, 360.

26. Sargent, *Technique of the Photoplay,* 3d ed., p. 173.

27. The implication is that the close-up, far from drastically isolating a figure, includes enough space to show other characters' entrances and exits; to accomplish this

the framing need only cut off the legs of the figure. This seems to have been what Griffith meant in an interview when he claimed that his "close-ups" were criticized because they make "the characters come swimming in on the scene"; Robert E. Welsh, "David W. Griffith Speaks," in *Spellbound in Darkness: A History of the Silent Film,* ed. George C. Pratt (Greenwich, Conn.: New York Graphic Society, 1966), p. 111.

28. Charles Musser, *The Emergence of Cinema: The American Screen to 1907* (New York: Scribner's, 1990), pp. 193–223. Yuri Tsivian has suggested that in Russia the program, not the film, remained the relevant unit of audience experience throughout the first decade of the century; *Early Cinema in Russia and Its Cultural Reception,* trans. Alan Bodger (London: Routledge, 1994), pp. 126–133.

29. Musser, *Emergence of Cinema,* pp. 297, 316; Charles Musser, *Thomas A. Edison and His Kinetographic Motion Pictures* (New Brunswick, N.J.: Rutgers University Press, 1995), pp. 31–34.

30. Robert C. Allen, *Vaudeville and Film, 1895–1915: A Study in Media Interaction* (New York: Arno Press, 1980), pp. 212–220.

31. See Charles Musser, *Before the Nickelodeon: Edwin S. Porter and the Edison Manufacturing Company* (Berkeley: University of California Press, 1991), pp. 394–396; and André Gaudreault, "Showing and Telling: Image and Word in Early Cinema," in Elsaesser, *Early Cinema,* pp. 276–277.

32. Gaudreault and Gunning, "Le cinéma des premiers temps."

33. Tom Gunning, "The Cinema of Attractions: Early Film, Its Spectator and the Avant-Garde," in Elsaesser, *Early Cinema,* pp. 56–60.

34. Tom Gunning, "Cinéma des attractions et modernité," *Cinémathèque* no. 5 (Spring 1994): 130.

35. Tom Gunning, "What I Saw from the Rear Window of the Hotel des Folies-Dramatiques, or the Story Point of View Films Told," in *Ce que je vois de mon ciné,* ed. André Gaudreault (Paris: Klincksieck, 1988), pp. 36–38.

36. Gunning, "Cinema of Attractions," pp. 57–58.

37. Tom Gunning, "I film Vitagraph e il cinema dell'integrazione narrativa," in Cherchi Usai, *Vitagraph Co. of America,* pp. 225–239.

38. Tom Gunning, "'Now You See It, Now You Don't': The Temporality of the Cinema of Attractions," *Velvet Light Trap* no. 32 (1993): 10–11.

39. Tom Gunning, "Passion Play as Palimpsest: The Nature of the Text in the History of Early Cinema," in *Une invention du diable? Cinéma des premiers temps et religion,* ed. Roland Cosandey, André Gaudreault, and Tom Gunning (Sainte-Foy: Les Presses de l'Université Laval/Lausanne: Payot, 1992), p. 107.

40. Gunning offers an excellently explicit account of these presuppositions in "'Now You See It,'" pp. 3–4.

41. Tom Gunning, "The Whole Town's Gawking: Early Cinema and the Visual Experience of Modernity," *Yale Journal of Criticism* 7, no. 2 (1994): 189.

42. For a review of research, see Pierre Jenn, *Georges Méliès cinéaste: Le montage cinématographique chez Georges Méliès* (Paris: Albatros, 1984), pp. 15–93, 116–126. See also Abel, *Ciné Goes to Town,* pp. 71–86.

43. Jacques Malthête, "Méliès, technicien du collage," in *Méliès et la naissance du spectacle cinématographique,* ed. Madeleine Malthête-Méliès (Paris: Klincksieck, 1984), pp. 171–184; idem, "Georges Méliès: Montage . . . et collage," *CinémAction* no. 72 (1994): 16–20.

44. Barry Salt, "The Evolution of Film Form up to 1906," in Holman, *Cinema*

1900–1906, 1: 286; Pierre Jenn, "Le cinéma selon Georges Méliès," in Malthête-Méliès, *Méliès et la naissance du spectacle cinématographique,* pp. 143–148.

45. André Gaudreault, "'Théatralité' et 'narrativité' de G. Méliès," in Malthête-Méliès, *Méliès et la naissance du spectacle cinématographique,* pp. 212–218.

46. See Tom Gunning, "Le récit filmé et l'idéal théâtral: Griffith et les 'films d'art' français," in *Les premiers ans du cinéma français,* ed. Pierre Guibbert (Perpignan: Institut Jean Vigo, 1985), p. 128; idem, "'Primitive' Cinema: A Frame-Up? Or, the Trick's on Us," in Elsaesser, *Early Cinema,* pp. 97–100.

47. Porter quoted in Musser, *Before the Nickelodeon,* p. 230.

48. Charles Musser, "The Early Cinema of Edwin S. Porter," in Holman, *Cinema 1900–1906,* 1: 273–278. See also Musser, *Before the Nickelodeon,* p. 100.

49. Musser, *Before the Nickelodeon,* pp. 205–211.

50. Marguerite Engberg points out similar repetitions in early Danish filmmaking in "Le cinéma de fiction au Danemark avant 1908," *Iris* 2, no. 1 (1984): 128.

51. See André Gaudreault, "Detours in Film Narrative: The Development of Cross-Cutting," in Elsaesser, *Early Cinema,* pp. 133–144. How did the inaccurate version enter the canon? The Museum of Modern Art had preserved it, and Lewis Jacobs used the print as the basis of his influential account of Porter in *The Rise of the American Film* ([New York: Harcourt Brace, 1939], pp. 43–46). It is generally agreed that this print is the result of recutting sometime after 1910, when orthodox cross-cutting had become more common. Jacques Deslandes had some years before pointed out the disparity between the Edison catalogue description and a strip of stills published in Jacobs' *Rise of the American Film;* see Deslandes, *Histoire comparée du cinéma,* vol. 2: *Du cinématographe au cinéma 1896–1906* (Paris: Casterman, 1968), pp. 372–375, 385–386.

52. Musser, *Before the Nickelodeon,* p. 226. For a contrasting view, which considers Porter's presentation of the whole action twice as the first step toward true alternating editing, see Gaudreault, "Detours," p. 144.

53. Musser, *Before the Nickelodeon,* pp. 416, 403–405.

54. Henry Stephen Gordon, "The Story of D. W. Griffith," part 1, *Photoplay* 10, no. 1 (June 1916): 30.

55. Orson Welles and Peter Bogdanovich, *This Is Orson Welles,* ed. Jonathan Rosenbaum (New York: HarperCollins, 1992), p. 21.

56. Review of *Enoch Arden, Motography* 6, no. 1 (July 1911): 38.

57. See Eileen Bowser, *The Transformation of Cinema: 1907–1915* (New York: Scribner's, 1990), pp. 60–62.

58. For a discussion and illustration of one possible source for Griffith, see Barry Salt, "The Physician of the Castle," *Sight and Sound* 54, no. 4 (Autumn 1985): 284–285.

59. The example is from *The House of His Family* (1909), discussed in Joyce E. Jesniowski, *Thinking in Pictures: Dramatic Structure in D. W. Griffith's Biograph Films* (Berkeley: University of California Press, 1987), pp. 67–71.

60. On Griffith's cross-cutting, see in particular André Gaudreault, "De 'L'arrivée d'un train' à 'The Lonedale Operator': Une trajectoire à parcourir," in *D. W. Griffith,* ed. Jean Mottet (Paris: L'Harmattan, 1984), pp. 57–71; Jesniowski, *Thinking in Pictures,* pp. 127–137, 176–179; Bowser, *Transformation of Cinema,* pp. 258–266; and Tom Gunning, *D. W. Griffith and the Origins of American Narrative Film: The Early Years at Biograph* (Urbana: University of Illinois Press, 1991), pp. 95–103, 130–138, 190–206.

61. Henry Stephen Gordon, "Story of D. W. Griffith," part 3, *Photoplay* 10, no. 3 (August 1916): 87–88.

62. See Gunning, *D. W. Griffith,* pp. 189, 265–270; Jesniowski, *Thinking in Pictures,* pp. 34–39; Bowser, *Transformation of Cinema,* pp. 95–98. Charles Keil discusses Griffith's 1913 films in "Transition through Tension: Stylistic Diversity in the Late Griffith Biographs," *Cinema Journal* 28, no. 3 (Spring 1989): 22–41.

63. For example, the Dane Benjamin Christensen used a series of close-ups to show the wind blowing a trapdoor shut in *The Mysterious X* (1913). The development of editing in Danish films of this period is discussed in Ron Mottram, *The Danish Cinema before Dreyer* (Metuchen, N.J.: Scarecrow, 1988), pp. 85, 104, 116, 142, 175.

64. Jesniowski, *Thinking in Pictures,* pp. 117–118, 126. See also Jacques Aumont, "Griffith, le cadre, la figure," in *Le cinéma américain: Analyses de films,* ed. Raymond Bellour (Paris: Flammarion, 1980), pp. 57–60; Gunning, *D. W. Griffith,* pp. 109–123, 293–295; and Scott Simmon, *The Films of D. W. Griffith* (Cambridge: Cambridge University Press, 1993), pp. 34–35. In an earlier essay ("Textual Analysis, Etc.," p. 134) I speculated that this device might have been conventional during Griffith's period; alas, it apparently was not.

65. Griffith discusses this use of the switchback in "Weak Points in a Strong Business," *Motion Picture News* 11, no. 18 (8 May 1915): 39.

66. See Russell Merritt, "Mr. Griffith, *The Painted Lady,* and the Distractive Frame," *Image* 19, no. 4 (December 1976): 26–30; and Jesniowski, *Thinking in Pictures,* pp. 72–75.

67. Gunning, *D. W. Griffith,* pp. 35–43, 70–80.

68. Astute comments on this era can be found in Richard Koszarski, ed., *The Rivals of D. W. Griffith: Alternate Auteurs, 1913–1918* (Minneapolis: Walker Art Center, 1976).

69. Bowser, *Transformation of Cinema,* pp. 266–269.

70. Kristin Thompson, "The Formulation of the Classical Style, 1909–28," in David Bordwell, Janet Staiger, and Kristin Thompson, *The Classical Hollywood Cinema: Film Style and Mode of Production to 1960* (New York: Columbia University Press, 1985), pp. 196–212.

71. Ibid., pp. 161–162.

72. See, for instance, Kristin Thompson, "Fairbanks without the Moustache: A Case for the Early Films," in *Sulla via di Hollywood,* ed. Paolo Cherchi Usai and Lorenzo Codelli (Pordenone: Biblioteca dell'Immagine, 1988), pp. 168–176.

73. Thompson, "Formulation of the Classical Style," pp. 195–196.

74. Mitry, *Histoire du cinéma,* 1: 370–400.

75. See, for example, Kristin Thompson, "Early Alternatives to the Hollywood Mode of Production: Implications for Europe's Avant-Gardes," *Film History* 5, no. 4 (December 1993): 386–396; Miriam Tsikounas, "Russes et soviétiques: Des conceptions différentes," *CinémAction* no. 72 (1994): 28–30.

76. Urban Gad, *Filmen: Dens Midler og maal* (Copenhagen: Gyldendal, 1919), p. 129; Colette, "*L'Outrage*" (1917), in *Au cinéma,* ed. Alain and Odette Virmaux (Paris: Flammarion, 1975), p. 43.

77. Kristin Thompson has discovered a curious variant of shot/reverse-shot cutting in a 1917 Argentine film, in which during a dialogue every reverse shot is preceded by a return to the master framing; "The International Exploration of Cinematic Expressivity," in *Film and the First World War,* ed. Karel Dibbets and Bert Hogenkamp (Amsterdam: Amsterdam University Press, 1995), pp. 69–70.

78. Tom Gunning points out that Sjöström employed such cutting even earlier, in *The Girl from Stormycroft* (1917); "Notes and Queries about the Year 1913 and Film Style: National Styles and Deep Staging," *1895*, special issue: "L'année 1913 en France" (1993): 203.

79. See Charles Musser, "Rethinking Early Cinema: Cinema of Attractions and Narrativity," *Yale Journal of Criticism* 7, no. 2 (1994): 216–225.

80. See Barry Salt, "What We Can Learn from the First Twenty Years of Cinema," *Iris* 2, no. 1 (1984): 83–85.

81. See, for example, Robert C. Allen, "Film History: The Narrow Discourse," in *1977 Film Studies Annual: Part Two* (Pleasantville, New York: Redgrave, 1977), pp. 9–17; Rick Altman, "Towards a Historiography of American Film," *Cinema Journal* 16, no. 2 (Spring 1977): 1–25.

82. For discussion see Vincent Descombes, *Modern French Philosophy,* trans. L. Scott-Fox and J. M. Harding (Cambridge: Cambridge University Press, 1980), chaps. 1 and 2.

83. Such a taxonomy is offered in Burch and Dana's "Propositions," pp. 46–48. The most influential typology of this sort is Jean-Louis Comolli and Jean Narboni, "Cinema/Ideology/Criticism (1)," (1969), in *Screen Reader 1: Cinema/Ideology/Politics* (London: SEFT, 1977), pp. 2–11.

84. Further discussions of the rise of Grand Theory can be found in Noël Carroll, *Mystifying Movies: Fads and Fallacies in Contemporary Film Theory* (New York: Columbia University Press, 1988), pp. 1–8; David Bordwell, "Contemporary Film Studies and the Vicissitudes of Grand Theory," in *Post-Theory: Reconstructing Film Studies,* ed. David Bordwell and Noël Carroll (Madison: University of Wisconsin Press, 1996), pp. 3–36; Carroll, "Prospects for Film Theory: A Personal Assessment," ibid., pp. 37–68.

85. On this process see David Bordwell, *Making Meaning: Inference and Rhetoric in the Interpretation of Cinema* (Cambridge, Mass.: Harvard University Press, 1989), pp. 13–42, 71–104.

86. For an example see Judith Mayne, "'Primitive' Narration," in *The Woman at the Keyhole* (Bloomington: Indiana University Press, 1990), pp. 157–183.

87. See Bordwell, "Contemporary Film Studies," pp. 8–12.

88. Walter Benjamin, "The Work of Art in the Age of Mechanical Reproduction," in *Illuminations,* ed. Hannah Arendt (New York: Schocken, 1968), p. 222. Benjamin cites Riegl and Wickhoff's study of "the organization of perception" at various periods, as reflected in art (ibid.). On Benjamin's debt to Riegl, see Thomas Y. Levin, "Walter Benjamin and the Theory of Art History: An Introduction to 'Rigorous Study of Art,'" *October* no. 47 (Winter 1988): 77–83.

89. See Heinrich Wölfflin, *Principles of Art History: The Problem of the Development of Style in Later Art,* trans. M. D. Hottinger (New York: Dover, n.d.), p. 11. E. H. Gombrich has shown that Hegel's thought decisively influenced Burckhardt, Riegl, Dvořák, and other cultural historians of art. See Gombrich, "In Search of Cultural History," in *Ideals and Idols: Essays on Values in History and in Art* (Oxford: Phaidon, 1979), pp. 24–59; idem, "'The Father of Art History': A Reading of the *Lectures on Aesthetics* of G. W. F. Hegel (1770–1831)," in *Tributes: Interpreters of Our Cultural Tradition* (Oxford: Phaidon, 1984), pp. 51–69; and his review of two works by Panofsky, "Icon," *New York Review of Books* (15 February 1996): 29–30.

90. Benjamin, "Work of Art," pp. 239–242.

91. David Frisby's *Fragments of Modernity: Theories of Modernity in the Work of*

Simmel, Kracauer, and Benjamin (Cambridge, Mass.: MIT Press, 1986) traces this idea from Baudelaire through Simmel and Nietzsche to Benjamin and Kracauer.

92. The history-of-vision proponent may reply that biological evolution is irrelevant to claims about the new modes of perception in modernity. I am not so sure, for two reasons. First, proponents of the position often write about perceptual change rather loosely, as if within a few decades people could start to rely automatically upon haptic cues instead of visual ones. Yet this sort of change requires something in the nature of evolutionary mutation.

Still, the point of departure for many of these theorists—the confusion a person feels when adrift in the modern city—does seem phenomenologically convincing. If you come from a small town, a day in Times Square or Piccadilly Circus can leave you with a feeling of sensory overload. But we might hypothesize that this confusion has an evolutionary explanation. Over several million years, humans evolved in a savannah environment, with its open spaces, unobstructed views of danger and shelter, and the possibility of easily retreating some distance from other humans. We have not had sufficient time to adapt (in the strong, biological sense) to the challenges of life in any city, ancient, medieval, or modern. The densely packed industrial city, as an environment for which we were not made, should seem particularly threatening. An explanation along these lines would treat the perceptual skills that help us cope with this environment as acquired through experience, with all the ephemerality and all the variations among individuals that any such learned skills display.

93. The best example I know is Michael Baxandall's *Painting and Experience in Fifteenth-Century Italy* (London: Oxford University Press, 1972). Baxandall carefully explains how the cultivation of certain habits and skills in appreciating painting developed out of particular social practices, such as preaching and measuring by eye. He has no need to posit an all-pervading Renaissance "mode of vision"; his case for the development of contrasting domains of pictorial expertise would suffer if he did.

94. Benjamin, "Work of Art," pp. 238, 250.

95. For example, Wolfgang Schivelbusch claims that the railroad created a specifically modern reorganization of space, time, and vision. This was further exploited in the diorama, the department store, and moving pictures; *The Railway Journey: The Industrialization of Time and Space in the Nineteenth Century* (Berkeley: University of California Press, 1986), pp. 165–194.

96. Miriam Hansen, "Benjamin, Cinema, and Experience: The Blue Flower in the Land of Technology," *New German Critique* no. 40 (Winter 1987): 185. See also Jacques Aumont, *L'oeil interminable: Cinéma et peinture* (Paris: Séguier, 1989), pp. 44–56.

97. Tom Gunning, "An Aesthetic of Astonishment: Early Film and the (In)Credulous Spectator," in *Viewing Positions: Ways of Seeing Film,* ed. Linda Williams (New Brunswick, N.J.: Rutgers , 1995), p. 128.

98. Gunning, "The Whole Town's Gawking," pp. 197–199.

99. Gunning, "The Aesthetics of Astonishment," pp. 197–199.

100. The criticisms which I pursue in the text presume that Gunning takes attractions to be, among other things, results of processes at work within modernity. I believe that the points already cited in my text make this a plausible inference. In a response to my text, however, Gunning has said that he does not believe attractions to be effects produced by modernity. "I have claimed in my principal essay on this topic . . . simply

that the concept of attractions could be fruitfully extended to an analysis of the cultural forms of modernity, especially of commercial culture . . . I find a rich congruence in these forms of modern culture, which I propose are areas of investigation that should help us to describe the relation between early cinema and the culture of modernity. I never make a causal claim, which indeed I would find very dubious in its simplistic sense of how culture and style interact, bereft of mediation" (letter to author).

I am grateful to Gunning for clarifying his position. Still, after reexamining the article he highlights ("The Whole Town's Gawking"), I cannot agree that it does not make causal claims. True, the essay does frequently treat the concept of attractions as a methodological tool for describing neglected aspects of modernity. But the article also treats attractions as consequences of forces in modern life.

Most often the essay claims that attractions reflect or express the new visual culture: "If the experience of modernity finds its locus classicus in big city streets and their crowds, the unique stimulus offered by this new environment discovers its aesthetic form in attractions . . . Attractions express the fugitive nature of modern life, with their brief form and lack of narrative development, as well as their aggressivity" (p. 193). This last sentence indicates that the fugitive nature of modern life is somehow causally linked to the brief, fragmentary nature of attractions. Furthermore, talk of reflection or expression often harbors a tacit causality. Because I feel euphoric, I express that feeling in a smile; a mirror reflects my image because I stand before it and because photons behave in certain ways.

The causal nature of the process seems still more evident when Gunning treats attractions as a result of urban commercial culture: "The variety of factors that converge to create an emerging culture of consumption affect the appearance of attractions as both a form of entertainment and a means of promoting consumption." In turn, attractions themselves have causal powers: "Attractions do more than reflect modernity; they provide one of its specific methods" (p. 194). At its close the article invokes a biological metaphor of growth: "The concept of attractions reveals a common seedbed for both the experience of modernity and aspects of the aesthetic of modernism" (p. 199). This seedbed (presumably, urban life) would appear to be one causal precondition for modernity, modernism, and attractions.

For all these reasons, I take Gunning's article to be proposing that certain aspects of modernity, through causal mechanisms yet to be specified, produce or favor the development of attractions. This is not to say that the causality in question is linear or unmediated. And certainly there may be mutual interactions among the elements we pick out. But surely we are on the terrain of some sort of causal explanation, not simply descriptions of similarities between cinematic attractions and other phenomena.

Even if Gunning no longer holds this view, it is available in print and is likely to be adopted by sympathetic readers—which is why I analyze it here and in the text. Finally, I do not see that the line of inquiry Gunning proposes will avoid matters of causality. Why would we search for congruences unless they led us toward some explanatory hypotheses? We can find similarities between a great many events that have no historical relationship to one another. (You may have Caesar's nose, but that's of no interest to a historian of ancient Rome.) The similarities between cinematic attractions and aspects of modern urban culture which a historian finds striking are likely to be ones that intuitively suggest either a common cause or some causal interaction among themselves.

101. Benjamin, "Work of Art," p. 217.

102. One theorist has faced this point, declaring that after the changeover has been made to modern consciousness, stimuli associated with earlier stages of consciousness simply no longer register. See Schivelbusch, *The Railway Journey,* p. 165.

103. I am grateful to Charles Keil for suggesting this idea to me. He has developed this point in "'Fatal Attractions': The Problems Transitional Cinema Poses for Spectatorship" (forthcoming).

104. Gunning, "Cinema of Attractions," p. 134.

105. Gunning discusses the rise of classical narrative cinema as an analogue for bourgeois theater in *D. W. Griffith,* pp. 38–41. In another essay, "Urban Spaces in Early Silent Film" (Working Papers, Center for Urbanity and Aesthetics, University of Copenhagen, 1995), Gunning relates *Traffic in Souls* (1913) to various conceptions of vision in the modern city, but he does not treat this relation as depending on the attraction; implicitly he treats the film as a "classical" text (p. 23), a predecessor of the urban thrillers of Lang and Hitchcock.

106. Inventories of these features are provided in Steven Connor, *Postmodernist Culture: An Introduction to Theories of the Contemporary* (Oxford: Blackwell, 1989), pp. 44–56; and David Harvey, *The Condition of Postmodernity: An Enquiry into the Origins of Cultural Change* (Oxford: Blackwell, 1989), pp. 39–65.

107. Fredric Jameson, *Postmodernism, or, the Cultural Logic of Late Capitalism* (Durham, N.C.: Duke University Press, 1991), pp. 1, 6, 7.

108. Ibid., pp. 38–39.

109. Régis Debray, *Vie et mort de l'image: Une histoire du regard en Occident* (Paris: Gallimard, 1992), p. 18.

110. Ibid., pp. 374–375, 178.

111. Ibid., pp. 283–358. This chapter has been translated into English as "The Three Ages of Looking," *Critical Inquiry* 21, no. 3 (Spring 1995): 529–555.

112. Debray, *Vie et mort,* p. 228.

113. Ibid., pp. 437–440.

114. For commentary on this and other problems of postmodernist theory, see Noël Carroll, "Periodizing Postmodernism?" *Clio* 26, no. 2 (Winter 1997): 143–165.

115. Fincher quoted in Amy Taubin, "The Allure of Decay," *Sight and Sound* 6, no. 1 (January 1996): 34.

116. Jean-Luc Godard, "*Pierrot* My Friend," in *Godard on Godard: Critical Writings by Jean-Luc Godard,* ed. Jean Narboni and Tom Milne (New York: Viking Press, 1972), p. 214.

117. Michael Podro usefully traces modern developments of this idea in German-language art historiography; *Critical Historians of Art,* pp. 34–36, 56–58, 68–97.

118. James Ackerman, "Style," in *Distance Points: Essays in Theory and Renaissance Art and Architecture* (Cambridge, Mass.: MIT Press, 1991), pp. 7–11.

119. Ernst Gombrich and Didier Eribon, *Looking for Answers: Conversations on Art and Science* (New York: Abrams, 1993), p. 168.

120. Noël Carroll, "Film History and Film Theory: An Outline for an Institutional Theory of Film," in *Theorizing the Moving Image* (Cambridge: Cambridge University Press, 1996), pp. 375–391. For refinements in this argument see idem, "Art, Practice and Narrative," *The Monist* 71 (1988): 140–156; idem, "Identifying Art," in *Institutions of Art,* ed. Robert Yanal (State College: Pennsylvania State University Press, 1993), pp. 3–38; and idem, "Historical Narratives and the Philosophy of Art," *Journal of Aesthetics and Art Criticism* 51, no. 3 (Summer 1993): 313–326.

121. Gombrich, *Art and Illusion,* pp. 146–178. Gombrich also uses the term "schema" to denote a skeletal, diagrammatic depiction of an object or a spatial array.

122. David Bordwell, *Narration in the Fiction Film* (Madison: University of Wisconsin Press, 1985), pp. 205–310.

123. Interestingly, Henri Colpi, the director of *Une aussi longue absence,* served as editor on *Marienbad.*

124. See Ernst Gombrich, *The Story of Art* (London: Phaidon, 1950), pp. 190–201, 234.

125. Cinematographer John Bailey complains of being expected "to cook up slick and quick images for 'lite' film appetites"; "Can We Save the Shot?" *American Cinematographer* 77, no. 1 (1996): 13.

126. See my case for a "historical poetics" of cinema in *Ozu and the Poetics of Cinema* (Princeton: Princeton University Press, 1988), pp. 17–18, 31–33, and elsewhere; and in *Making Meaning,* pp. 263–274.

6. Exceptionally Exact Perceptions

Several techniques of staging discussed in this chapter are reviewed in chapters 6 and 7 of David Bordwell and Kristin Thompson's *Film Art: An Introduction,* 5th ed. (New York: McGraw-Hill, 1996). Steven D. Katz has written two intriguing manuals on staging: *Film Directing Shot by Shot: Visualizing from Concept to Screen* (Studio City, Calif.: Michael Wiese, 1991) and *Film Directing—Cinematic Motion: A Workshop for Staging Scenes* (Studio City, Calif.: Michael Wiese, 1992). Peter Ward provides a useful survey of contemporary principles of shot design in *Picture Composition for Film and Television* (London: Focal Press, 1996).

A pioneering overview of pictorial depth in film is Charles Harpole's *Gradients of Depth in the Cinema Image* (New York: Arno, 1978).

Until quite recently, students of pre-1920 cinema have paid more attention to the consolidation of editing techniques than to aspects of staging. For an overview of stylistic changes in general, with particular emphasis on editing, see Charles Andrew Keil, "American Cinema from 1907 to 1913: The Nature of Transition" (Ph.D. diss., University of Wisconsin–Madison, 1995). Much of the study of staging in early cinema was initiated by Kristin Thompson, Ben Brewster, and Barry Salt. Specific references can be found in the notes below.

An ambitious, if highly prescriptive, exploration of how cinematic composition guides eye movements is Victor Oscar Freeburg's *Pictorial Beauty on the Screen* (New York: Macmillan, 1923). More recently, Noël Carroll has suggested that the idea of attention can explain certain cross-cultural regularities in cinematic communication; see "Film, Attention, and Communication," in *The Great Ideas Today* (Chicago: Encyclopaedia Britannica, 1996).

The remark by Jacques Rivette on page 237 comes from "The Age of *Metteurs en Scène,*" in *Cahiers du Cinéma: The 1950s: Neo-Realism, Hollywood, New Wave,* ed. Jim Hillier (Cambridge, Mass.: Harvard University Press, 1985), p. 278.

1. Jean-Louis Comolli, "Technique et idéologie: Caméra, perspective, profondeur de champ," *Cahiers du cinéma* no. 233 (November 1971): 41–43.

2. Jean-Louis Comolli, "Technique et idéologie," *Cahiers du cinéma* no. 234–235 (December 1971–February 1972): 96–99.

3. Jean-Louis Comolli, "Technique et idéologie," *Cahiers du cinéma* no. 231 (August–September 1971): 45–46.

4. Jean-Louis Comolli, "Technique et idéologie," *Cahiers du cinéma* no. 230 (July 1971): 53. The comment refers to an illustration from *Ossessione.* It is probably worth mentioning that many of the illustrations accompanying Comolli's text are production stills, not frame enlargements, and so do not necessarily indicate what the actual shot looked like.

5. Comolli, "Technique et idéologie," *Cahiers* no. 233: 41.

6. Comolli, "Technique et idéologie," *Cahiers* no. 230: 56.

7. See Gary Hatfield, *The Natural and the Normative: Theories of Spatial Perception from Kant to Helmholtz* (Cambridge, Mass.: MIT Press, 1990), p. 46.

8. Comolli, "Technique et idéologie," *Cahiers* no. 230: 52.

9. Comolli, "Technique et idéologie," *Cahiers* no. 233: 44.

10. Ibid.

11. Roman art of the pre-Christian era offers many examples of size diminution along parallel, rather than receding, planes; this system does not imply a fixed point of view. A famous example is the Pompeian mosaic *Alexander's Victory over Darius* (c. 100 B.C.), probably a copy of a Greek original. For a complete discussion of the tendency, see Miriam Schild Bunim, *Space in Medieval Painting and the Forerunners of Perspective* (New York: AMS Press, 1970).

12. For a discussion of alternative projective systems, see Margaret A. Hagen, *Varieties of Realism: Geometries of Representational Art* (Cambridge: Cambridge University Press, 1986).

13. On this score Comolli's view differs from another promulgated at the period. Jean-Louis Baudry argued that the very optics and machining of the movie camera make it necessarily and incorrigibly a vehicle for bourgeois ideology. Although Baudry leaves some room for doubt, his position seems to rule out the sort of "subversion" of the perspective image that Comolli believes possible. See Jean-Louis Baudry, "Ideological Effects of the Basic Cinematographic Apparatus," in *Narrative, Apparatus, Ideology,* ed. Philip Rosen (New York: Columbia University Press, 1986), pp. 286–298.

14. For a discussion of the perspective implications of long lenses, see David Bordwell, *Narration in the Fiction Film* (Madison: University of Wisconsin Press, 1985), pp. 107–110.

15. For a clear review of the issues, see Robert L. Solso, *Cognition and the Visual Arts* (Cambridge, Mass.: MIT Press, 1994), pp. 129–155. A superb application of eye-movement theory to the study of a single painting is Michael Baxandall's "Fixation and Distraction: The Nail in Braque's *Violin and Pitcher* (1910)," in *Sight and Insight: Essays on Art and Culture in Honour of E. H. Gombrich at 85,* ed. John Onians (London: Phaidon, 1994), pp. 398–415.

16. In 1911 Louis Reeves Harrison wrote in *Moving Picture World:* "While [our attitudes and thoughts] can be imparted by other means, the eyes and the lips are most effective in facial expression of any kind, whether the emotion be open or subdued" (quoted in Janet Staiger, "The Eyes Are Really the Focus: Photoplay Acting and Film Form and Style," *Wide Angle* 6, no. 4 [1985]: 20). Compare cinematographer Sven Nykvist: "The truth of the characters is in the eyes; that's how the audience gets to know them as human beings" (quoted in Bob Fisher, "ASC Salutes Sven Nykvist," *American Cinematographer* 77, no. 2 [1996]: 48). And film editor Walter Murch: "The determining factor for selecting a particular shot is frequently, 'Can you register the

expression in the actor's eyes?'" (Walter Murch, *The Blink of an Eye: A Perspective on Film Editing* [Los Angeles: Silman-James, 1995], p. 88).

17. I am grateful to Noël Carroll for this point.

18. Such an unexceptionable claim would seem unnecessary, but at least one history-of-vision theorist has hinted that attention was invented by modernity. Jonathan Crary, in "Unbinding Vision: Manet and the Attentive Observer in the Late Nineteenth Century" (in Leo Charney and Vanessa R. Schwartz, eds., *Cinema and the Invention of Modern Life* [Berkeley: University of California Press, 1995], p. 48), writes: "Part of the cultural logic of capitalism demands that we accept as *natural* the switching of our attention from one thing to another." But for evolutionary reasons it *is* natural for primates like us to search the environment through saccadic eye movements, and in this sense we do "switch our attention" from point to point.

19. I discuss this conception of "social construction" in "Convention, Construction, and Cinematic Vision," in *Post-Theory: Reconstructing Film Studies,* ed. David Bordwell and Noël Carroll (Madison: University of Wisconsin Press, 1996), pp. 87–107.

20. A. Lumière and L. Lumière, "La photographie oeuvre d'art," in Bernard Chardère, *Lumières sur Lumière* (Lyon: Institut Lumière/Presses Universitaires de Lyon, 1987), p. 102.

21. Noël Burch, *Life to Those Shadows,* trans. and ed. Ben Brewster (Berkeley: University of California Press, 1990), p. 154.

22. Charles Musser makes this point in *The Emergence of Cinema: The American Screen to 1907* (New York: Scribner's, 1990), p. 383.

23. Patrick G. Loughney, "In the Beginning Was the Word: Six Pre-Griffith Motion Picture Scenarios," *Iris* 2, no. 1 (1984): 26–29.

24. This example is discussed and illustrated in Kristin Thompson, "The Formulation of the Classical Style," in David Bordwell, Janet Staiger, and Kristin Thompson, *The Classical Hollywood Cinema: Film Style and Mode of Production to 1960* (New York: Columbia University Press, 1985), p. 174 and figs. 15.1, 15.2.

25. As Burch points out of the PMR generally, "This early 'system' is also the 'simplest' way a film camera could have been used"; *Life to Those Shadows,* p. 139.

26. Rudolf Arnheim, *The Power of the Center: A Study of Composition in the Visual Arts,* 2nd ed. (Berkeley: University of California Press, 1988), p. 67.

27. Heinrich Wölfflin, *Principles of Art History: The Problem of the Development of Style in Later Art,* trans. M. D. Hottinger (New York: Dover, 1950), p. 73.

28. Most early lenses were borrowed from still photography, and cinematographers seem to have been content with apertures of f/8, f/4.5, and wider. According to Vincent Pinel, for instance, the still-photography Darlot lens used on the Cinématographe could be stopped down only to f/8 (*Louis Lumière: Inventeur et cinéaste* [Paris: Nathan, 1994], p. 108). Lumière, however, insisted that his engineer design the diaphragm so that it could be closed down to f/12.5, f/18, and even f/22 (Auguste Lumière and Louis Lumière, *Correspondances 1890–1953,* ed. Jacques Rittaud-Hutinet and Yvelise Dentzer [Paris: Cahiers du Cinéma, 1994], p. 134).

29. Wölfflin, *Principles,* pp. 75–82.

30. Joyce Jesniowski offers an illuminating discussion of the spatial dynamics of the chase film in *Thinking in Pictures: Dramatic Structure in D. W. Griffith's Biograph Films* (Berkeley: University of California Press, 1987), pp. 21–22.

31. Lumière and Lumière, "La photographie," p. 104.

32. See the illustrations from *Den Hvide slavinde* (1906) and *Anarkistens Svigermoder* (both 1906) in Paolo Cherchi Usai, ed., *Schiave bianche allo specchio: Le origini del cinema in Scandinavia (1896–1918)* (Pordenone: Studio Tesi, 1986), p. 51; see also Ron Mottram, *The Danish Cinema before Dreyer* (Metuchen, N.J.: Scarecrow, 1988), pp. 21–22, 29.

33. Jon Gartenberg, "Vitagraph before Griffith: Forging Ahead in the Nickelodeon Era," *Studies in Visual Communication* 10, no. 4 (Fall 1984): 13–16.

34. Ken Dancyger comments on this in *The Technique of Film and Video Editing* (Boston: Focal Press, 1993), pp. 261–263.

35. For discussion of the narrative implications of such staging, see Marshall Deutelbaum, "Structural Patterning in the Lumière Films," in *Film before Griffith*, ed. John Fell (Berkeley: University of California Press, 1983), pp. 299–310.

36. Ben Brewster, "Deep Staging in French Films 1900–1914," in *Early Cinema: Space, Frame, Narrative*, ed. Thomas Elsaesser (London: British Film Institute, 1990), pp. 46–48.

37. This point is developed in Ben Brewster and Lea Jacobs, *Theatre to Cinema: Stage Pictorialism and the Early Feature Film* (Oxford: Oxford University Press, 1997).

38. Thompson, "Formulation of the Classical Style," p. 216.

39. A modern handbook suggests that entrances and exits from the side of the frame still seem weaker dramatically than those involving depth. See Mike Crisp, *The Practical Director* (Oxford: Focal Press, 1993), p. 11.

40. A critic praises *Captain Kate* (1911) for presenting "detail so clearcut all over the picture that faces can be seen not merely in the near foreground but also in the middle and even in the distance"; *Moving Picture World* 9, no. 3 (29 July 1911): 211. I thank Charles Keil for this reference.

41. See Colin N. Bennett, *The Guide to Kinematography for Camera Men, Operators, and All Who "Want to Know"* (London: Heron, 1917), p. 28. See also Frederick A. Talbot, *Practical Cinematography and Its Applications* (Philadelphia: Lippincott, 1913), p. 47; Herbert C. McKay, *The Handbook of Motion Picture Photography* (New York: Falk, 1927), p. 271. Later discussions are Jean Mitry, *Histoire du cinéma: Art et industrie*, vol. 4: *Les années 30* (Paris: Delarge, 1980), pp. 41, 56; Barry Salt, "Film Lighting in 1913," *Griffithiana* no. 50 (May 1994): 193. Thanks to Ben Brewster for help on this point.

42. Bennett, *Guide to Kinematography*, p. 45.

43. Quite early, Danish directors were using mirrors to create depth; see Mottram, *Danish Cinema before Dreyer*, pp. 85–87, 138–140. On mirrors in Russian films of the era see Yuri Tsivian, "Portraits, Mirrors, Death: On Some Decadent Clichés in Early Russian Films," *Iris* no. 14–15 (1992): 70–78. Kristin Thompson discusses the mirrors of the 1910s as means of enhancing expressive qualities of the story. See "The International Exploration of Cinematic Expressivity," in *Film and the First World War*, ed. Karel Dibbets and Bert Hogenkamp (Amsterdam: Amsterdam University Press, 1995), pp. 73–74.

44. Urban Gad, *Filmen: Dens midler og maal* (Copenhagen: Gyldendal, 1919), pp. 122–125.

45. Lev Kuleshov, *The Art of the Cinema*, in *Selected Works: Fifty Years in Films*, trans. Dmitri Agrachev and Nina Belenkaya (Moscow: Raduga, 1987), pp. 110–111.

46. Leon Battista Alberti, *On Painting*, trans. John R. Spencer (New Haven: Yale University Press, 1956), pp. 46–47.

47. Gad, *Filmen,* p. 122.

48. Kuleshov, *The Art of the Cinema,* p. 142.

49. Lev Kuleshov, "On the Artist's Work in Films," in *Selected Works,* p. 31.

50. The trapezoidal playing area is discussed in several sources of the 1910s. A detailed account can be found in J. Berg Esenwein and Arthur Leeds, *Writing the Photoplay* (Springfield, Mass.: Home Correspondence School, 1913), pp. 157–160 (although the trigonometry seems to be miscalculated). See also James Slevin, *On Picture-Play Writing: A Hand-Book of Workmanship* (Cedar Grove, N.J.: Farmer Smith, 1912), pp. 85–86; Epes Winthrop Sargent, *Technique of the Photoplay* (New York: Moving Picture World, 1912), p. 8, as well as the second edition of the same book (New York: Moving Picture World, 1913), p. 163; J. Arthur Nelson, *The Photo-Play: How to Write, How to Sell,* 2nd ed. (Los Angeles: Photoplay, 1913), pp. 46–47; Frances Agnew, *Motion Picture Acting* (New York: Reliance Newspaper Syndicate, 1913), pp. 72–74. Later discussions include Henri Diamant-Berger, *Le cinéma* (Paris: Renaissance du Livre, 1919), p. 24; Carl Louis Gregory, ed., *A Condensed Course in Motion Picture Photography* (New York: New York Institute of Photography, 1920), pp. 225–226.

51. Rob Wagner, *Picture Values from an Artist's Viewpoint* (Los Angeles: Palmer Photoplay, 1920), pp. 4–5. Other contemporary sources are William Roy Mott, "White Light for Motion Picture Photography," *Transactions of the Society of Motion Picture Engineers* no. 8 (14–16 April 1919): 8–9; and Gregory, *Condensed Course,* p. 226.

52. They consider this subject in detail in *Theatre to Cinema.* See also Lea Jacobs, "Belasco, DeMille and the Development of Lasky Lighting," *Film History* 5, no. 4 (December 1993): 406; Tom Gunning, "Notes and Queries about the Year 1913 and Film Style: National Styles and Deep Staging," *1895,* special issue: "L'année 1913 en France" (1993): 202.

53. Vachel Lindsay, *The Art of the Moving Picture,* rev. ed. (New York: Liveright, 1922), p. 112.

54. Quoted in Bengt Forslund, *Victor Sjöström: His Life and His Work,* trans. Peter Cowie, Anna-Maija Marttinen, and Christopher Frunck (New York: Zoetrope, 1988), p. 47.

55. Yhcam, "Cinematography," in *French Film Theory and Criticism: A History/Anthology, 1907–1939,* ed. Richard Abel, vol. 1 (Princeton: Princeton University Press, 1988), pp. 72–74.

56. Lindsay, *Art of the Moving Picture,* p. 49.

57. This development aroused some criticism for its distortion of the figures; examples may be found in Thompson, "Formulation of the Classical Style," p. 222. Gad advises that because lenses of short focal length give unnatural perspective, they should be used only when backgrounds are unimportant or architectural details need to be included in the image; *Filmen,* p. 84.

58. See Gad, *Filmen,* p. 128; Bennett, *Guide to Kinematography,* p. 55; Karl Brown, *Adventures with D. W. Griffith,* ed. Kevin Brownlow (New York: Farrar, Straus and Giroux, 1973), pp. 15–16.

59. Most silent films we see today, even in archival prints, have suffered some cropping of the original frame through successive generations of printing. Thus frame enlargements such as mine here sometimes only approximate what the original frame edges were. In addition, some frames pictured here suffer from previous efforts to crop them; as a result, horizontal lines slice across the top and bottom of the picture area.

60. On the nine-foot line, see James Morrison's reminiscences in Kevin Brownlow,

The Parade's Gone By (New York: Knopf, 1969), p. 16. Thompson cites a 1911 article suggesting that eight feet is a common camera-to-foreground distance "with those who amputate the lower limbs to show us facial expression" ("Formulation of the Classical Style," p. 215). For a general discussion, see Eileen Bowser, *The Transformation of Cinema: 1907–1915* (New York: Scribner's, 1990), p. 252.

61. Barry Salt, "Vitagraph, un tocco di classe," in *Vitagraph Co. of America: Il cinema prima di Hollywood,* ed. Paolo Cherchi Usai (Pordenone: Studio Tesi, 1987), pp. 171–202; Bowser, *Transformation of Cinema,* pp. 88–95. A thorough discussion of the scale of front lines can be found in Barry Salt, *Film Style and Technology: History and Analysis,* 2nd ed. (London: Starword, 1992), pp. 87–91.

62. Slevin, *On Picture-Play Writing,* p. 86.

63. George Pratt records several objections in *Spellbound in Darkness: A History of the Silent Film* (Greenwich, Conn.: New York Graphic Society, 1973), pp. 95–99.

64. Sargent, *Technique of the Photoplay,* 2nd ed., p. 22.

65. I discuss Feuillade's staging in more detail in "*La Nouvelle Mission de Feuillade;* or, What Was *Mise en Scène?*" *Velvet Light Trap* no. 37 (Spring 1996): 10–29.

66. Kristin Thompson analyzes the subsequent scene in a similar way in "International Exploration," pp. 66–68; and Kristin Thompson and David Bordwell, *Film History: An Introduction* (New York: McGraw-Hill, 1994), p. 67.

67. John Fullerton, "Contextualizing the Innovation of Deep Staging in Swedish Film," in Dibbets and Hogenkamp, *Film and the First World War,* pp. 87–93. See also Jan Olssen, "'Classical' vs. 'Pre-Classical': *Ingeborg Holm* and Swedish Cinema," *Griffithiana* no. 50 (May 1994): 113–123.

68. Jesniowski, *Thinking in Pictures,* p. 77.

69. "We would undoubtedly find scattered among the works of others elements of nonexpressionistic cinema in which montage plays no part—even including Griffith" (Bazin, "The Evolution of the Language of Cinema," in *What Is Cinema?* ed. and trans. Hugh Gray [Berkeley: University of California Press, 1967], p. 27). On Griffith's use of depth, see Jacques Aumont, "L'écriture Griffith-Biograph," in *D. W. Griffith,* ed. Jean Mottet (Paris: L'Harmattan, 1984), pp. 238–240, and Tom Gunning, *D. W. Griffith and the Origins of American Narrative Film* (Urbana: University of Illinois Press, 1991), pp. 207–214.

70. "He marked new limit lines, and had us stand so close to the camera that it seemed the result would certainly look foolish"; Christy Cabanne, quoted in Henry Stephen Gordon, "The Story of D. W. Griffith," Part III, *Photoplay* 10, no. 3 (August 1916): 87.

71. See Richard Abel, "Before *Fantômas:* Louis Feuillade and the Development of Early French Cinema," *Post Script* 7, no. 1 (1987): 4–26; and Thompson, "International Exploration."

72. Burch, *Life to Those Shadows,* p. 74. For Burch, films like *Fantômas* and *Afgrunden* perfectly exemplify the Primitive Mode of Representation (p. 186), while I argue that they are sophisticated examples of the depth aesthetic I have been exploring here. Gunning makes a similar point in suggesting that "the most talented European directors did not approach deep staging as a simple return to the earlier dramatic style of linked tableaux"; "Notes and Queries," p. 202.

73. See Thompson, "Formulation of the Classical Style," pp. 194–213.

74. Henri Fescourt and Jean-Louis Bosquet, "Idea and Screen: Opinions on the Cinema," in Abel, *French Film Theory and Criticism,* p. 374.

75. Homer Croy, *How Motion Pictures Are Made* (New York: Harper, 1918), p. 100.

76. Kuleshov, *The Art of the Cinema,* pp. 132–136.

77. Janet Staiger, "The Hollywood Mode of Production to 1930," in Bordwell, Staiger, and Thompson, *The Classical Hollywood Cinema,* pp. 87–153.

78. Richard Abel, *The Ciné Goes to Town: French Cinema, 1896–1914* (Berkeley: University of California Press, 1994), pp. 182, 299–300.

79. Sargent, *Technique of the Photoplay,* 3d ed. (New York: Moving Picture World, 1916), pp. 175, 178.

80. John Fullerton, "Spatial and Temporal Articulations in Pre-Classical Swedish Film," in Elsaesser, *Early Cinema,* p. 375; Abel, *The Ciné Goes to Town,* pp. 300, 429. Thomas Elsaesser and Adam Barker go the furthest in this direction. They propose to treat the entirety of fictional European filmmaking as "a cinema of non-continuity," which developed "the 'primitive' style of narrativity" in ways that led to "a different way of reading the frame, different skills in 'following' the narrative"; Elsaesser, *Early Cinema,* p. 309. They do not, however, indicate what these different activities involve.

81. Tom Gunning has suggested that a conception of nationally distinct styles solidified around 1913. See "Notes and Queries," p. 196.

82. See Kristin Thompson, "Early Alternatives to the Hollywood Mode of Production: Implications for Europe's Avant-Gardes," *Film History* 5, no. 4 (December 1993): 386–404.

83. E. Rubinstein discusses Keaton as a long-shot, deep-space director in *Filmguide to The General* (Bloomington: Indiana University Press, 1973).

84. See Carroll's Ph.D. dissertation, "An In-Depth Analysis of Buster Keaton's *The General*" (New York University, 1976), especially pp. 105–177, and his essay "Buster Keaton, *The General,* and Visual Intelligibility," in *Close Viewings: An Anthology of New Film Criticism,* ed. Peter Lehman (Tallahassee: Florida State University Press, 1990), pp. 125–140.

85. Bazin, "Evolution," p. 33; translation slightly modified.

86. See, for a contemporary discussion, Joseph Dubray, "Large Aperture Lenses in Cinematography," *Transactions of the Society of Motion Picture Engineers* no. 33 (1928): 205.

87. I analyze the spatial organization of *The New Babylon* in *Narration in the Fiction Film,* pp. 249–268.

88. See Thompson, "Formulation of the Classical Style," pp. 287–293.

89. For a good general discussion of Borzage's visual style, see Jean Mitry, *Histoire du cinéma: Art et industrie,* vol. 3: *1923–1930* (Paris: Editions Universitaires, 1973), p. 440.

90. See David Bordwell, *Ozu and the Poetics of Cinema* (Princeton: Princeton University Press, 1988), pp. 105–108.

91. Matthew Josephson wrote in 1926 of the "distorted" and "uncanny" shots of *Greed,* evoking "a nameless fear"; quoted in Pratt, *Spellbound in Darkness,* pp. 336–337.

92. Adrian Brunel, *Film Production* (London: Newnes, 1936), p. 47.

93. See David Bordwell, *The Cinema of Eisenstein* (Cambridge, Mass.: Harvard University Press, 1993), p. 98.

94. Tamar Lane, *New Technique of Screen Writing* (New York: Whittlesey, 1936), p. 78.

95. For detailed analyses of these scenes, see David Bordwell, "Mizoguchi and the

Evolution of Film Language," in *Cinema and Language,* ed. Stephen Heath and Patricia Mellencamp (Los Angeles: American Film Institute, 1983), pp. 107–117; and Donald Kirihara, *Patterns of Time: Mizoguchi and the 1930s* (Madison: University of Wisconsin Press, 1992), pp. 109–111.

96. See André Bazin, "Le mythe de Staline dans le cinéma soviétique," in *Le cinéma française de la libération à la nouvelle vague (1945–1958)* (Paris: Editions de l'Etoile, 1983), pp. 232–242.

97. Lev Kuleshov, "The Banner of Cinematography," in *Selected Works,* pp. 49–50.

98. Kuleshov, *The Art of the Cinema,* pp. 176–181.

99. Vladimir Nilsen, *The Cinema as a Graphic Art,* trans. Stephen Garry (New York: Hill and Wang, 1959), pp. 36, 59–60, 85–100.

100. Vladimir Nizhny, *Lessons with Eisenstein,* trans. and ed. Ivor Montagu and Jay Leyda (New York: Hill and Wang, 1962), pp. 63–92.

101. I analyze these aspects of Eisenstein's theory of staging in *The Cinema of Eisenstein,* pp. 139–162.

102. For broad-ranging discussions of this trend, see Matthew Cullerne Bown, *Art under Stalin* (London: Phaidon, 1991); and Igor Golomstock, *Totalitarian Art,* trans. Robert Chandler (New York: HarperCollins, 1990). The tendency is most evident in Soviet architecture. See Vladimir Paperny, "Moscow in the 1930s and the Emergence of a New City," in *The Culture of the Stalin Period,* ed. Hans Günther (New York: St. Martin's, 1990), pp. 229–239; and Alexei Tarkhanov and Sergei Kavtaradze, *Stalinist Architecture* (London: Laurence King, 1992).

103. Boris Groys makes a case for the continuity between the Constructivist avant-garde and Socialist Realism in *The Total Art of Stalinism: Avant-Garde, Aesthetic Dictatorship, and Beyond,* trans. Charles Rougle (Princeton: Princeton University Press, 1992).

104. Much of the ensuing discussion of Toland's work derives from arguments made in more detail in "Film Style and Technology, 1930–1960," in Bordwell, Staiger, and Thompson, *Classical Hollywood Cinema,* pp. 339–364; and in David Bordwell and Kristin Thompson, "Technological Change and Classical Film Style," in Tino Balio, *Grand Design: Hollywood as a Modern Business Enterprise 1930–1939* (New York: Scribner's, 1993), pp. 109–141. See also Harpole, *Gradients of Depth in the Cinema Image,* pp. 161–193.

105. "After dinner every night for about a month, I'd run *Stagecoach,* often with some different technician or department head from the studio, and ask questions: 'How was this done?' 'Why was this done?' It was like going to school"; Orson Welles and Peter Bogdanovich, *This Is Orson Welles,* ed. Jonathan Rosenbaum (New York: HarperCollins, 1992), p. 29.

106. According to Rick Altman, however, "deep-focus sound" was not exploited because filmmakers were not sure how to differentiate sonic planes; "Deep-Focus Sound: *Citizen Kane* and the Radio Aesthetic," *Quarterly Review of Film and Video* 15, no. 3 (1994): 1–33.

107. E. H. Gombrich, *Art History and the Social Sciences* (Oxford: Clarendon Press, 1975), pp. 37–40.

108. The trick work in *Kane* is discussed in Peter Bogdanovich, "The *Kane* Mutiny," *Esquire* 77(October 1972): 99–105, 180–190. See also Robert L. Carringer, *The Making of Citizen Kane* (Berkeley: University of California Press, 1985), pp. 81–99.

109. Welles and Bogdanovich, *This Is Orson Welles,* p. 79.

110. See "Orson Welles: Once a Child Prodigy, He Has Never Quite Grown Up," *Life* (26 May 1941): 110–116.

111. Gregg Toland, "Realism for *Citizen Kane,*" *American Cinematographer* 22, no. 2 (1941): 80.

112. See Bordwell, "Film Style and Technology," pp. 348–349.

113. I suspect, however, that Toland couldn't keep focus on both Regina in the foreground and Horace's collapse in the rear, so Wyler capitalized on this limitation.

114. Olivier quoted in Russell Campbell, ed., *Practical Motion Picture Photography* (London: Tantivy, 1970), p. 179. The cinematographer Desmond Dickinson reports that he did not use wide-angle lenses, preferring instead to light the foreground bright and hard so that the plane seemed sharper than it was.

115. Sidney Lumet, *Making Movies* (New York: Knopf, 1995), pp. 76–77, 84.

116. Welles told Alexandre Astruc that he learned from Toland that wide-angle lenses, stopped down to f/16 and positioned at a steep low angle, could create nightmarish distortions; Astruc, *La tête la première* (Paris: Orban, 1975), p. 59.

117. In "The Cinematic Invention of Mexico: The Poetics and Politics of the Fernández-Figueroa Style" (in Chon A. Noriega and Steven Ricci, eds., *The Mexican Cinema Project* [Los Angeles: UCLA Film and Television Archive, 1994], pp. 13–24), Charles Ramirez Berg argues along Comolli's lines that the director and his cinematographer challenged Renaissance perspective. He claims that Fernández and Figueroa react against Hollywood by using "two-point perspective" and "curvilinear perspective," both violations of Hollywood's "linear perspective" (pp. 16–20). The result is a "fracturing" of capitalist ideology and a new status for "the viewing subject" (p. 23).

The case will not stand, I think, for the following reasons. (1) Berg's diagram exemplifies not two-point (angular) perspective but three-point (oblique) perspective. (2) Both two-point and three-point perspective are *types* of linear perspective, not alternatives to it. (Ramirez Berg has conflated linear perspective with central, one-point perspective.) (3) Curvilinear perspective is not, as Berg claims, the use of curved shapes across the upper part of the image (as in the clouds in Figueroa's skies). Curvilinear perspective is a cylindrical or spherical distortion of the entire picture plane; painters developed this in an effort to imitate the curvature of the retina. Wide-angle lenses, focusing on a flat film plane, do not produce curvilinear perspective. (4) Once these confusions are sorted out, nothing in Berg's description of the Fernández-Figueroa films (p. 19) would not apply as well to American films in the Welles/Wyler line: considerable depth of field with big foregrounds left or right, action on several planes, low-angle compositions, diagonal movement, and the like. The optics and composition of Fig. 6.177, a typical Fernández image, resemble the Hollywood "deep-focus" norm.

118. I have discussed these strategies in *The Cinema of Eisenstein,* pp. 208–210, 243–248.

119. On the development of color filmmaking in the United States, see Gorham A. Kindem, "Hollywood's Conversion to Color: The Technological, Economic, and Aesthetic Factors," *Journal of the University Film Association* 31, no. 2 (Spring 1979): 29–36.

120. Joe Valentine, "Lighting for Technicolor as Compared with Black and White Photography," *International Photographer* 20, no. 1 (1948): 8.

121. Ron Rose and Vic Heutschy, "Cameraman's Comments," *International Photographer* 25, no. 11 (1953): 10.

122. See the remarks of Charles G. Clarke in Clarke, "And Now 55mm," *American Cinematographer* 36, no. 12 (1955): 707; and in Walter R. Greene, "New CinemaScope '55,'" *International Photographer* 28, no. 3 (1956): 6.

123. See Frederick Foster, "Photography Sharp, Clear, and Incisive," *American Cinematographer* 40, no. 8 (1959): 504.

124. Cameron quoted in Paula Parisi, "'Larger than Life,' Widescreen Rules Film," *Hollywood Reporter* (18 April 1995): 8. I am grateful to Mike Pogorzelski for this reference

125. Cukor quoted in Ronald Haver, *A Star Is Born: The Making of the 1954 Movie and Its 1983 Restoration* (New York: Knopf, 1988), p. 133.

126. *Kazan on Kazan,* ed. Michel Ciment (New York: Viking, 1974), pp. 122–123.

127. Rudy Behlmer, ed., *Memo from Darryl F. Zanuck: The Golden Years at Twentieth Century–Fox* (New York: Grove, 1993), p. 235.

128. Cukor quoted in Haver, *A Star Is Born,* p. 133. Actually, during the 1930s Cukor knew very well how to line up people in rows (see, for example, *Holiday,* 1938). Perhaps after he had mastered diagonal depth arrangements in such films as *Adam's Rib* (1949) and *The Marrying Kind* (1952), the return to lateral staging for CinemaScope seemed a step backward.

129. Jacques Rivette, "The Age of Metteurs en Scène," in *Cahiers du Cinéma: The 1950s: Neo-Realism, Hollywood, New Wave,* ed. Jim Hillier (Cambridge, Mass.: Harvard University Press, 1985), p. 278.

130. *Kazan on Kazan,* p. 123.

131. I analyze the scene of the missing rifle in "Mise-en-Scène Criticism and Widescreen Aesthetics," *Velvet Light Trap* no. 21 (Summer 1985): 118–25.

132. Richard Rush quoted in Paul Joannides, "The Aesthetics of the Zoom Lens," *Sight and Sound* 40, no. 1 (Winter 1970/71): 42.

133. For an example, see Thompson and Bordwell, *Film History,* p. 501.

134. The zoom is thus different from a camera movement, such as a tracking shot, which transports the camera toward or from the object filmed. It seems that before the zoom lens came into wide use, the word "zoom" was used for a fast tracking shot forward. See, for example, John Paddy Carstairs, *Movie Merry-Go-Round* (London: Newnes, 1937), p. 139.

135. For historical accounts of the zoom lens, see John Belton, "The Bionic Eye: Zoom Aesthetics," *Cineaste* 9, no. 1 (Winter 1980–81): 20–27; and Salt, *Film Style and Technology,* pp. 232, 244, 258–259.

136. Liu Shi, "Ng See-Yuen: An Interview," in *A Study of the Hong Kong Martial Arts Film,* ed. Lau Shing-Han (Hong Kong: Urban Council, 1980), p. 144.

137. Belton, "Bionic Eye," p. 26.

138. Andrzej Wajda, *Double Vision: My Life in Film,* trans. Rose Medina (New York: Henry Holt, 1989), pp. 86–87.

139. I borrow the term "searching and revealing" from Bern Levy, "Zoom Lenses," in *American Cinematographer Manual,* ed. Rod Ryan, 7th ed. (Hollywood: ASC Press, 1993), p. 157.

140. For an analysis of Jancsó's construction of space in *The Confrontation,* see Bordwell, *Narration in the Fiction Film,* pp. 130–146.

141. Bob Fisher, "*Jurassic Park:* When Dinosaurs Rule the Box Office," *American Cinematographer* 74, no. 6 (1993): 44.

142. To get depth of this sort, the Coen brothers have often employed a "swing and

tilt" bellows lens set at an oblique angle to the film plane. See Al Hassell, "Personality Prevails in *Killing Zoe*," *American Cinematographer* 76, no. 4 (1995): 73.

143. "Anamorphobia: Martin Scorsese in Conversation with Gregory Solman," in *Projections 4: Film-makers on Film-making*, ed. John Boorman, Tom Luddy, David Thomson, and Walter Donohue (London: Faber, 1995), p. 31.

144. Perhaps rapid panning movements of this sort adjust for the eventual "pan-and-scan" rereading of the widescreen image that will be executed when the film passes to the squarish video format.

145. Zsigmond quoted in David E. Williams, "Shooting to Kill," *American Cinematographer* 76, no. 11 (1995): 56. "We shot the entire film almost wide open," recalls the cinematographer of *Seven* (1995). "That made it extremely difficult for focus-pulling, but gave a precise plane to the action, so we could direct the viewer's eye" (David E. Williams, "The Sins of a Serial Killer," *American Cinematographer* 76, no. 10 [1995]: 40). On the video-driven urge for tight close-ups, see the comments of Phil Méhaux in David E. Williams, "Reintroducing Bond . . . James Bond," *American Cinematographer* 76, no. 12 (1995): 39.

146. Panavision's new Frazier lens system is discussed by cinematographer John Schwartzman in Eric Rudolph, "*The Rock* Offers No Escape," *American Cinematographer* 77, no. 6 (1996): 72.

147. I argue for Angelopoulos' revision of Antonioni's style in "Modernism, Minimalism, Melancholy: Angelopoulos and Visual Style," in *The Last Modernist: The Films of Theo Angelopoulos*, ed. Andrew Horton (London: Flicks Books, 1997), pp. 11–26.

148. Hou Hsiao-Hsien quoted in Tony Rayns, "The Sandwich Man," *Monthly Film Bulletin* no. 653 (June 1988): 164.

149. As, for example, Robert Lepage does in *Le confessional* (1995) by shooting planimetric compositions with short lenses; or as Wong Kar-Wai does in pushing wide-angle depth to grotesque extremes in *Fallen Angels* (1995).

150. I try to support this idea in "Convention, Construction, and Cinematic Vision," pp. 87–107.

151. On this point, see Noël Carroll, "The Power of Movies," in *Theorizing the Moving Image* (Cambridge: Cambridge University Press, 1996), pp. 78–93.

152. I am thinking of Blur's "To the End," which parodies *L'année dernière à Marienbad*, and Milla's "The Gentleman Who Fell," a pastiche of Maya Deren's *Meshes of the Afternoon*.

Index